Introducing Affordable Housing

The issue of affordable housing has never been more important – and so it has never been more important to be well-...ormed about it! This book – in its ...elfth year and now fully updated – ...mines the history and role of social and ...rdable housing in the UK and how it is ... and managed. It explains the key tasks ...ssionals have to undertake and is an ... for students and practitioners alike.
...00 CIH Non-member: £35.00
...: September 2009

Homelessness in the UK: problems and solutions

Homelessness is one of the most distressing and visible of social problems. This book examines the contemporary nature of homelessness in the UK and responses to it. It is research-based but policy-focused – emphasising those issues which are most relevant to housing students, policy-makers, and practitioners. It considers not only the 'problems' associated with homelessness, but also the 'solutions' that have been identified as effective means to prevent and/or address homelessness.
*CIH Member: £24.00 CIH Non-member: £30.00
Code: 129 Published: June 2009

...quality, Diversity and Good ...elations in Housing – practice ...rief

This practice brief illustrates how equality, diversity, good relations and community cohesion impact on the housing sector. It focuses on the seven strands of diversity: age, disability, gender, race, religion or belief, sexual orientation and transgender. For each strand it demonstrates how discrimination can occur in a housing context, shows examples of innovative practice and provides practice checklists.
*CIH Member: £8.00 CIH Non-member: £10.00
Code: 801 Published: April 2009

Suspending Housing Applicants: a practical guide (Scotland)

Suspending housing applicants is a common tool used by landlords to restrict access to housing for some households. This can prove challenging for landlords, who are expected to strike a balance between the sometimes competing objectives of managing anti-social behaviour and rent arrears on the one hand, and promoting inclusion and access on the other. This revised guidance is intended for those working in housing policy and strategy, those who allocate housing and those advising housing applicants.
*CIH Member: £24.00 CIH Non-member: £30.00
Code: 530 Published: January 2010

ORDER FORM – Please send me the following:

Code no.	Title	Price	Quantity	Total

 # Postage and packing: 1 book – £3.00 (min. charge); thereafter p&p will be charged at an additional £1.00 per book. Rest of Europe and overseas at cost. Bulk orders at cost.

Post and packing#

TOTAL

Customer details

Contact name	Job title
Organisation	Membership no. (if applicable)
Address	
Postcode Date	Email
Signature	Telephone

Is this a home ☐ or work ☐ address?

Payment details

Note: Individuals may pay by personal cheque or online with a credit/debit card. Organisations may be invoiced.

To place a credit card order visit our Online Bookshop: **http://members.cih.org/bookshop/catalogue.aspx**

Alternative payment options are:

Invoice organisation   Purchase order number

I enclose a cheque for £   (made payable to the *Chartered Institute of Housing*)

Payment made by BACS Sort Code 20-23-55 Account No. 50177628   Ref Pubf06/10

* NOTE FOR ALL MEMBERS: The **CIH Member price** applies when chosen as part of your flexible benefits package and payment is made by cheque or credit/debit card. If you have not yet chosen your flexible benefits, please visit **www.cih.org/members**.

Return to: Publications, Chartered Institute of Housing, Octavia House, Westwood Way, Coventry, CV4 8JP. Tel: 024 7685 1700. E-mail: pubs@cih.org
See the full publications list online at www.cih.org/publications

Publications
from the Chartered Institute of Housing

Promoting Homeownership – practice brief

Promoting homeownership is an important activity for many social housing providers, whether they are engaged in low-cost homeownership schemes or simply responding to right to buy and right to acquire applications. This practice brief deals with all the 'pre-sale' aspects of homeownership, including government policies, the different 'products', marketing properties and all the legal aspects of the right to buy/right to acquire.

*CIH Member: £12.00 CIH Non-member: £15.00
Code: 804 Published: June 2010

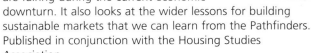

Building Sustainable Housing Markets

Have the Housing Market Renewal Pathfinders in nine areas of the North and Midlands arrested the collapse in prices and demand? This book assesses the effectiveness of the initiatives, and asks how the nine areas are fairing during the current economic downturn. It also looks at the wider lessons for building sustainable markets that we can learn from the Pathfinders. Published in conjunction with the Housing Studies Association.

*CIH Member: £24.00 CIH Non-member: £30.00
Code: 123 Published: June 2010

Allocations and Local Flexibility – practice brief

Allocations and Local Flexibility provides a full briefing on how to implement the Department for Communities and Local Government's latest statutory guidance. It is essential reading for local authorities, but will also be of interest to registered providers more widely as well as those seeking a concise and jargon-free introduction to the topic.

*CIH Member: £12.00 CIH Non-member: £15.00
Code: 803 Published: March 2010

Guide to Housing Benefit and Council Tax Benefit

This publication covers all the rules across the United Kingdom and contains many practical examples and useful tables. The Guide has a strong reputation for clear, impartial and accurate advice and is used by local councils, social landlords, advisers, tribunal members and housing professionals. It is updated annually to incorporate all the changes over the past year.

*CIH Member: £20.80 CIH Non-member: £26.00
Code: 368 Published: Annually in May

UK Housing Review

The UK Housing Review provides the key information for busy managers and policy-makers. It brings together the most up-to-date housing statistics available for England (and its regions), Wales, Scotland and Northern Ireland. Updated annually, it is the key resource for anyone interested in housing policy and finance, in both the public and private sectors.

*CIH Member: £36.00 CIH Non-member: £45.00 Code: 367 Published: Annually in December

www.cih.org/publications

CIH publications

UK Housing Review

2010/2011

Published by the Chartered Institute of Housing

Hal Pawson and Steve Wilcox

Contents of the *UK Housing Review 2010/2011*

UK Housing Review 2010/2011
Hal Pawson and Steve Wilcox
© CIH, Heriot-Watt University and University
of York 2011

Published by the Chartered Institute of Housing

ISBN: 978-1-905018-89-5
Layout by Jeremy Spencer
Editorial management: John Perry
Cover photograph by Reuters/Cathal McNaughton
Printed by Hobbs the printers, Totton, Hants on
FSC certified papers

Chartered Institute of Housing
Octavia House
Westwood Way
Coventry CV4 8JP
Tel: 024 7685 1700
Website: www.cih.org

The facts presented and views expressed in the
Review, however, are those of the author(s) and
not necessarily those of the CIH

UK Housing Review website: www.ukhousingreview.org.uk

Acknowledgements

This annual compilation of statistical data would not have been possible without the substantial help and guidance of a host of civil servants, at the Department for Communities and Local Government, the Department for Work and Pensions, the Treasury, the Welsh Assembly Government, the Scottish Government, the Northern Ireland Executive, the Office for National Statistics, and elsewhere.

Similar assistance was given from the Council of Mortgage Lenders, the Homes and Communities Agency, the Northern Ireland Housing Executive, and many others. The enormous help they have all once again provided in the compilation of this year's edition of the *Review* is most readily and gratefully acknowledged.

Much of the statistical data presented here is generally available in a variety of published, or publicly available, statistical series, and sources are comprehensively acknowledged against each Table in the *Review*. Thanks are again due to Alan Lewis for his help in updating much of the Compendium of tables in the *Review*.

This year the *Review* has again been produced by the Chartered Institute of Housing. Thanks are thus variously due to John Perry and Jeremy Spencer for their hard work, support and creative contributions in producing this edition. Thanks are also due to colleagues at York University, Jane Allen and Nicholas Please, for their work on the website for the *Review*.

There are many to thank for their financial support for the *Review* this year, including the Department for Communities and Local Government, the Welsh Assembly Government and the Scottish Government. The support of all these government agencies for the *Review*, representing all parts of the UK, is particularly welcome given that from time to time the *Review* will inevitably raise issues that are challenging for one or another of those agencies. The authors and the Chartered Institute of Housing are very grateful to Savills, the housing consultancy, for their support for the *Review's* production costs.

Thanks are due to the University of York and Heriot-Watt University, who have this year covered some of the costs of the *Review*. Thanks are also due to Genworth for their support for the work on the deposit barrier chapter, and to the Joseph Rowntree Foundation for their support for work on the universal credit chapter.

For all the diverse help provided, and despite every attempt that has been made to check and double check all the figures included in the *Review*, and the construction put upon them, the final responsibility for any errors, omissions or misjudgements is entirely that of the editors. The views expressed in the *Review* are the responsibility of the respective authors.

Finally it should be noted that this year the *Review* is under new management, with Hal Pawson from Heriot-Watt joining Steve Wilcox as co-editor. We hope this is the beginning of a beautiful partnership. And as this new partnership begins we would also like to place on record our thanks to both Alan Dearling and Peter Williams for all their work and help on previous editions of the *Review*.

December 2010

Professor Steve Wilcox
Centre for Housing Policy
University of York
Heslington, York YO10 5DD
Telephone: 01823 323891
Email: stevewpwilcox@aol.com

Professor Hal Pawson
Heriot-Watt University
Edinburgh
Scotland EH14 4AS
Telephone: 0131 449 5111
Email: H.Pawson@hw.ac.uk

List of figures and tables

The main tables included in the *Review* are located in Section 3: Compendium of tables. Table numbers 1-122 all refer to this Compendium. Other figures and tables are included in Section 1: Contemporary issues, and Section 2: Commentary, and the reference numbers refer to the Section, Chapter and specific table or figure (e.g., Table 1.3.2 is the second table in the Contemporary issues Section 1 Chapter 3).

Data in tables and figures are frequently rounded and/or updated and therefore will not always add up exactly.

The majority of the tables contain UK-based figures, but sometimes figures for Great Britain are used, depending upon the sources. All other tables will refer to the country(ies) concerned. Where English regional figures are shown, this is usually indicated in the title. Tables showing any breakdowns between England, Wales, Scotland and/or Northern Ireland are indicated with a single *, and those showing international comparisons with two **.

Housing, the economy and public expenditure

Dwellings, stock condition and households

Social housing expenditure plans

Housing needs, homelessness, lettings and housing management

Introduction

Introduction

The primary objective of this, the 19th edition of the *UK Housing Review* (initially called the *Housing Finance Review*), remains simply to draw together key current financial and related data about both public and private housing in the United Kingdom, and rapidly assemble them in a coherent and accessible format.

To that end the *Review* draws on a wide range of Expenditure Plans and Departmental Reports, as well as statistical volumes, survey reports, and other more occasional research reports. The *Review* also includes several tables constructed from databases that are not routinely published elsewhere.

The structure of the *Review*, and the sparse text, aim above all to provide a swift guide to the data, with detailed analysis confined to the Section 1: Contemporary Issues chapters at the beginning of the *Review*. This year, two of those chapters focus on welfare benefit issues, one examining the immediate proposals for housing benefit reform, and the other the medium-term proposals for wider welfare reform. Of the other two chapters, one focuses on housing management performance issues, while the other explores the implications of the 'deposit barrier' to owner-occupation.

The six chapters of Section 2: Commentary offer a brief introduction to and discussion of the key developments in policy, financial provision and output, that are reflected in the tables and figures in the main Compendium of tables. They also provide a reference to other publications and data that offer further useful insights into current policy issues. This year, Commentary Chapters 1 and 4 examine the general and housing implications of the 2010 Comprehensive Spending Review. Of the six Commentary Chapters, Hal Pawson wrote 2, 4 and 5, while Steve Wilcox wrote 1, 3 and 6.

A longer perspective

Many of the tables in the *Review* provide data over a long time-period. Wherever possible those tables start in 1970, providing data at five-year intervals for the years to 1990, with annual data for more recent years. The precise range of the years covered varies from table to table, depending both on data availability and the practicality of setting out data on a single page. Even with its landscape format, there are limits to the number of years' data that the *Review* can fit onto a single page.

Readers can consult earlier editions of the *Review* for data for the individual years between 1981 and 1989 that are no longer published in the current edition.

However, readers should exercise care as in some cases data for those earlier years may subsequently have been revised, primarily as a result of changes in definitions. A cross-check of the data for those years still published in the current edition of the *Review* will generally indicate whether or not this is an issue.

Regions

The *Review* contains several tables providing data for the regions of England. Many of those tables provide data for the long-established standard statistical regions. Government statistics are, however, now published primarily on the basis of government office regions. This presents difficulties in providing a consistent long run of regional data. Wherever possible, current data for standard regions have been sought, in order to provide a consistent data series. This has not, however, always been possible: equally long back-series of data for government office regions are not always available. In some cases, therefore, the *Review* includes recent data for government office regions, together with earlier data for standard regions. This is clearly indicated in the tables concerned.

There has also been a change in the nomenclature of government office regions. The Eastern region is now the East of England, and Yorkshire and Humberside is Yorkshire and The Humber. The government office regions are now generally shown under their current names. However, these names are not always used in our source documents or datasets, and we have followed the practice in the latest editions of our sources, rather than impose a uniform usage.

The North West government office region now includes Merseyside, and in many cases separate figures for Merseyside are no longer available. However, where Merseyside figures continue to be available these continue to be provided in the *Review*.

Government departments

Over the course of time, government departments are restructured or simply change their name. Thus over the years of the *Review's* publication the department responsible for housing policy in England has evolved from the Department of the Environment, through the Department of the Environment, Transport and the Regions, the Office of the Deputy Prime Minister, to now being the Department for Communities and Local Government, with the coalition government having reinstated the departmental prefix to the name.

Where data series have been made available continuously over that period, the reference given for that data in the tables of the *Review* is the current form and name of the responsible department. Where, however, reference is made to historical data the reference will be to the form and name of the responsible department at the time they were initially published or otherwise made available to the *Review*.

The UK Housing Review website

The whole body of tables in the *Review*, together with the commentaries, are available linked to the University of York website. An interim update to the tables in this year's edition of the *Review* will be available on the website in the Spring of 2011.

The address for the Review website is:
www.ukhousingreview.org.uk

Comments and suggestions

Finally, the editors would welcome any comments or suggestions on the current and future format and contents of the *Review*, and they can be contacted by email, phone or letter (see page 3).

Section 1   Contemporary issues 1

Post-millennium dividends?

Assessing recent trends in social housing management efficiency and effectiveness

Hal Pawson

Introduction

Aspirations for improved housing services were an important aspect of the stated commitment to public service reform which remained an overriding priority throughout the New Labour era. Since the 2010 general election, however, the coalition government has signalled a radical break with the Blair-Brown approach to public service management. Ministers moved quickly to distance themselves from what was seen as a centralised 'command and control' policy model slavishly devoted to performance targets and which stifled both managerial creativity and local accountability. The sharp divergence from the pre-2010 status quo has been symbolised by the abolition of the Audit Commission and by the all-pervading emphasis on 'localism'.

Specifically in the social housing field, the coalition's distinctly new approach has been embodied in ministerial plans for a fresh approach to regulation as primarily concerned with economic objectives rather than consumer protection.[1] And, with the November 2010 announcement that decent homes funding would no longer be restricted to councils with well-rated arms length management organisations (ALMOs),[2] the new administration has underscored its divergence from the New Labour 'rules of the game' which explicitly linked housing management performance with resource allocation (as further discussed below).

Against this backdrop, this seems an appropriate moment to review recent trends in social landlords' efficiency and effectiveness. How far has the target-driven, interventionist approach of the past decade actually borne fruit in terms of improved value for money and higher quality service delivery?

Before moving to the substantive discussion, however, two important points must be made. First, it should be recognised that – at least in relation to social housing – the new public service management model unveiled since the 2010 general election is not entirely novel. Rather, in certain respects, it continues and extends trends already under way under the previous administration (and paralleled in Scotland). Having terminated the Best Value Performance Indicators framework (in 2008), the Brown government was continuing to scale back housing inspection from its earlier peak (see Figure 1.1.1). Influenced both by the Cave Review and by other critics of 'heavy-handed' and 'burdensome' techniques, the regulatory model being installed by the Tenant Services Authority from 2009 placed greater reliance on self-regulation and a lighter touch approach than the previous regime.[3]

Secondly, while coalition government decisions on public spending and welfare reform affect the whole of the UK, social housing funding and regulatory frameworks are devolved matters not directly affected by Westminster thinking. Hence, the remit of the Cameron government's 'radical localism' agenda is limited to England. Nevertheless, at least in Scotland, the 2007-10 period saw social housing regulation evolving in a similar direction to that in England, with a transition from a substantially inspection-focused approach to a slimmed-down,

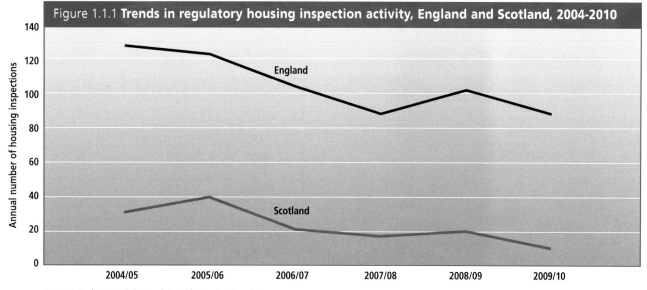

Figure 1.1.1 **Trends in regulatory housing inspection activity, England and Scotland, 2004-2010**

Sources: Audit Commission and Scottish Housing Regulator.

risk-based oversight model.[4] Unfortunately, given the paucity of data for Wales, the analytical focus of this article is concentrated on England and Scotland. The main body of the article looks first at efficiency trends, before moving on to a consideration of changing management effectiveness.

Tracking housing service efficiency

An explicit central government pre-occupation with promoting the efficiency and effectiveness of public service organisations can be traced back to the Treasury's Financial Management Initiative and the establishment of the Audit Commission in the early 1980s. An important development here was the creation of the local government performance indicators regime under John Major's 1991 Citizens' Charter. The main stated justification for the system was to strengthen municipal accountability to service users and taxpayers. In highlighting poor or declining provision, it was asserted, annual publication of performance scores would inform popular demands for service improvement. In practice, however, most of the specified indicators were focused more on process efficiency rather than service outputs or outcomes.

The council housing service activity measures within the 1991 framework were largely incorporated within the wider Best Value system introduced under the Blair government from 1998 and applicable to both local authorities and housing associations. However, many would contend that, particularly as it evolved over the subsequent decade, this framework was shaped mainly by the interests of regulators and policymakers rather than by tenants, directly. Now, with the 2010 DCLG review of regulation, we have come full circle with the government's declared aspiration that the prime role in assuring consumer protection in social housing should rest with tenants rather than the regulator. Hence the review's emphasis on the need for tenants to be able to scrutinise landlord performance.[5]

The housing management performance indicators which have become familiar over many years have focused on the three main functions of managerial activity, as shown in Table 1.1.1. While these can be criticised as rather narrow ratings of process efficiency, a trend-over-time analysis of these measures can nonetheless form a useful element of a more broadly based assessment of social landlords' service delivery performance.

Housing management performance data for individual local authorities and housing associations have been published annually for many years. However, there have been few officially commissioned studies which have sought to analyse and explain trends in these measures over time. One such assessment conducted a few years ago found little evidence of any clear trend of performance change among social landlords in England in the decade to 2001/02.[6] Against this backdrop it is striking to observe from Figures 1.1.2-1.1.4 that the past few years have shown a distinct and fairly consistent improving trend across all three of the functions examined, for all of the sectors included. For example, in the six years to 2008/09, English local authorities reduced uncollected rent by a third, cut the time taken to let empty properties by almost a quarter, and halved the proportion of urgent repairs failing to be completed on time.

In England, a specific driver of local authority performance improvement has been the ALMO funding regime. As established in 2001/02, this framework provided councils with the opportunity

---

Table 1.1.1 **Traditional housing management performance indicators**

Housing management function	Key measure(s)
Rent collection and arrears control	Current tenants' arrears at year end as a proportion of rent due in year Former tenants' arrears as a proportion of rent due in year Rent collected in year as a proportion of rent due in year
Empty property management	Number of empty properties at year-end as a proportion of total housing stock Average inter-tenancy interval for properties re-let in year
Response repairs	Proportion of repairs completed within specified target response time Average time taken to complete non-urgent repairs

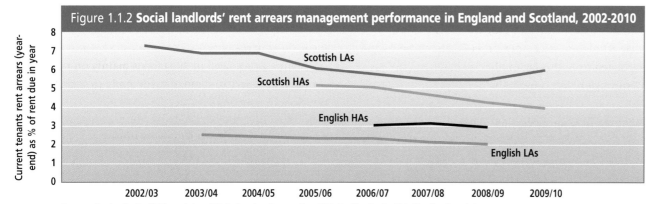

Figure 1.1.2 **Social landlords' rent arrears management performance in England and Scotland, 2002-2010**

Sources: England – Audit Commission, DCLG, Housing Corporation, TSA; Scotland – Scottish Housing Regulator.
Notes: 1. Figures show national median values for all landlords in each dataset. 2. Precise PI definitions vary across sectors on this indicator.

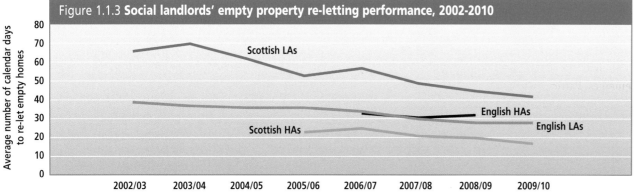

Figure 1.1.3 **Social landlords' empty property re-letting performance, 2002-2010**

Sources: England – Audit Commission, DCLG, Housing Corporation, TSA; Scotland – Scottish Housing Regulator.
Note: Figures show national median values for all landlords in each datase.

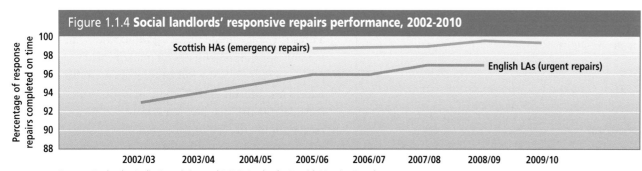

Figure 1.1.4 **Social landlords' responsive repairs performance, 2002-2010**

Sources: England – Audit Commission and DCLG; Scotland – Scottish Housing Regulator.

to access additional public funding to underpin decent homes investment.[7] At the outset, eligibility was dependent on having delegated housing management to an ALMO assessed as an excellent performer via Audit Commission inspection. Initially, it seemed that access to this route would be confined to traditionally high-performing local authorities among those in need of substantial stock investment. Traditionally weak performers in these circumstances would have no alternative but to opt for stock transfer in order to access additional resources, through private borrowing. In practice, research evidence has demonstrated that this 'adverse selection' hypothesis did not operate: local authorities achieving 'funded ALMO' status by 2009 included a number which had been among the least efficient and effective landlords in England only a few years earlier.[8]

The corollary of these findings is that the ALMO performance threshold indeed incentivised improved housing management performance among English local authorities retaining a landlord function. Detailed analysis focusing on performance indicator scores for the period 2002/03-2008/09 has shown that the gains recorded over this period by authorities with ALMOs tended to be greater than those registered by their non-ALMO counterparts.[9] At the same time, however, the period also saw aggregate performance gains recorded by non-ALMO councils, albeit to a slightly lesser extent in respect of the chosen indicators. This suggests that factors other than the ALMO funding regime have played some role in boosting council housing management performance in England over this period. And, indeed, the existence of the ALMO funding incentive can have played no role in stimulating the generally positive performance trends seen for English housing associations and for Scottish social landlords in Figures 1.1.2-1.1.4.

Another efficiency measure is unit management expenditure. Partly because accountancy conventions are not standard across all sectors, it is risky to compare different types of landlords, or landlords of the same type operating in different jurisdictions. However, the inclusion of Table 1.1.2 is mainly to illustrate within-sector change over time.

At least over the most recent four-year period, English local authorities recorded reduced real-terms management expenditure per dwelling – see Table 1.1.2. For English housing associations and Scottish local authorities, however, real-terms management spend increases were quite substantial during the

period. For local authorities, a factor here will be the shrinking stock base resulting from right to buy sales. However, since housing associations are largely insulated from this factor, their rising management costs must reflect other influences.

With recent indications that future affordable house building will need to be funded substantially through revenue contributions (either directly, or by supporting prudential borrowing),[10] social landlords are likely to face intensified pressures to restrain management expenditure.

So, taking together the evidence on 'process efficiency' housing management performance indicators and management expenditure rates, a somewhat mixed picture of the sector's recent record emerges. Particularly with respect to rent arrears, there must also be concerns as to whether it will be possible to sustain improved performance in future.

First, the proposed reforms to the housing benefit regime could impact negatively on rent arrears in the medium-term future. While the modifications to the HB regime announced in 2010 focus mainly on the private rented sector, some of them apply to social housing. In particular:

- Increased non-dependent deductions.
- Limiting HB payments to the appropriate amount for a property of the required size – while this proposal relates to working-age households only, survey evidence shows that this could nevertheless affect 22 per cent of all social renter households in England.[11]
- Reducing HB payments by 10 per cent for households receiving jobseeker's allowance for more than 12 months.

Whereas the first of these is due for implementation from April 2011, the latter two will come into force only in 2013. Hence, the full influence of these reforms on social landlords' rent arrears performance could be felt only some way into the future.

On top of these changes, however, with the prospect of rents for new tenants being raised to 80 per cent of market levels in England,[12] social landlords are facing a drastic change in the sector's ground rules with possibly substantial impacts on management performance. While the full consequences of this reform are difficult to predict, there must be a considerable risk that it will result in a serious escalation in arrears and bad debts, as well as possibly damaging void management performance in some localities by creating difficult-to-let housing.

Table 1.1.2 **Weekly per unit management expenditure – at 2010 prices**

	2003/04 £	2004/05 £	2005/06 £	2006/07 £	2007/08 £	2008/09 £	2009/10 £	Change – 2005/06-2009/10[2] %
England – LAs	15.03	16.28	16.40	15.90	15.77	16.52	15.29	- 7
England – HAs	–	–	15.85	16.22	16.78	18.03	–	14
Scotland – LAs	10.99	11.08	11.95	13.45	13.21	14.08	13.76	15
Scotland – HAs	–	–	18.74	18.90	17.77	19.49	–	4

Sources: England – LAs: Business Plan Statistical Annex (DCLG); England – HAs: Housing Association Global Accounts (TSA); Scotland – LAs: Scottish Government Statistical Bulletin; Scotland – HAs: Scottish Housing Regulator annual financial statistics tables.

Note: 1. Except for English housing associations, all figures are sector-wide median values.
2. 2005/06-2008/09 for housing associations.

Monitoring housing service effectiveness

Rating housing service effectiveness, or quality, is inherently much more challenging than measuring efficiency. However, reflecting the official priority given to improving service outcomes, the past decade has seen considerable activity here. The most visible part of this has been the large volume of housing inspection activity. In England, the need for clear inspection benchmarks led the Audit Commission to develop its intricate Key Lines of Enquiry (KLoE) criteria. Again, this approach can be criticised as embodying an excessive focus on landlord compliance with highly detailed processes and procedures. Nevertheless, by including techniques such as mystery shopping and complaints analysis, and by involving tenants directly – e.g. via focus groups – standard inspection techniques have also sought to assess services from a consumer viewpoint.

Table 1.1.3 sets out the Audit Commission's judgements on housing management services taken from over 300 inspections in the six years to 2009/10. Unfortunately, because of the Commission's methods for selecting organisations for inclusion, these statistics cannot be treated as a true cross-section of social housing suitable for simple inter-sector comparisons. In Scotland, however, because local authority inspections were staged as a comprehensive programme, it is at least possible to treat them as a sector-wide picture (albeit one spanning a relatively lengthy period). As shown in Table 1.1.4, half of all inspected authorities were well-rated on housing management whereas this was true for under a fifth of homelessness services.

Nevertheless, because inspections have never been undertaken on any regular cycle (e.g. three-yearly), inspectors' judgements cannot inform the monitoring of housing management effectiveness trends over time. In any case, the ultimate measure of service quality must surely be that of the consumer – in this case the social housing tenant population. This is where survey evidence of tenant satisfaction can play an important role. Drawing on large-scale national surveys, Figure 1.1.5 reveals somewhat contrasting trends for England and Scotland. Whereas satisfaction rates remain lower in England, the past few years have seen an encouragingly consistent pattern of improvement. No such trend has been apparent in Scotland. In part, this may reflect different points on the cycle of Decent Homes Standard and Scottish Housing Quality Standard property upgrading. Whereas the English compliance deadline was 2010, Scottish landlords have until 2015 to complete their associated works programmes (see Commentary Chapter 2).

Table 1.1.3 Housing management inspection ratings, England, 2004-2010

	Excellent	Good	Fair	Poor	Total
ALMO	4	27	15	1	47
HA	4	75	117	21	217
LA (non-ALMO)	1	7	47	23	78
Total	9	109	179	45	342

Source: Audit Commission website www.audit-commission.gov.uk/
Notes. 1. Figures exclude 're-inspections'.
2. 'Housing management' is defined broadly, e.g. including inspections focused specifically on 'repairs and maintenance' and 'allocations'; and including all ALMO (first) inspections.

Table 1.1.4 Housing inspection ratings for Scottish local authorities, 2004-10

	Excellent	Good	Fair	Poor	Total
Housing management	5	8	10	2	25
Asset management and repairs	3	7	14	1	25
Homelessness	1	5	22	4	32

Source: Scottish Housing Regulator (SHR). Note that the grade descriptions have been translated by the author to match those used in England – official SHR grades are A-D.

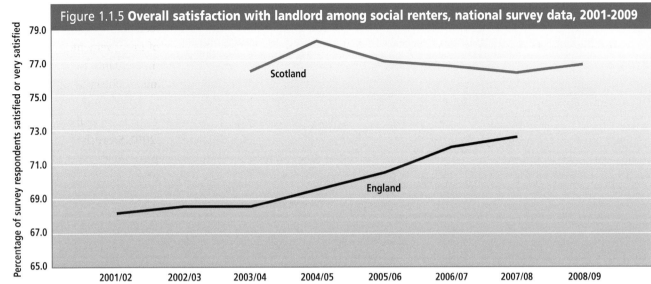

Figure 1.1.5 **Overall satisfaction with landlord among social renters, national survey data, 2001-2009**

Sources: England – Survey of English Housing; Scotland – Scottish House Condition Survey (special tabulations).
Note: SHCS figures post 2005/06 are for calendar years. Figure for 2006/07 is interpolated.

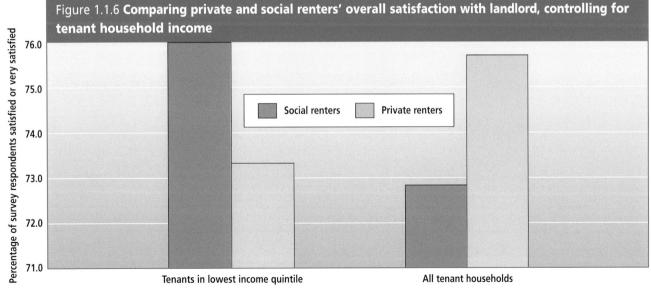

Figure 1.1.6 **Comparing private and social renters' overall satisfaction with landlord, controlling for tenant household income**

Source: Survey of English Housing 2007/08 (special tabulations).

While tenant satisfaction has been gradually rising in England, should social landlords regard ratings in the mid-70s as acceptable? One critical perspective on this was offered by John Hills who pointed out that private tenants' satisfaction ratings remain substantially higher than those for social renters.[13] Looking at Survey of English Housing figures from 2007/08, for example, the proportion of all private tenants who are 'overall satisfied' or 'very satisfied' with their landlord was 76 per cent as compared with only 73 per cent of social renters.

One response to the Hills observation is that private tenants are, by and large, a highly mobile component of the population and that their expectations of their landlord may in consequence be lower. Also potentially important is that the Hills comparison takes no account of the very different economic status and property quality profiles of the two sectors. While the social rented sector is relatively homogeneous in these terms, the private rented sector is nowadays highly diverse and incorporates a substantial up-market component. Exploring this further, Figure 1.1.6 illustrates the effect of controlling for income differences by comparing 'overall satisfaction with landlord' ratings for social and private tenants in the lowest quintile of household incomes. This illustrates that, if we focus on what is likely to be the more 'downmarket' end of private renting – more properly comparable with social housing – satisfaction ratings are in fact higher in the latter, albeit to a relatively modest extent.

Over the past few years, reflecting the regulatory emphasis on consumer protection, tenant satisfaction ratings have also come to play an enhanced role in official judgements of housing management effectiveness with respect to *individual* landlords. These have informed housing inspection ratings. They have also acquired a potential business significance for landlords as emphasized in the 2008 statement by the then head of the Tenant Services Authority that 'The [TSA] can and will direct the Homes and Communities Agency to stop funding landlords who fail to satisfy their existing tenants'.[14]

Using tenants' survey evidence in this way of course calls for a data collection framework sufficiently robust to generate statistics which are both reliable and properly comparable across organisations. While the National Housing Federation's STATUS methodology helped to provide such a basis in England, there are a number of respects in which the pre-2010 STATUS-based regime could have been made more rigorous.[15]

However, far from looking to enhance the STATUS-based framework, the coalition government looks set to dismantle it. Reflecting an overriding commitment to 'localism', ministers have made clear their disenchantment with the concept of nationally applicable performance measures for public services. In the social housing field, for example, it is argued that 'government should avoid being prescriptive about the precise form that performance information should take; instead, this should be agreed between landlords and tenants as part of local offers'.[16]

Statements of the kind cited above raise questions about the ongoing central collection of the 'traditional' housing performance indicators shown in Figures 1.1.2-1.1.4. More specifically on tenant satisfaction assessment, although there has as yet been no definitive statement on future regulatory requirements in this regard, the likely direction of travel has been signalled in the following: 'Whilst we would expect that you will still wish to measure periodically levels of tenant satisfaction…how and when you do so is up to you' (letter to local authorities from Department for Communities and Local Government, 4 August 2010).

Conclusions

The past decade has seen generally encouraging trends in social landlords' efficiency as measured by traditional indicators focusing on managerial processes. Among English local authorities this has been paralleled by falling real management expenditure per dwelling. In other sectors, however, unit management expenditure has risen substantially ahead of inflation. For England, steadily rising tenant satisfaction rates have provided heartening evidence of improving service effectiveness, although it seems likely that this also reflects the decent homes investment programme.

There is a concern that, at a time when regulatory inspection is continuing to be wound down, the Westminster government is looking to dismantle rather than strengthen the national framework for tenant satisfaction assessment. Given the risk that such reforms will lead social landlords to downgrade 'service delivery excellence' as a key corporate priority, they are a retrograde step.

Notes and references

1   DCLG (2010) *Review of Social Housing Regulation*. London: DCLG. www.communities.gov.uk/publications/housing/socialhousingregulation

2   Hardman, I. (2010) 'Decent Homes cash opened up to councils', *Inside Housing*, 11 November. www.insidehousing.co.uk/news/housing-management/decent-homes-cash-opened-up-to-councils/6512482.article

3   Tenant Services Authority (2009) *Building a New Regulatory Framework*. London: TSA. www.tenantservicesauthority.org/upload/pdf/Building_a_new_reg_framework_disc_paper.pdf

4   Scottish Government (2007) *Firm Foundations: The future of housing in Scotland*. Edinburgh: Scottish Government.

5   See para. 4.11 of DCLG (2010) *Review of Social Housing Regulation*. London: DCLG. www.communities.gov.uk/publications/housing/socialhousingregulation

6   More, A., Pawson, H. & Scott, S. (2005) *Evaluation of English Housing Policy 1975-2000: Management Effectiveness*. London: DCLG. www.communities.gov.uk/publications/housing/evaluationenglish

7   National Audit Office (2010) *The Decent Homes Programme – Report by the Comptroller and Auditor General*. London: The Stationery Office. www.nao.org.uk/publications/0910/the_decent_homes_programme.aspx

8   Pawson, H., Davidson, E., Smith, R. & Edwards, R. (2009) *The Impacts of Housing Stock Transfer in Urban Britain*. Coventry: Chartered Institute of Housing (for the Joseph Rowntree Foundation) www.jrf.org.uk/publications/impacts-housing-stock-transfers-urban-britain

9   Pawson, H. (2010) *Analysis of English local authority housing management performance 2008/09*. Briefing. York: Housing Quality Network.

10 Department for Communities and Local Government (2010) *Local Decisions: A Fairer Future for Social Housing*. London: DCLG. www.communities.gov.uk/publications/housing/socialhousingreform

11 Special tabulations from Survey of English Housing by Steve Wilcox.

12 See DCLG (2010) *op.cit.*

13 Hills, J. (2007) *Ends and Means: The Future Roles of Social Housing in England*. London: CASE/DCLG. http://sticerd.lse.ac.uk/dps/case/cr/CASEreport34.pdf

14 Social Housing (2008) 'Tenant Services Authority boss warns developers over grant complacency', *Social Housing*, December, p.5.

15 Pawson, H., Sosenko, F. & Ipsos MORI (2010) *Assessing Resident Satisfaction; A report for London & Quadrant Housing Group* www.lqgroup.org.uk/_assets/files/L&Q-report-V4.pdf; Pawson, H. (2010) 'A measure you can't trust', *Inside Housing*, 5th February.

16 Para. 4.17 of DCLG (2010) *Review of Social Housing Regulation*. London: DCLG. www.communities.gov.uk/publications/housing/socialhousingregulation

Section 1   Contemporary issues 2

The deposit barrier to homeownership

Steve Wilcox

Introduction

For the last three decades, following the deregulation of the mortgage market, it has been generally possible for households to become first-time buyers without first having to acquire a capital sum to provide a deposit.

Mortgages to cover 100 per cent of the purchase price have been widely available, alongside mortgages with relatively high loan-to-value ratios (LTVs), so that households with no savings, or only limited savings, could readily become homeowners provided only that they had a sufficient income to cover their mortgage repayments.

So over those decades, the primary discussions about the 'affordability' of homeownership, and the financial capacity for households to become homeowners, focused almost exclusively on the incomes which households required to access the market.

However, the housing market has now changed fundamentally in the wake of the post-2007 'credit crunch'. High LTV mortgages have virtually disappeared from the market since then. While this is due partly to cyclical factors they will remain scarce in future as a consequence both of the new FSA regulatory requirements and of the continuing constraints on the overall availability of mortgage finance.

Whereas in the past the availability of capital for a deposit could ease the affordability requirements for first-time buyers, the lack of such capital was not, in itself, an absolute barrier to homeownership.

However, unless there is some innovation in policies or products, the 'deposit barrier' to accessing homeownership is now set to become just as important as the more familiar and continuing 'income barrier'.

First-time buyer deposits

Average loan advances for first-time buyers, as a proportion of purchase prices, peaked at 90 per cent in 1996, before falling for the following seven years. While they rose again from 2003 to 2006, they only averaged 83 per cent in 2006, before falling to historically low levels following the credit crunch (see Compendium Table 42a).

Various factors are involved in this moving average over time, including affordability constraints, the gradual rise of inherited wealth, and the numbers of households returning to homeownership for a second time – but included as first-time buyers on the basis that their immediate previous residence was not another owner-occupied dwelling.

However, a key point to note is that even in 2006 and 2007, at the peak of the pre-crunch housing market, average deposits as a percentage of value (the obverse of LTV ratios) were higher than was the case throughout the whole of the 1980s, as shown in Figure 1.2.1.

Nonetheless, for a substantial proportion of first-time buyers, access to a mortgage with a high loan-to-value ratio, and thus a limited requirement for a deposit, was a critical factor in their being able to enter the homeowner market.

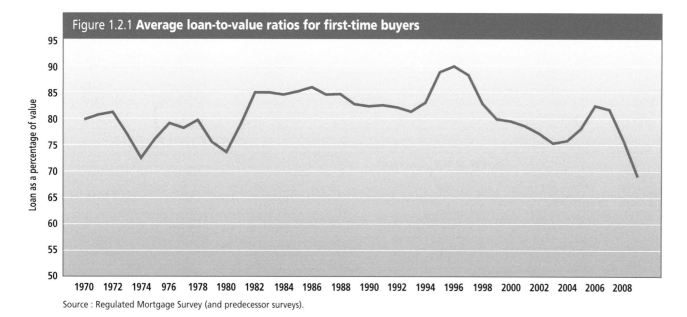

Figure 1.2.1 **Average loan-to-value ratios for first-time buyers**

Source : Regulated Mortgage Survey (and predecessor surveys).

The distribution of deposits as a proportion of purchase price for first-time buyers, for the years 2005 to 2009, is set out in Figure 1.2.2. The key point to note is just how important a feature of the market in those years were mortgage advances with LTVs in excess of 90 per cent, in that they represented over half of all mortgage advances to first-time buyers in the period 2005-2007, before falling to 44 per cent in 2008, and then plummeting to just 14 per cent in 2009 as the market responded to the credit crunch.

This translates into very substantial numbers – 218,000 first-time buyers managed to become homeowners in 2005 with LTVs of 90 per cent or more. This rose to 245,000 in 2006 before easing back to 214,000 in 2007, and then falling more sharply to 85,000 in 2008 and then just 28,000 in 2009.

Post-credit crunch, high LTV mortgages (i.e. those at more than 90 per cent of the purchase price) have become very scarce, and even 90 per cent advances are only available at a very significant premium. While mortgages of 90 per cent or more comprised three-fifths of all those on the market at the beginning of 2008, the great majority of such products were withdrawn from the market during that year. Since the beginning of 2009 such loans have comprised less than one in ten of the mortgages on offer.

Latest FSA data for the first three-quarters of 2010 also show that mortgage advances with an LTV of 90 per cent or higher now represent just two per cent of all new mortgage business. This is a further marked decline in the proportion of high LTV mortgage advances compared to 2009.

The fall in numbers and proportions of mortgage advances to first-time buyers with an LTV of 95 per cent or above has been even more dramatic. In the years from 2005 to 2007 these represented around a third of all advances to first-time buyers, but in 2008 this fell to a fifth, before dropping to under two per cent in 2009. Again, the numbers involved are substantial. Some 118,000 first-time buyers were able to enter the market in 2007 with LTV advances of 95 per cent or above, as against 38,000 in 2008 and just 3,000 in 2009.

In the course of the withdrawal of high LTV mortgages from the market, the Bank of England discontinued the data series showing the average interest rates for 95 per cent LTV mortgages – as they had virtually disappeared. It now shows series for 75 per cent and 90 per cent LTV mortgages, and in April 2010 the average interest rate for 90 per cent mortgages was 6.61 per cent, compared to just 3.83 per cent for a 75 per cent mortgage.

In a market downturn, when there are higher risks of falling property values, it is logical that the financial sector should be far more cautious about the risks associated with high LTV mortgages, and both restrict their availability – and price those still available – accordingly.

However, that rational, cyclical market caution is now set to be reinforced by new regulatory requirements to be introduced by the Financial Services Authority. Under proposals now out for consultation, the FSA does not propose an outright ban on high LTV mortgages. However, the regulatory

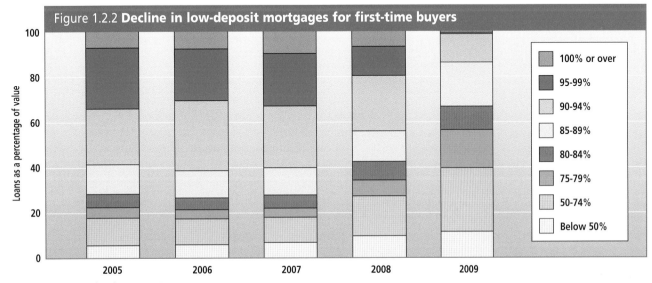

Figure 1.2.2 **Decline in low-deposit mortgages for first-time buyers**

Loans as a percentage of value

100% or over
95-99%
90-94%
85-89%
80-84%
75-79%
50-74%
Below 50%

2005   2006   2007   2008   2009

Source: Regulated Mortgage Survey.

framework it proposes – and, in particular, the higher capital provisions lenders would have to make against any high LTV advances – will be a clear constraining factor limiting the return of high LTV advances even when the market recovers.

While the FSA itself may be restructured, the regulatory framework it sets for the mortgage market is likely to remain in place, and in the medium term it is also likely to be reinforced by continuing constraints on the overall availability of mortgage finance, and an anticipated period of relatively modest economic and housing market growth.

Raising deposits

Even with the availability of relatively high LTV mortgages, the overwhelming majority of first-time buyers had to provide some level of deposit. Even in 2007 only ten per cent of all mortgage advances to first-time buyers were for 100 per cent (or more) of the purchase price (see Figure 1.2.2). And, with the sharp rise in prices over the past decade, the level of deposit required – even with a 90 per cent or 95 per cent advance – rose sharply.

For the UK as a whole, a deposit of over £9,000 was required, even with a 95 per cent advance, to purchase a dwelling at the average first-time buyer price in the second quarter of 2010. Some £18,600 was required with a 90 per cent advance. In London, and to a lesser extent the South East, typical deposit requirements were far higher. Almost £30,000 is now required in London as an average first-time buyer deposit with a 90 per cent advance (Table 1.2.1).

First-time buyers raise the funds for deposits in a number of ways, of which saving from income over time is the most important but not the only source. The latest survey evidence available shows that three-fifths of all first-time buyers who purchased in the three years to 2007 had some savings; while about a third either received a gift or loan from members of their family or friends, or had the benefit of some inheritance or other windfall (see Table 1.2.2 for further details).

More recent analysis by the Council of Mortgage Lenders has estimated that some four in five of younger first-time buyers (aged under 30) in the post-credit crunch market in 2009 received parental help with deposits. This compares with an estimate of just two in five younger first-time buyers receiving

---

Table 1.2.1 Deposits required with 90% and 95% mortgage advances in 2010

Region & Country	90% loan-to-value ratio	95% loan-to-value ratio	First-time buyer prices
United Kingdom	18,623	9,311	186,228
North East	11,649	5,824	116,489
North West	12,932	6,466	129,324
Yorkshire and the Humber	12,964	6,482	129,644
East Midlands	13,281	6,640	132,809
West Midlands	14,121	7,061	141,210
East	18,311	9,156	183,112
London	29,662	14,831	296,617
South East	20,915	10,457	209,148
South West	17,550	8,775	175,504
England	19,440	9,720	194,402
Wales	12,580	6,290	125,795
Scotland	12,934	6,467	129,341
Northern Ireland	12,345	6,172	123,448

Source: Prices from Regulated Mortgage Survey, 2nd Quarter 2010.

Table 1.2.2 Sources of contributions towards deposits for first-time buyers

Percentages of first-time buyers who purchased in the last three years

	1995	1998	2001	2004	2007
Savings	69	69	68	68	60
Gift/loan family/friends	22	22	24	22	29
Inheritance	6	6	6	8	6
Windfall	1	2	1	1	0
None	9	7	11	13	15

Source: Survey of English Housing.
Note: Multiple sources of contributions may be indicated in the survey

parental help in 2006, and less than one in ten before house prices began their sharp rise in the late 1990s.[1]

While the average age of first-time buyers (at 31) has remained stable post-credit crunch, a much wider gap has developed between the ages of those assisted to purchase, and those not receiving assistance. By April 2009 the average age for unassisted first-time buyers had risen sharply to 36, from an average age of 33 in October 2007. Consequently by 2009 there was a six-year difference between the average age of unassisted and assisted purchasers, whose average age was just 30.

Assisted purchasers are not only able to make fuller use of mortgages requiring a more substantial deposit, they can also afford to buy with lower incomes. In the second quarter of 2008, assisted purchasers were, on average, able to provide a 25 per cent deposit, compared to a five per cent deposit for unassisted purchasers. The average income of assisted purchasers was £29,420, but it was £36,490 for unassisted purchasers.[2]

Assisted purchasers were also, by virtue of their larger deposits, able to secure mortgage advances with higher income multiples (an average of 3.56 compared to 3.37), and also mortgages with lower initial gross interest rates (5.79 per cent compared to 6.12 per cent). Moreover, as seen above, by 2010 the gap between the interest rates on 75 per cent and 90 per cent LTV mortgages had substantially widened.

If a far higher proportion of first-time buyers are currently receiving parental assistance, this is in the context of a much reduced flow of first-time buyers overall – partly a function of the market downturn but also resulting from a disproportionate reduction in the numbers of unassisted purchasers in the post-credit crunch years.

Indeed, between 2006 and 2009 there was no significant change in the number of younger, assisted first-time buyers – running at somewhat over 80,000 in both years. But over the same period the numbers of younger, unassisted first-time buyers fell by over 100,000 a year – to just over 20,000 (see Table 1.2.3).

The CML estimates, however, relate solely to younger households (those under 30). In overall terms, the number of first-time buyers with mortgages with LTVs of 90 per cent or more fell by some 218,000

Table 1.2.3 **The decline in numbers of younger unassisted first-time buyers**
Numbers of first-time buyers aged under 30

	2006	2009
Assisted	80,200	80,700
Unassisted	120,900	20,200
Total	211,100	100,900

Source : Based on CML estimates of the percentage of assisted first-time buyers under the age of 30.

between 2006 and 2009, while there was a small increase in the numbers of advances to households with lower LTVs (of some 15,000). Younger households accounted for some 125,000 of the reduction in mortgages with an LTV of 90 per cent or more – with the balance relating to older households.

The CML has not estimated the proportion of older buyers that were assisted to purchase over the years. In part, this is a more complex analysis, not least due to the far higher proportions of older 'first-time buyers' that have previously been homeowners, but are now classified as buying 'first-time' because they made their new purchase when they were resident in another tenure.

In overall terms, it has been estimated that in any one year these 'returning' homeowners represent some 20 per cent of all first-time buyers, but are predominantly older first-time buyers.[3] Indeed only some two per cent of younger first-time buyers are 'returners', compared to just over a third of older ones (those aged 30 and above).

While many (but by no means all) of the returners will have retained equity from their previous period as a homeowner, those with such assets are less likely to require a high LTV mortgage. However, even if all the returners are disregarded, this still leaves a fall of some 50,000 in the numbers of older first-time buyers able to purchase with a high LTV mortgage between 2006 and 2009; a substantial proportion of these are likely to be those excluded from the market due to their inability to secure a high LTV mortgage.

The overall reduction in the numbers of 'unassisted' first-time buyers able to enter the market is thus rather higher than indicated by the 100,000 a year decline clearly shown for younger first-time buyers. Moreover, it should be recognised that while this represents a significant annual flow of households unable to access the market due to deposit constraints, over time this flow will grow cumulatively into an ever larger body of households excluded from homeownership.

While, eventually, some of those households will be able to save for a deposit, there are constraints on how far this prospect is a realistic one – discussed further below.

Renting and buying

In effect, the decline in the availability of high LTV mortgages is substantially affecting the ability of younger, working households, who do not have access to parental help, to become first-time buyers. Rather, it is forcing them to remain in the private rented sector for many more years than their contemporaries who *can* access parental help.

With the growth in the private rented sector over the last decade there has been a decline in the proportion of all households below retirement age living in the owner-occupied sector, and that decline has been most marked for younger households. Just over a half of those aged under 25 now reside in the private rented sector, just over a third of those aged from 25-29, and a fifth of those aged 30-34 (Table 1.2.4).

The growth of the private rented sector has had both push and pull impacts on the housing options of young households. On the one hand, it has contributed to the upward pressures on house prices, and thus exacerbated the price constraints for first-time buyers. A report from the (now abolished) National Housing and Planning Advisory Unit, for example, estimated that buy to let investments increased house prices by seven per cent in the years to 2007.[4]

On the other hand, buy to let investment has provided an increased supply of market rented housing, and over the last decade it has typically become cheaper to rent than to buy an equivalent sized dwelling,[5] as the costs of house purchase rose more rapidly than private rents.[6]

Private renting has the advantage of short-term flexibility for households. It has low transaction costs, and typically involves modest (returnable) deposits of one month's rent. While this may suit younger households in the short term, CML survey evidence shows that the overwhelming majority still aspire to homeownership in the medium term (Table 1.2.5). The private rented sector, with the very limited security it offers, is not in the UK a long-term household choice.

Table 1.2.4 Distribution of households by tenure and age

Percentages

	Homeowners	Private renters	Social renters
Aged 20-24			
1997	26	45	29
2002	28	42	30
2007	18	52	30
Aged 29-30			
1997	55	23	22
2002	51	28	21
2007	47	35	19
Aged 30-34			
1997	66	15	20
2002	67	16	17
2007	60	23	17

Source: Survey of English Housing.

Table 1.2.5 Households preferring homeownership

Percentages

	Under 25	25-34	35-54
In two years time			
1991	60	83	87
1999	59	77	84
2003	37	76	83
2007	50	75	83
In ten years time			
1991	90	91	89
1999	86	89	86
2003	76	87	87
2007	84	86	86

Source: CML, *Improving attitudes to home-ownership. Housing Finance*, March 2007.

However, there is a very substantial mismatch between aspiration and outcomes. Half of private tenants aged 20-24 would prefer to be homeowners in two years' time; in practice, by 2007, less than one in five had achieved this objective. Three-quarters of private tenants aged 25-34 would prefer to be homeowners in two years' time; in practice, by 2007, just 54 per cent had succeeded in becoming homeowners.

Moreover, there is no evidence to suggest any difference in aspirations towards homeownership as between assisted and unassisted first-time buyers. The deposit barrier to homeownership is thus set to require households – especially those without access to parental or family help with a deposit – to remain in the private rented sector for much longer than they would wish.

There is a view that younger households should be content to be private tenants while they save for a deposit; but this value judgement takes no account of the evidence on realistic household savings patterns, or the limited impact of schemes designed to encourage households to save for deposits.

The capacity of private tenants to save for a deposit is also likely to be squeezed by more recent moves in private rents back towards parity with the costs of purchase, because demand has risen (not least due to the homeownership deposit barrier) and housing supply has stalled.[7]

Wealth, savings and inheritance

The re-emergence of a deposit barrier for entry to homeownership raises questions about the extent and distribution of younger households' own wealth, and the potential scope for future growth in inheritances and parental support for would-be first-time buyers.

A recent report shows that levels of wealth are clearly linked with age, and that younger households have very limited financial wealth.[8] Indeed, the mean position for those aged under 29 is of having net debt, rather than net financial wealth, while those aged 30-34 have average net wealth of only some £3,000.

It should be stressed that while the data are the latest available, they relate to 2005 and thus do not yet fully reflect the impact of student loans (introduced in 2006/07) on the overall net financial position of younger households. Even so, the data show that only just over one in ten of those aged 25-29 have net financial wealth in excess of £11,700, while only a quarter have more than £1,100. Similarly, only just over one in ten of those aged 30-34 have net financial wealth in excess of £16,300, while only a quarter of have more than £3,600.

The same report also shows that younger households do not, typically, save. Data for 2000 to 2005 show that those aged under 25 have a negative median savings rate, while for those aged 25 to 34 the median savings rate is zero. These figures exclude savings in the form of housing equity for those that have succeeded in becoming homeowners. If housing equity is included, the savings rate for those aged under 25 is zero, while for those aged 25-29 it increases to just over 20 per cent, and for those aged 30-34 it rises to just over 35 per cent.

The essential point from this is that considerable caution is needed in considering the extent to which younger households can realistically be expected to save towards a deposit for homeownership while living in the private rented sector, particularly if account is taken of the rising burden of student loans.

The same point has also been forcefully made in a recent report from Oxford Economics. This makes projections, based on savings rate data from the Expenditure and Food Survey, suggesting that if younger households were required to save for a 20 per cent deposit it would take them an average of 40 years to do so.[9] It follows from this that even to save for a ten per cent deposit would involve a period of decades, not just a few years.

Conversely, the data from the wealth survey strongly make the point that becoming a homeowner is the most significant way for younger households to save – in the form of growing housing equity. While the level of growth in house prices between 2000 and 2005 was atypically high, the key point is that on average this was the only form of net saving by younger households.

Another recent report shows that the likelihood of households inheriting wealth will increase only modestly in the coming decades, despite the very substantial rise in the value of the housing wealth of older homeowner households over the last 15 years.[10] This research estimates the value of unmortgaged equity held by older homeowners (aged 60 and over) at £1,000 billion in 2006. If house prices continued to rise in line with inflation over the period, this was projected as rising to £1,400 billion (in real terms) by 2006. If house prices increased in line with earnings over the period, the value was projected as rising to £2,300 billion.

However, despite these very substantial sums, the report also shows how long it takes for housing equity to filter through to younger households in the form of inheritances. In part, this is because improving life expectancy is slowing down the point at which inheritance transfers. Taking this into account, inheritances are expected to grow from £16 billion in 2006 to between £19-30 billion in 2026.

If this will gradually become a rather more important factor, it does not represent a radical transformation, given that over the last two decades inheritances have only contributed towards six per cent of first-time buyer deposits (Table 1.2.2 above).

There is a similar caution to expectations of growth in future levels of parental assistance towards first-time buyer deposits. Clearly, in the short term the economic and housing market constraints do not create a positive context for parents considering the release of housing equity, or other funds, to assist with deposits. As noted above, while the proportion of first-time buyers assisted with their deposits has risen sharply in the last few years, this has been because of an even sharper fall in the proportions of unassisted first-time buyers able to access the market; it has not involved any significant change in the numbers of first-time buyers being assisted in each year.

There are also medium- and longer-term pressures on the housing assets held by older households, both in terms of supplementing retirement incomes and providing for the costs of care given the increasing likelihood of households living beyond the age of 75. Those factors have not been considered in the estimates of growth in inheritances outlined above.

Household preferences

As already seen in Table 1.2.5 above, the regular CML surveys have confirmed that – despite the rise in short-term private renting – younger households continue to aspire to homeownership, in both the medium and longer term.

A new household survey undertaken in July 2010[11] has also confirmed that the lack of mortgages available to first-time buyers with small deposits is now seen as the largest single barrier to becoming a homeowner: two-thirds of the sample of households aspiring to homeownership cited this as an obstacle. Moreover, almost half also cited the difficulties involved in trying to save for a deposit, given low interest rates on savings and the current economic situation.

The survey also found that just over two-fifths of the households primarily wanted to buy because they did not want to 'throw money away' on private renting. This was by far the most frequent reason cited by households for aspiring to ownership.

Conclusions

The credit crunch has seen a re-emergence of a deposit barrier to entry to homeownership, operating alongside the income-based affordability barrier. From now onwards, the deposit barrier is set to become institutionalised by the new regulatory regime being proposed by the FSA.[12]

While FSA's concern to ensure that risk is managed prudently in the mortgage markets is entirely proper, given the experience of recent years, it will have far-reaching implications for the wider economy not just for the housing market. It also represents a major development in housing policy which has dimensions that go well beyond the narrow regulatory remit of the FSA.

The deposit barrier acts as a constraint on first-time buyers entering the market – and can currently be said to have reduced the potential demand by younger first-time buyers alone by an order of

100,000 in 2009. It thus substantially exacerbates the housing market downturn. It is also evident that the excluded first-time buyers are predominantly those unable to obtain family help to fund their deposits, and that they are continuing to occupy private rented dwellings as a necessity rather than as a positive, long-term choice.

The existing evidence on household savings and inherited wealth also provides a strong caution about expectations that younger households will simply be able to save for a while longer as private tenants before making a slightly later entry to homeownership. Only a limited proportion of younger households will be able to make that deferred progression and, as seen above, the average period of deferral is likely to be measured in terms of decades rather than merely years.

Policy issues and options

For many years governments have sought to encourage and support younger households to become homeowners, and the new government has clearly indicated that, in principle, it continues to support those aspirations. In giving effect to such support, there are a number of steps that the government can take. There is an immediate need for it to engage with the FSA so that a regulatory framework emerges that properly meets the authority's prudential requirements, but without unnecessarily inhibiting the return of 90-100 per cent mortgages provided they are subject to appropriate standards of household risk assessment.

Beyond that, ministers need to reconsider the instruments of housing policy currently being applied to support entry to homeownership. The most widespread current instrument is shared ownership (and its variants). However, this is structured to deal primarily with the income (affordability) barrier to homeownership, rather than the deposit barrier.

The re-emergence of a deposit barrier requires a different instrument, and there are a number of options that could be considered. For example, in the years before the mortgage market was deregulated, mortgage guarantees were offered by local authorities to building societies, to back the provision of 100 per cent mortgages, both for key workers and for other local authority nominees.

Private sector-based insurance guarantees for high LTV mortgages are another option. There are forms of mortgage indemnity guarantee that provide cover to both borrowers and lenders. The cover for lenders avoids the risk to them of default, that is a proper concern for the regulatory regime, and can also replace the requirement for lenders to set aside increased capital cover.

Finally, the deposit barrier represents an important new obstacle to social mobility: the sons and daughters of tenant households are now disadvantaged in the housing market compared to the sons and daughters of homeowner parents, who are able to help them overcome the deposit barrier.

If this is to be addressed, government needs to reconsider policies advocated elsewhere,[13] which would either enable social renters to share in the equity growth of their homes, or to benefit from equity grants to enable them to move into the homeowner sector (and thus release a vacancy in the social sector for another household).

Without such policy developments, the level of owner-occupation will continue to decline, and it will be increasingly restricted to the sons and daughters of existing owners who are able to assist their children with deposits.

For all the (overly) prudential regulation of new mortgages, the mortgage market as a whole will remain unstable. The homeowners that run into difficulties with mortgage payments overwhelmingly do so as a result of unforeseen changes in personal circumstances. While the regulation of new mortgages threatens to be unnecessarily restrictive, far more intervention is required in terms of support and regulation at the 'back end' of the business when mortgagees run into difficulties (see Commentary Chapter 3).

Notes and references

1   CML (2009) 'First-time buyers – are they getting older?', *CML News & Views*, August; CML (2008) 'Family help for first-time buyers continues to grow', *CML News & Views*, November; CML (2007) 'Affordability – are parents helping?', *CML Housing Finance*, May.

2   CML (2008) *CML News and Views*, November.

3   Holmans, A. (2008) *Recent trends in numbers of first time buyers: A review of recent evidence*. CML Research.

4   Taylor, R. (2008) *Buy-to-let mortgage lending and the impact on UK house prices: A technical report*. Fareham: National Housing and Planning Advisory Unit. www.communities. gov.uk/documents/507390/pdf/684943.pdf

5   Wilcox, S. (2008) *Can't supply, Can't buy: the affordability of private housing in Great Britain*. London: Hometrack.

6   Wilcox, S. (2008) 'Where next for private renting?' in: Wilcox, S. (Ed) *UK Housing Review 2008/09*. Coventry and London: Chartered Institute of Housing and Building Societies Association.

7   Donnell, R. (2010) 'Lack of high LTV finance – implications for the housing market', *Estates Gazette*, 6 February.

8   Crossley, T. and O'Dea, C. (2010) *The Wealth and Savings of UK Families on the Eve of the Crisis*. London: Institute for Fiscal Studies.

9   Oxford Economics (2010) *Analysis of the likely age of a first-time buyer*. Oxford: Oxford Economics.

10   Holmans, A. (2008) *Prospects for UK housing wealth and inheritance*. London: Council of Mortgage Lenders.

11   One Poll Survey of 2,000 prospective first-time buyers, 2010.

12   Financial Services Agency (2010) *Mortgage Market Review: Responsible Lending*. www.fsa.gov.uk/pages/Library/Policy/ CP/2010/10_16.shtml

13   Hills, J. (2007) *Ends and Means: the future roles of social housing in England*. London: Centre for Analysis of Social Exclusion, London School of Economics and Political Science; Terry, R., Simpson, M. & Regan, S. (2005) *HomeSave: Increasing choices for tenants to own assets*. Coventry and London: CIH and Shelter.

Constraining choices: the housing benefit reforms

Steve Wilcox

Introduction

Proposals for wide-ranging and radical reforms to the housing benefit system were put forward in the June 2010 Budget. The proposals are intended to substantially reduce housing benefit expenditure and, in particular, to cut the level of support provided to private tenants through the local housing allowance (LHA) framework. Nevertheless, while reduced entitlements bear most heavily on those renting from private landlords, the reform package also includes provisions that apply to the social rented sector.

The proposed changes to LHA entitlements are clearly driven to a large degree by the government's imperative to reduce levels of public spending. However, they are also justified by

ministers on the basis that they will prevent claimants from securing high-value dwellings that are beyond the means of low-income working households, and that they will provide better value for money to the government by restraining the rents charged by private landlords to housing benefit claimants.

This article begins by tracing the rapid rise in housing benefit costs in recent years, and the underlying causes of this trend. It then sets out the proposed changes, as modified in response to a critical appraisal by the Social Security Advisory Committee,[1] and discusses the evidence on their likely impact, taking into account the potential behavioural responses by claimants, landlords and local authorities.

The rising costs of housing benefit

Housing benefit spending has almost doubled over the last decade, rising from £11.5 billion in 2000/01 to a forecast £21.5 billion in 2010/11. Only about half of that increase can be accounted for by inflation: Figure 1.3.1 shows that over the same period expenditure has risen by virtually 50 per cent in real terms.

Rents in both the social and private rented sectors have increased in real terms – broadly in line with earnings. Housing benefit caseloads have also grown in the last few years as a result of the economic downturn. The last five years have also seen a particularly sharp rise in the numbers of claimants securing private tenancies; not least due to proactive homelessness prevention policies in England aimed at reducing pressures on the limited supply of social rented housing (see Commentary Chapter 5). An element of recent increases is attributable to additional costs associated with the disregard of child benefit when calculating housing benefit entitlement.

The government has argued that increased rents charged to claimants reflect exploitation of the housing benefit regime by private landlords, and that this has also been a substantial factor accounting for rising programme costs.[2] However, the evidence for those claims is not robust. Even if it is assumed that all of the above-inflation rise in private rents for housing benefit claimants from 2000 can be attributed to landlord 'action', this would account for just £1.1 billion of the £10.5 billion total cash increase in housing benefit costs over the decade to

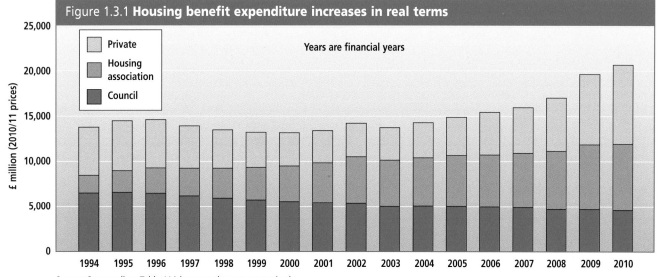

Figure 1.3.1 Housing benefit expenditure increases in real terms

Legend: Private, Housing association, Council

Years are financial years

Y-axis: £ million (2010/11 prices) — 0, 5,000, 10,000, 15,000, 20,000, 25,000

X-axis: 1994 1995 1996 1997 1998 1999 2000 2001 2002 2003 2004 2005 2006 2007 2008 2009 2010

Source: Compendium Table 114 (converted to constant prices).

2010/11. This view of rising costs is discussed further below, as it is related to the view propounded by ministers and other reform advocates that the lower levels of LHA rates will elicit a substantial reduction in rents charged by landlords, thus softening the impact on claimants.[3]

The reforms in detail

While the rising costs of housing benefit can be seen to be very largely explicable in terms of economic fundamentals and government policies, they are nonetheless an understandable cause for concern at a time when ministers are committed to substantial and widespread reductions in public spending to contain the overall government budget deficit.

However, while that imperative is reflected in the proposed housing benefit reforms, these have also been shaped by a policy focus on the relative position of claimants compared with low-income working households. That focus particularly relates to the proposals to reduce the levels of LHA available to claimants securing private tenancies.

The proposed reforms that relate exclusively to the private rented sector are as follows:

- restricting the maximum bedroom entitlement to the four-bedroom rate;
- capping maximum LHA weekly rates at £250 (shared room and one bedroom), £290 (two bedrooms), £340 (three bedrooms) and £400 (four bedrooms) respectively;

- setting LHA rates based on the 30th percentile of private sector rents (rather than the median);
- removing the provisions for claimants to retain a maximum of up to £15 per week, in cases where their contractual rent is below the LHA rate.

All these measures will apply to new claimants from April 2011; with some limited transitional protection for existing claimants that will mean that they will largely begin to be affected from January 2012 onwards. Then, from April 2013, LHA rates will be uprated based on the Consumer Price Index, rather than on the basis of assessments of actual local rents by the Valuation Office Agency (VoA).

In a subsequent announcement, the government said that it also proposes to extend the age range for single person households that only qualify for the 'single room' LHA rate, so that it covers all those aged up to 35.

In addition, a number of measures have been proposed that will impact on claimants in all rented tenures, including social sector tenants. They are as follows:

- The size criteria will be adjusted to provide for an additional bedroom for a carer where there is an established need for overnight care, from April 2011;
- 'Appropriate property size' criteria will also be applied to working-age claimants in the social rented sector from April 2013. Hence, council and housing association tenants other than those

of pension age will find their benefit limited to the rent chargeable for a dwelling with an 'appropriate' number of bedrooms;
- The rates of non-dependent deductions will be increased in three annual steps from April 2011, so that they reach levels reflecting increases in rents and council tax since 2001;
- Jobseeker's allowance claimants will only receive full housing benefit entitlements for a period of 12 months. Thereafter their HB entitlement will be reduced by ten per cent. This will apply from April 2013.

In recognition of the potential hardships that will arise for some households as a result of all the changes, the government has also made provision for increased expenditure on discretionary housing payments (sums that may be paid to tenants facing a gap between LHA entitlement and actual rental charges). The initial provision of £10 million in 2011/12 and £40 million a year thereafter was subsequently increased by a further £50 million spread over the spending review period.

Likely reform impacts

The initial DWP assessment of the impact of the housing benefit reforms to the local housing allowance regime was essentially limited to the 'first round' impacts on existing HB recipients, and included no consideration of the potential behavioural responses to the reforms, either by landlords or by tenants.[4] Key findings from that initial assessment are summarised in the following paragraphs. A wider discussion of the evidence on the likely impacts of the housing benefit reforms, including discussion of the evidence on the potential behavioural responses to them, then follows.

The initial DWP assessment included three sets of analyses. The first considered the impact of the changes set out in the March 2010 Budget. The second focused on the measures proposed in the June 2010 Budget. The third analysed the additional impact of the changes resulting from the June budget as compared with the consequences of the previously announced proposals. In all cases the assessments were set out in terms of their potential impact on customers receiving HB under the current LHA regime, as at March 2010.

The full assessment provides a range of alternative analyses and includes details of initial impacts for each individual local authority area. At the same time, detailed indicative figures for the proposed 30th percentile-based LHA rates have been set out on the VoA website for each month since March 2010, enabling these to be compared with the current median-based LHA rates.

Here, we provide a summary of the assessed effects of the LHA changes set out in the June 2010 Budget, showing their overall impact, and also showing separately the specific impact of the four-bedroom maximum rate and the maximum caps, and of setting rates based on the 30th percentile level of market rents.

The overall impact

Table 1.3.1 shows the overall impact by size of dwelling, and for households with and without dependents. It should be noted that all tables slightly understate the numbers of households affected, as the DWP analysis is based on the 939,220 cases for which full data were available, out of the total 1,015,330 LHA claimants at March 2010.

Table 1.3.1 clearly shows the substantially greater cash impact of the overall changes on households with dependents and, in particular, those requiring larger accommodation. The cash impact is relatively uniform across the country, but much more marked in London (averaging £22 per week for all claimants), partly as a result of the impact of the national caps in central London.

Within that overall impact, 414,000 households (44 per cent) were projected as facing losses of up to £10 per week, 469,000 (50 per cent) were set for losses of between £10 and £20 per week, while 44,000 (five per cent) faced losses of over £20 per week.

Impact of setting LHA rates at 30th percentile of market rents

Within the overall package of measures, Table 1.3.2 shows the impact of just setting LHA rates based on 30th percentile market rents by size of dwelling, and for households with and without dependents. Once again, this shows the greater cash impact of this specific measure on households with dependents, and those requiring larger accommodation. Similarly, while the effect is relatively uniform across the UK, average losses are far higher in London (at

Table 1.3.1 **Overall impact of 2010 LHA reform package by size of dwelling and household type**					
Impact group	LHA caseload	Average maximum HB £pw	Estimated number of losers	Estimated percentage of losers	Average loss per loser £pw
Shared room	74,690	69	73,610	99	- 7
One bedroom	387,740	107	386,560	100	- 11
Two bedrooms	328,250	139	328,250	100	- 12
Three bedrooms	112,550	164	112,550	100	- 15
Four bedrooms	27,900	201	27,900	100	- 22
Five bedrooms	8,100	260	8,100	100	- 57
With dependents	450,650	151	450,650	100	- 14
No dependents	488,570	103	486,310	100	- 10
Total impact	939,220	126	936,960	100	- 12

Source: See note (4).

an average of £17), reflecting the higher rent levels there, and the greater difference between median and 30th percentile rents.

Table 1.3.2 also highlights just how wide the effects of this measure will be across the claimant caseload – potentially affecting almost five out of six claimant households. Within the overall impact of the 30th percentile reform, 512,000 households (55 per cent) face losses of up to £10 per week and 223,000 (24 per cent) losses of between £10 and £20 per week, while 40,000 (four per cent) face losses of over £20 per week. This measure accounts for the greatest part of the reductions in expenditure within the total reform package.

Impact of the maximum four-bedroom rate and the maximum weekly caps

Table 1.3.3 shows the impact of the maximum four-bedroom rate and the maximum weekly caps by size of dwelling, and for households with and without dependents. The table shows the very substantial impact of these changes for the (albeit relatively small) numbers of households affected. Once again, the greatest impact is in London, with the national maximum caps in London affecting far more households than the maximum four-bedroom rate. Altogether, only 3,650 households outside London are affected by the maximum four-bedroom rate.

Behavioural responses to the housing benefit reforms

In practice, however, the net impact of the housing benefit changes will be mediated by the actions

Table 1.3.2 Impact of 30th percentile LHA rates by size of dwelling and household type

Impact group	LHA caseload	Average maximum HB £pw	Estimated number of losers	Estimated percentage of losers	Average loss per loser £pw
Shared room	74,690	69	70,430	83	- 6
One bedroom	387,740	107	298,700	94	- 7
Two bedrooms	328,250	139	294,490	77	- 10
Three bedrooms	112,550	164	94,680	90	- 12
Four bedrooms	27,900	201	13,500	84	- 20
Five bedrooms	8,100	260	8,100	48	- 36
With dependents	450,650	151	384,860	39	- 14
No dependents	488,570	103	390,110	85	- 11
Total impact	939,220	126	774,970	80	- 7

Source: See note (4).

Table 1.3.3 Impact of four-bedroom rate and maximum caps by size of dwelling and household type

Impact group	LHA caseload	Average maximum HB £pw	Estimated number of losers	Estimated percentage of losers	Average loss per loser £pw
Shared room	74,690	69	–	–	–
One bedroom	387,740	107	3,230	1	- 83
Two bedrooms	328,250	139	8,290	3	- 52
Three bedrooms	112,550	164	2,900	3	- 103
Four bedrooms	27,900	201	1,080	4	- 135
Five bedrooms	8,100	260	5,570	69	- 75
With dependents	450,650	151	16,970	4	- 72
No dependents	488,570	103	4,100	1	- 83
Total impact	939,220	126	21,600	2	- 74

Source: See note (4).

of landlords, claimants and local authorities. The critical questions are how far will landlords maintain the supply of lettings to claimants at lower rents; how far will claimants be able to move to cheaper accommodation; and how far will local authorities be able to deal with the net hardships for claimants within their increased budgets for discretionary housing payments. These are discussed in turn below.

Landlord responses

There is widespread agreement that the reduced LHA rates are likely to have some impact on landlord rents, and that the impact is likely to vary from one area to another. However, there is less agreement on the extent of such an impact, and very limited robust data on which to base such an assessment.

The government has argued that it expects to see a substantial impact on rents; albeit that it is likely to be more limited in areas of high housing demand where the housing benefit sub-sector is a relatively small part of the market. Ministers' case here is founded on the argument that overall the housing benefit sub-sector is now a very large part of the total market, citing in support evidence that rents in the HB sub-sector have been growing more rapidly than in the rest of the market. As ministers see it, this demonstrates that landlords have been taking advantage of the current regime at the expense of the public purse. The government has also presented evidence that landlords' rents are increasingly clustering around LHA rates. However,

none of that evidence is quite as compelling as might appear at first sight.

The case is made that between 2000 and 2007 rents in the housing benefit sector rose by 25 per cent in real terms, while in the wider sector they rose by just 15 per cent. These figures are not disputed. Further, both are drawn from robust sources. However, while the index of private rents relates exclusively to *assured tenancies*, the housing benefit rent figures include both *assured and regulated tenancies*, and the proportion of housing benefit cases for regulated tenancies fell from 14 per cent to seven per cent over that period. The proportion of HB cases for single person households also fell over the period – more rapidly than was the case for the wider private rented sector.

Moreover, it was only in 2008 that the LHA regime was rolled out nationally. In the preceding years, eligible rents for housing benefit were capped in a number of ways, including a cap based on Rent Service assessments of a reasonable market rent for the specific dwelling. It was under that regime, with the safeguards in place to protect the scheme against any landlord action, that the relative rise in HB sub-sector rents took place between 2000 and 2007.

The government also cites more recent evidence of HB rents rising while wider market rents have been falling. However, in this case it cites a web-based index of 'asking' rather than 'achieved' rents, that does not have any established methodological provenance. In contrast, the Valuation Office Agency

assessment of market rents led it to *increase* the levels at which the LHA rates were set.

If the data source quoted by the government cannot be regarded as robust, it must be acknowledged that there is a problem – in that there is currently no reliable index of private sector rents. But even if it were the case that rents in the private rented sector as a whole did not rise as rapidly, or as consistently, as rents for claimants this is not, in itself, evidence of landlord 'abuse'. The market for private rented housing has been subject to a number of pressures in the post-credit crunch years, and the changes in the LHA regime since 2008 are only one factor in a changing market.

While (at the time of writing) the full report of the two-year evaluation of the national roll-out of the LHA regime is yet to be published, Lord Freud indicated in evidence to the House of Commons Select Committee that the evaluation suggested that landlords were increasing rents towards LHA levels. In part, this involved local authority HB officers indicating that in some instances this was happening. Additionally, evidence was provided to show that there had been a degree of convergence of contractual rents for dwellings let to claimants around the LHA rates,[5] and this is set out in Table 1.3.4 opposite. However, in considering these findings, two points should be noted. The first is that there is more 'downward' convergence of rents that are above the LHA rate than there is 'upward' convergence of rents below the LHA rate. Secondly, these changes result from actions and decisions by claimants as well as by landlords.

Table 1.3.4 **Distribution of claimants' contractual rents relative to LHA rates**

Difference between rent and LHA	Apr 2009	Aug 2009	Apr 2010	Aug 2010
+ £15 to £20	26	29	30	31
+ £10 to £15	21	23	25	25
+ £5 to £10	14	16	17	17
+ £0 to £5	6	7	8	8
Equal to LHA rate	7	8	8	9
- £0 to £5	7	8	7	8
- £5 to £10	14	16	15	15
- £10 to £15	21	23	23	23
- £15 to £20	25	27	27	26

Source : DWP analysis of the Single Housing Benefit Extract.

The evaluation of LHA pathfinders found even less evidence of upward convergence of rents.[6] The authors also argued that the identified downward convergence of rents towards the LHA rate could be just as readily explained in terms of tenants' choices – in the light of the more transparent information the LHA rate provided on the level of benefit available – as it could in terms of any decisions by landlords to reduce rents towards LHA levels.

In overall terms, the modest net downward convergence of claimants' rents towards LHA rates does not suggest that landlords increasing their rents towards LHA rates is a significant factor in the rising costs of housing benefit for private tenants; nor is the slightly higher increase in claimant rents relative to LHA rates over a similar period.

Evidence on landlords' likely responses to the changes in LHA rates was also provided to the House of Commons Select Committee reviewing the proposals. Of particular note were a survey conducted on behalf of London Councils,[7] and an excellent analysis undertaken by the Cambridge Centre for Housing and Planning Research (CCHPR).[8]

The London Councils research involved a survey of landlords accredited under the London Landlords' Accreditation Scheme. While this was a small sample of a selective sub-set of landlords, it nonetheless suggested that a substantial minority of them would be willing to reduce rents to the LHA rates if the required reduction was of modest proportions. Almost two-fifths of landlords suggested they would

be prepared to reduce rents by up to £10 a week for smaller properties, while just over a third suggested that they would be prepared to reduce rents by up to £20 on larger properties. The survey also suggested that landlords would be far less likely to make any larger adjustments in the rent.

The CCHPR analysis based its assessment of likely landlord responses on the much larger representative surveys of landlords undertaken as part of the LHA pathfinder evaluation for DWP.[9] That survey was also based on landlords' accounts of actions they had taken in response to the new LHA regime, rather than hypothetical speculation on what they might do in the future.

The LHA evaluation found that, where the LHA rate was lower than the contractual rent, then one in six landlords had reduced the rent charged. In just over half of all cases the tenant made up the shortfall between the LHA and the rent, while almost 30 per cent failed to do so. In the latter cases the resulting rent arrears did not lead to any landlord action; and thus they de facto accepted the lower level of rent set by the LHA rates. Overall, the pathfinder evaluation suggests that just over 30 per cent (16 + 15 per cent) of all landlords had been explicitly, or implicitly, prepared to reduce their rents in response to LHA rates.

While these survey data are the best available on the 'landlord behaviour' consequences of the LHA system, they cannot conclusively show how landlords will react to the changes to the LHA regime now proposed: these involve a substantial reduction in LHA rates, and will come into effect in a very different market context.

When the LHA regime was first introduced, claimants comprised just over a quarter of all households in the private rented sector; now the proportion is closer to two-fifths. At the same time, the changing housing market conditions, the acute mortgage constraints on access to owner-occupation (see Contemporary Issues Chapter 2), and the continuing shortfall in new house building rates (see Commentary Chapter 2), add to the competitive pressures within the private rented sector.

To encourage landlords to reduce rents charged to claimants, the government announced in late 2010 a temporary measure whereby housing benefit could be paid direct to the landlord in cases where the landlord agreed to reduce the contractual rent to match the new, lower LHA rate. While this measure will reinforce the likelihood of landlords responding to lower LHA rates, the extent of that response cannot be precisely predicted. Within that context there is, however, agreement that the landlord response will vary from area to area depending on local market conditions, and the degree to which landlords have choice in securing tenants not reliant on HB. Given that the proportion of claimants within local private rented markets ranges from less than ten to over 80 per cent, then a similarly marked local variation in landlord responses to the new regime might also be anticipated.

Claimant responses

Claimants can respond to the lower LHA rates in a number of ways. They can seek to negotiate a lower rent from their landlord; make good the shortfall from their own resources; seek to move to cheaper accommodation, or seek local authority help.

The previous section has indicated that the extent to which landlords are prepared to reduce rents charged to claimants will be limited, notwithstanding the (temporary) direct payments incentive. The capacity for claimants to absorb shortfalls from their own resources is also limited; and it must be recognised that, even before the LHA changes, almost half of all claimants already face shortfalls.

This will leave a substantial proportion of existing claimants who are under pressure to move; and a smaller pool of dwellings available to them that will not involve an unsustainable shortfall in benefit entitlement. In some cases, and especially in inner London and some other high-value areas, the changes will effectively require households to move to areas with lower property values. This will clearly have an impact in terms of social polarisation. This will be most marked in central London, where it is estimated that only seven per cent of all properties in the private rented sector will have rents below the level of the capped LHA rates.[10]

The government argues that this is an appropriate outcome of a 'rebalancing' reform such that claimants should not be enabled to secure

accommodation unaffordable to low-income working households. This raises an important issue of 'horizontal equity' amongst lower-income households. Recently commissioned research has shown that low-income working households do, on average, reside in accommodation with rents slightly below current LHA rates.[11] However, this is also true for many claimants. Moreover, this is something of a false polarity as many claimants are also in low-paid work, and the non-claimant, low-income working households include a substantial minority that are eligible for housing benefit, but fail to claim.

But a further point that is made by the Walker and Niner study is that low-income working households are also competing, and will continue to compete, for lower-cost rented housing. That competition will constrain the extent to which claimant households can locate and secure dwellings in the cheapest third of the market.

There will be a particular squeeze in outer London, where not only will many existing local claimants be looking to trade down to cheaper properties, but the competition for places will be swelled by claimant households no longer able to maintain or secure private rented housing in central London.

The position will vary from area to area, but the net impact is almost certainly going to mean that not only will some claimants be effectively compelled to move, but that fewer will be able to secure a private tenancy of any kind. The various symptoms of housing market pressures for lower-income households are all likely to be worsened – from overcrowding and sharing of accommodation through to homelessness.

Local authority responses
It will fall to local authorities to mitigate the impact of the LHA reforms, in the first instance by allocating discretionary housing payments either to households who would otherwise be unable to continue in their existing tenancy or to assist households to secure otherwise unaffordable lettings.

Beyond that, councils will face additional demands in the form of homelessness applications from households unable to retain or secure private tenancies. These two dimensions are linked, and inevitably local authorities will look to use their increased DHP budgets to contain the potential demand from homeless applicants.

It is notable that, in recent years, numbers of homeless applications have fallen, and much of this has been a result of local authorities' proactive approach to homelessness prevention, with over 50,000 households assisted to secure accommodation in the private rented sector in 2009/10 in England alone (see Commentary Chapter 5). The CCHPR analysis estimated that the proposed LHA reforms will result in some 130,000 households being unlikely to remain in their existing accommodation. Of these, some 70,000 would be families with children, while some 20,000 would be single people or couples aged over 60. The estimated

cost (in terms of DHPs) to keep those households in their accommodation would be almost £60 million a year. In some cases, councils may be able to edge those costs downwards by negotiating a lower rent, either on the basis of guarantees or by agreeing to pay housing benefit direct to the landlord.

These estimates raise questions not just about authorities' capacity to cope with the transitional impacts of the LHA reforms, but their capacity to manage the demands of homeless households in the future.

Uprating LHA rates
From 2013 onwards it is proposed that LHA rates be uprated in line with the CPI (consumer price index), rather than in line with movements in private sector rents. On past trends this would further depress LHA rates relative to market averages, and year-by-year further reduce the proportion of dwellings in the sector effectively accessible to claimant households.

However the precise impact of this reform cannot be predicted, not least as the CPI measure itself is due for revision in the near future to include an element related to homeowners' housing costs. Moreover, it has been acknowledged by the government that CPI uprating cannot be left to run for many years before there is a more fundamental review of LHA rates, and the outturn impact of the new reforms.

Other measures
In the space available in this chapter it has only been possible to examine the housing benefit

reforms relating exclusively to the private rented sector. However, important aspects of the reform package will impact substantially on the social rented sector. In addition to the new size limits, the social sector will also be affected by the new 30th percentile-based LHA rates and caps, particularly for future 'affordable rent' social sector lettings (see Commentary Chapter 4).

Moreover, the ability of low-income households to secure or maintain accommodation in either the social or private rented sectors will be further constrained by the government proposals to impose a 'total benefits cap' based on average earnings. While this will apply only to working-age households not in work, it implies a far more restrictive limit on the maximum housing benefit available for the families concerned than the more immediate LHA caps.

The levels of the caps, and the maximum amounts available for help with housing costs, are illustrated in Figure 1.3.2 overleaf. For larger families in high-value areas these limits will not only have a far more dramatic impact than the LHA caps in the private sector, but will also limit their ability to meet either social or 'affordable' level rents.

Beyond those national caps, the whole welfare benefit regime is due to be recast in the form of the 'universal credit', and this will also impact on the structure and administration of housing benefit. Those reforms are considered in Contemporary Issues Chapter 4.

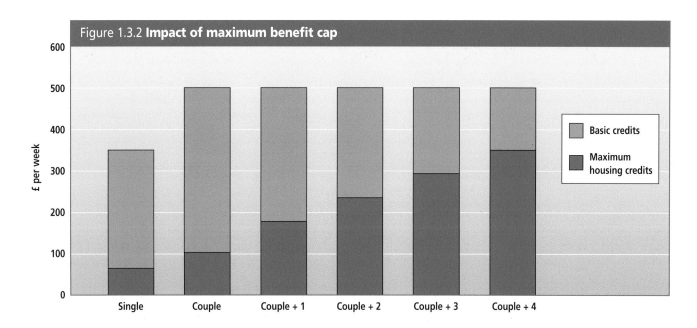

Figure 1.3.2 **Impact of maximum benefit cap**

£ per week

Legend:
- Basic credits
- Maximum housing credits

Categories: Single, Couple, Couple + 1, Couple + 2, Couple + 3, Couple + 4

10 Rhodes, D., Rugg, J. and Wilcox S. (2006) *The housing and labour market impacts of the Local Housing Allowance*. London: Department for Work and Pensions.

11 Walker, B. & Niner, P. (2010) *Low income working households in the private rented sector*. London: Department for Work and Pensions. http://campaigns.dwp.gov.uk/asd/asd5/rports2009-2010/rrep698.pdf

Notess and references

1 Social Security Advisory Committee (2010) *The Housing Benefit (Amendment) Regulations 2010 (S.I. no. 2010/2835), the Rent Officers (Housing Benefit Functions) Amendment Order 2010 (S.I. no. 2010/2836): report by the Social Security Advisory Committee under section 174 (1) of the Social Security Administration Act 1992 and the statement by the Secretary of State for Work and Pensions in accordance with sections 174 (2) of that Act*. London: The Stationery Office.

2 Wintour, P. (2010) 'Welfare Minister seeks a new definition of homelessness', *The Guardian*, 3 November. www.guardian.co.uk/society/2010/nov/03/welfare-minister-new-definition-homeessness?INTCMP=SRCH

3 Roe, P. (2010) 'Housing benefit cap was needed', *The Guardian*, 24 June. www.guardian.co.uk/commentisfree/2010/jun/24/housing-benefit-cap-needed

4 Department for Work and Pensions (2010) *Impacts of Housing Benefit proposals: Changes to the Local Housing Allowance to be introduced in 2011-12*. www.dwp.gov.uk/docs/impacts-of-hb-proposals.pdf

5 Department for Work and Pensions (2010) *Impact of the changes to housing benefit announced in the June 2010 Budget. Analytical Supplement submitted to the House of Commons Work and Pensions Select Committee Inquiry following the Oral Evidence Session on the 3rd November 2010*.

6 Rhodes, D., Rugg, J. and Wilcox S. (2006) *The housing and labour market impacts of the Local Housing Allowance*. London: Department for Work and Pensions.

7 London Councils (2010) *The Impact of Housing Benefit Changes in London – Analysis of findings from a survey of landlords in London*. www.londoncouncils.gov.uk/policylobbying/housing/benefit/landlordsurvey.htm

8 Fenton, A. (2010) *How will changes to Local Housing Allowance affect low-income tenants in private rented housing?* Cambridge Centre for Housing and Planning Research. www.cchpr.landecon.cam.ac.uk/Downloads/lha_reform_effects_prs-fenton-Sep2010.pdf

9 Rhodes, D. and Rugg, J. (2006) *Landlords and Agents in the private rented sector: the baseline experience in the LHA Pathfinders*. London: Department for Work and Pensions.

Section 1 Contemporary issues 4

Universal credit: issues, opportunities and the housing dimension

Steve Wilcox

Beyond the more immediate challenges of the housing benefit reforms lie Iain Duncan Smith's wider 2010 proposals for longer-term reform of the entire structure of welfare benefits in the UK, including the support that assists low-income households with their housing costs.

These are radical and ambitious plans which, if carried through, would be the most significant changes to the overall welfare benefits regime for forty years. The central proposal is to unify a wide range of current benefits for households in and out of work, to create a single 'universal credit'. The outline proposals were developed by the Centre for Social Justice,[1] and have now been taken forward in the Department for Work and Pensions 2010 White Paper, *Universal Credit: welfare that works*.

The universal credit is proposed to replace working tax credits, child tax credits, housing benefit, income support, and the income-related jobseeker's allowance and employment and support allowance. While the original CSJ report envisaged that universal credit would also include council tax benefit (CTB), current government thinking sees CTB being devolved to local authorities.

These changes are not put forward as administrative simplification for its own sake, but are aimed at both improving work incentives and making the potential gains to households entering low-paid work more transparent. Hence, as described by the Secretary of State, the new regime 'will ensure that work always pays and is seen to

pay'.[2] Central to this is that, with a single unified benefit structure, there will be a single 'taper rate' through which the universal credit is withdrawn as household earned incomes rise. This will replace the complex overlapping tapers of tax credits and housing benefits incorporated within the present system; mechanisms that can result in cumulative benefit deductions of 96 pence for every additional £1 in earned income.

The outline proposals for the universal credit are based on a taper rate of 65 per cent applied to households' net earnings. With tax and national insurance at standard rates, this results in a cumulative 77 per cent deductions rate. Not only is this far lower than the maximum under current arrangements, it is far more straightforward. Nevertheless, while the withdrawal rate is much lower than the cumulative rates that apply when tax credits, housing and council tax benefits overlap, it is still higher than the rate for households that do *not* receive housing cost benefits as well as tax credits, as seen in Figure 1.4.1.

Figure 1.4.1 shows how the universal credit would operate with council tax benefit continuing as a separate scheme, with the current 20 per cent taper rate. Clearly, if the universal credit scheme also incorporated council tax benefit, as originally proposed, it would be much simpler; its impact in reducing cumulative net deductions from gross earnings would be that much greater.

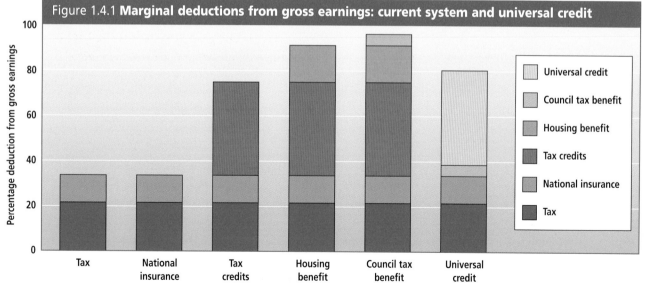

Figure 1.4.1 **Marginal deductions from gross earnings: current system and universal credit**

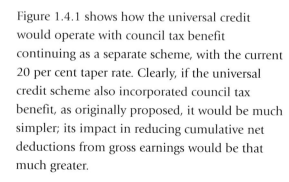

Remarkably, given the overall financial constraints on government spending, the current universal credit proposals are, in many circumstances, more generous than current benefits, and would provide most households in low-paid work with *more financial support* than received under present arrangements. While households not receiving help with their housing costs will face a marginally higher taper rate, in such cases the proposal is to offset this by disregarding a higher level of their earnings.

Through the overall increase in benefits, together with the relative simplicity and transparency of the scheme, and some sanctions on out-of-work payment programmes, it is hoped that a reduction in future numbers of out-of-work households will be achieved, thereby generating overall savings in benefits expenditure.

Just how the universal credit scheme will compare to the current benefits structure will depend on the final detailed form that it takes, but the potential gains are illustrated in Figure 1.4.2. This is constructed on the basis of the current 2009/10 benefits scheme, and assumes that the universal credit is founded on the level of income support allowances. It shows the impact for a couple with two children and an £80 per week rent, based on their having work with earnings at the level of the 2010 minimum wage.

This graph assumes that council tax benefit continues to be operated as a separate benefit by local councils, following current rules, rather than becoming part of the universal credit. If, as initially envisaged, council tax benefit were to be included within the universal credit scheme, then the income

range where households are better off under *current* arrangements would almost disappear.

Under the universal credit regime, those working just a few hours each week would be better off since, under income support rules which apply to people working less than 16 hours per week, a household loses benefit based on 100 per cent of their earnings after the first £10. Universal credit would thus improve the incentives for households to work even for a few hours each week, while at the same time easing the pressure for individuals to work for more than 16 hours a week.

In overall terms, the proposed approach has been broadly welcomed, but there are many issues of detailed policy design yet to be resolved, and aspects of the proposals that are problematic: no more so than in respect of the plans to restructure help with housing costs. This article first comments briefly on some aspects of the overall universal credit, before considering in more detail the issues involved with the approach to help with housing costs.

Some critical design issues

The integration of tax credits and welfare benefits is a major logistical challenge in terms of IT requirements and administrative reform. The proposals require the IT systems for HM Revenue & Customs and for universal credit offices to be linked, so that changes in earned incomes can be automatically picked up through the PAYE system, and immediately translated into variations in universal credit payments.

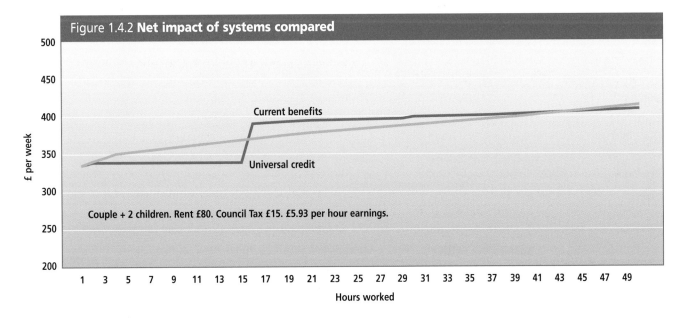

Figure 1.4.2 **Net impact of systems compared**

Couple + 2 children. Rent £80. Council Tax £15. £5.93 per hour earnings.

Current benefits

Universal credit

£ per week

Hours worked

This would minimise issues around under- and over-payments resulting either from administrative delays, or delays in reporting changes of circumstance on the part of claimants. There would also only be one office, and one set of rules for households to meet, in terms of reporting other changes of circumstance.

The practical challenges of this approach, however, should not be underestimated, especially given the evidence of the very substantial short-term volatility in many households' incomes and circumstances.[3] There are particular complexities for households with more than one earner, households where the single earner has two or more part-time jobs rather than a single employment, and for self-employed households entirely outside the PAYE system.

It also has to be said that HM Revenue & Customs does not have an entirely happy recent history in administering either taxes or tax credits, and there is a long litany of complex public sector IT developments being less than fully effective (or not arriving on time and within budget).

The exclusion of council tax benefit from the proposals is also problematic, as any means test applied by local authorities to CTB would increase the cumulative rate at which benefits are reduced as net earnings rise. If the current 20 per cent taper for CTB continues to apply, this would increase the overall rate of deductions from gross earnings from 76 per cent to 81 per cent (as shown in Figure 1.4.1 above). Moreover, as seen in Figure 1.4.2, the exclusion of CTB from the universal credit reduces the extent to which households would be better off compared to the current scheme.

While, in the main, the earnings disregards proposed under the universal credit regime are higher than under current arrangements, this is not so for single people, where no earnings disregard at all is envisaged. They will thus face the full costs of entering work (travel, meals away from home, etc) without any 'buffer' before the tax credit taper applies. Even with the higher earnings disregards for other households, there will still be those that face work-related costs in excess of the standard disregard provisions (see Table 1.4.2 below).

While the same issues arise under the existing benefit system, this weakness will take on potentially greater significance in the context of the tougher sanctions proposed for households refusing to take up offers of employment.[4] How will those sanctions be applied in cases where the offered employment involves substantial travel and other working costs, that would leave the household worse off?

The universal credit proposals are also problematic for lone parents in several ways. For their out-of-work benefits, the allowances they receive are essentially those for a single person with a child (or children). In contrast, for tax credits their allowances are those for a couple with children. The universal credit is proposed to be based on the levels of out-of-work benefits, and this will reduce the positive work incentives for lone parents. In addition, the provisions for assistance with childcare costs as part of the tax credit regime are also being scaled back.

There are many other important design features involved in the universal credit proposals, such is the extent of the change it involves compared to the current regime. But for all the challenges and complications, the potential promise of a simplified and more transparent benefit system is considerable. However, if that promise is to be realised, there needs to be a convincing approach to the issues arising from the complexities of the highly variable housing costs experienced by different households.

The housing cost issues

It should first be acknowledged that fitting help with housing costs into the wider welfare benefit scheme has always been problematic – dating all the way back to Beveridge. The failure to provide for an adequate gap between national insurance and welfare benefits meant that, from the beginning, out-of-work households were embroiled in means testing, rather than solely receiving an out-of-work benefit as an entitlement based on their national insurance contributions.

Similarly, the complexities of the overlap between housing benefit and tax credits date back to the early 1970s, when family income supplements and rent rebates and allowances were introduced as separate schemes within years of each other. It must count as a notable missed opportunity that an integrated, in-work benefit for child and housing costs was not introduced at that point.

The New Labour emphasis on boosting in-work benefits incorporated a whole series of reforms to the tax credit regime, all conducted without any attempt to deal with the issues around the overlap between tax credit and housing benefit systems. While the extent of these overlaps was reduced by the increased generosity of the tax credit regime, for those households that remained dependent on both tax credits and housing benefit, the interactions between the schemes became ever more complex and confusing.

The clear advantage of the universal credit scheme is that it removes the confusing overlap that is characteristic of the current schemes. However, the initial proposals about how to accommodate housing costs within the universal credit are not without their complexities and limitations.

Help with mortgage costs

On a positive note, it is proposed that the universal credit includes provision for help with homeowners' mortgage interest costs, as well as tenants' rental costs. This is potentially a major step towards a more tenure-neutral welfare system; albeit that full details have yet to be revealed. It will be much less significant if it time-limits help with mortgage interest costs as now applies to new claims under the support for mortgage interest (SMI) scheme (see Commentary Chapter 3 – Private Housing). There are also some doubts about whether this proposal will find its way into the eventual scheme. That said, it may be noted that an early proposal to provide help with housing costs for homeowners in low-paid

work was put forward nearly two decades ago in a report co-authored by Steve Webb, now Minister for Pensions at DWP.[5]

Despite the caveats, the proposal to incorporate help with mortgage costs within the universal credit would potentially provide assistance to homeowners in low-paid work, and would remove the current 'unemployment trap' which can leave homeowners who move into low-paid work worse off, as a result of losing SMI (in the absence of any in-work help with mortgage costs to supplement tax credits). This is not the case for all homeowners in low-paid work, as, for those with moderate mortgages, tax credit

---

Table 1.4.1 Gross earnings required for an after-mortgage-cost net income at the level of income support allowances

Based on 2009/10 benefit rates

Household type	Mortgage costs	
	All buyers £125 pw[1]	2009 buyers £145 pw[2]
Single person	£223	£270
Couple	£243	£310
Lone parent + 1	£120	£180
Couple + 1 child	£253	£319
Couple + 2	£302	£368

Notes: 1. A mortgage payment of £125 a week was the average in 2007/08 for all homebuyers with a mortgage.
2. A mortgage payment of £145 per week represents the median mortgage costs for a new advance to first-time buyers in 2009 (DCLG website live tables).

---

entitlements can be sufficient to ensure they are better off in work, even at relatively low levels of earnings, as shown in Table 1.4.1 below.

Nonetheless, this still leaves a significant gap in the support for homeowners' housing costs, leaving the system unable to ensure that low-paid households will always be better off in work.

Nor are the numbers involved insignificant. There were some 1.6 million homeowner households in receipt of tax credits in 2005/06 (excluding those that qualified only for the family element available to those with higher incomes). Of those, some 850,000 had weekly mortgage interest costs in excess of £50 per week, and some 260,000 had weekly mortgage interest costs in excess of £100 per week.

Plugging this gap in the system is also important in providing a route back into employment for homeowners that become unemployed, and as such would contribute towards stabilising the housing market in economic downturns.

Help with rental costs

Eligibility for the proposed help with rental costs is, at least initially, to be based on current arrangements for the private and social rental sectors. Social rents would be eligible in full (excluding ineligible service charges and non-dependent deductions); but they would be subject to the same local housing allowance (LHA) caps that apply in the private rented sector (see Contemporary Issues Chapter 3 for a discussion of the new LHA caps).

However, households receiving help with rents or mortgage interest will have the level of earnings they are entitled to receive – before their universal credit entitlement is reduced – set at a lower level. Households not receiving help with their housing costs will have the benefit of a higher earnings disregard.

Those receiving help with their housing costs will have their earnings disregard reduced by a multiple of their rent – and in the initial proposals that multiple is set at 1.5 times their eligible housing costs. This is subject to a 'floor' of minimum earnings disregards for those with higher levels of housing costs.

The higher and lower levels of proposed earnings disregards, plus the level of housing costs that will mean households receive only the 'floor level' earnings disregard, are set out in Table 1.4.2.

A first point to note is that even the lower earnings disregards are slightly higher than those that currently apply for housing benefit. The exception is for single people, who will no longer get an earnings disregard under universal credit, but do qualify for a disregard of (just) £5 under current housing benefit rules.

A second point to note is the very modest level of housing costs required before households will be eligible only for the lower-level earnings disregard. A third point is the oddity that families with more children will obtain only the minimum earnings disregard with a lower level of housing costs than families with fewer children. Given that larger families require larger accommodation, in practice they will also typically face higher housing costs.

In effect, this complex formula that scales down the level of earnings disregards in relation to levels of housing costs, mirrors the current complexities where housing benefit and tax credit tapers overlap. This serves to ensure that households not requiring help for their housing costs maintain the same advantages now available to them under the current tax credits regime. However:

- Maintaining the status quo in this way leaves in place arrangements where the positive financial incentives for households with housing costs are lower than for those with no, or very limited, housing costs.
- The highly complex nature of these arrangements cuts across the desire for a simple and transparent scheme that not only provides work incentives, but clearly delivers the message that 'work pays'.

An alternative model would be to set the earnings disregard at a single standard rate for each household type, whether or not they also qualify for help with housing costs as part of the universal credit. By comparison with the existing universal credit proposals, this approach would have two key advantages. First, its simplicity and transparency: it more clearly delivers the 'work pays' message, i.e. *'you can earn £xx pounds a week before you begin to see any reduction in the level of universal credit you receive'*.

Secondly, this alternative model provides improved work incentives for households with higher housing costs. They do face the universal credit taper applying over a greater range of earnings – but even with modest pay there would be a clear and more substantial gap between their in-work and out-of-work incomes.

Table 1.4.2 **Proposed earnings disregards for the universal credit scheme**

| Household type | Earnings disregard | | Housing costs that trigger the lower earnings disregard |
	Higher	Lower	
Couple	£57.70	£10	£31.80
Couple + 1 child	£109.60	£20	£59.80
Couple + 2 children	£109.60	£25	£56.40
Lone parent + 1 child	£148.10	£40	£72.10
Lone parent + 2 children	£148.10	£45	£68.70

Note: All figures rounded to nearest 10 pence.

Conclusion

While there are many advantages to the universal credit, as proposed, there are also many complex issues to be resolved in finalising the scheme, and considerable challenges in preparing the administrative and IT systems required to operate it (especially against the suggested timetable).

The issues around the treatment of housing costs, including CTB, are among the most significant matters needing to be resolved in the scheme's final design.

Universal credit offers a major potential gain for homeowner households if, as proposed, its scope includes mortgage costs. However, the complicated mechanisms for differential and variable earnings disregards for households receiving help with housing costs are perhaps the scheme's weakest element. The complexity and confusion of those proposals fly in the face of the overall objectives of simplicity and transparency, and clearly communicating the 'work pays' message.

Notes and references

1 Centre for Social Justice (2009) *Dynamic Benefits: Towards Welfare That Works*. London: CSJ. www.centreforsocialjustice.org.uk/default.asp?pageref=266

2 See p.1 of Department for Work and Pensions (2010) *Universal Credit: welfare that works*. London: DWP. www.dwp.gov.uk/docs/universal-credit-full-document.pdf

3 Hills, J., Sefton, T. & Stewart, K. (2009) *Towards a More Equal Society? – Poverty, inequality and policy since 1997*. Bristol: The Policy Press.

4 As detailed in Chapter 3 of Department for Work and Pensions (2010) – see previous reference.

5. Webb, S. & Wilcox, S. (1991) *Time for mortgage benefits*. York: Joseph Rowntree Foundation.

Section 2   Commentary

Chapter 1
Economic prospects
and public expenditure

Introduction

Managing and responding to the effects of the credit crunch remain central to both UK economic prospects and public expenditure plans. The year 2010 has been a busy one for UK government, which has seen two Budgets, one by the outgoing government and one by the new coalition government. They have been followed by a Comprehensive Spending Review and by major shifts in government policy across virtually all departments.

The focus of this Chapter is first on the prospects for the UK economy, and then on the overall implications for the spending review for public sector services. The specific implications of the spending review for housing expenditure and policy are discussed in Commentary Chapter 4.

Economic prospects

The credit crunch has led both to the sharpest economic downturn in the UK for many decades (see Figure 2.1.1), and to an unprecedented rise in levels of UK debt (Compendium Table 12c). In that context, government economic policy faces a difficult balancing act between the objectives of sustaining economic recovery and of containing and reducing levels of government debt.

Before the 2010 general election the previous administration had already indicated that there would be substantial reductions in public spending in the years ahead. The new coalition government has taken the view that it is necessary to accelerate and deepen the level of public spending cuts in order to retain international confidence in the UK government's fiscal policies. So far it has achieved that objective, and the UK has avoided the acute difficulties that have confronted both the Greek and Irish governments, and still remains a threat for other European governments.

The price of failure on that front would be higher costs for UK borrowing which, given the historically high level of UK government debt, would have further severe impacts on other aspects of government expenditure. As seen in this Chapter in last year's *Review*, while the level of UK debt is at an historically high level this is currently offset by the relatively low cost of UK borrowing, so that the costs of servicing that debt, as a percentage of GDP, are even now lower than during the 1980s.

However, by putting a stronger emphasis on the deficit reduction objective, the government has weakened the support for economic recovery, increasing its dependence on private sector economic growth to offset the deeper cuts now planned in public expenditure programmes.

The newly established Office for Budget Responsibility (OBR) got off to a shaky start, but is now acknowledged to be properly independent of HM Treasury. Following the Comprehensive Spending Review, it has reduced its forecast for economic growth in 2011 and 2012 (to 2.1 per cent and 2.6 per cent respectively), compared to the slightly higher forecast given in its (June) Pre-Budget Report (Compendium Table 11). Nonetheless, even allowing for standard measures of uncertainty in such forecasts, the OBR does not envisage a 'double dip' recession.

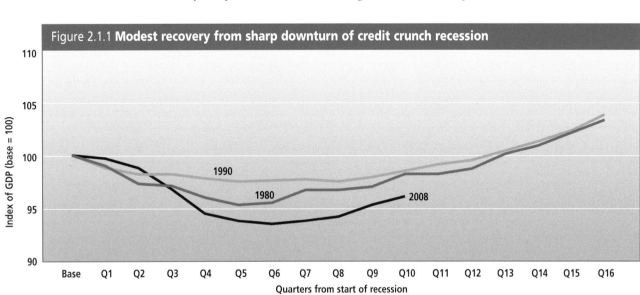

Figure 2.1.1 **Modest recovery from sharp downturn of credit crunch recession**

Index of GDP (base = 100)

1990

1980

2008

Quarters from start of recession

Source : Computed from ONS Quarterly GDP data (ABMI).

That said, uncertainty still remains. Concerns about job losses in the public sector, and by private companies reliant on public sector contracts, as well as tax rises and the sluggish housing market, will all constrain levels of household consumption. Housing equity withdrawal has plummeted post-credit crunch, and 2009 saw positive housing equity investment equivalent to almost three per cent of household consumption expenditure in 2009, compared to equity withdrawal of over six per cent of household consumption expenditure in 2007 (Figure 2.1.2).

And, as ever, prospects for the UK economy will depend to a large extent on developments in the wider international economy, and in China and the USA in particular. Neither the UK nor the world economy can yet be judged to have successfully navigated their way out of the post-credit crunch economic and fiscal difficulties, let alone to have put in place effective reforms which would significantly reduce the chances of financial dislocation in the future.

The Comprehensive Spending Review

The main tables in the Compendium set out the public expenditure plans, and forecast levels of government debt and borrowing, included in the second 2010 Budget Report, together with their related public spending analyses. However, those plans have now been significantly recast by the November 2010 Comprehensive Spending Review, which has confirmed the severity of the government's plans to reduce public spending over the next four years.

Overall government spending plans are shown in Table 2.1.1. In cash terms, total spending is set to rise over the period, but by less than the anticipated rate of inflation. The real-terms reduction in Departmental Expenditure Limits is rather sharper, as this is required to offset the increase in levels of Annually Managed Expenditure (AME). The two main growing elements within AME are central government gross debt interest, set to rise from £43.3 billion in 2010-11 to £63 billion in 2014/15, and spending on benefits and pensions, set to rise from £151.5 billion in 2010-11 to £163.7 billion in 2014/15. The growth in benefits and pension spending reflects the impact of the recession (and is due to occur despite several new measures to reduce benefit costs).

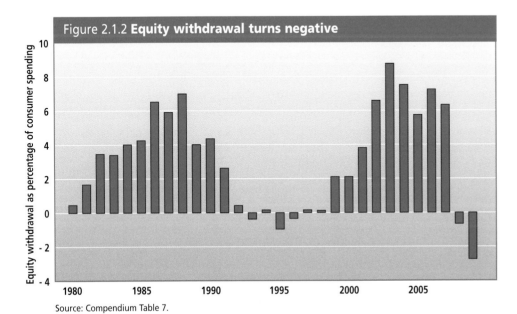

Figure 2.1.2 **Equity withdrawal turns negative**

Source: Compendium Table 7.

Table 2.1.1 **Comprehensive Spending Review 2010: Total Managed Expenditure**

£ billion

	2010-11 plans	2011-12 forecast	2012-13 forecast	2013-14 forecast	2014-15 forecast
Current Expenditure					
Resource Annually Managed Expenditure	294.6	307.8	319.5	329.1	344.0
Resource Departmental Expenditure Limits	342.7	343.3	345.0	349.6	348.7
Total public sector current expenditure	637.3	651.1	664.5	678.6	692.7
Capital Expenditure					
Capital Annually Managed Expenditure	7.8	7.3	6.7	6.4	6.9
Capital Departmental Expenditure Limits	51.6	43.5	41.8	39.2	40.2
Total public sector gross investment	59.5	50.7	48.5	45.6	47.1
Total Managed Expenditure	696.8	701.8	713.0	724.2	739.8

Source: Cm 7942.

Table 2.1.2 **Comprehensive Spending Review 2010: Departmental Programme and Administration Budgets**

	2010-11 baseline £ bn	2011-12 plans £ bn	2012-13 plans £ bn	2013-14 plans £ bn	2014-15 plans £ bn	Cumulative real growth Percentage
Departmental Programme and Administration Budgets						
Education	50.8	51.2	52.1	52.9	53.9	- 3.4
NHS (Health)	98.7	101.5	104.0	106.9	109.8	1.3
Transport	5.1	5.3	5.0	5.0	4.4	- 21
DCLG Communities	2.2	2.0	1.7	1.6	1.2	- 51
DCLG Local Government	28.5	26.1	24.4	24.2	22.9	- 27
Business, Innovation and Skills	16.7	16.5	15.6	14.7	13.7	- 25
Home Office	9.3	8.9	8.5	8.1	7.8	- 23
Justice	8.3	8.1	7.7	7.4	7.0	- 23
Law Officers Departments	0.7	0.6	0.6	0.6	0.6	- 24
Defence	24.3	24.9	25.2	24.9	24.7	- 7.5
Foreign and Commonwealth Office	1.4	1.5	1.5	1.4	1.2	- 24
International Development	6.3	6.7	7.2	9.4	9.4	37
Energy and Climate Change	1.2	1.5	1.4	1.3	1.0	- 18
Environment, Food and Rural Affairs	2.3	2.2	2.1	2.0	1.8	- 29
Culture, Media and Sport	1.4	1.4	1.3	1.2	1.1	- 24
Olympics	–	0.1	0.6	0.0	–	–
Work and Pensions	6.8	7.6	7.4	7.4	7.6	2.3
Scotland	24.8	24.8	25.1	25.3	25.4	- 6.8
Wales	13.3	13.3	13.3	13.5	13.5	- 7.5
Northern Ireland	9.3	9.4	9.4	9.5	9.5	- 6.9
HM Revenue and Customs	3.5	3.5	3.4	3.4	3.2	- 15
HM Treasury	0.2	0.2	0.2	0.2	0.1	- 33
Cabinet Office	0.3	0.4	0.3	0.2	0.4	28
Single Intelligence Account	1.7	1.7	1.7	1.7	1.8	- 7.3
Small and Independent Bodies	1.8	1.8	1.6	1.5	1.4	- 27
Reserve	2.0	2.3	2.4	2.5	2.5	–
Special Reserve	3.4	3.2	3.1	3.0	2.8	–
Green Investment Bank	–	–	–	1.0	–	–
Total	326.6	326.7	326.9	330.9	328.9	- 8.3

Source: Cm 7942.

Notes: Excludes depreciation. Devolved budgets are impacted by different arrangements for deferral of 2010-11 budget cuts.

The reduction in the DCLG Communities budget would be lower, at -33%, if grants moving to local government were included.

Table 2.1.3 **Comprehensive Spending Review 2010: Departmental Capital Budgets**

	2010-11 baseline £ bn	2011-12 plans £ bn	2012-13 plans £ bn	2013-14 plans £ bn	2014-15 plans £ bn	Cumulative real growth Percentage
Departmental Capital Budgets						
Education	7.6	4.9	4.2	3.3	3.4	- 60
NHS (Health)	5.1	4.4	4.4	4.4	4.6	- 17
Transport	7.7	7.7	8.1	7.5	7.5	- 11
DCLG Communities	6.8	3.3	2.3	1.8	2.0	- 74
DCLG Local Government	0.0	0.0	0.0	0.0	0.0	–
Business, Innovation and Skills	1.8	1.2	1.1	0.8	1.0	- 52
Home Office	0.8	0.5	0.5	0.4	0.5	- 49
Justice	0.6	0.4	0.3	0.3	0.3	- 50
Law Officers Departments	0.0	0.0	0.0	0.0	0.0	- 46
Defence	8.6	8.9	9.1	9.2	8.7	- 7.5
Foreign and Commonwealth Office	0.2	0.1	0.1	0.1	0.1	- 55
International Development	1.6	1.4	1.6	1.9	2.0	20
Energy and Climate Change	1.7	1.5	2.0	2.2	2.7	41
Environment, Food and Rural Affairs	0.6	0.4	0.4	0.4	0.4	- 34
Culture, Media and Sport	0.2	0.2	0.2	0.1	0.1	- 32
Olympics	1.0	1.1	0.2	0.0	- 0.1	–
Work and Pensions	0.2	0.2	0.3	0.4	0.2	- 5.5
Scotland	3.4	2.5	2.5	2.2	2.3	- 38
Wales	1.7	1.3	1.2	1.1	1.1	- 41
Northern Ireland	1.2	0.9	0.9	0.8	0.8	- 37
HM Revenue and Customs	0.2	0.3	0.1	0.1	0.1	- 44
HM Treasury	0.0	0.1	0.0	0.0	0.0	- 30
Cabinet Office	0.0	0.0	0.0	0.0	0.0	- 28
Single Intelligence Account	0.3	0.4	0.3	0.3	0.3	- 3
Small and Independent Bodies	0.1	0.1	0.1	0.1	0.1	- 52
Reserve	2.1	1.0	1.0	1.0	1.1	–
Special Reserve	0.7	0.7	0.8	0.8	0.8	–
Total	51.6	43.5	41.8	39.2	40.2	- 29

Source: Cm 7942.

Note: Devolved budgets are impacted by different arrangements for deferral of 2010-11 budget cuts. Departmental Expenditure Limits do not include prudential borrowing by local authorities.

The impact of the spending review on individual departments is shown in Table 2.1.2 (which sets out resource and administration budgets), and Table 2.1.3 (which sets out capital budgets). What is immediately clear is that the DCLG Communities resource and capital budgets will face the most severe of all the departmental budget cuts, and that the English local government resource budget is amongst those facing real budget reductions of over 20 per cent in the four years to 2014/15.

In contrast, the NHS resource budget increases by 1.3 per cent over the period, while the Education resource budget is to be cut by 3.4 per cent over the period. The overall resource budgets for the devolved administrations fall by marginally less than the overall UK average, and it will be for the devolved administrations to decide how they will distribute those reductions between different services. The implications of the spending review for housing expenditure programmes are considered in Commentary Chapter 4.

Notes and references

HM Treasury (2010) *Budget 2010*. London: The Stationery Office.

HM Treasury (2010) *Spending Review 2010*, Cm 7942. London: The Stationery Office.

HM Treasury (2010) *Public Expenditure, Statistical Analyses 2010*, Cm 7890. London: The Stationery Office.

Office for Budget Responsibility (2010) *Economic and Fiscal Outlook*, Cm 7979. London: The Stationery Office.

OECD (2009) *Economic Outlook 84*. Paris: OECD.

Office for National Statistics (2010) *Economic and Labour Market Review*. London: The Stationery Office.

Office for National Statistics (2010) *Financial Statistics*. London: The Stationery Office.

A very substantial volume of economic and financial data can now also be accessed from the Office for National Statistics website.

Section 2   Commentary

Chapter 2
Dwellings, stock condition and households

The changing structure of the private housing market

Dwelling stock trends for recent years reveal some striking developments with important longer-term implications for the UK housing system. Nationally, owner-occupation contracted in 2008 and 2009 – both numerically and as a proportion of the dwelling stock. Never before in the past 40 years has the UK seen falling owner-occupier numbers for more than a single, isolated year. In the last major housing market downturn in the 1990s, by contrast, the growth of homeownership (used here as a synonym for owner-occupiers) dipped into negative territory only for a single year – 1991.

The contrasting pattern of private housing market restructuring seen in the last two recessions is illustrated in Figure 2.2.1. As confirmed here, the past two years have seen an intensification of a declining homeownership *rate* which had been evident for several years towards the end of the pre-2007 housing market boom. This probably reflects growing affordability constraints as house prices continued to race ahead of incomes. The feasibility of government policy aspirations to expand homeownership significantly beyond 70 per cent remains very much in question.

The absolute contraction of homeownership post-2007 suggests that the number of formerly owner-occupied dwellings being rented out has been exceeding the expansion of the owner-occupied stock via new house building or sitting tenant sales of former social rented housing. This is partly about the falling output of the recession-hit private construction industry. However, while private sector house building has fallen sharply since 2007, developers still completed some 270,000 homes in 2008 and 2009. Falling homeownership numbers suggest that a substantial proportion of these homes have either remained unsold or have been immediately rented out, rather than being purchased by prospective owner-occupiers.

Another factor underlying the different patterns shown in Figure 2.2.1 is the dramatically reduced rates of right to buy (RTB) sales to sitting tenants over recent years. While annual sales of former social rented homes (in Great Britain) never dropped below 60,000 in the 1988-94 market downturn, the number recorded in 2009 fell to under 5,000. As shown in Figure 2.2.2, rapidly declining RTB sales have been seen in all of the constituent countries of Great Britain, although to a slightly lesser extent in Scotland where post-2002 restrictions on discount entitlement have been more limited.[1]

As illustrated in Figure 2.2.1, private rented sector growth has continued without interruption through the post-2007 housing market downturn. On the supply side, as noted above, this probably reflects the growing incidence of formerly owner-occupied homes being rented out by owners wishing to defer sales in the hope of a market recovery. Additionally, while immediate prospects of capital growth currently remain poor, buy to let (BTL) investment has continued to finance the purchase of homes for renting out – albeit that BTL mortgage lending has

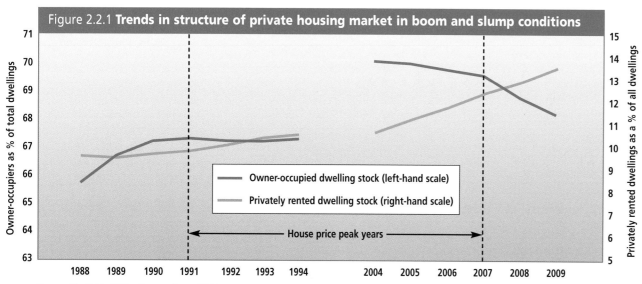

Figure 2.2.1 **Trends in structure of private housing market in boom and slump conditions**

Owner-occupied dwelling stock (left-hand scale)
Privately rented dwelling stock (right-hand scale)

House price peak years

Sources: See Table 17(d) – Compendium of Tables.
Note: Reflecting data availability, 1988-1994 figures relate to England only, whereas the 2004-2009 series is for the UK.

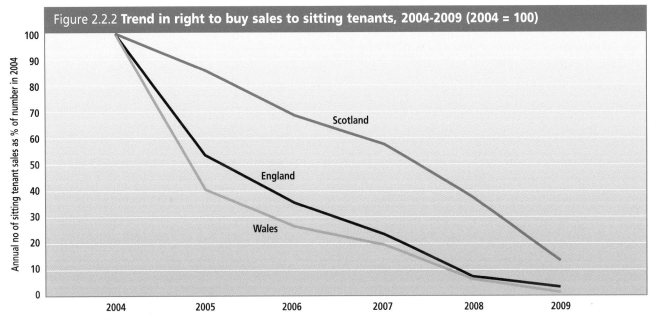

Figure 2.2.2 **Trend in right to buy sales to sitting tenants, 2004-2009 (2004 = 100)**

Sources: see Table 20d, Compendium of Tables.

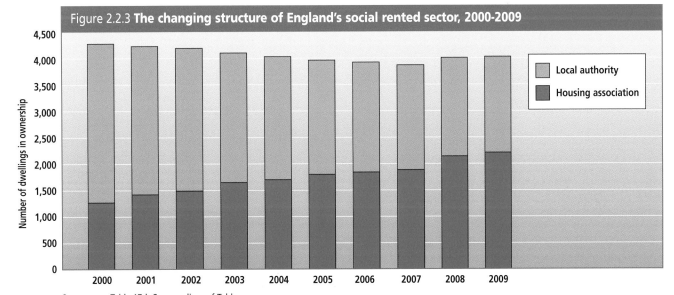

Figure 2.2.3 **The changing structure of England's social rented sector, 2000-2009**

Sources: see Table 17d, Compendium of Tables.

declined substantially from its 2007 peak. The 94,000 new BTL advances in 2009 represented only a third of the numbers recorded two years earlier. Moreover, it is important to recognise that over 40 per cent of recent BTL investment has re-financed traditional PRS stock rather than expanding the sector through the purchase of brand new or previously owner-occupied property.[2]

On the demand side, the expanding private rented sector is likely to reflect both the ongoing restrictions on mortgage availability for prospective first-time buyers, and the needs of homeowners needing to move but unable to sell their existing homes. Another factor may be the significant scale of local authority 'homelessness prevention' action in facilitating low-income households' access to private rented homes (see Commentary Chapter 5).

Social renting expansion

Across Great Britain, but more particularly in England, the past two years have witnessed a long-predicted milestone with housing associations taking over from local authorities as the majority providers at a national level. Thanks to a flurry of stock transfers in recent years, Wales is also approaching the same point. More broadly, the virtual cessation of right to buy sales (see Figure 2.2.2) coinciding with relatively high housing association house building activity, has resulted in Britain's social rented sector posting its first net expansion for 30 years. Both of these trends are illustrated for England in Figure 2.2.3.

However, if – as prefigured in the October 2010 Comprehensive Spending Review – public funding for new social housing is terminated in 2011, the recent reversal in the sector's decline will prove very short-lived.

Upgrading social rented housing stock

The past 15 years have seen significant improvements in the condition of the UK's dwelling stock. Measured in terms of the official Decent Homes Standard, the proportion of problematic dwellings in England has been reduced from 45 per cent to 33 per cent (see Compendium Tables 23a and 23b). As summarised in Figure 2.2.4, this trend has been evident across all housing tenures. Similarly, in Wales, the all tenure 'unfitness' rate was cut from

19.5 per cent in 1986 to 4.8 per cent in 2004 and in Scotland the proportion of dwellings failing one or more of the Scottish Housing Quality Standard criteria was reduced from 77 per cent in 2002 to 64 per cent in 2008 (see Compendium Tables 25a and 26b).

In policy terms, most attention has been focused on eliminating the repairs and modernisation backlog in the social rented sector. The starting point here was the establishment of official minimum standards in England, Wales and Scotland around 2001, with targets set to bring all social landlord properties up to these standards by 2010, 2012 and 2015, respectively. While the three standards were very similar, they were not identical (e.g. in relation to

their treatment of energy efficiency and the immediate surroundings of social housing). For the sake of simplicity, however, we refer below to the three standards as though they were equivalent to one another.

Evaluating the progress of the decent homes programme (and its Welsh and Scottish counterparts) is complicated by inconsistencies between different stock condition data sources. Figure 2.2.5 shows the extent to which social landlord statistical returns tell a more positive story than the trend suggested by the English House Condition Survey (and, latterly, English Housing Survey). As recounted by the National Audit Office,[3] possible explanations for the lower non-decency rates shown by landlord returns include the fact that these can exclude homes:

- where the current tenant has opted for their home to be omitted from relevant works programmes;
- where the homes concerned are scheduled for demolition.

Another factor is that Housing Health and Safety Rating System (HHSRS) category 1 defects are likely to be dealt with by social landlords as urgent responsive repairs. Taking all of these factors into account, the Westminster government announced in 2008 that, in monitoring ongoing progress in meeting the standard, it would rely primarily on landlord returns. Even on this basis, the programme remained incomplete in 2010 and it was expected that, as far into the future as 2015, a small number of social rented dwellings would remain non-decent.[4]

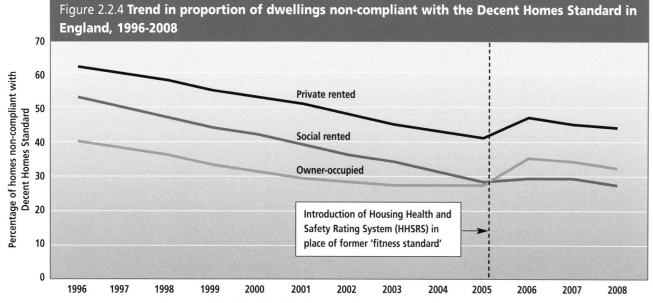

Figure 2.2.4 **Trend in proportion of dwellings non-compliant with the Decent Homes Standard in England, 1996-2008**

Y-axis: Percentage of homes non-compliant with Decent Homes Standard

Lines: Private rented, Social rented, Owner-occupied

Introduction of Housing Health and Safety Rating System (HHSRS) in place of former 'fitness standard'

Sources: English House Condition Surveys 1996, 2001, 2004, 2006, 2007 and English Housing Survey 2008.

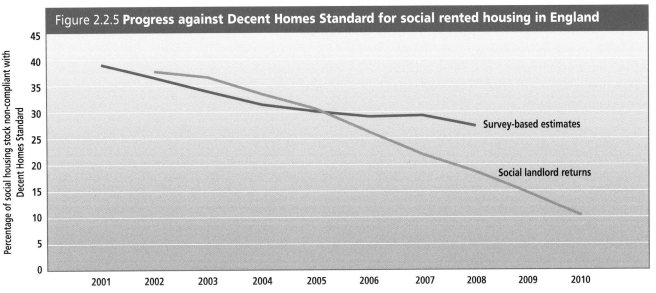

Figure 2.2.5 **Progress against Decent Homes Standard for social rented housing in England**

Percentage of social housing stock non-compliant with Decent Homes Standard

Survey-based estimates

Social landlord returns

2001 2002 2003 2004 2005 2006 2007 2008 2009 2010

Sources: Survey-based estimates – see Table 23a, Compendium of Tables; Social landlord returns – DCLG Live Table 119.

Table 2.2.1 **Social landlords in England: views on standard of 'decent homes' works implemented by comparison with actual DHS criteria**

Social landlord type	Refurbishment standard adopted as compared with DHS		
	Similar (%)	A little higher (%)	Much higher (%)
Stock transfer housing association	9	50	41
Traditional housing association	22	62	17
Arms length management organisation	8	70	23
Retained stock local authority	50	35	15

Source: National Audit Office.

At the time it was devised in 2002/03, a survey-based measure showed more than three-quarters of Scotland's social housing (77 per cent) as non-compliant with the Scottish Housing Quality Standard. As shown in Compendium Table 26b, there has been subsequent sector-wide progress, with the (survey-based) national non-compliance rate having been cut to 61 per cent by 2008. As in England, landlord monitoring returns paint a more positive picture, with these indicating a compliance rate of 50 per cent in 2008/09. Nevertheless, local authority progress has been considerably slower than anticipated by authorities themselves. While it had been estimated in 2005 that non-compliance would be cut to 45 per cent by 2009, the actual proportion at that time was 63 per cent.[5]

In evaluating the impact of the works programmes triggered by the Decent Homes Standard (and Welsh and Scottish equivalents), it should be borne in mind that the specified criteria acted as minimum thresholds rather than providing a fixed template. Provided they could access the required resources, landlords were free to negotiate with their tenants on locally defined enhancements to the relevant national standard. According to Table 2.2.1, the standards actually adopted have tended to vary according to the type of landlord concerned – at least in England. On this assessment, stock transfer landlords and arms length management organisations (ALMOs) have tended to be more ambitious than traditional local authorities and housing associations. As far as transfer associations are concerned, this confirms evidence from other research.[6] Such 'discretionary enhancements' have tended to involve higher standard security works and energy efficiency measures.

Commentary chapter 4 (on housing expenditure trends and plans) analyses the extent to which Decent Homes Standard activity (and equivalent work in Wales and Scotland) has resulted in increased repairs and maintenance expenditure by social landlords and how such 'extra spending' has been financed.

Household projections

The latest set of (2008-based) household projections for England forecast an average annual increment of 232,000 households for the 2008-2033 period.[7] While this is slightly down on the equivalent 252,000 figure published in the last set of (2006-based) projections, it remains substantially higher than the 160,000 homes built annually in England in the ten years to 2007. This would suggest continuing pressure on housing supply arising from household growth - with probable consequences including a resumption of long-term house price inflation.

Among the factors contributing to household growth, the most volatile is international migration. For the UK, the annual balance between immigration and emigration has resulted in net immigration being recorded consistently since 1993. However, while gross immigration has levelled off since 2005, net immigration has remained in the range 163,000-233,000 persons per year over this period. Latest figures show a slight increase in net immigration in 2009 resulting mainly from a sharp reduction in emigration from the UK, which fell back from a 2008 peak of 427,000 to 368,000 persons.[8]

For Wales, the latest population projections cover the period 2008-2033. As in England, the expected average annual growth in households - at almost 13,000 - exceeds 'normal' new construction output as seen prior to 2008.[9]

Latest household projections for Scotland (2008-based) anticipate a slightly faster growth rate than previously estimated. Across the 25-year period, an annual increment of over 19,000 is now expected – as compared with only 17,000 estimated by the previous 2006-based figures.[10] Even so, the new average annual projected increase remains slightly below the typical yearly house building numbers recorded for Scotland in the 20 years to 2007.

In Northern Ireland, 2008-based household projections[11] suggest that, on average, the number of households will grow by just over 8,000 per year over the period to 2023 – well below pre-credit crunch house building rates.

Even for Scotland, the 2008-based projections remain fairly similar to the previous 2006-based figures. For a more detailed analysis of 2006-based projections in England, Wales, Scotland and Northern Ireland, see the 2009/10 edition of the *Review*.

Notes and references

1   Wilcox, S. & Fitzpatrick, S. (2010) *The Impact of Devolution: Housing and Homelessness*. York: Joseph Rowntree Foundation. www.jrf.org.uk/sites/files/jrf/impact-of-devolution-long-term-care-housing.pdf

2   HM Treasury (2010) *Investment in the UK Private Rented Sector*. London: HM Treasury. www.hm-treasury.gov.uk/d/consult_investment_ukprivaterentedsector.pdf

3   National Audit Office (2010) *The Decent Homes Programme – Report by the Comptroller and Auditor General*. London: Stationery Office. www.nao.org.uk/publications/0910/the_decent_homes_programme.aspx

4   Local authority estimates included in 2010 Business Plan Statistical Annex returns to DCLG suggested that 100,000 council properties would remain non-compliant with the Standard at this date. www.communities.gov.uk/publications/corporate/statistics/bpsanondecenthomes0910

5   Scottish Housing Regulator (2010) *Scottish Housing Quality Standard Progress Update 2008/09*. www.communities scotland.gov.uk/stellent/groups/public/documents/webpages/shr_shqs2010progressreport.pdf

6   Pawson, H., Davidson, E., Smith, R. & Edwards, R. (2009) *The Impacts of Housing Stock Transfer in Urban Britain*. Coventry: Chartered Institute of Housing (for the Joseph Rowntree Foundation). www.jrf.org.uk/publications/impacts-housing-stock-transfers-urban-britain

7   DCLG (2010) *Household projections 2008-2033*. www.communities.gov.uk/publications/corporate/statistics/2033household1110

8   Office for National Statistics (2010) *Migration Statistics 2009*. www.statistics.gov.uk/pdfdir/miga1110.pdf

9   Welsh Assembly Government (2010) *Household projections for Wales, 2008-based*. http://wales.gov.uk/docs/statistics/2010/100929hseholdproj2008en.pdf

10 General Register Office for Scotland (2010) *Household projections for Scotland – 2008-based*. www.gro-scotland.gov.uk/statistics/publications-and-data/household-projections-statistics/hproj-08-based/index.html

11 Northern Ireland Statistics and Research Agency (2010) *Statistical report: 2008-based household projections for areas within Northern Ireland*. www.nisra.gov.uk/archive/demography/population/household/NI08_House_Projs.pdf

Section 2   Commentary

Chapter 3
Private housing

Introduction

This chapter focuses on the continuing downturn in the housing market, the *Review's* regular Affordability Index, and issues related to mortgage repossessions and private renting. A discussion of the future prospects for the mortgage market, and in particular the likelihood that high deposits will be an enduring requirement for first-time buyers going forward, can be found in Contemporary Issues Chapter 2.

Recovery not yet in sight

There were few signs of housing market recovery in 2009, or going into 2010. Levels of housing market transactions and mortgage advances for house purchase both bumped along at levels well below those in the pre-crunch years.

Property transactions did begin to pick up through 2009, although still well down on the pre-crunch years, but fell back again in the first half of 2010 (Figure 2.3.1). There was a similar pattern with mortgage advances for house purchase, but the latest figures for the months to September 2010 show that levels of mortgage advances have now stalled (Figure 2.3.2).

With limited levels of housing market activity, house prices also appeared to have 'bottomed out'; but showed no substantial signs of recovery (Figure 2.3.3). Clearly various factors underlie this position, and in particular the considerable uncertainty about the wider prospects for economic recovery (see Commentary Chapter 1).

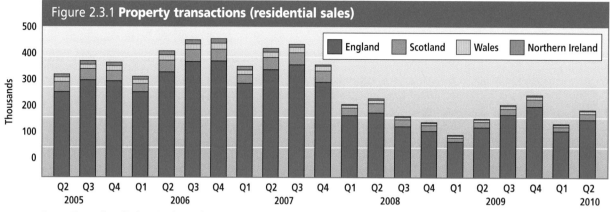

Figure 2.3.1 **Property transactions (residential sales)**

Source: Economic and Labour Market Review, ONS.

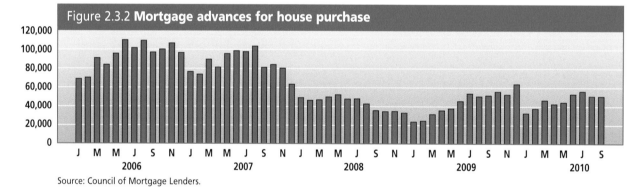

Figure 2.3.2 **Mortgage advances for house purchase**

Source: Council of Mortgage Lenders.

Figure 2.3.3 **House prices bottom out**

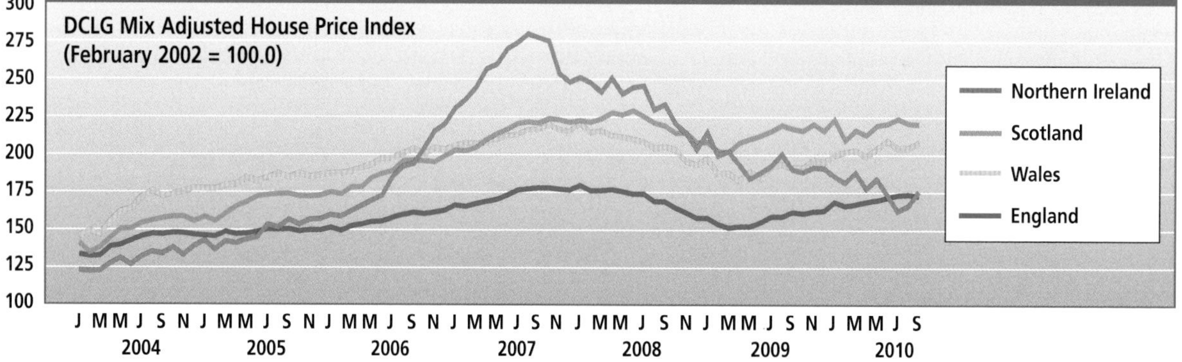

DCLG Mix Adjusted House Price Index (February 2002 = 100.0)

Table 2.3.1 **Affordability Index**
Based on mortgage costs for first-time buyers and average incomes for all working households

Country/Region	1994	1995	1996	1997	1998	1999	2000	2001	2002	2003	2004	2005	2006	2007	2008	2009
United Kingdom	100.0	94.3	95.2	110.5	120.0	122.9	133.3	123.8	143.8	139.0	186.7	181.9	185.7	209.5	196.2	164.8
North East	100.0	92.8	96.4	103.6	122.9	121.7	128.9	109.6	114.5	116.9	175.9	179.5	189.2	218.1	207.2	175.9
North West	100.0	93.9	90.8	105.1	111.2	109.2	123.5	112.2	120.4	108.2	152.0	160.2	174.5	196.9	183.7	152.0
Yorkshire and The Humber	100.0	95.8	92.6	106.3	117.9	116.8	126.3	108.4	120.0	116.8	162.1	167.4	181.1	203.2	189.5	162.1
East Midlands	100.0	95.7	93.5	114.1	119.6	119.6	128.3	117.4	134.8	140.2	194.6	190.2	185.9	213.6	196.6	160.2
West Midlands	100.0	93.6	89.0	98.2	101.8	104.6	112.8	110.1	122.9	116.5	154.1	153.2	155.0	168.8	156.9	130.3
East	100.0	94.5	95.5	113.6	118.2	120.0	137.3	136.4	152.7	148.2	185.5	184.5	186.4	209.1	193.6	154.5
London	100.0	104.5	102.7	122.5	136.0	148.6	155.9	149.5	163.1	159.5	212.6	203.6	221.6	251.4	232.4	186.5
South East	100.0	91.6	91.6	105.0	118.5	117.6	134.5	131.1	152.1	150.4	189.9	168.9	167.2	185.7	173.1	140.3
South West	100.0	93.8	93.8	113.3	123.0	126.5	140.7	137.2	158.4	159.3	208.0	192.9	189.4	210.6	191.2	156.6
England	100.0	92.7	92.7	109.2	117.4	121.1	130.3	125.7	142.2	140.4	187.2	180.7	184.4	207.3	192.7	161.5
Wales	100.0	89.0	91.0	101.0	116.0	116.0	123.0	119.0	125.0	112.0	167.0	171.0	178.0	200.0	187.0	153.0
Scotland	100.0	100.0	103.8	115.4	142.3	144.9	143.6	132.1	134.6	121.8	166.7	157.7	167.9	203.8	200.0	175.6
Northern Ireland	100.0	115.5	118.3	143.7	170.4	169.0	184.5	167.6	176.1	159.2	200.0	225.4	271.8	387.3	340.8	240.8

Source: Computed from Regulated Mortgage Survey house prices for first-time buyers and household earnings data from the Expenditure & Food Survey.
Note: Mortgage costs assume a constant 82% mortgage advance to house price ratio, in line with the average over the period. They are based on average mortgage lender rates for new mortgages in the last quarter of the year, and assume a standard 25-year repayment mortgage.

Table 2.3.2 **Mortgage cost to income ratios**
Based on first-time buyer house prices and average incomes for all working households

Country/Region	1994	1995	1996	1997	1998	1999	2000	2001	2002	2003	2004	2005	2006	2007	2008	2009
United Kingdom	10.5	9.9	10.0	11.6	12.6	12.9	14.0	13.0	15.1	14.6	19.6	19.1	19.5	22.0	20.6	17.3
North East	8.3	7.7	8.0	8.6	10.2	10.1	10.7	9.1	9.5	9.7	14.6	14.9	15.7	18.1	17.2	14.6
North West	9.8	9.2	8.9	10.3	10.9	10.7	12.1	11.0	11.8	10.6	14.9	15.7	17.1	19.3	18.0	14.9
Yorkshire and The Humber	9.5	9.1	8.8	10.1	11.2	11.1	12.0	10.3	11.4	11.1	15.4	15.9	17.2	19.3	18.0	15.4
East Midlands	9.2	8.8	8.6	10.5	11.0	11.0	11.8	10.8	12.4	12.9	17.9	17.5	17.1	18.8	17.3	14.1
West Midlands	10.9	10.2	9.7	10.7	11.1	11.4	12.3	12.0	13.4	12.7	16.8	16.7	16.9	18.4	17.1	14.2
East	11.0	10.4	10.5	12.5	13.0	13.2	15.1	15.0	16.8	16.3	20.4	20.3	20.5	23.0	21.3	17.0
London	11.1	11.6	11.4	13.6	15.1	16.5	17.3	16.6	18.1	17.7	23.6	22.6	24.6	27.9	25.8	20.7
South East	11.9	10.9	10.9	12.5	14.1	14.0	16.0	15.6	18.1	17.9	22.6	20.1	19.9	22.1	20.6	16.7
South West	11.3	10.6	10.6	12.8	13.9	14.3	15.9	15.5	17.9	18.0	23.5	21.8	21.4	23.8	21.6	17.7
England	10.9	10.1	10.1	11.9	12.8	13.2	14.2	13.7	15.5	15.3	20.4	19.7	20.1	22.6	21.0	17.6
Wales	10.0	8.9	9.1	10.1	11.6	11.6	12.3	11.9	12.5	11.2	16.7	17.1	17.8	20.0	18.7	15.3
Scotland	7.8	7.8	8.1	9.0	11.1	11.3	11.2	10.3	10.5	9.5	13.0	12.3	13.1	15.9	15.6	13.7
Northern Ireland	7.1	8.2	8.4	10.2	12.1	12.0	13.1	11.9	12.5	11.3	14.2	16.0	19.3	27.5	24.2	17.1

Sources and Notes: As Table 2.3.1.

A further factor is the continuing constraints on the terms on which mortgage advances can be secured by would-be first-time buyers, and the very limited availability of mortgages that do not require a substantial deposit. These issues, and their potential implications for the future of homeownership in the UK, are discussed in Contemporary Issues Chapter 2.

The Affordability Index

However, for those households able to secure a mortgage, affordability improved markedly in 2009. This was not because of falling prices (which were little changed from 2008), but because of the sharp reduction in average interest rates for mortgages which fell from 5.6 per cent to 4.2 per cent between the fourth quarter of 2008 and the fourth quarter of 2009.

Table 2.3.2 shows that UK mortgage cost-to-income ratios fell to 17.3 per cent in 2009, down from the peak level of 22.0 per cent in 2007. Unlike other indices, the UKHR Index is based on gross household earnings – not individual earnings. This is important given the high proportion of first-time buyer mortgages that are based on two incomes. Data series based on individual earnings taken at face value exaggerate (as if it was necessary) the extent of affordability issues.

The UKHR Index only begins in 1994, primarily due to data constraints on the availability of household earned incomes in previous years. An analysis based on individual earnings can, however, show the relative movements in affordability over a longer run of years. Figure 2.3.4 shows that on that basis the mortgage cost-to-income ratios for first-time buyers in 2007 were very close to the 1990 level at the peak of the last housing market boom. This is despite the much lower level of interest rates in 2007 (6.1 per cent, compared to 14.5 per cent in 1990). In effect, lower interest rates have now been factored into house prices.

While, in practice, mortgage advance-to-income ratios vary from year-to-year, and have been higher in recent years, the Index applies a constant (82 per cent) assumption over the period so that it represents a single measure of the relative affordability of house purchase by homebuyers.

Similarly, average levels of deposits vary from region to region, but the constant average deposit assumption enables the Index to provide a single measure of the relative affordability of house purchase between the regions. In practice, however, it must be recognised that there are both wealth and income barriers constraining the ability of households to enter the homeowner sector, and that these apply in a highly variable mix between one homebuyer and another.

The Affordability Index also shows the exceptional volatility in the Northern Ireland housing market. Historically, Northern Ireland has been one of the most affordable parts of the UK. By 2007, however, mortgage cost-to-income ratios in Northern Ireland were more or less at the same levels as in London. While by 2009 they had fallen back to a little below the UK average, the Index shows that, even so, mortgage cost-to-income ratios remained far higher, relative to the 1994 base year, than for any other part of the UK.

Mortgage repossessions

The recession and rising unemployment (Compendium Table 1) continued to take their toll in terms of rising levels of mortgage arrears and repossessions in 2009 (Compendium Table 51), but they remain well below the levels experienced in the housing market 'bust' of the early 1990s (Figure 2.3.5). However, as mentioned last year in this chapter, it should be noted that the CML repossession data do not include repossessions of dwellings as a result of legal actions by non-mortgage creditors, and consequently tend to underestimate repossessions by some 20 per cent.

While there was a sharp rise in the numbers of substantial arrears cases (12+ months in arrears) in 2009, to just over 60,000 cases, since then in the first half of 2010 arrears and repossession levels have stabilised.

The fall in interest rates, together with the wide range of measures introduced by the previous government to support the housing market through the downturn, have clearly played a part in containing repossession levels. Those measures were detailed in this chapter in last year's *Review*.

While most of those measures remain in place, the new government has now reduced the interest rate level at which payments of Support for Mortgage Interest (SMI) have been made. This was maintained at 6.08 per cent for two years despite the sharp fall in average interest rates over that period, but from October 2010 it has been reduced

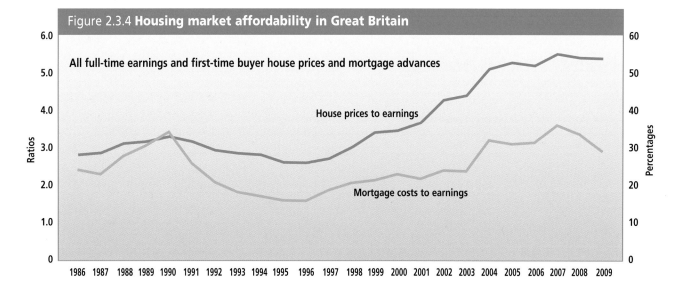

Figure 2.3.4 **Housing market affordability in Great Britain**

All full-time earnings and first-time buyer house prices and mortgage advances

House prices to earnings

Mortgage costs to earnings

Ratios

Percentages

1986 1987 1988 1989 1990 1991 1992 1993 1994 1995 1996 1997 1998 1999 2000 2001 2002 2003 2004 2005 2006 2007 2008 2009

to 3.63 per cent, based on the Bank of England average mortgage rate.

This reduced level of support will have a negative impact on households with mortgages with above-average interest rates. The overall average is depressed by the low rates for those households fortunate to have continuing tracker mortgages linked to the Bank of England base rate. Average fixed mortgage rates for outstanding mortgages were 5.2 per cent in October 2010, compared to just 2.7 per cent as the average for variable rate mortgages.[1]

The use of a standard interest rate for SMI has always involved 'swings and roundabouts' as the cost of administrative simplicity. But in the currently fractured mortgage market those swings and roundabouts will be rather more problematic than they were in the pre-crunch years.

For the time being, the short period of delay before claimants can get SMI has been left in place. There are, however, few signs of government engagement in considering the construction of a more enduring safety net for homeowners to replace the failed policy regime of the pre-crunch years. These issues are considered further in Contemporary Issues Chapter 4 on the government's wider welfare reforms.

Private renting

The latest figures from the new English Housing Survey show that the sector continued to grow in 2008/09, despite the sharp decline in the numbers of new buy to let mortgage advances in 2008

(Compendium Table 55 and Figure 2.2.1 in Commentary Chapter 2). The survey shows the number of private tenants in England rising to just over 3 million in the year – compared to just 2 million in 2000. Unfortunately, due to changes in the methodology for the new survey we are unable this year to update Compendium Table 54, which shows the trends in tenancy types within the private rented sector.

The property industry has argued that private rented housing could be made more attractive to financial institutions through taxation changes including VAT reliefs and reform of stamp duty land tax (SDLT) on the bulk purchase of housing.[2] However, the coalition government quickly moved to rule out any new incentives for investment in private rented homes.[3] On the contrary, changes to the tax regime for capital gains tax for business investments introduced by the June 2010 Budget have increased the impact of capital gains tax on private landlords, and thus worsened their position relative to homeowner households (see Commentary Chapter 6).

The coalition government has also now announced that it will not proceed with the reforms advocated in the 2008 Rugg Review.[4]

References

1 Source: *Effective Interest Rates*. Bank of England Statistics. www.bankofengland.co.uk/statistics

2 Property Industry Alliance (2010) *Investment in the UK Private Rented Sector – Response to Treasury Consultation*. www.rics.org/site/download_feed.aspx?fileID=6504&fileExtension=PDF

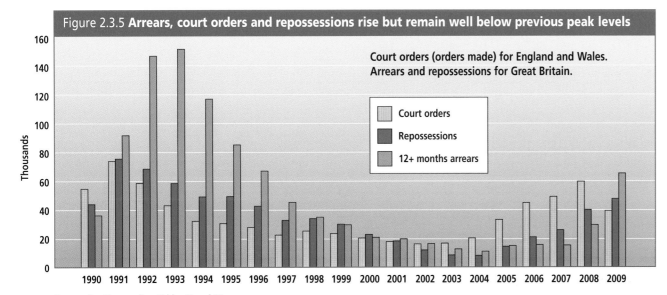

Figure 2.3.5 **Arrears, court orders and repossessions rise but remain well below previous peak levels**

Court orders (orders made) for England and Wales.
Arrears and repossessions for Great Britain.

Court orders
Repossessions
12+ months arrears

Sources: See Compendium Tables 51 and 53.

3   HM Treasury (2010) *Government Response to the Consultation on Investment in the Private Rented Sector.* www.hm-treasury.gov.uk/d/investment_in_the_uk_ private_rented_sector_response_summary.pdf

4   Rugg, J. & Rhodes, D. (2008) *The private rented sector: its contribution and potential.* York: Centre for Housing Policy, University of York.

Key Reading

Council of Mortgage Lenders (1997) *Compendium of Housing Finance Statistics.* London: Council of Mortgage Lenders.

Section 2   Commentary

Chapter 4
Housing expenditure trends and plans

This chapter is structured in four main sections. It begins by focusing on housing investment over the recent past; in particular, the extent to which the Decent Homes Standard (and its Scottish equivalent) have been associated with additional capital spending over the past few years. Picking up from the global analysis set out in Commentary Chapter 1, the second main section explores some key housing investment implications arising from the October 2010 Comprehensive Spending Review. The penultimate section then provides an update on the reform of the local authority Housing Revenue Account system. Finally, the chapter outlines government plans for housing-related revenue expenditure.

Housing investment – recent trends
Overview

Overall gross social housing investment in Great Britain rose again slightly in 2009/10, to the highest level in real terms for almost 20 years – up by over 80 per cent since the previous decade (see Figure 2.4.1). Within that total the strongest annualised growth was seen in Scotland – reflecting increases in both HRA spending (a real increase of 21 per cent on the previous year) and housing association grant (up by 30 per cent). Special factors involved here included the growing momentum of the local authority Scottish Housing Quality Standard (SHQS) modernisation programme and the bringing forward of housing association construction subsidy.

It should be noted, however, that the data underlying Figure 2.4.1 do not include the private finance which now forms such a substantial part of the investment programme for new housing association dwellings (£3.2 billion for Great Britain in 2009/10 – see Compendium Table 59). Nor do the underlying numbers include the substantial investment in stock improvements by stock transfer landlords. Taking account of both these factors, the last two years have seen overall investment in social housing at *its highest sustained level (in real terms) for three decades.*[1]

Repairs and maintenance investment
As highlighted in Commentary Chapter 2 (and associated Compendium Tables), the past ten years have seen a marked improvement in the condition of social rented housing across Britain. This has so far been particularly evident in England, where – according to administrative estimates – the proportion of total stock non-compliant with the official Decent Homes Standard has been cut from over 35 per cent in 2002 to some ten per cent in 2009.

This raises questions on the extent to which the associated activity has resulted in increased repairs and maintenance expenditure by social landlords, as well as on how such 'extra spending' has been financed. As a partial answer to the first of these questions, Tables 2.4.1 and 2.4.2 show trends in local authority housing capital expenditure (provision for investment in Scotland) over the period 1997/98 to 2010/11. Adjusting the raw figures both for inflation and for the changing size of the local authority

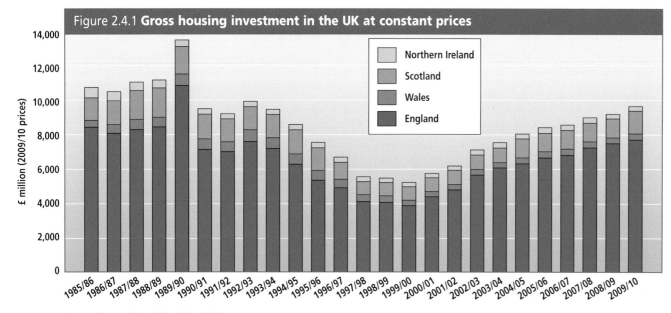

Figure 2.4.1 **Gross housing investment in the UK at constant prices**

Legend:
- Northern Ireland
- Scotland
- Wales
- England

y-axis: £ million (2009/10 prices)

Sources: Compendium Tables 57b and 88.

housing portfolio shows that municipal housing capital spending in England increased almost threefold between the base year and the 2007/08 peak. The later Scottish Housing Quality Standard (SHQS) starting date and the longer timescale for achieving compliance is reflected in the Scottish figures, which show provision for investment (per dwelling) rising steadily from 2003/04 and sharply from 2009/10 (see Table 2.4.2). These trends are summarised in Figure 2.4.2 overleaf.

The overall cost of the decent homes and equivalent stock upgrade programmes cannot be precisely quantified. However, it has been estimated by DCLG that, even by 2010/11, the overall figure for England would total some £37 billion. While this is far in excess of the original 'disrepair backlog' estimate – £19 billion[2] – the National Audit Office attributes that partly to the fact that this latter figure included only local authority housing.[3] In addition, the £19 billion figure took no account of costs

associated with further homes which *fell into disrepair* after 2001. This leads to the question about how the decent homes and equivalent stock upgrade programmes have been funded. An indication of the sums invested by central government in England can be gained from Table 2.4.3 (overleaf).

In Scotland, while local authority SHQS work was initially funded mainly from right to buy receipts, this has changed over time such that, by 2008/09,

Table 2.4.1 Local authority housing capital expenditure in England, 1997/98-2010/11

	1997/98	1998/99	1999/00	2000/01	2001/02	2002/03	2003/04	2004/05	2005/06	2006/07	2007/08	2008/09	2009/10	2010/11
Cash prices – £ million	2,346	2,513	2,406	2,779	3,110	3,828	3,485	3,987	4,534	4,507	5,008	4,901	4,516	4,230
2010 prices – £ million	3,423	3,444	3,262	3,647	4,013	4,856	4,302	4,775	5,290	5,077	5,424	5,056	4,726	4,230
Stock of LA dwellings	3,401	3,309	3,178	3,012	2,812	2,706	2,457	2,335	2,166	2,086	1,987	1,870	1,820	1,820
Capital expenditure per dwelling (£) – 2010 prices	1,007	1,041	1,026	1,211	1,427	1,795	1,751	2,045	2,442	2,434	2,730	2,704	2,597	2,324

Source: Local Authority Capital Expenditure and Receipts, DCLG website.
Notes: 1. Expenditure figures are outturn statistics except for 2009/10 which is provisional and 2010/11 which is a forecast.
2. Local authority stock figure for 2010/11 is an estimate.

Table 2.4.2 Provision for local authority housing revenue account investment in Scotland, 1997/98-2010/11

	1997/98	1998/99	1999/00	2000/01	2001/02	2002/03	2003/04	2004/05	2005/06	2006/07	2007/08	2008/09	2009/10	2010/11
Cash prices – £ million	320	352	345	351	367	401	312	364	427	462	453	501	606	647
2010 prices – £ million	467	482	468	461	474	509	385	436	498	520	491	517	634	647
Stock of LA dwellings	668	630	608	583	553	531	416	389	374	362	347	330	326	326
Capital expenditure per dwelling (£) – 2010 prices	699	766	769	790	857	959	925	1,120	1,332	1,438	1,415	1,566	1,945	1,985

Source: see Compendium Table 82.
Notes: 1. Provision for investment figures are outturn statistics except for 2009/10 which is provisional and 2010/11 which is a forecast.
2. Local authority stock figure for 2010/11 is an estimate.

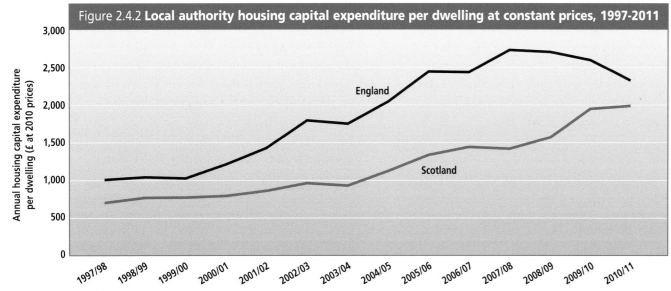

Figure 2.4.2 **Local authority housing capital expenditure per dwelling at constant prices, 1997-2011**

Annual housing capital expenditure per dwelling (£ at 2010 prices)

England

Scotland

Sources: See Tables 2.4.1 and 2.4.2.
Note: Scottish figures refer to provision for capital investment.

Table 2.4.3 **Central government funding for social housing upgrade investment in England, 2001-2011**
£ billion

	2001-2009	2009-11	Total
	Actual	Planned	
Departmental funding specifically for decent homes			
ALMOs	4.41	1.68	6.09
Private Finance Initiative	1.32	1.04	2.36
Stock transfer gap funding	0.24	0.22	0.46
Local authority debt write-off	2.50	0.13	2.63
Departmental spending for major housing repairs including decent homes			
Major Repairs Allowance	11.12	2.39	13.51
Supported Capital Borrowing	4.79	0.53	5.32
Total	24.38	5.99	30.37

Based on National Audit Office (2010) but also including local authority debt write-off expenditure.

almost half of SHQS funding was derived from prudential borrowing, with right to buy receipts reduced to only 20 per cent (from over 60 per cent in 2005/06).[4] As shown in Compendium Table 82, total local authority housing capital investment funded from borrowing increased more than threefold in the five years to 2010/11. The scope for taking on new debt in this way is attributable to the freedom of Scottish local authorities to borrow against rental income streams – in contrast with their English and Welsh counterparts who currently remain constrained within redistributive subsidy systems.

For the most part, housing associations have been expected to finance compliance with decent homes and equivalent standards from their own resources. However, in England, Wales and Scotland, public money has been made available for some stock transfer landlords able to convince government of their need for 'gap funding'[5] – see also Compendium Table 68.

Housing investment – future prospects
Some forms of investment may hold up fairly well during 2010/11. Indeed, the Homes and Communities Agency anticipated a further 25 per cent increase in its net capital expenditure over 2009/10 (see Compendium Table 64), while Scottish local authorities planned a further 7 per cent hike in investment spending (associated with expanding new build housing activity, as well as SHQS programmes – see Compendium Table 82). Thanks to the 2010 Comprehensive Spending Review,

however, a period of rapidly shrinking public housing investment appears inevitable from 2011/12. While overall public spending is set to contract by some eight per cent in the period 2010/11-2014/15,[6] much larger reductions in housing investment were always inevitable as a knock-on consequence of the ring fence erected around NHS spending.

While detailed figures on future housing expenditure remain unavailable at the time of writing, it is understood that the Homes and Communities Agency (HCA) National Affordable Housing Programme is to be cut from £8.4bn for the period 2008-11 to just £4.5bn in the three years from 2011/12.[7] Accounting for the inclusion of mortgage rescue and the recovery of empty homes, this represents a cash terms cut of 50 per cent. Moreover, because of the need to allow for existing commitments, only some £2bn will be available for new schemes to be commissioned in the four years from 2011/12. In Scotland, meanwhile, the draft

budget for 2011/12 prefigures a cut in housing and regeneration spending from £488m to £393m.[8] While this is a cash cut of just 19 per cent, the Scottish Federation of Housing Associations estimates that allowance for spending brought forward in 2010/11 means that the real reduction in 2011/12 will be over 30 per cent.

Significant cuts are also in prospect for centrally funded local authority housing investment programmes. As shown in Table 2.4.1, total spend of this kind is set to decline from just over £1bn in 2010/11 to £0.78bn in 2014/15 – a real terms cut of 29 per cent. While substantial progress towards decent homes targets has been made in recent years (see Commentary Chapter 2), the cuts in programme funding shown in Table 2.4.4 mean the original 2010 full compliance target is effectively deferred well into the future. This is in spite of an authoritative view that decent homes benchmarks constitute no more than a 'low standard', and calls for urgent consideration of a successor programme.[9]

According to the Chartered Institute of Housing, the £1.6bn decent homes allocation for the spending review period (see Table 2.4.4) falls £1.2bn short of the amount required to complete the existing project. As argued by the CIH, there is a strong case for this shortfall being factored into the proposed local authority HRA reform settlement now expected to be concluded by 2012 (see below). However, ministers' immediate response has been to stipulate that future official investment planning will incorporate an assumption that landlords with less than 10 per cent of their stock remaining non-decent in 2011/12 will 'self-fund' the remaining investment required to fulfil decent homes obligations.[10]

One other important housing-related investment programme not included in Table 2.4.4 is the Housing Market Renewal (HMR) programme initiated in 2002 to 'rebuild housing markets in areas with low demand for housing' in England.[11] While HMR activity has included demolition and replacement of obsolete privately owned stock, it has also involved a wide range of other policy instruments. However, while central government has invested some £2.2bn in the HMR programme since 2002, ministers decided in 2010 to restrict future funding to existing 'committed schemes': an announcement interpreted as effectively bringing the programme to an end.

In an associated move, the coalition government has announced an end to specific allocations for private sector housing renewal. In keeping with ministers' overriding commitment to 'localism', any continuing

Table 2.4.4 CSR 2010 spending plans: centrally funded local authority housing investment activity
£ million

Programme	2010/11	2011/12	2012/13	2013/14	2014/15	Total: 2011/12-2014/15
Local Authority Social Housing Grant	212	65	0	0	0	65
Disabled Facilities Grant	169	180	180	180	185	725
Decent homes	625	260	352	389	594	1,595
Total	1,006	505	532	569	779	2,385

Source: letter from Eric Pickles to local authority leaders, 20 October 2010. www.communities.gov.uk/documents/localgovernment/pdf/1745945.pdf

element of central funding associated with such needs will cease to be specified or ring-fenced. Private renewal investment is now therefore entirely at local discretion and, given overall funding constraints, is bound to decline sharply or even end in many areas, except for investment associated with the remaining specific initiatives to promote energy efficiency and with promised investment through the Green Deal.[12]

Rent-funded house building
In an attempt to mitigate reduced government funding for new house building in England, it is proposed that social landlords (initially, housing associations only) will be empowered to collect additional revenue via higher rents. These charges, set at a maximum of 80 per cent of local market rents, will apply to all new-build housing association homes, as well as to 'some' of their existing homes being re-let. 'Affordable rent' lettings will involve a new 'affordable rent' tenancy where security of tenure is provided only for a minimum of two years.

However, the affordable rent plan raises a number of important questions. First, there is the matter of ensuring that additional rental income generated by higher rental charges is, in fact, devoted to new investment in house building. Here, it is proposed that rents be brought firmly within the remit of social housing regulation so that the HCA – in a regulatory guise – will have to 'sign off' a landlord's plans in this field, and will subsequently monitor compliance:

'Housing associations will be able to convert vacant properties to Affordable Rent where they have reached an investment agreement with the Homes and Communities Agency about how additional rental income will be reinvested in the supply of new affordable housing.'[13]

Related to this aspect of the affordable rent regime, the Tenant Services Authority envisages revisions to its Tenancy Standard to include new guidance defining key operational matters such as rent-setting methodology and provisions for subsequent rent changes.[14]

A second, and larger, question arising from the affordable rent proposals is whether the additional rental income generated as a result will in fact fill the gap resulting from the sharp reductions in government funding detailed above. The current range of unknowns here means that it is very difficult to judge whether this aspiration will be fulfilled. For example, the point at which local authorities, as well as housing associations, will be empowered to grant affordable rent tenancies has yet to be revealed. Similarly, there is uncertainty about the proportion of existing homes being re-let which will be offered to applicants on 'affordable rent' terms.

In any event, however, the feasibility of the affordable rent regime as a mechanism for underpinning new house building will vary substantially by region. This reflects the fact that the private rent benchmarks against which affordable

rents will be set vary dramatically across the country (see Figure 2.4.3). The consequence, according to one respected commentator, is that the new framework could be workable in London and the South of England.[15] Elsewhere, however, substantially lower market rents will mean that the additional income gained under the new system will be sufficient to fund new house building only on the basis of higher grant rates. This could result in the counter-intuitive need to concentrate government funding in the Midlands and the North.

A third issue raised by the affordable rent model is that the rents chargeable under the '80 per cent of market rent' formula may in fact be 'affordable' only to relatively high-income households. This is because households eligible for housing benefit will be subject to maximum payment caps – not just in relation to the HB component of income, but also in relation to their benefit income in total (see Contemporary Issues Chapter 3).

Recent Scottish research looked at the extent to which continuing rent increases at the conventional RPI+1 per cent norm could underpin ongoing social house building in the context of nil management cost inflation.[16] Given the historic tendency for landlords' management costs to rise significantly above RPI, such a scenario would represent a significant break with the past. Nevertheless, the research found that both local authorities and housing associations were increasingly asserting their ability to do so – e.g. by

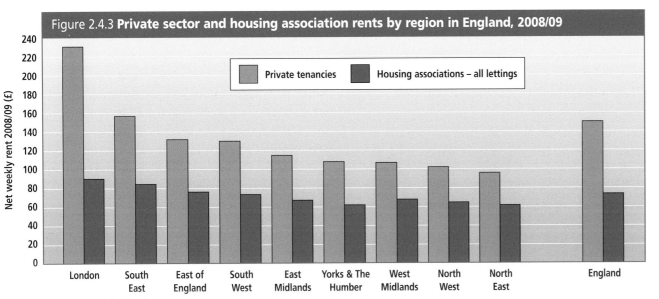

Figure 2.4.3 Private sector and housing association rents by region in England, 2008/09

Net weekly rent 2008/09 (£)

Legend: Private tenancies | Housing associations – all lettings

Regions: London, South East, East of England, South West, East Midlands, Yorks & The Humber, West Midlands, North West, North East, England

Sources: Private rents – Family Resources Survey (special tabulations); Housing association rents – Dataspring, Cambridge University (original data from CORE returns).

holding staff numbers constant while growing stock numbers through new construction. Particularly given the advantaged position of Scottish local authorities in relation to prudential borrowing,[17] achieving this objective could provide substantial capacity for new council and housing association house building, even within the context of reduced government grant expenditure.

The lending environment
Another factor with an important bearing on housing associations' ability to participate in the brave new world of rent-funded house building is the broader lending environment. By comparison with the pre-credit crunch era, conventional loan finance has become considerably more expensive in

terms of margins over the standard LIBOR benchmark. More importantly, while the range of lenders active in the market has recovered from the nadir of 2007/08, loan finance is now tending to be offered on 7-10-year terms – considerably shorter loan durations than the traditional 25-year norm.[18] This is important because it increases associations' need to hedge against refinancing risk. One response to these developments has been the burgeoning interest in bond finance. However, the nature of bond funding is such that medium-sized and smaller associations can participate only via complex consortia arrangements.

Research evidence also suggests tendencies towards tightening loan covenants and more demanding

lender expectations around management accounts and business plans.[19] And, while 2009/10 saw English associations successfully reducing liabilities associated with unsold low-cost homes, the unit proceeds of such sales continued to decline in 2010, reflecting the general weakness of the market.[20]

Restructuring local authority housing revenue accounts in England

As noted in last year's *Review*, proposed radical reforms to local authority Housing Revenue Accounts (HRAs) in England were finally published in 2009. Under these plans, a one-off 'debt redistribution' settlement would bring to an end the HRA subsidy system and, in its place, establish a self-financing regime where each council keeps both its rental income and right to buy receipts.[21] The plans reflect concerns that the existing system has become unsustainable. For many authorities, for example, its continuation would lead to a situation where there is insufficient funding to retain hard-won compliance with the Decent Homes Standard.[22]

Following the 2010 general election the newly installed coalition government confirmed an intention to proceed with the HRA reform plans announced by the former administration, albeit with some modifications to the fine detail. The new scheme is now proposed to come into effect from April 2012. While full details remain unavailable at the time of writing, it is now anticipated that the terms of the debt-restructuring will be somewhat tougher than previously expected. This is partly due to the exercise starting a year later than originally intended (by which time annual net HRA surpluses in England will have risen), and partly due to a harder stance by the coalition government on public sector expenditure and debt. In addition, at least initially, councils will be required to continue to remit 75 per cent of the receipts from right to buy sales to central government. However, estimates for the resulting loss of income to councils will be built into the valuation exercise underpinning initial debt redistribution.

While current council rents are expected to 'converge' with housing association rents by 2015/16, there is no suggestion at this stage that the debt restructuring will automatically factor in the option of moving to 'affordable rents' for lettings to new tenants. Also, as re-confirmed in December 2010,[23] the reforms will provide for higher levels of management and maintenance allowances, and increased major repairs allowances, reflecting the recommendations of independent research commissioned by DCLG (as yet unpublished). It is estimated that altogether this provides an increase in council budgets of almost 12 per cent. This will be reflected in the estimates of sustainable debt for each council to be factored into the debt redistribution settlement.

Following the settlement, councils will be free from the national subsidy regime with its annual determinations of the amounts which most councils must pay into the system (and a minority receive back as subsidy). Over time their financial position

should improve as increases in rental income outstrip any increases in management and maintenance costs. This, and the increased certainty, are the main prizes for councils in the debt restructuring exercise.

However, HM Treasury has insisted that councils will not be free to increase their borrowing beyond the level of their opening debt following the restructuring exercise. The Treasury has also retained the power to revisit the debt-restructuring exercise at a later date in the event that future policy changes have a significant material effect on council costs or incomes. In consequence, the annual improvements in councils' finances cannot be regarded as immutably protected in the longer term. The emerging framework also falls some way short of the initial reform prospectus in that councils remain subject to borrowing controls, and the regular uncertainties of the annual subsidy determination are replaced by the lesser (but still hovering) possibility of future reviews of the initial financial settlement.

While they are specific to local authorities in England, the proposals described above have some implications for Wales in that any future reforms to the Welsh HRA system will be expected by the Treasury to take the English settlement as a starting position. Welsh Assembly Government ministers have put forward the case for Wales to receive the same treatment as Scotland in respect of council housing finances. This would end the requirement for transfers of HRA surpluses from Wales to HM

Treasury, as well as providing greater freedom of action over council HRA borrowing.

For both Scotland and Wales, one indirect implication of the English reform plan may be an end to the provision for local authority debt write-off in 'overhanging debt' stock transfers. Since the reform settlement explicitly proscribes such arrangements in England, it is difficult to see how such 'subsidies' could continue to be offered elsewhere in Britain.

Revenue funding plans

Much of this chapter has been occupied with a catalogue of capital spending cuts and with measures intended to mitigate the consequences. However, while they may be relatively modest in absolute terms, there are certain central government housing-related programmes where funding is set to remain steady or even increase in coming years. In particular, as shown in Table 2.4.5, ministers decided to protect the homelessness prevention grants budget which underpins local authority staff and other costs involved in running schemes such as landlord liaison and rent deposit guarantee projects (see Commentary Chapter 5). This is consistent with the increased provision for spending on discretionary housing payments as detailed in Commentary Chapter 1. Nevertheless, since the bulk of local authority homelessness staff costs are met from General Fund resources, overall homelessness services will be vulnerable to the sharp cuts in Formula Grant resulting from the Comprehensive Spending Review.

Table 2.4.5 Government spending plans: housing-related (non-investment) programmes

£ million

Programme	2010/11	2011/12	2012/13	2013/14	2014/15	Total: 2011/12-2014/15
Supporting People	1,636	1,625	1,620	1,620	1,590	6,455
Homelessness prevention	71	90	90	89	88	357
New Homes Bonus	0	196	250	250	250	946

Source: letter from Eric Pickles to local authority leaders, 20 October 2010. www.communities.gov.uk/documents/localgovernment/pdf/1745945.pdf

It is a similar story for the Supporting People budget. While specified funding is set for a real terms cut of 'only' 11 per cent over the spending review period, it must be recognised that, since this is no longer a ring-fenced budget, stresses on councils' General Funds are likely to result in substantial 'leakage' of SP-associated resources to underpin the costs of other council services.

Table 2.4.5 also identifies the New Homes Bonus (NHB) as a programme freshly created by the coalition government. This is intended to incentivise local authorities to support and promote the construction of new housing. At present it is argued that the local government finance system provides no such incentive: increases in the council tax base bring forth balancing reductions in central funding. Under the NHB, central government will match-fund the additional council tax for each new home and property brought back into use, for each of the six years after that home is built.[24] The resources will not be additional, however: the NHB is to be funded

by 'top-slicing' the Formula Grant which DCLG pays to local authorities. This means that the NHB will effectively redistribute funds to authorities that successfully promote new build, from those who do not.

Notes and references

1   Going right back to the 1970s, in only one earlier year – 1989/90 – was expenditure higher. This resulted from a coincidence of exceptional factors – peaking right to buy receipts in the late 1980s housing market boom, together with landlord action to pre-empt government spending restrictions that were announced before they took effect.

2   It is believed that the original source of this figure was: Moody, G. (1998) *Council Housing: Financing the Future*. Coventry: Chartered Institute of Housing. However, the £19 billion estimate was subsequently officially adopted in: DETR and DSS (2000) *Quality and Choice: A Decent Home for All – The Housing Green Paper*. www.communities.gov.uk/archived/publications/housing/qualitychoice2

3   National Audit Office (2010) *The Decent Homes Programme – Report by the Comptroller and Auditor General*. London: The Stationery Office. www.nao.org.uk/publications/0910/the_decent_homes_programme.aspx

4   Scottish Housing Regulator (2010) *Scottish Housing Quality Standard – Progress Update 2008/09*. www.scottishhousingregulator.gov.uk/stellent/groups/public/documents/webpages/shr_shqs2010progressreport.pdf

5   Pawson, H. & Mullins, D. (2010) *After Council Housing: Britain's New Social Landlords*. Basingstoke: Palgrave Macmillan.

6   HM Treasury (2010) *Spending Review 2010*. http://cdn.hm-treasury.gov.uk/sr2010_completereport.pdf

7   National Housing Federation (2010) *Comprehensive Spending Review 2010 – Briefing for NHF Members*. www.housing.org.uk/Uploads/File/Policy%20briefings/Research%20Futures/CSR%20member%20brief%20-%20regn2010br07.pdf

8   Scottish Government (2010) *Scotland's Spending Plans and Draft Budget 2011/12*. www.scotland.gov.uk/Resource/Doc/331661/0107923.pdf

9   House of Commons (2010) *Beyond Decent Homes*. Communities and Local Government Committee, Fourth report of session 2009/10. www.publications.parliament.uk/pa/cm200910/cmselect/cmcomloc/60/60i.pdf

10 Hardman, I. & Hilditch, M. (2010) 'ALMOs could stop decent homes work', *Inside Housing*, 19 November.

11 Long, R. (2010) *Housing Market Renewal Pathfinders*. House of Commons Library briefing. www.parliament.uk/briefingpapers/commons/lib/research/briefings/snsp-05520.pdf

12 A measure included in the Energy Bill presented to Parliament in December 2010. See www.decc.gov.uk/en/content/cms/what_we_do/consumers/green_deal/green_deal.aspx

13 DCLG (2010) *Localism Bill and Social Housing*. Ministerial Statement by Grant Shapps MP, Minister for Housing and Local Government. www.communities.gov.uk/statements/newsroom/localismbillsocialhousing

14 Tenant Services Authority (2010) *Affordable Rent: Revisions to the Tenancy Standard – A statutory consultation*. London: TSA. www.tenantservicesauthority.org/upload/pdf/Affordable_Rent_-_Revs_tenancy_standard.pdf

15 Joseph, D. (2010) 'Sector must deliver new development model before private firms eat into social market', *Social Housing*, November, p11.

16 Bramley, G., Pawson, H., Morgan, J., Wilcox, S. & Williams, P. (2010) *A Study into the Housebuilding Capacity of Local Authorities and RSLs in Scotland*. Edinburgh: Scottish Government. www.scotland.gov.uk/Publications/ 2010/11/11115938/0

17 Wilcox, S. (2007) Commentary Chapter 4 – 'Housing Expenditure Plans' in: Wilcox, S. (ed) *UK Housing Review 2007/08*. Coventry and London: Chartered Institute of Housing and Building Societies Association.

18 Bramley *et al.* (2010) – see previous reference.

19 Bramley *et al.* (2010) – see previous reference.

20 Tenant Services Authority (2010) *Quarterly Survey of Housing Associations October 2010*. www.tenantservices authority.org/upload/pdf/Quarterly_survey_of_housing_ associations_October_2010.pdf

21 Perry, J. (2009) 'A New future for council housing?' in Wilcox, S. (ed) *UK Housing Review 2009/10*. Coventry and London: Chartered Institute of Housing and Building Societies Association.

22 Pawson, H. & Mullins, D. (2010) *After Council Housing: Britain's New Social Landlords*. Basingstoke: Palgrave.

23 DCLG (2010) *Next Steps in Delivering a Better Deal for Council House Tenants*. Press Release 13 December. www.communities.gov.uk/news/corporate/1795389

24 DCLG (2010) *New Homes Bonus: Consultation*. www.communities.gov.uk/publications/housing/ newhomesbonusconsult

Section 2   Commentary

Chapter 5
Housing needs, homelessness and lettings

Homelessness and its prevention

As detailed in last year's edition of the *Review*, homelessness is an area which has seen marked policy divergence across the UK since devolution. The Westminster government has prioritised the reduction in official homelessness numbers through a prevention-focused agenda, an approach largely reflected in Wales. Conversely, Scotland's 2003 decision to phase out the 'priority need' test by 2012 was made in the conscious expectation that this would result in an increased volume of households owed the main rehousing duty.[1]

Headline impacts of the divergent policies outlined above can be seen in Figure 2.5.1 and Table 2.5.1. The most striking feature here is the remarkable reduction in statutory homelessness numbers in England. In the seven years to 2009/10, this total has been reduced by over 70 per cent to its lowest level on record. On the face of it, this cannot be attributed to a more 'hard line' interpretation of the homelessness legislation. As a proportion of all formal assessment decisions, the number of applicants assessed as 'unintentionally homeless and in priority need' has remained remarkably steady throughout this period (at around 45 per cent). Given that most of this period also coincided with a booming housing market and declining levels of housing affordability, it is implicit that the observed trend has resulted from more prevention-centred local authority practices. Statistical modelling of the factors which contribute to homelessness has demonstrated that, in the absence of prevention measures, headline homelessness rates would have continued to increase in the period to 2007 rather than – as recorded – having fallen back sharply during these years.[2]

The nature and impacts of 'prevention-centred practice' around homelessness has been explored in detail elsewhere.[3] Since 2008/09, however, DCLG has been directly monitoring such action. Summary national statistics collected under this framework are presented in Table 2.5.2. This shows actions undertaken by English local authorities outside the statutory homelessness framework. Hence, the instances where applicants are assisted to obtain private or social sector tenancies do not constitute

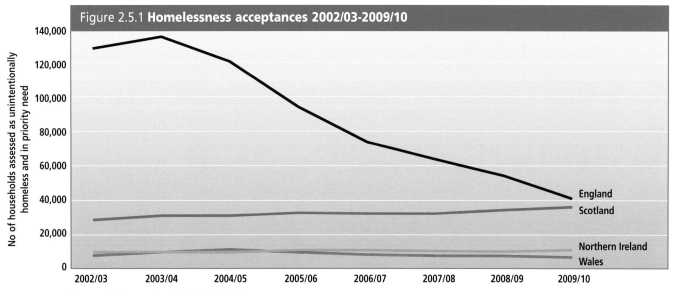

Figure 2.5.1 **Homelessness acceptances 2002/03-2009/10**

Sources: See Compendium Tables 90 and 104.
Note: Figures for Wales and Northern Ireland are for calendar years.

Table 2.5.1 **Change in homelessness acceptances, 2002/03-2009/10**

	England	Scotland	Wales	N Ireland
2003/04	135,430	30,029	8,512	8,594
2009/10	40,020	35,239	5,430	9,914
% change - 2003/04 to 2009/10	- 70.4	17.3	- 36.2	15.4

Sources: See Compendium Tables 90 and 104. Note: Figures for Wales and Northern Ireland are for calendar years.

Housing needs, homelessness and lettings

Table 2.5.2 Homelessness prevention and relief activity by local authorities in England, 2009/10

Local authority action	No. of households	% of total
Household assisted to remain in existing home via:		
Mediation or conciliation to resolve intra-household tensions	9,800	5.9
Debt advice and/or payments from homelessness prevention fund	7,300	4.4
Resolving rent arrears (including help on housing benefit claims)	9,000	5.4
Sanctuary provision to ward off threat of domestic violence	5,200	3.1
Crisis intervention – emergency support	2,300	1.4
Other help (including legal advocacy) to enable retention of tenancy	20,300	12.3
Mortgage arrears interventions or mortgage rescue	3,600	2.2
Other	6,800	4.1
Sub-total	*64,300*	*38.9*
Household assisted to obtain alternative accommodation in the form of:		
Hostel or HMO	9,500	5.8
Private tenancy (with or without landlord incentive scheme)	50,700	30.7
Home of friends or relatives	5,200	3.1
Supported housing	11,600	7.0
Social housing – management transfer	1,200	0.7
Social housing – not within homelessness provisions	19,600	11.9
Other	3,100	1.9
Sub-total	*100,900*	*61.1*
Overall total	165,200	100.0

Source: DCLG statistics on homelessness prevention and relief - www.communities.gov.uk/publications/corporate/statistics/homelessnessprevention200910

formal 'discharges of duty' as is the case when an authority arranges a tenancy for a homeless household owed the main rehousing duty.

It is instructive to set the figures shown in Table 2.5.2 within the context of statistics on local authority homelessness actions recorded as undertaken *within* the statutory framework. The total number of recorded 'homelessness and relief' cases in 2009/10 – some 165,000 – was almost double the gross number of statutory assessment decisions (accepted as priority homeless or otherwise) recorded in the same year (89,000). This could be read as illustrating that, in England, two-thirds of local authority homelessness work is now being undertaken via purely informal procedures.

Taking the comparison between statutory and non-statutory activity on homelessness a little further, Table 2.5.3 on the next page focuses on local authority actions leading to independent tenancies. Two important observations emerge from this. First, the number of private tenancies being arranged via informal procedures is slightly in excess of the number of 'discharge of duty' social sector tenancies allocated under the statutory framework.

Secondly, the number of *social sector* tenancies (including supported housing) being arranged for potentially homeless people outside the statutory provisions is very substantial. Although we cannot be certain, it seems likely that this is largely a new phenomenon. This may help to 'explain' the dramatic downward trend of homelessness acceptances in England shown in Figure 2.5.1. Part of this reduction may have been achieved by 'intercepting' potential homelessness applicants before they have made a formal application and facilitating their entry into the social rented sector on a 'discretionary' rather than a statutory basis. In other words, the sharply reduced numbers of households being recorded as statutory homeless somewhat overstate the impact of the policy in terms of preventing access to social housing.

Another striking aspect of Figure 2.5.1 is that, by 2009/10, statutory homelessness in Scotland had risen close to the level recorded in the whole of England. However, as shown in Figure 2.5.2, recorded homelessness *applications* peaked in Scotland in 2005/06. Hence, the ongoing increase in

Table 2.5.3 Local authority action to rehouse homeless households in independent tenancies in England: comparing scale of statutory and non-statutory action

	Under statutory framework	Outside statutory framework
Local authority tenancy (incl. introductory tenancies)	26,314	**
HA tenancy via nomination	20,766	**
LA/HA tenancies via mobility schemes	58	**
Subtotal – social rented sector tenancies	*47,138*	*32,400*
Private tenancy and other	3,118	50,700
Total	50,256	83,100

Sources: Column 1 – local authority HSSA returns; column 2 – DCLG monitoring statistics – see Table 2.5.2.
Note: Figures in column 1 relate to 2008/09 while those in column 2 are for 2009/10. Where marked ** figures are not separately collected.

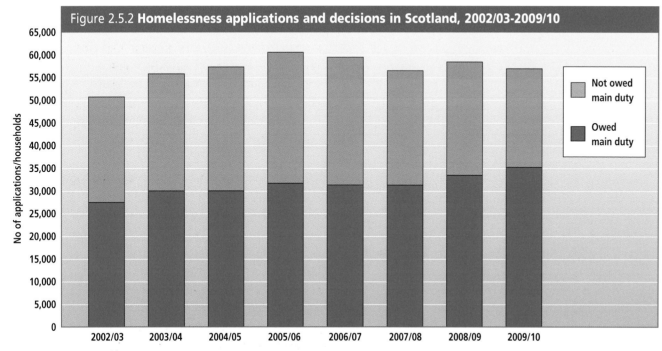

Figure 2.5.2 Homelessness applications and decisions in Scotland, 2002/03-2009/10

Source: Scottish Government.

the number of households owed the main (rehousing) duty reflects other factors. Probably the most important of these is the phased abolition of the 'priority need' test – due for full abolition in 2012. Henceforward, applicants found unintentionally homeless will be owed the main rehousing duty irrespective of their household characteristics (i.e. whether the household contains a child, pregnant woman or 'vulnerable person'). This is likely to be the main cause of the growing *proportion* of applications assessed as 'owed the main duty' – as seen in Figure 2.5.2. In the three years to 2009/10 this proportion rose from 53 per cent to 62 per cent of all applications.

Key consequences of trends in homeless applicants 'owed the main duty' (see Figure 2.5.1 and Table 2.5.1) include changes in the scale of temporary accommodation placements. As shown in Figure 2.5.3, the declining trend recorded in England appears on track to fulfil the ministerial target set in 2005 to reduce placements to below 50,000 by (the end of) 2010. In Scotland, by contrast, rising statutory homeless numbers (see Table 2.5.1) have contributed to a doubling in the number of temporary housing placements since 2003.

Waiting list numbers as a housing needs indicator

Homelessness is clearly an important and extreme form of housing need. Traditionally, therefore, official homelessness statistics have been seen as a key measure of the incidence of housing stress. At least in England and Wales, however, the past few

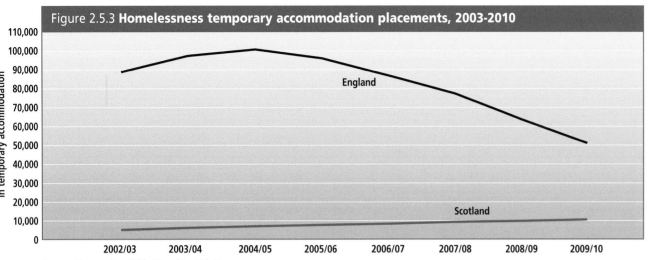

Figure 2.5.3 **Homelessness temporary accommodation placements, 2003-2010**

Sources: Compendium Table 91 and Scottish Government.
Note: Figures relate to financial year-end.

Table 2.5.4 **Relative scale of waiting list registrations in 2010**

	Waiting list (WL) totals 2010 – 000s	Total household population 2006 – 000s	WL registrations as % of existing households
England			
North East	77	1,110	6.9
North West	254	2,931	8.6
Yorkshire & The Humber	259	2,181	11.9
East Midlands	124	1,849	6.7
West Midlands	157	2,237	7.0
East of England	156	2,371	6.6
London	362	3,178	11.4
South East	215	3,447	6.2
South West	148	2,211	6.7
England – total	1,752	21,515	8.1
Wales	71	1,272	5.6
Scotland	161	2,291	7.0
Great Britain	1,984	25,078	7.9

Sources: Waiting list numbers: England – HSSA returns; Wales – Welsh Assembly Government *In Figures: Housing*; Scotland – Scottish Government housing statistics website; Household projections: DCLG live tables 401 and 403.
Note: Waiting list figures generally relate to 31 March; Wales figure is for 2009.

years have seen sharp reductions in the recorded numbers of homeless households 'owed the main duty'. Even in Scotland, the number of recorded homelessness applications has been falling since 2005. Given that few would suggest that these trends indicate declining levels of underlying *housing need* there has been renewed interest in monitoring housing waiting list registrations as an alternative indicator.

While waiting list numbers are often held up by campaigning bodies as a critical yardstick of unmet housing need, eligibility to join a list is not usually limited to those with an assessed housing problem. To put it at its strongest, therefore, it is probably more appropriate to see housing waiting list numbers as a proxy for expressed demand for social housing. Nevertheless, as an indicator of housing stress, and because they represent a conceptually simple measure, trends in waiting list numbers still command considerable political and media attention.

As shown in Table 2.5.4, by 2010 waiting list registrations across Britain totalled almost two million households. Such figures are often translated as an equivalent number of persons – e.g. in the frequently made assertion that the 1.8 million households on English waiting lists equate to 4.5 million people. In fact, there is no sound basis for such estimates: English local authorities' HSSA returns suggest that the majority of all registered households are single people and childless couples (52 per cent of the 2010 total were classed as in need of one-bedroom homes).

At a national level, the rate of recorded waiting list applications as a percentage of existing households is relatively similar in England, Wales and Scotland. However, the somewhat curious English regional rankings highlight possible shortcomings in the reliability of such data as an index of housing need. While the rate for Yorkshire and The Humber is unexpectedly higher than that for all other regions including London, this is highly influenced by just one local authority entry – that for Sheffield. This contributes no less than 97,000 to the national total – substantially more than the 2009 figure for the whole of Wales (see Table 2.5.4). Although this figure relates to a large city it remains somewhat hard to credit. Historically, national and regional

waiting list figures could be cross-checked via the Survey of English Housing. Unfortunately, however, the deletion of the relevant SEH question some years ago removed what had been a potentially useful validation benchmark.

Setting on one side doubts about their validity as a measure of housing need, recorded waiting list numbers in England have grown considerably in recent years. While the national total fell back slightly in 2009 and 2010, it still represented an increase of 60 per cent on the figure eight years earlier. In Scotland, by contrast, waiting list registrations remained almost static over these years. It is worth noting that this period coincided with a policy push

to introduce common housing registers (CHRs) across Scotland in place of the purely municipal lists which have traditionally fed into the national waiting list total. By 2010, CHRs had been established in about half of all local authority areas.[4] Given that this process involved amalgamation of previously separate local authority and housing association registers, this would have been expected to inflate the new combined lists which now inform many councils' returns. In practice, however, the Scotland-wide total has remained fairly flat. At least at a national level, therefore, it is hard to argue on the basis of waiting list figures that unmet demand for social housing has been demonstrably expanding over the past few years.

There are also reasons for questioning whether the recorded scale of increased waiting list demand seen in England over recent years is entirely a reflection of growing housing stress. Potentially significant here has been the ongoing roll-out of choice-based lettings (CBL) since 2001. CBL enables people seeking a social housing tenancy to view and 'bid' for vacant properties. The advertising of social housing vacancies clearly raises the sector's public profile as a possible source of accommodation for people seeking a new home. Research focusing on the period 2000-2004 found that total waiting list numbers for councils adopting CBL during this period rose by 79 per cent in the five years to 2005, as compared with an increase of only 40 per cent for other councils.[5] Crudely, this might suggest that only about half of the increase in national waiting list figures recorded in England over the past few years is, in fact, the product of an underlying rise in demand.

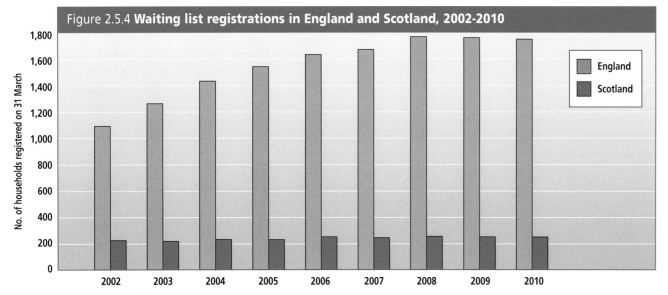

Figure 2.5.4 **Waiting list registrations in England and Scotland, 2002-2010**

Sources: DCLG, Scottish Government.
Notes: 1. Figures for Scotland include transfer applicants.
2. Figures are for the start of the financial year.
3. Estimates have been included to allow for the impacts of housing stock transfers in Scotland.
4. Historical figures for Wales unavailable.

Relevant here is the concept, heavily promoted by the previous Westminster government, of a 'housing options approach'. This is defined as 'a standard procedure whereby all new housing applicants participate in an initial interview to review their housing circumstances and prospects …to discuss, in detail, the feasibility of securing the applicant's existing accommodation or, failing that, to examine the full range of possible routes to accessing a new tenancy'.[6] Vigorous implementation of this model should enable local authorities to manage down excessive waiting list numbers by counselling low priority applicants on their limited chances of obtaining a social rented tenancy. In a recently cited example of such a strategy, Portsmouth City Council reduced its housing waiting list from 12,500 to 2,500.[7]

The coalition government sees the rise in waiting list numbers recorded over recent years in England as resulting partly from the 'open waiting lists' provision within the Homelessness Act 2002. In its view, these changes encouraged people to register even when they had 'no real need of social housing'. Accordingly, the government welcomes measures of the kind taken by Portsmouth (see above). It also envisages restoring to local authorities the power to determine 'who should qualify to be considered for social housing' and suggests this might be used to exclude potential applicants unless they are in housing need.[8] Other possible exclusion criteria might include residency, previous tenancy record or income. To the extent that such powers are utilised by local authorities, the value of waiting list figures as a reliable trend-over-time indicator of housing demand will be further reduced.

While neither homelessness nor waiting list figures provide credible evidence of rising rates of housing need over the past few years, statistical modelling work drawing on a range of surveys and administrative data sources demonstrates that the proportion of England's households experiencing various forms of housing need rose sharply in the five years to 2009 – up from around 6 per cent of all households to almost 9 per cent of the total.[9]

Lettings

Combined with modest rates of new social housing construction, the shrinking size of the social rented sector since 1980 has inevitably resulted in a reduced flow of properties becoming available to let. While the impact of contracting stock numbers on relet numbers has lagged considerably,[10] by the late 1990s the effects began to kick-in to a marked extent. In England, for example, during the ten years to 2006/07, the supply of properties becoming available for letting (as measured by lettings to new tenants) contracted by 38 per cent. This resulted not only from the diminished size of the social housing stock but also from the declining 'relet rate' – i.e. the number of existing homes falling vacant each year as a proportion of the total stock. As compared with the position ten years earlier, this latter factor alone resulted in a 'loss' of over 50,000 lettings in England in 2006/07.[11]

However, as shown in Table 2.5.5, new supply in the social rented sector has remained fairly steady over more recent years. In part, this reflects the fact that – at least in many parts of England – the relet rate has 'bottomed out' close to its lowest possible level. Also of some significance will have been the gradually increasing rates of new social housing construction seen in the period 2003-2009. Albeit from a low base, housing association completions across Great Britain almost doubled (they rose by 92 per cent) during this period – see Compendium Table 19h.

Table 2.5.5 Social landlord lettings to new tenants, 2002/03-2009/10
(000s)

	2002/03	2003/04	2004/05	2005/06	2006/07	2007/08	2008/09	2009/10
England	308	266	257	229	220	206	212	222
Wales	–	–	–	–	19	19	21	–
Scotland	–	–	50	48	48	46	45	48
Northern Ireland	9	8	8	8	8	7	8	9

Sources: Compendium Tables 97, 102-104.
Note: Housing association supported tenancy lettings are excluded.

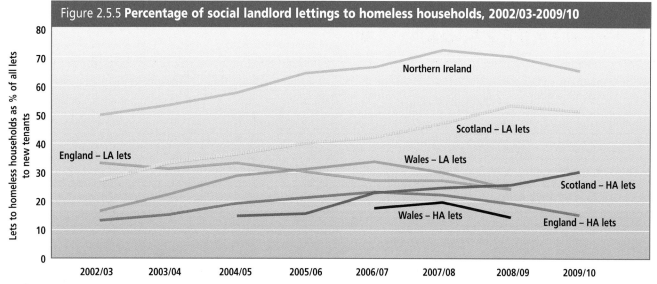

Figure 2.5.5 **Percentage of social landlord lettings to homeless households, 2002/03-2009/10**

Lets to homeless households as % of all lets to new tenants

Northern Ireland

Scotland – LA lets

England – LA lets

Wales – LA lets

Scotland – HA lets

Wales – HA lets

England – HA lets

Sources: Compendium Tables 96, 98, 102, 103 and 104.

In combination with falling rates of homelessness acceptances in England and Wales (see above), relatively steady rates of new supply in these jurisdictions (see Table 2.5.5) have been reflected in recently declining proportions of new tenancies allocated to homeless households – see Figure 2.5.5. At the same time, there has been a notable divergence in the relevant trend between Scotland, on the one hand, and England and Wales, on the other. And while the proportion of lets to the homeless in Northern Ireland has fallen somewhat in the two most recent years, the level remains very high by comparison with other parts of the UK.

Footnotes

1   Pawson, H. & Davidson, E. (2008) 'Radically divergent? Homelessness policy and practice in post-devolution Scotland', *European Journal of Housing Policy*, 8(1) pp.39-60.

2   Bramley, G., Pawson, H., White, M., Watkins, D. & Pleace, N. (2010) *Estimating Housing Need*. London: DCLG. www.communities.gov.uk/documents/housing/pdf/ 1776873.pdf

3   Pawson, H. (2007) 'Local authority homelessness prevention in England: Empowering consumers or denying rights?', *Housing Studies*, 22(6) pp.867-884; Pawson, H., Netto, G., Jones, C., Wager, F., Fancy, C. & Lomax, D (2007) *Evaluating Homelessness Prevention*. London: DCLG. www.communities.gov.uk/publications/housing/prevent homelessness

4   Scottish Housing Best Value Network (2010) *Common Housing Registers Position Study 2010.* www.sbe.hw.ac.uk/ shbvn/CHR/PDFs/Position%20Study%20Report_F.pdf

5   Pawson, H., Donohoe, A., Jones, C., Watkins, D., Fancy, C., Netto, G., Clegg, S. & Thomas, A. (2006) *Monitoring the Longer-term Impact of Choice-based Lettings*. London: DCLG. www.communities.gov.uk/publications/housing/ monitoringlonger

6   Pawson, H., Netto, G. & Jones, C. (2006) *Homelessness Prevention: A Guide to Good Practice*. London: DCLG. www.communities.gov.uk/documents/housing/pdf/ 150973.pdf

7   Richardson, J. (2010) *Housing and the Customer*. Coventry: Chartered Institute of Housing/Housing Studies Association.

8   Department for Communities and Local Government (2010) *Local Decisions: A Fairer Future for Social Housing.* London: DCLG. www.communities.gov.uk/publications/ housing/socialhousingreform

9   See Figure 7.8 in Bramley, G., Pawson, H., White, M., Watkins, D. & Pleace, N. (2010) *Estimating Housing Need*. London: DCLG. www.communities.gov.uk/documents/ housing/pdf/1776873.pdf

10 Pawson, H. (1998) 'Gravity Defied: Local authority lettings and stock turnover in the 1990s'; in S. Wilcox (Ed.) *Housing Finance Review 1998/99*. York: Joseph Rowntree Foundation.

11 Pawson, H. & Watkins, D. (2008) *Analysing Key Trends in the Supply and Distribution of Social Housing Lettings*. Housing Corporation Sector Study 62. London: Housing Corporation. www.housingcorp.gov.uk/server/show/ nav.001010001005

Section 2   Commentary

Chapter 6
Help with housing costs

The coalition government has made a number of significant changes in the approach to help with housing costs in both the private and social rented sectors. While partly driven by budget restrictions, the new approaches are also infused with concerns about economic efficiency and horizontal equity, particularly as between out-of-work households and those in low-paid work.

Proposals have been introduced to reduce substantially the levels of assistance available to private sector tenants, along with other short-term housing benefit reforms. These are discussed in Contemporary Issues Chapter 3. Outline proposals have also been set out for a very radical restructuring of the overall system of welfare benefits. These raise far more wide-ranging issues, but would also result in major changes to the way assistance is provided towards housing costs for households in all tenures. These are discussed in Contemporary Issues Chapter 4.

In that context, this chapter of the *Review* focuses this year on two main issues, as well as drawing out some key developments from the body of tables on help with housing costs in the Compendium. The chapter begins by expanding the regular analysis of the composition of the principal taxes and tax reliefs that apply for private homeowners. It then considers some of the issues involved in the move to intermediate rents for new affordable house building in England, as well as the proposal to provide only short-term, rather than secure, tenancies for new tenants in the social rented sector.

The net tax position of homeowners

The abolition of mortgage interest tax relief for homeowners in 2000 significantly reduced the long-standing fiscal bias in favour of owning rather than renting, that was one of the factors in the continuing decline of the private rented sector in the UK throughout the twentieth century.

However, there is still a continuing, if less pronounced, fiscal bias in favour of homeownership relative to private renting, as demonstrated in this chapter in last year's *Review*. The current extent of the net favourable tax position for homeowners is set out in Table 2.6.1.

This shows the annual yield from the two taxes that do bear on homeowners – stamp duty and inheritance tax. Both these taxes go rather wider than just homeowners. The stamp duty figures relate to all residential property transactions, while the estimates of the yield from inheritance tax (IHT) are based on the proportion of wealth in residential property held by all individuals subject to IHT, including non-corporate private landlords.

The figures thus tend to overstate the yield that relates exclusively to homeowners. Council tax is not included, as this is a tax that applies to households in all tenures, and is thus (relatively) tenure neutral.

The table also shows estimates of the two primary continuing forms of tax relief enjoyed by homeowners – capital gains tax relief and tax relief on the imputed rental value of the home which the owner occupies. This imputed value was taxed until 1963 (albeit at a very low value), and was the logical counterpart to mortgage interest relief, as an offset. This was in parallel to the arrangements for private landlords, in that the rental value of owners' homes is an income 'in kind' equivalent to the cash income which landlords receive from their tenants.

It would have been logical for mortgage interest tax relief to have been abolished at the same time as Schedule A tax, but in fact it was another 37 years before that occurred. While this belated move reduced the fiscal advantages of homeownership it did not remove them, as the absence of Schedule A tax (based on realistic values) has a very substantial net value even after full allowance is made for mortgage interest against the gross imputed rental values. The author estimates that the net value of Schedule A tax relief rose to over £17 billion in 2003/04, before falling back to £11 billion in 2009/10.

While the methodology for these estimates could be refined, it is robust enough to give a ballpark indication of the very substantial value of that relief. However it should be noted that if such a tax were ever to be levied, it would reduce house prices; and this would in turn reduce the net income from the tax.

Table 2.6.1 also includes figures for the value of capital gains tax (CGT) relief. The gross figures are those published by HM Revenue and Customs. However these assume that the tax is levied at the full

Table 2.6.1 **Private owner taxes and tax reliefs**

£ million

	1995/96	1996/97	1997/98	1998/99	1999/00	2000/01	2001/02	2002/03	2003/04	2004/05	2005/06	2006/07	2007/08	2008/09	2009/10
Taxes															
Inheritance tax	429	440	480	496	611	684	769	870	999	1,166	1,300	1,409	1,486	1,141	958
Stamp duty	465	675	830	1,065	1,825	2,145	2,690	3,525	3,710	4,620	4,585	6,375	6,680	2,950	3,290
Gross Tax	894	1,115	1,310	1,561	2,436	2,829	3,459	4,395	4,709	5,786	5,885	7,784	8,166	4,091	4,248
Tax Reliefs															
Imputed rental return tax relief (net)	- 7,500	- 8,300	- 7,400	- 9,800	- 12,700	- 14,000	- 14,600	- 16,700	- 17,300	- 14,500	- 14,100	- 12,600	- 9,200	- 10,300	- 11,000
Capital gains tax relief (gross)	- 500	- 600	- 800	- 1,400	- 3,000	- 3,300	- 6,000	- 10,000	- 10,500	- 13,000	- 12,500	- 15,800	- 14,500	- 4,900	- 3,800
Capital gains tax relief (net)	- 200	- 240	- 320	- 560	- 1,200	- 1,320	- 2,400	- 4,000	- 4,200	- 5,200	- 5,000	- 6,320	- 5,800	- 2,940	- 2,280
Total Net Tax Reliefs	- 7,700	- 8,540	- 7,720	- 10,360	- 13,900	- 15,320	- 16,400	- 20,700	- 21,500	- 19,700	- 19,100	- 19,920	- 15,000	- 13,240	- 13,280
Net tax position	- 6,806	- 7,425	- 6,410	- 8,799	- 11,464	- 12,491	- 12,941	- 16,305	- 16,791	- 13,914	- 13,215	- 12,136	- 6,834	- 9,149	- 9,032

Source: Inland Revenue Statistics (various years).

Notes: Up to 2007/08, estimates of capital gains tax relief are set at 40% of Inland Revenue estimates to provide for roll over and taper relief provisions. From 2008/09 they are based on 60% of Inland Revenue estimates to provide for roll over relief provisions. It should also be noted that the stamp duty and Inheritance Tax yields are for all residential dwellings, and not just those occupied by home owners. The imputed rental return tax relief are based on the asset values and mortgage debt figures from Table 45, average mortgage interest rates, net residential yield figures from the IPD Index and standard rates of income tax.

rate, without any provisions for 'taper relief', or the 'roll over relief' which defers the application of the tax when the proceeds from the sale of a home are fully re-invested in another home; this is typically a feature of the tax in those countries, such as Sweden, where it is applied to homeowners.

The estimated net values for CGT relief for homeowners shown in Table 2.6.1 take into account the 'taper relief' provisions of the UK CGT regime, and also make provision for roll over relief. The estimates do not, however, make any adjustment for the potential impact of the levying of CGT on house prices.

The credit crunch has seen a fall both in the yield from property taxes, and in the value of the continuing tax reliefs. Nevertheless, as shown in Table 2.6.1, homeownership enjoyed a £9 billion net advantage in terms of its tax position – even without making any deduction from the proportion of stamp duty and inheritance tax revenues that are based on rented rather than owner-occupied dwellings.

There are no immediate prospects of any UK government fundamentally reducing the very substantial net tax advantages these reliefs provide for homeowners. This is partly politics, and partly

their low visibility – particularly in respect of the tax relief on the 'in-kind' benefit of rental values, which is an unfamiliar idea outside economic and taxation theory and history.

But the practical importance of those reliefs does need to be recognised, especially when there are debates about the more visible elements of the tax package for homeowners, or about the respective tax treatment of private landlords. It should also be emphasised that these reliefs are almost entirely regressive and favour households that own the most expensive dwellings in the country.

Lower subsidies for social sector tenants

Last year this chapter of the *Review* set out the continuing levels of economic subsidy to social sector tenants, based on the differences between current and social sector rents, and contrasted those with the much more limited current cash public expenditure grants and subsidies for the sector. Indeed, as shown in Compendium Table 109, there is now a substantial net *negative* cash subsidy for council housing in England and Wales, albeit that this is heavily underpinned by government expenditure on housing benefit (which is shown in Compendium Table 114).

New policies in England will substantially change this position.[1] New affordable housing will now have rents at the levels previously applied to 'intermediate' tenancies targeted on households that could afford to pay significantly more than social sector rents, but could not afford to buy in the private sector.

Intermediate rents are based on 80 per cent of the market rent for the dwelling; although this is now proposed to be subject to caps based on the new local housing allowance (LHA) rates, and the national maximum LHA rates being set as part of the proposed housing benefit reforms (See Contemporary Issues Chapter 3).

The potential difference between current social sector rents and intermediate rents will vary significantly across the country, given that current rents reflect local differences in earnings to a much greater extent than differences in property values. This is illustrated in Figure 2.6.1, which compares housing association rents with intermediate and market rents computed on the basis of 2007/08 housing association stock and rent levels.

As can be seen, the difference between current social rents and intermediate rents is much more substantial in London and the south of England, than in the Midlands and the north of England.

In time, these rents will result in higher housing benefit costs, and issues around work incentives. In the short term, however, they will enable the output of new sub-market rented housing to be maintained despite the sharp cutback in the grant budget announced in the October 2010 Comprehensive Spending Review. Analysis for the review of the English HRA also showed that, while the costs of housing benefit are not insignificant, there are still net savings for government budgets associated with a higher rent regime.[2] Even at market rents it was estimated (based on DWP modeling) that just under three-quarters of current social sector tenants would receive housing benefit, and that the expenditure on housing benefit would amount to just under two-thirds of the total rental income.

The issues around the application of higher rent levels to relets of existing social sector stock are more complex. In the case of new-build dwellings, government is assured of the up-front savings in the form of lower grant rates. It is less clear how it will ensure that the additional revenue from higher relet rents is just as effectively directed towards

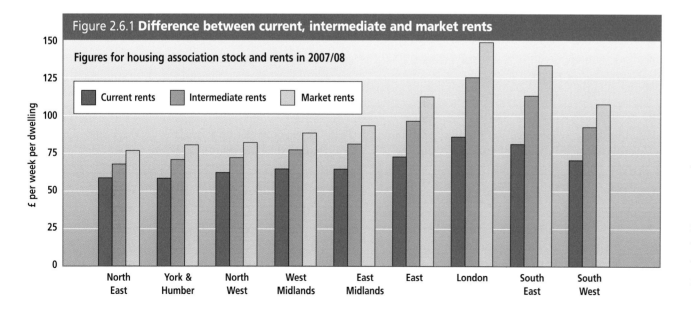

Figure 2.6.1 **Difference between current, intermediate and market rents**

Figures for housing association stock and rents in 2007/08

Legend: Current rents, Intermediate rents, Market rents

£ per week per dwelling

North East, York & Humber, North West, West Midlands, East Midlands, East, London, South East, South West

priority investments. One suggestion has been that this could be achieved by a contractual component within social housing regulation.[3]

The new policy has also created a marked differential between the rents and tenancy conditions for existing social sector tenants, and the rules that will apply to post-2011 new tenants. This does not sit very easily alongside the concerns expressed about horizontal equity in the context of the proposed housing benefit reforms. It is also proposed that new tenancies should be for a fixed period, and that if a household's financial position improves they should be asked to leave. While there is a case for targeting economic subsidies only on those households where it is required, this does not logically require the removal of security of tenure.

Even in those countries (including Australia and Canada) that have a smaller and more residual public housing sector, rents are simply fixed as a proportion of incomes.[4] If incomes rise sufficiently then rents are simply increased to market levels. While, in common with 'tenancy duration linked to need', such a regime risks dampening work incentives, it has the advantage that the subsidy is moved on to other households that require it – without the household in improved circumstances being required to move.

To return to the issues explored at the beginning of this chapter: the rapid introduction of the intermediate rent and tenancy regime is in marked contrast to the inaction on the continuing subsidies to existing homeowner households. A radical – and consistent – market-orientated reform package of the kind now being floated in the Netherlands[5] would logically require very substantial changes for homeowners as well as for social sector tenants.

References

1   Department for Communities and Local Government (2010) *Local Decisions: A fairer future for social housing.* London: DCLG.

2   Wilcox, S. (2009) *Costs and savings from higher rents.* Housing Revenue Account Review Rents and Service Charges Working Paper. London: DCLG.

3. Tickell, J. (2010) 'Call for change', *Inside Housing,* 10 September; Bramley, G., Pawson, H., Morgan, J., Wilcox, S. & Williams, P. (2010) *A Study into the Housebuilding Capacity of Local Authorities and RSLs in Scotland.* Edinburgh: Scottish Government.

4   Fitch, J., Lewis, A. & Wilcox S. (2009) *Social housing, tenure and housing allowances.* London: DWP.

5. Priemus, H. (2010) 'Housing Finance Reform in the Making: The Case of the Netherlands', *Housing Studies,* 25(5) pp.755-764.

Key Reading

Department for Work and Pensions (2010) *Business Plan.* London: DWP.

HM Government (2010) *Resource Accounts 2009-10.* HC 296. London: The Stationery Office.

A note on key reading

Following the general election, DWP have not this year published an annual report. They have, however, published resource accounts and a business plan, and a number of the tables (such as those on expenditure) that were previously included within the annual report are now available on their website (www.dwp.gov.uk).

The DWP quarterly summary statistics on housing benefit and council tax benefit are available at http://campaigns.dwp.gov.uk/asd/

HMRC statistics are available at www.hmrc.gov.uk/thelibrary/national-statistics.htm

Section 3   Compendium of tables

Housing, the economy and public expenditure

Table 1 **Key economic trends**

	1970	1975	1980	1985	1990	1995	1996	1997	1998	1999	2000	2001	2002	2003	2004	2005	2006	2007	2008	2009
Gross Domestic Product																				
£ billion (Cash)	51.7	106.7	233.2	361.8	570.3	733.3	781.7	830.1	879.1	928.7	976.5	1,021.8	1,075.6	1,139.7	1,203.0	1,254.1	1,325.8	1,398.9	1,448.4	1,395.9
£ billion (2005 prices)	544.0	605.3	660.1	732.9	863.0	936.2	963.2	995.1	1,031.0	1,066.8	1,108.5	1,135.8	1,159.6	1,192.2	1,227.4	1,254.1	1,289.8	1,322.8	1,330.1	1,264.6
% annual real growth	2.6	2.3	1.8	2.2	3.5	3.0	2.9	3.3	3.6	3.5	3.9	2.5	2.1	2.8	3.0	2.2	2.8	2.6	0.6	- 0.9
Claimant unemployment																				
000s	–	789.5	1,351.0	2,997.3	1,648.1	2,289.7	2,087.5	1,584.5	1,347.8	1,248.1	1,088.4	969.9	946.6	933.0	853.3	861.8	945	864.5	905.8	1,528.5
%	2.5	2.9	4.8	10.3	5.5	7.6	6.9	5.3	4.5	4.1	3.6	3.1	3.1	3.0	2.7	2.7	3.0	2.7	2.8	4.7
Inflation %	6.4	24.2	18.0	6.1	9.5	3.5	2.4	3.1	3.4	1.5	3.0	1.8	1.7	2.9	3.0	2.8	3.2	4.3	4.0	- 0.5
Interest rates %	7.0	11.5	16.3	12.1	14.6	6.6	5.9	6.6	7.2	5.3	6.0	5.1	4.0	3.7	4.4	4.7	4.6	5.5	4.7	0.6

Sources: UK National Accounts, Economic & Labour Market Review, Bank of England.

Notes: Gross Domestic Product is shown at current (YBHA) and 2005 prices (ABMI). For the years to 1990 the annual real growth rates are averages for the preceding five year period. Claimant unemployment figures are seasonally adjusted (BCJD & BCJE). Inflation is the General Index of Retail Prices (CZBH). Interest rates are average bank rate for the year.

Table 2 **Average male and female earnings in Great Britain**

	1970	1975	1980	1985	1990	1995	1996	1997	1998	1999	2000	2001	2002	2003	2004	2005	2006	2007	2008	2009
£ per week																				
All full-time men	30.0	60.8	124.5	192.4	295.6	374.6	391.3	408.7	427.1	442.4	464.1	490.5	511.3	525.0	559.3	568.0	591.6	606.1	631.1	645.8
All full-time women	16.3	37.4	78.8	126.4	201.5	269.8	283.0	297.2	309.6	326.5	343.7	366.8	382.1	396.0	421.3	435.6	453.6	462.8	485.5	502.4
Full-time manual men	26.8	55.7	111.7	163.6	237.2	291.3	301.3	314.3	328.5	335.0	344.8	359.9	366.6	–	–	–	–	–	–	–
Full-time manual women	13.4	32.1	68.0	101.3	148.0	188.1	195.2	201.1	210.8	221.9	229.1	241.8	250.3	–	–	–	–	–	–	–
Percentages																				
All women's earnings as a % of all men's earnings	54.3	61.5	63.3	65.7	68.2	72.0	72.3	72.7	72.5	73.8	74.1	74.8	74.7	75.4	75.3	76.7	76.7	76.4	76.9	77.8
All manual women's earnings as a % of all manual men's earnings	50.0	57.6	60.9	61.9	62.4	64.6	64.8	64.0	64.2	66.2	66.4	67.2	68.3	–	–	–	–	–	–	–

Sources: Regional Trends, New Earnings Surveys, Annual Survey of Hours and Earnings.

Notes: Earnings figures are inclusive of overtime. Because of classification changes, figures for manual and non-manual earnings are no longer available from 2003. There were also changes of methodology in 2004 and 2006, which both slightly reduced average figures compared to the previous years.

Table 3 **Household disposable income, consumer spending and savings[1]**

	1970	1975	1980	1985	1990	1995	1996	1997	1998	1999	2000	2001	2002	2003	2004	2005	2006	2007	2008	2009
£ billion																				
Household disposable income	32.3	68.3	147.3	223.9	365.1	503.6	536.9	573.3	599.1	623.7	657.3	700.1	725.3	760.9	782.6	817.5	845.3	873.9	915.0	957.1
− Consumer spending	31.2	64.6	136.4	215.4	354.8	465.3	500.4	532.1	568.0	604.6	640.1	672.9	707.4	742.3	779.1	815.0	849.5	893.0	928.5	910.6
= Savings	1.1	3.7	10.8	8.6	10.4	38.2	36.5	41.2	31.1	19.2	17.2	27.2	17.9	18.6	3.5	2.5	- 4.2	- 19.1	- 13.5	46.5
Savings ratio[2] (%)	3.4	5.4	7.4	3.8	2.8	7.6	6.8	7.2	5.2	3.1	2.6	3.9	2.5	2.4	0.4	0.3	- 0.5	- 2.2	- 1.5	4.9
Increases over previous years:[3]																				
Household disposable income																				
% (Cash)	–	22.3	23.1	10.4	12.6	7.6	6.6	6.8	4.5	4.1	5.4	6.5	3.6	4.9	2.8	4.5	3.4	3.4	4.7	4.6
% (Constant prices)	–	3.3	2.5	1.8	4.5	2.4	3.1	4.2	2.1	2.9	4.2	4.4	2.0	3.0	1.1	2.0	0.7	0.5	1.6	3.2
Consumer spending																				
% (Cash)	–	21.4	22.2	11.6	12.9	6.2	7.5	6.3	6.7	6.4	5.9	5.1	5.1	4.9	5.0	4.6	4.2	5.1	4.0	- 1.9
% (Constant prices)	–	2.7	1.9	2.4	5.3	1.3	3.9	3.8	4.3	5.2	4.7	3.1	3.5	3.0	3.1	2.2	1.5	2.1	0.9	- 3.2

Sources: UK National Accounts; UK Economic Accounts, Economic & Labour Market Review and Financial Statistics for latest data.

Notes: 1. Households include non-profit institutions serving households.

2. The 'savings ratio' is the ratio of savings to household disposable income.

3. For the years to 1995 the increases are the average annual increase over the previous five years.

Table 4 Measures of employment and unemployment in the UK

Thousands

	1979	1984	1989	1990	1991	1992	1993	1994	1995	1996	1997	1998	1999	2000	2001	2002	2003	2004	2005	2006	2007	2008	2009
Employees	23,092	20,942	22,504	22,710	22,330	21,540	21,353	21,460	21,744	22,099	22,661	23,030	23,456	23,901	24,139	24,331	24,418	24,498	24,863	25,062	25,122	25,412	24,836
+ Self-employed	1,833	2,688	3,494	3,531	3,374	3,472	3,391	3,470	3,543	3,482	3,450	3,349	3,311	3,241	3,266	3,320	3,537	3,650	3,592	3,680	3,763	3,810	3,796
+ Training programmes	–	318	496	471	436	364	342	319	280	242	218	164	158	147	145	105	91	122	112	94	113	112	104
+ Unpaid family workers	–	–	–	–	–	177	155	148	143	122	115	99	98	110	93	95	86	95	98	90	97	110	96
= Total in employment	24,925	23,974	26,502	26,717	26,154	25,554	25,241	25,397	25,711	25,945	26,444	26,642	27,023	27,399	27,643	27,852	28,132	28,365	28,665	28,926	29,095	29,444	28,832
of which																							
Full-time	–	–	–	–	–	19,469	19,110	19,126	19,348	19,394	19,721	19,881	20,177	20,413	20,617	20,679	20,818	20,957	21,300	21,541	21,666	21,898	21,215
Part-time	–	–	–	–	–	6,052	6,099	6,263	6,354	6,544	6,714	6,754	6,840	6,977	7,016	7,161	7,298	7,388	7,353	7,369	7,407	7,495	7,566
+ ILO unemployed	1,528	3,209	2,059	1,959	2,391	2,743	2,898	2,705	2,418	2,315	2,026	1,764	1,710	1,559	1,423	1,472	1,420	1,394	1,397	1,649	1,621	1,641	2,408
= Total economically active	26,453	27,183	28,561	28,676	28,545	28,297	28,138	28,103	28,129	28,261	28,470	28,405	28,733	28,958	29,066	29,324	29,552	29,759	30,062	30,575	30,715	31,084	31,240
Economically inactive	15,727	16,557	16,146	16,133	16,350	16,699	16,884	16,969	17,076	17,101	17,050	17,285	17,172	17,195	17,402	17,426	17,489	17,632	17,761	17,642	17,930	17,953	18,178
Claimant unemployed	1,070	2,860	1,790	1,574	2,208	2,691	2,912	2,651	2,307	2,153	1,618	1,351	1,275	1,104	971	951	944	859	853	951	870	815	1,535

Sources: Economic & Labour Market Review, Labour Force Survey Historical Supplement, Office for National Statistics.

Notes: Claimant unemployment figures are seasonally adjusted for the second quarter of the year. This series relates only to claimants aged 18+, and is based on the current definition of claimant unemployment. All other figures are from the Labour Force Survey for all those aged from 16 to retirement ages, and are not seasonally adjusted. For the years to 1991 they are for the April of the year; from 1992 they are for the second quarter of the year. The Labour Force definitions of unemployment and inactivity apply for 1979. Thereafter the ILO definition (based on a four-week instead of a one-week job search period) applies.

Table 5 **Regional claimant unemployment rates at 1st quarter in year**

Percentages

Region	1970	1975	1980	1985	1990	1991	1992	1993	1994	1995	1996	1997	1998	1999	2000	2001	2002	2003	2004	2005	2006	2007	2008	2009	2010
North East	–	3.7	6.9	15.4	9.1	9.8	11.0	12.0	12.1	11.0	10.3	8.4	7.3	7.2	6.6	5.8	5.2	4.7	4.2	3.7	3.9	4.1	3.9	6.3	7.0
Yorkshire & The Humber	2.7	2.2	3.9	11.2	6.2	7.3	9.0	9.9	9.5	8.3	7.7	6.5	5.5	5.3	4.6	4.0	3.6	3.4	3.0	2.7	3.2	3.2	2.9	5.1	5.9
North West	–	3.0	4.9	12.6	7.0	7.8	9.6	10.2	9.8	8.4	7.5	6.3	5.1	4.8	4.3	3.8	3.5	3.3	3.0	2.7	3.2	3.3	3.0	4.8	5.5
West Midlands	1.8	2.0	3.9	12.1	5.4	6.7	9.4	10.6	10.0	8.0	7.1	5.7	4.6	4.6	4.1	3.9	3.5	3.5	3.4	3.1	3.7	4.0	3.4	5.7	6.3
East Midlands	2.1	1.9	3.2	9.3	4.6	5.9	8.1	9.2	8.6	7.3	6.8	5.2	3.9	3.7	3.4	3.2	2.9	2.8	2.6	2.3	2.7	2.8	2.4	4.4	4.9
East	–	1.6	2.5	7.5	2.9	4.8	7.4	9.1	8.2	6.4	6.1	4.6	3.3	3.0	2.6	2.1	2.0	2.1	2.0	2.0	2.2	2.3	1.9	3.6	4.1
London	–	1.4	2.5	8.2	4.4	6.3	9.2	10.9	10.5	9.1	8.7	7.0	5.2	4.6	4.0	3.3	3.5	3.6	3.5	3.4	3.5	3.3	2.7	3.8	4.6
South East	–	1.4	2.1	6.7	2.4	4.2	6.8	8.4	7.4	5.8	5.2	3.8	2.7	2.4	2.0	1.6	1.6	1.7	1.7	1.5	1.8	1.7	1.4	2.9	3.4
South West	2.7	2.4	3.5	8.5	3.6	5.4	8.1	9.3	8.2	6.7	6.2	4.8	3.4	3.2	2.7	2.1	2.0	1.9	1.7	1.5	1.7	1.7	1.3	3.0	3.3
England	–	2.1	3.5	9.7	4.8	6.2	8.6	9.9	9.2	7.7	7.1	5.6	4.4	4.1	3.6	3.1	2.9	2.9	2.7	2.5	2.8	2.8	2.4	4.1	4.8
Wales	3.9	3.0	5.1	13.0	6.3	7.6	9.3	9.9	9.4	8.2	7.9	6.7	5.5	5.3	4.5	4.2	3.6	3.4	3.1	2.8	3.1	2.9	2.7	5.0	5.5
Scotland	3.8	2.9	5.7	12.0	8.0	7.8	8.6	9.3	9.1	7.8	7.2	6.5	5.4	5.2	4.8	4.0	3.9	3.7	3.6	3.2	3.1	2.9	2.5	4.0	4.9
Great Britain	2.4	2.2	3.8	10.1	5.1	6.4	8.6	9.8	9.2	7.8	7.2	5.8	4.5	4.2	3.7	3.2	3.0	3.0	2.8	2.6	2.9	2.8	2.4	4.2	4.8
Northern Ireland	6.5	4.6	8.0	15.3	13.0	12.5	13.5	13.9	12.9	11.6	10.8	8.7	7.5	6.9	5.5	5.0	4.6	4.1	3.8	3.3	3.2	2.9	2.7	4.7	6.2
United Kingdom	2.5	2.2	3.9	10.2	5.3	6.6	8.8	9.9	9.3	7.9	7.3	5.8	4.6	4.3	3.8	3.2	3.1	3.0	2.8	2.6	2.9	2.8	2.4	4.2	4.9

Source: Economic & Labour Market Review.

Notes: Figures are seasonally adjusted. Figures from 1997 are affected by the introduction of the jobseeker's allowance. Figures for government office regions are unavailable for the years prior to 1975, except where they coincide with standard regions.

Table 6 **Personal housing wealth, borrowing and net equity**

£ billion

	1970	1975	1980	1985	1990	1995	1996	1997	1998	1999	2000	2001	2002	2003	2004	2005	2006	2007	2008	2009
Net equity	36.5	104.0	258.3	423.0	850.3	697.6	786.7	870.1	1,048.2	1,223.9	1,431.5	1,525.1	1,892.9	2,094.4	2,343.8	2,369.1	2,617.5	2,890.1	2,462.5	2,591.0
+ House loans	11.5	25.2	52.6	127.4	294.7	390.9	409.6	431.3	456.7	495.0	536.4	591.4	675.2	774.6	877.5	967.0	1,078.8	1,187.2	1,226.3	1,235.5
= Gross assets	48.0	129.2	310.9	550.4	1,145.0	1,088.5	1,196.3	1,301.4	1,504.9	1,718.9	1,967.9	2,116.5	2,568.1	2,869.0	3,221.3	3,336.1	3,696.3	4,077.3	3,688.8	3,826.5
Index of growth of gross assets	15.4	41.6	100.0	177.0	368.3	350.1	384.8	418.6	484.0	552.9	633.0	680.8	826.0	922.8	1036.1	1,073.0	1,188.9	1,311.5	1,187.8	1,230.8
Deflator for gross domestic capital formation (YBFU)	24.3	50.7	100.0	129.4	174.2	184.9	188.3	187.1	185.7	186.9	188.1	188.3	191.0	195.5	199.7	204.0	207.8	213.0	219.8	223.6
Index of real growth of gross assets	63.5	82.0	100.0	136.8	211.4	189.4	204.3	223.7	260.7	295.8	336.5	361.5	432.5	472.0	518.8	526.0	572.1	615.7	540.4	550.5

Sources: UK National Accounts, Office for National Statistics; Bank of England Statistics.

Notes: The personal sector includes non-corporate private landlords. See Table 45 for net equity estimates for homeowners.

There is a break in the series of data for the value of private residential dwellings following a change in accounting conventions. The new series (CGRI) runs from 1987. Data from the old series (ALLN) has been used for earlier years, with minor adjustments to avoid a discontinuity with the new series. The deflator for gross domestic capital formation (YBFU) has been rebased to 1980.

Table 7 **Equity withdrawal**

£ million

	1975	1980	1985	1990	1995	1996	1997	1998	1999	2000	2001	2002	2003	2004	2005	2006	2007	2008	2009
Net mortgage lending	3,613	7,368	19,034	33,296	15,165	19,107	23,636	25,234	37,747	40,756	53,892	78,827	101,083	100,706	91,220	110,450	108,278	41,124	11,625
+ Private housing grants	78	159	697	519	564	533	414	391	382	343	357	398	334	326	340	381	310	322	320
− Domestic capital formation	2,725	6,115	9,683	16,867	18,860	20,205	22,011	23,317	23,921	25,604	27,085	31,455	34,804	40,926	43,844	49,273	51,865	46,310	35,475
− Council house sales	132	800	1,477	2,894	1270	1110	1,394	1,604	2,170	2,511	2,410	2,887	3,934	3,741	2,592	2,174	2,080	1,078	505
= Equity withdrawal	834	612	8,571	14,054	- 4,401	- 1,675	645	704	12,038	12,984	24,754	44,883	62,679	56,365	45,124	59,384	54,643	- 5,942	- 24,035
Consumer spending £billion	63.0	133.2	209.4	343.0	448.7	482.0	512.5	546.9	582.4	616.6	647.8	681.0	714.6	749.9	784.1	819.6	861.7	892.2	873
Equity withdrawal as % of consumer spending	1.32	0.46	4.09	4.10	- 0.98	- 0.35	0.13	0.13	2.07	2.11	3.82	6.59	8.77	7.52	5.75	7.25	6.34	- 0.67	- 2.75

Sources: Mortgage lending – Financial Statistics (AAPR); Private housing grants – Housing and Construction Statistics; Domestic capital formation – Economic Trends (DFDF); Public Corporation house sales – UK National Accounts (A4LG); Consumer spending – Economic Trends (ABPB).

Notes: Equity withdrawal previously peaked in 1988, when it was £19.5 billion and 6.8 per cent of consumer spending. The private housing grants figures for 2003 to 2008 are for the financial years. The 2009 grant figures are estimates.

Table 8 **Gross fixed capital formation in housing as a percentage of Gross Domestic Product**

Percentages

	1970	1975	1980	1985	1990	1991	1992	1993	1994	1995	1996	1997	1998	1999	2000	2001	2002	2003	2004	2005	2006	2007	Average 1991-2007
Denmark	7.9	6.6	5.1	4.2	3.6	3.1	3.1	3.0	3.2	3.5	3.6	3.9	3.9	4.0	4.2	3.9	3.8	4.3	4.7	5.3	5.9	–	4.0
France	7.2	7.4	6.7	5.3	4.7	4.5	4.3	4.3	4.4	4.3	4.2	4.1	4.1	4.2	4.1	4.1	4.1	4.2	4.3	4.6	4.8	–	4.3
Germany	6.8	5.9	6.9	5.7	6.0	6.2	6.7	7.1	7.8	7.7	7.6	7.4	7.2	7.2	6.8	6.3	5.8	5.7	5.5	5.2	5.5	5.6	6.5
Greece	12.0	12.4	17.8	10.3	12.0	11.4	9.2	8.4	7.2	7.1	6.8	7.0	7.4	7.5	6.8	6.8	7.4	7.7	7.3	6.9	8.6	7.7	7.7
Ireland	3.7	5.3	5.9	4.6	4.3	4.3	4.7	4.1	5.0	5.3	6.0	6.7	7.2	8.0	8.3	8.6	8.8	10.6	12.2	13.6	14.0	12.5	8.2
Italy	7.7	6.9	6.1	5.5	4.7	4.8	4.8	4.7	4.5	4.3	4.1	3.9	3.7	3.7	3.8	3.8	3.8	3.9	4.0	4.2	4.4	–	4.2
Netherlands	6.7	6.0	7.0	5.4	5.5	5.1	5.4	5.5	5.7	5.6	5.7	5.8	5.8	5.9	5.9	6.1	5.8	5.7	5.9	6.1	6.3	6.4	5.8
Norway	15.1	20.5	17.8	16.6	13.9	13.6	13.6	13.6	13.2	13.4	13.5	14.3	16.4	14.3	11.7	11.9	11.9	11.9	12.3	12.9	13.4	15.3	13.4
Spain	5.4	6.0	5.3	4.1	4.9	4.6	4.3	4.2	4.2	4.4	4.8	4.7	5.0	5.5	6.1	6.5	7.1	7.8	8.4	8.9	9.4	9.3	6.2
Sweden	5.7	4.1	4.8	4.2	5.6	5.8	5.2	3.3	2.0	1.5	1.6	1.4	1.4	1.5	1.7	1.9	2.1	2.1	2.5	2.8	3.2	3.3	2.5
United Kingdom	3.6	4.4	3.7	3.4	3.7	3.1	3.0	3.0	3.1	3.1	2.9	2.9	2.9	2.8	2.8	2.9	3.2	3.4	3.7	3.8	4	4.1	3.2
Australia	5.1	5.9	7.0	5.9	5.7	5.7	6.3	6.7	6.8	5.7	5.5	6.1	6.3	7.1	5.9	6.7	7.6	8.0	7.6	7.0	–	–	6.6
Canada	5.2	6.5	5.8	5.3	6.2	5.5	5.8	5.5	5.5	4.5	4.8	5.0	4.7	4.6	4.5	5.0	5.7	6.0	6.5	6.6	6.8	7.1	5.5
Japan	7.0	7.6	6.8	4.8	5.9	5.4	5.1	5.2	5.5	5.2	5.7	5.0	4.3	4.3	4.3	4.0	3.9	3.8	3.8	3.8	3.8	–	4.6
New Zealand	–	6.9	3.7	4.4	4.7	4.1	4.2	4.7	5.5	5.6	5.8	5.9	5.0	5.7	4.8	4.6	5.7	6.6	6.9	6.7	6.5	–	5.5
USA	–	–	4.4	4.5	3.9	3.5	3.8	4.0	4.3	4.1	4.3	4.2	4.5	4.6	4.6	4.7	4.9	5.3	5.8	6.2	5.8	–	4.4

Source: OECD Factbook 2009: Economic, Environmental and Social Statistics.

Note: Averages are based on those years for which data is available.

Table 9 **Growth of real Gross Domestic Product**

Average annual percentage changes from previous period

	1975	1980	1985	1990	1995	1996	1997	1998	1999	2000	2001	2002	2003	2004	2005	2006	2007	Estimates and projections			
																		2008	2009	2010	2011
Japan	2.9	3.6	5.0	4.9	2.0	2.6	1.6	-2.0	-0.1	2.9	0.2	0.3	1.4	2.7	1.9	2.0	2.3	-0.7	-5.3	1.8	2.0
USA	-1.3	-0.5	3.2	3.3	2.5	3.7	4.5	4.4	4.8	4.1	1.1	1.8	2.5	3.6	3.1	2.7	2.1	0.4	-2.5	2.5	2.8
Belgium	-1.4	4.3	0.8	3.1	2.4	1.1	3.9	1.9	3.5	3.7	0.8	1.4	0.8	3.1	2.0	2.8	2.8	0.8	-3.1	0.8	1.7
France	-0.3	1.6	1.9	3.2	2.2	1.0	2.2	3.5	3.2	4.1	1.8	1.1	1.1	2.3	1.9	2.4	2.3	0.3	-2.3	1.4	1.7
Germany	-1.3	1.0	2.0	3.4	2.0	1.0	1.9	1.8	1.9	3.5	1.4	0.0	-0.2	0.7	0.9	3.4	2.6	1.0	-4.9	1.4	1.9
Ireland	3.7	0.7	2.6	4.8	9.6	8.1	11.5	8.4	10.7	9.4	5.8	6.5	4.4	4.6	6.2	5.4	6.0	-3.0	-7.5	-2.3	1.0
Italy	-2.7	4.1	2.6	2.9	2.9	1.0	1.9	1.3	1.4	3.9	1.7	0.5	0.1	1.4	0.8	2.1	1.5	-1.0	-4.8	1.1	1.5
Netherlands	-0.1	0.9	2.6	3.1	3.1	3.4	4.3	3.9	4.7	3.9	1.9	0.1	0.3	2.2	2.0	3.4	3.6	2.0	-4.3	0.7	2.0
Spain	0.6	1.3	2.6	4.5	2.8	2.4	3.9	4.5	4.7	5.0	3.6	2.7	3.1	3.3	3.6	4.0	3.6	0.9	-3.6	-0.3	0.9
Sweden	2.7	1.7	1.9	2.5	4.2	1.5	2.7	3.7	4.3	4.5	1.2	2.4	2.0	3.5	3.3	4.5	2.7	-0.4	-4.7	2.0	3.0
UK	-0.7	-2.2	3.8	3.3	3.0	2.9	3.3	3.6	3.5	3.9	2.5	2.1	2.8	3.0	2.2	2.9	2.6	0.6	-4.7	1.2	2.2
Euro area			1.4	3.3	2.5	1.5	2.6	2.8	2.8	4.0	1.9	0.9	0.8	1.9	1.8	3.1	2.7	0.5	-4.0	0.9	1.7

Source: Annex Table 1, OECD Economic Outlook, December 1991 and November 2009, OECD Economic Outlook No. 86.

Note: The figures for 1975, 1980, 1985, 1990 and 1995 are the annual average percentage changes over the previous five years. Euro area figures were not available for years before 1985.

Table 10 **General Government Financial Balances as a percentage of Gross National Product**

Surpluses (+) or Deficits (-)

	1975	1980	1985	1990	1995	1996	1997	1998	1999	2000	2001	2002	2003	2004	2005	2006	2007	2008	Estimates and projections 2009	2010	2011	Difference 2009 and EMU Criterion
Japan	- 2.8	- 4.4	- 0.6	2.1	- 4.7	- 5.1	- 4.0	- 11.2	- 7.4	- 7.6	- 6.3	- 8.0	- 7.9	- 6.2	- 6.7	- 1.6	- 2.5	- 2.7	- 7.4	- 8.2	- 9.4	- 4.4
USA	- 4.1	- 1.3	- 5.0	- 4.2	- 3.3	- 2.3	- 0.9	0.3	0.7	1.5	- 0.6	- 4.0	- 5.0	- 4.4	- 3.3	- 2.2	- 2.8	- 6.5	- 11.2	- 10.7	- 9.4	- 8.2
Belgium	- 5.3	- 9.3	- 10.2	- 6.7	- 4.5	- 4.0	- 2.3	- 1.0	- 0.7	- 0.1	0.4	- 0.2	- 0.2	- 0.4	- 2.8	0.2	- 0.2	- 1.2	- 5.7	- 5.6	- 5.2	- 2.7
France	- 2.4	0.0	- 3.0	- 1.8	- 5.5	- 4.0	- 3.3	- 2.6	- 1.8	- 1.5	- 1.6	- 3.2	- 4.1	- 3.6	- 3.0	- 2.3	- 2.7	- 3.4	- 8.2	- 8.6	- 8.0	- 5.2
Germany	- 5.6	- 2.9	- 1.1	- 2.0	- 9.7	- 3.3	- 2.6	- 2.2	- 1.5	1.3	- 2.8	- 3.6	- 4.0	- 3.8	- 3.3	- 1.6	0.2	0.0	- 3.2	- 5.3	- 4.6	- 0.2
Ireland	- 11.1	- 12.1	- 10.3	- 2.8	- 2.0	- 0.1	1.4	2.3	2.6	4.8	0.9	- 0.3	0.4	1.4	1.7	3.0	0.2	- 7.2	- 12.2	- 12.2	- 11.6	- 9.2
Italy	- 12.9	- 8.6	- 12.7	- 11.4	- 7.4	- 7.0	- 2.7	- 3.1	- 1.8	- 0.9	- 3.1	- 3.0	- 3.5	- 3.6	- 4.4	- 3.3	- 1.5	- 2.7	- 5.5	- 5.4	- 5.1	- 2.5
Netherlands	- 2.8	- 3.9	- 4.1	- 5.7	- 9.2	- 1.9	- 1.2	- 0.9	0.4	2.0	- 0.3	- 2.1	- 3.2	- 1.8	- 0.3	0.5	0.2	0.7	- 4.5	- 5.9	- 5.3	- 1.5
Spain	- 0.5	- 2.2	- 5.5	- 4.1	- 6.5	- 4.9	- 3.4	- 3.2	- 1.4	- 1.0	- 0.7	- 0.5	- 0.2	- 0.4	1.0	2.0	1.9	- 4.1	- 9.6	- 8.5	- 7.7	- 6.6
Sweden	2.8	- 4.0	- 3.9	3.4	- 7.3	- 3.3	- 1.6	1.2	1.2	3.7	1.7	- 1.4	- 1.2	0.6	2.0	2.4	3.8	2.5	- 2.0	- 3.0	- 2.0	1.0
UK	- 4.5	- 3.4	- 2.9	- 1.8	- 5.8	- 4.2	- 2.2	- 0.1	0.9	3.7	0.6	- 2.0	- 3.7	- 3.6	- 3.3	- 2.7	- 2.7	- 5.3	- 12.6	- 13.3	- 12.5	- 9.6

Source: Annex Table 28, OECD Economic Outlook, December 1991 and Annex Table 27, OECD Economic Outlook, November 2009.

Note: The EMU Convergence Criterion is for annual General Government Financial Deficits of no more than 3 per cent of Gross Domestic Product.

Table 11 Office for Budget Responsibility Pre-Budget Economic Forecast[1]

	2009 outturn	2010	2011	2012 forecasts	2013	2014
Gross Domestic Product at constant prices	- 4.9	1.3	2.6	2.8	2.8	2.6
Expenditure components of GDP						
Household consumption[2]	- 3.2	0.4	1.6	1.8	2.0	2.0
Business investment	- 19.3	1.3	8.0	9.8	10.6	9.1
General government consumption	2.2	1.9	- 0.5	- 1.5	- 2.0	- 2.3
General government investment	15.7	- 3.1	- 19.0	- 8.5	- 6.6	0.6
Net trade[3]	0.7	- 0.5	0.7	0.8	0.6	0.5
Inflation CPI Q4	2.1	2.3	1.6	2.0	2.0	2.0
Labour market						
Employment (millions)	29.0	28.8	29.0	29.3	29.6	29.9
Wages and salaries	- 1.0	1.2	2.8	3.5	4.9	5.3
Average earnings[4]	1.0	2.1	2.2	2.6	3.8	4.3
ILO unemployment (percentage)	7.6	8.1	7.9	7.4	6.8	6.3
Claimant count (Q4 millions)	1.6	1.5	1.4	1.3	1.2	1.1
Household sector						
Real household disposable income	3.2	0.6	2.0	1.6	1.9	2.0
Savings ratio (level, percentage)	7.0	7.2	7.5	7.3	7.2	7.3
House prices	- 7.8	5.9	1.6	3.9	4.5	4.5
Fiscal aggregates (Percentage of GDP)[5]						
Public sector net borrowing	11.1	10.5	8.3	6.6	5.0	4.0
Public sector net debt	53.5	62.2	68.2	71.8	73.7	74.4
General government net borrowing[6]	9.2	8.0	6.1	4.8	3.7	3.0
General government net debt[6]	71.2	79.0	84.7	87.5	88.4	88.2

Source: Pre-Budget Forecast June 2010, Office for Budget Responsibility.

Notes: 1. Forecast is consistent with ONS output, income and expenditure data for the first quarter of 2010.

2. Includes households and non-profit institutions serving households.

3. Contribution to GDP growth, percentage points.

4. Wages and salaries divided by employees.

5. Fiscal aggregates are for the financial year (ie 2009 is 2009/10). The 2009/10 figures are estimates.

6. General government borrowing and debt measures on a Maastricht basis.

Table 12a **Total Managed Expenditure (TME)**

	£ billion							Percentages of Gross Domestic Product						
			Outturn			Estimate	Projection			Outturn			Estimate	Projection
	2004/05	2005/06	2006/07	2007/08	2008/09	2009/10	2010/11	2004/05	2005/06	2006/07	2007/08	2008/09	2009/10	2010/11
Departmental Expenditure Limits	278.7	297.4	312.5	333.8	357.6	386.7	393.4	22.9	23.4	23.2	23.5	24.9	27.5	26.9
+ Annually Managed Expenditure	213.6	226.6	237.5	248.9	272.0	287.4	310.6	17.6	17.8	17.6	17.6	19.0	20.4	21.2
= Totally Managed Expenditure	492.4	524.0	550.0	582.8	629.6	674.1	704.0	40.5	41.2	40.9	41.1	43.9	47.9	48.1
Gross Domestic Product	1,214.7	1,270.8	1,346.2	1,418.0	1,434.0	1,406.0	1,464.0	100.0	100.0	100.0	100.0	100.0	100.0	100.0

Sources: As Table 12b.

Table 12b **General government receipts**

	£ billion									Percentages of Gross Domestic Product								
				Outturn[1]				Estimate	Projection				Outturn[1]				Estimate	Projection
	2002/03	2003/04	2004/05	2005/06	2006/07	2007/08	2008/09	2009/10	2010/11	2002/03	2003/04	2004/05	2005/06	2006/07	2007/08	2008/09	2009/10	2010/11
Income tax (net of tax credits)	109.5	113.9	122.9	130.5	143.4	147.4	147.8	138.8	140.1	10.0	9.8	10.1	10.3	10.7	10.4	10.3	9.9	9.6
+ Value Added Tax	63.5	69.1	73.0	72.9	77.4	80.6	78.4	70.0	78.0	5.8	6.0	6.0	5.7	5.7	5.7	5.5	5.0	5.3
+ Corporation tax	29.3	28.1	33.6	41.8	44.3	46.4	43.7	36.0	42.1	2.7	2.4	2.8	3.3	3.3	3.3	3.0	2.6	2.9
+ Excise duties	38.8	39.8	40.7	40.6	41.1	42.8	49.3	51.8	55.4	3.6	3.4	3.4	3.2	3.1	3.0	3.4	3.7	3.8
+ Council tax and business rates	35.4	37.1	38.7	40.7	43.2	44.9	47.3	48.5	50.5	3.2	3.2	3.2	3.2	3.2	3.2	3.3	3.4	3.4
+ Other taxes and royalties	33.9	36.5	40.1	44.8	49.2	52.5	44.5	37.4	43.9	3.1	3.2	3.3	3.5	3.7	3.7	3.1	2.7	3.0
+ National insurance contributions	64.6	72.5	78.1	85.5	87.4	101.4	96.9	94.9	97.0	5.9	6.3	6.4	6.7	6.5	7.2	6.8	6.7	6.6
+ Interest, surplus and other adjustments	21.0	25.4	25.5	29.8	33.2	33.0	25.6	30.1	33.8	1.9	2.2	2.1	2.3	2.5	2.3	1.8	2.1	2.3
= Current receipts[2]	396.0	422.4	452.6	486.6	519.2	549.0	533.5	507.5	540.8	36.3	36.5	37.3	38.3	38.6	38.7	37.2	36.1	36.9

Sources: Various tables, Budget Report 2010, HC 451, HM Treasury 2010; Public Expenditure Statistics, HM Treasury website.
Notes: 1. Data for years to 2007/08 in Tables 12a and 12b from Public Expenditure Statistics; data for last three years Budget Report 2010.
2. Current receipts (and consequently the related measures) include windfall tax receipts and associated spending.

Table 12c **Public sector budgets and borrowing**

£ billion

	2002/03	2003/04	Outturn 2004/05	2005/06	2006/07	2007/08	2008/09	Estimate 2009/10	2010/11	2011/12	Projections 2012/13	2013/14	2014/15
Current receipts[1]	396.0	422.4	452.6	486.6	519.2	549.0	533.5	507.5	541.0	582.0	621.0	660.0	699.0
− Current expenditure	393.4	425.3	456.6	484.4	507.2	535.8	563.7	604.6	644.0	662.0	682.0	703.0	725.0
− Depreciation	14.5	14.9	15.6	16.4	17.3	17.9	18.7	19.5	20.0	21.0	22.0	23.0	24.0
= Current budget surplus (deficit)	− 11.9	− 17.8	− 19.6	− 14.2	− 5.3	− 4.7	− 48.9	− 116.6	− 124.0	− 102.0	− 84.0	− 67.0	− 51.0
Gross capital investment[2]	28.3	30.5	36.2	39.9	43.2	47.1	65.9	69.5	60.0	51.0	48.0	45.0	47.0
− Depreciation	14.5	14.9	15.6	16.4	17.3	17.9	18.7	19.5	20.0	21.0	22.0	23.0	24.0
= Net capital investment	13.8	15.6	20.6	23.5	25.9	29.2	47.2	50.0	40.0	29.0	26.0	22.0	23.0
Public Sector Net Borrowing	25.1	33.0	39.8	37.4	30.8	33.7	96.1	166.5	163.0	131.0	110.0	89.0	74.0
Public Sector Net Debt	346.0	381.5	422.1	461.7	497.8	527.2	617.0	776.6	952.0	1,095.0	1,218.0	1,320.0	1,406.0
General Government Net Borrowing[3]	27.0	37.3	42.3	38.7	35.0	38.4	96.7	171.5	164.0	132.0	111.0	91.0	77.0
General Government Gross Debt[3]	401.3	450.1	487.6	535.3	577.9	620.1	796.9	1,004.1	1,179.0	1,319.0	1,438.0	1,535.0	1,618.0
Gross Domestic Product	1092.1	1157.4	1214.7	1270.8	1346.2	1418.0	1435.0	1,406.0	1,464.0	1,533.0	1,621.0	1,720.0	1,824.0
Borrowing and Debt as a percentage of GDP													
Public Sector Net Borrowing	2.3	2.9	3.3	2.9	2.3	2.4	6.7	11.8	11.1	8.5	6.8	5.2	4.1
Public Sector Net Debt	31.7	33.0	34.7	36.3	37.0	37.2	43.0	55.2	65.0	71.4	75.1	76.7	77.1
General Government Net Borrowing[3]	2.5	3.2	3.5	3.0	2.6	2.7	6.7	12.2	11.2	8.6	6.8	5.3	4.2
General Government Gross Debt[3]	36.7	38.9	40.1	42.1	42.9	43.7	55.5	71.4	80.5	86.0	88.7	89.2	88.7

Sources: As Table 12b.

Notes: 1. Current receipts (and consequently the related measures) include windfall tax receipts and associated spending.

2. Gross capital investment is net of asset sales.

3. General Government Net Borrowing and Gross Debt are on a Maastricht Treaty basis.

Table 13 **Government expenditure and borrowing in cash and real terms, and as a percentage of Gross Domestic Product**

£ billion

	1970/71	1975/76	1980/81	1985/86	1990/91	1995/96	1996/97	1997/98	1998/99	1999/00	2000/01	2001/02	2002/03	2003/04	2004/05	2005/06	2006/07	2007/08	2008/09	2009/10	2010/11
Components of public expenditure																					
Public sector current expenditure	17.3	44.3	96.6	148.7	203.3	287.2	297.8	305.2	313.9	326.6	348.9	367.4	394.8	425.3	455.4	484.2	507.0	535.6	564.7	600.6	637.3
+ Depreciation	2.1	5.1	10.9	12.1	13.8	12.9	12.0	11.9	12.3	12.9	13.2	13.8	14.4	14.0	15.0	16.5	16.9	17.8	18.7	19.7	20.6
+ Public Sector Net Investment	3.2	6.1	4.3	4.5	8.2	10.3	5.9	5.6	6.4	4.1	5.0	9.4	9.8	15.0	20.7	22.7	25.8	29.3	46.4	49.0	38.9
= Total Managed Expenditure (TME)	22.6	55.5	111.8	165.3	224.5	310.5	315.6	322.7	332.7	343.6	367.1	390.5	418.9	454.3	491.0	523.4	549.8	582.7	629.8	669.3	696.8
Public expenditure at 2006/07 prices																					
Public sector current expenditure	195.0	262.6	289.0	326.9	331.9	400.1	399.9	399.4	402.3	410.5	432.8	445.8	464.1	486.2	506.6	529.0	535.9	550.4	564.7	591.7	609.6
Public Sector Net Investment	36.1	36.2	12.9	9.9	13.4	14.3	7.9	7.3	8.2	5.2	6.2	11.4	11.5	17.1	23.0	24.8	27.3	30.1	46.4	48.3	37.2
Total Managed Expenditure	254.7	329.0	334.5	363.4	366.5	432.5	423.8	422.3	426.4	431.9	455.4	473.8	492.4	519.4	546.2	571.8	581.2	598.8	629.8	659.4	666.5
Public sector borrowing and debt																					
Public Sector Net Borrowing (PSNB)	- 0.3	7.8	11.5	8.7	5.8	34.7	27.4	6.6	- 3.5	- 15.2	- 15.4	- 0.4	22.9	35.4	39.7	37.8	30.1	34.6	90.0	154.7	149.0
General Government Net Borrowing (GGNB)	- 1.1	5.3	9.1	9.5	7.9	36.9	29.6	7.9	- 2.8	- 14.4	- 15.2	- 0.4	22.3	35.4	38.5	35.9	34.0	39.4	102.7	158.0	149.6
General Government Gross Debt (GGD)	40.9	65.6	126.2	179.3	187.4	378.3	400.9	402.8	401.3	396.1	384.4	381.1	399.8	441.2	480.4	529.2	574.4	613.9	800.1	1002.8	1,162.2
Gross Domestic Product (GDP)																					
Cash GDP	53.1	112.1	239.0	369.9	576.8	744.1	792.4	843.1	890.3	944.6	989.6	1,031.5	1,092.1	1,157.4	1,214.7	1,273.6	1,348.4	1,423.6	1,434.1	1,401.6	1,474.0
GDP at 2007/08 prices	598.1	664.4	714.9	813.2	941.6	1,036.5	1,064.0	1,103.4	1,140.9	1,187.3	1,227.6	1,251.6	1,283.8	1,323.3	1,351.2	1,391.5	1,425.3	1,463.0	1,434.1	1,380.8	1,409.8
GDP deflator index	8.9	16.9	33.4	45.5	61.3	71.8	74.5	76.4	78.0	79.6	80.6	82.4	85.1	87.5	89.9	91.5	94.6	97.3	100.0	101.5	104.6
Public spending measures as a percentage of Gross Domestic Product																					
Total Managed Expenditure	42.6	49.5	46.8	44.7	38.9	41.7	39.8	38.3	37.4	36.4	37.1	37.9	38.4	39.3	40.4	41.1	40.8	40.9	43.9	47.8	47.3
Public Sector Net Borrowing	- 0.6	7.0	4.8	2.4	1.0	4.7	3.5	0.8	- 0.4	- 1.6	- 1.6	0.0	2.1	3.1	3.3	3.0	2.2	2.4	6.3	11.0	10.1
General Government Net Borrowing	- 2.1	4.7	3.8	2.6	1.4	5.0	3.7	0.9	- 0.3	- 1.5	- 1.5	0.0	2.0	3.1	3.2	2.8	2.5	2.8	7.2	11.3	10.1
General Government Gross Debt	77.1	58.5	52.8	48.5	32.5	50.8	50.6	47.8	45.1	41.9	38.8	36.9	36.6	38.1	39.5	41.6	42.6	43.1	55.8	71.5	78.8

Sources: Budget 2010, HC 61, HM Treasury 2010, HM Treasury website.

Note: Estimated GDP and borrowing forecasts for 2010/11 are given to the nearest £ billion.

Table 14 **Public sector gross capital expenditure**

£ million

	1970/71	1975/76	1980/81	1985/86	1990/91	1995/96	2000/01	2001/02	2002/03	2003/04	2004/05	2005/06	2006/07	2007/08	2008/09	2009/10 estimate	2010/11 plans
Central government	1,547	2,545	4,253	6,517	11,367	10,124	3,612	11,006	10,962	14,633	18,632	4,889	23,826	25,135	38,523	40,897	31,100
+ Local government	1,979	4,004	4,018	4,658	5,848	7,257	11,207	9,114	11,447	12,080	13,609	13,710	13,567	15,376	18,990	19,852	20,300
= General government	3,526	6,549	8,271	11,175	17,215	17,381	14,819	20,120	22,409	26,713	32,241	18,599	37,393	40,511	57,513	60,749	51,400
+ Public corporations	1,777	4,590	6,967	5,402	4,712	5,854	3,528	4,137	5,274	3,571	3,489	20,952	5,436	6,142	7,593	7,956	8,100
= Total public sector gross capital expenditure	5,303	11,139	15,238	16,577	21,927	23,235	18,347	24,257	27,683	30,284	35,730	39,551	42,829	46,653	65,106	68,705	59,500
- Depreciation	2,065	5,081	10,925	12,057	13,777	12,976	12,676	13,204	13,976	14,577	15,156	16,095	16,988	17,820	18,721	19,681	20,600
= Total public sector net investment	3,238	6,058	4,313	4,520	8,150	10,259	5,671	11,053	13,707	15,707	20,574	23,456	25,841	28,833	46,385	49,024	38,900
Total public sector gross capital expenditure at 2007/08 prices	59,762	66,024	45,590	36,441	35,796	32,365	22,761	29,434	32,543	34,624	39,745	43,212	45,273	47,942	65,106	67,686	56,910
Total public sector gross capital expenditure as a % of TME	23.5	20.1	13.6	10.0	9.8	7.5	5.8	7.5	8.3	8.8	9.7	10.1	10.2	10.3	13.3	13.1	10.8
Total public sector gross capital expenditure as a % of GDP	10.0	9.9	6.4	4.5	3.8	3.1	1.9	2.4	2.5	2.6	2.9	3.1	3.2	3.3	4.5	4.9	4.0

Sources: HM Treasury, Public Expenditure Statistical Analyses 2010.

Notes: Capital expenditure is shown on current sectoral definitions over the whole time series, to remove the effect of major classification changes. As a consequence, investment by public corporations excludes investments by the various industries that have been privatised over the years. Gross investment is shown net of asset sales, other than council house sales. Net investment is net of depreciation. Council HRA capital expenditure is now included within the public corporations' sector.

Table 15a **Total Managed Expenditure by function**

£ billion

| | 1980/81[1] | 1985/86 | 1990/91 | 1995/96 | 2000/01 | 2000/01 % of total | 2005/06 prices[3] | | | | | Real growth 1980/81 to 2000/01 |
| | | | | | | | 1980/81[1] | 1985/86 | 1990/91 | 1995/96 | 2000/01 | |
	outturn	outturn	outturn	outturn	outturn	expenditure	outturn	outturn	outturn	outturn	outturn	%
Social security	24.2	43.1	58.9	92.8	109.1	33.6	67.2	87.8	89.0	119.3	124.3	85.0
Health & personal social services	14.0	21.0	33.6	49.8	66.9	20.6	38.8	42.8	50.8	64.0	76.2	96.1
Education	12.8	16.8	26.3	35.6	44.2	13.6	35.5	34.2	39.7	45.8	50.3	41.7
Defence	11.5	18.0	21.5	21.6	24.9	7.7	31.9	36.7	32.5	27.8	28.4	- 11.1
Law, order & protective services	4.0	6.6	11.5	15.7	20.3	6.3	11.1	13.4	17.4	20.2	23.1	108.3
Trade, industry, energy & employment	4.8	8.0	9.0	9.5	10.6	3.3	13.3	16.3	13.6	12.2	12.1	- 9.4
Other environmental services	3.8	4.0	6.6	8.7	10.6	3.3	10.5	8.1	10.0	11.2	12.1	14.5
Transport	4.3	6.8	9.7	11.5	9.1	2.8	11.9	13.8	14.7	14.8	10.4	- 13.1
Culture, media & sport	1.0	1.7	2.8	3.5	5.2	1.6	2.8	3.5	4.2	4.5	5.9	113.4
Agriculture, fisheries, food & forestry	1.6	2.9	2.9	4.0	5.1	1.6	4.4	5.9	4.4	5.1	5.8	30.8
Overseas services & aid	1.3	1.6	2.4	3.3	4.1	1.3	3.6	3.3	3.6	4.2	4.7	29.5
HOUSING	5.6	4.2	4.9	5.0	3.1	1.0	15.5	8.6	7.4	6.4	3.5	- 77.3
Central administration etc.[2]	3.0	4.6	8.3	9.5	11.5	3.5	8.3	9.4	12.5	12.2	13.1	57.3
Total expenditure on services	92.0	139.4	198.3	270.5	324.8	100.0	255.3	283.9	299.6	347.7	369.9	44.9
+ Public sector debt interest	–	19.3	20.5	26.8	26.4	–	–	39.3	31.0	34.4	30.1	–
+ Other accounting adjustments	–	6.6	6.5	13.3	15.6	–	–	13.4	9.8	17.1	17.8	–
= Total Managed Expenditure	111.5	165.3	225.3	310.5	366.8	–	309.4	336.6	340.4	399.1	417.8	35.0

Sources: Public Expenditure, Cm 5901, HM Treasury 2003, Tables 3.2 & 3.3, additional data HM Treasury.

Notes: 1. The 1980/81 figures for expenditure on services are derived from earlier public expenditure plans, and figures for the adjustments between total expenditure on services and Total Managed Expenditure are not available.

2. Includes contributions to the European Communities and activities required for the general maintenance of government, such as tax collection and the registration of population.

3. Cash figures adjusted to 2005/06 price levels by excluding the effect of general inflation.

Table 15b Total expenditure on services by function

£ billion

	1987/88 outturn	1990/91 outturn	1991/92 outturn	1992/93 outturn	1993/94 outturn	1994/95 outturn	1995/96 outturn	1996/97 outturn	1997/98 outturn	1998/99 outturn	1999/00 outturn	2000/01 outturn	2001/02 outturn	2002/03 outturn	2003/04 outturn	2004/05 outturn	2005/06 outturn	2006/07 outturn	2007/08 outturn	2008/09 outturn	2009/10 estimated outturn
1. General public services	25.0	28.1	26.9	28.0	29.8	32.8	36.3	37.5	38.9	39.8	37.1	38.7	36.1	36.0	39.1	42.5	45.7	47.7	50.7	52.8	53.4
of which: public and common services	3.4	5.1	5.7	5.8	5.8	5.9	6.1	6.2	6.2	7.2	8.0	7.9	9.2	9.8	10.9	12.1	12.7	12.7	12.6	13.9	13.9
of which: international services	1.9	2.5	2.9	3.1	3.2	3.3	3.4	3.1	3.1	3.2	3.7	4.2	4.3	4.5	5.1	5.5	6.2	6.3	6.7	7.3	8.1
of which: public sector debt interest	19.7	20.5	18.3	19.0	20.8	23.5	26.8	28.1	29.7	29.4	25.4	26.6	22.7	21.7	23.0	24.9	26.7	28.7	31.4	31.6	31.4
2. Defence	19.1	22.0	23.2	23.8	23.5	23.3	22.5	22.1	21.7	24.5	25.1	25.7	25.4	27.0	28.8	29.8	30.9	32.1	33.6	36.7	38.2
3. Public order and safety	8.1	11.7	13.2	14.4	15.0	15.6	16.0	16.4	17.1	18.0	18.4	20.4	23.1	24.4	26.4	28.5	29.3	30.4	31.7	33.6	35.0
4. Economic affairs	19.0	21.6	21.4	23.3	23.8	23.9	23.4	23.3	21.5	19.6	21.5	23.8	27.8	30.8	33.1	33.7	35.5	37.7	38.9	48.1	45.6
of which: enterprise and economic development	6.5	6.9	5.4	5.4	5.5	4.7	4.5	4.3	4.3	3.1	4.4	4.9	5.1	5.9	6.0	6.5	6.5	6.5	6.9	15.6	9.1
of which: science and technology	1.0	1.2	1.3	1.4	1.5	1.1	1.2	1.4	1.4	1.4	1.4	1.4	1.7	2.1	2.3	2.5	3.0	2.8	3.2	3.2	3.5
of which: employment policies	3.0	2.4	2.7	2.9	3.1	3.2	3.1	2.8	2.5	2.9	3.5	3.8	3.3	3.0	3.2	3.2	3.3	3.3	3.3	3.1	3.8
of which: agriculture, fisheries and forestry	2.2	2.7	2.8	2.9	3.8	3.4	3.9	5.4	4.7	4.4	4.3	4.7	6.3	4.9	5.3	5.4	5.6	5.1	5.0	5.4	6.1
of which: transport	6.4	8.3	9.2	10.8	10.0	11.5	10.9	9.5	8.7	7.8	7.9	9.0	11.3	14.8	16.3	16.0	17.0	19.9	20.5	20.8	23.1
5. Environment protection	2.4	3.2	3.4	3.6	3.4	3.8	4.1	3.7	4.0	4.3	4.9	5.1	5.4	6.0	6.2	7.0	8.5	9.3	9.5	9.6	11.4
6. HOUSING AND COMMUNITY AMENITIES	4.6	6.0	6.8	7.1	6.2	6.2	6.0	5.7	4.9	5.5	4.7	5.5	6.2	5.4	6.7	8.0	10.6	11.5	12.9	15.0	15.6
7. Health	20.3	27.1	30.9	34.2	36.6	39.4	41.4	42.8	44.5	46.9	49.4	54.2	59.8	66.2	74.9	82.9	89.6	94.5	102.2	110.0	119.8
8. Recreation, culture and religion	3.5	4.8	5.0	5.1	5.1	5.2	5.5	5.7	6.4	7.2	7.7	7.8	8.6	9.3	9.7	10.0	10.8	11.4	12.2	13.1	14.1
9. Education (includes training)	21.2	28.1	31.3	33.2	34.7	36.2	37.0	37.8	38.6	40.0	42.2	45.9	51.2	54.7	61.0	65.1	69.7	72.9	78.1	82.6	88.3
10. Social protection	55.1	68.2	80.2	91.1	98.3	102.0	107.6	112.8	114.5	115.2	123.0	128.5	137.4	145.3	155.6	164.1	171.1	177.2	187.5	203.6	222.5
EU transactions	- 1.6	- 2.3	- 4.1	- 3.4	- 4.7	- 4.3	- 4.1	- 5.2	- 3.7	- 2.6	- 2.7	- 2.6	- 4.8	- 1.9	- 2.1	- 0.9	- 0.6	- 1.8	- 1.5	- 2.9	0.0
Unallocated[1]	–	–	–	–	–	–	–	–	–	–	–	–	–	–	–	–	–	–	–	–	- 2.5
Total expenditure on services	176.8	218.4	238.2	260.5	271.6	284.1	295.8	302.5	308.5	318.5	331.2	353.1	376.2	403.4	439.5	470.8	501.1	523.0	555.9	602.2	641.5
Accounting adjustments	6.5	9.1	16.0	13.7	14.7	15.1	15.6	13.4	13.5	12.4	11.8	10.9	13.0	17.8	16.0	21.6	22.9	27.0	26.7	27.7	27.8
Total Managed Expenditure (TME)	183.3	227.5	254.2	274.2	286.3	299.2	311.4	315.9	322.0	330.9	343.0	364.0	389.2	421.2	455.5	492.4	524.0	550.0	582.5	629.8	669.3

Source: Public Expenditure Statistical Analyses, Cm 7890, HM Treasury 2010, Tables 4.2 & 4.3.

Note: 1. Includes allowance for shortfall and departmental unallocated provision.

Table 15c Total expenditure on services by function in real terms[1]

£ billion (2008/09 prices)

	1987/88 outturn	1990/91 outturn	1991/92 outturn	1992/93 outturn	1993/94 outturn	1994/95 outturn	1995/96 outturn	1996/97 outturn	1997/98 outturn	1998/99 outturn	1999/00 outturn	2000/01 outturn	2001/02 outturn	2002/03 outturn	2003/04 outturn	2004/05 outturn	2005/06 outturn	2006/07 outturn	2007/08 outturn	2008/09 outturn	2009/10 estimated outturn
1. General public services	50.1	45.6	41.3	41.6	43.1	46.7	50.3	50.0	50.7	50.7	46.3	47.8	43.6	42.0	44.5	47.0	49.6	50.3	52.0	52.8	52.4
of which: public and common services	6.8	8.3	8.8	8.6	8.4	8.5	8.4	8.3	8.0	9.2	10.0	9.8	11.0	11.4	12.4	13.4	13.8	13.4	13.0	13.9	13.7
of which: international services	3.8	4.1	4.5	4.7	4.7	4.7	4.8	4.1	4.0	4.1	4.7	5.2	5.2	5.2	5.9	6.1	6.7	6.6	6.9	7.3	8.0
of which: public sector debt interest	39.6	33.2	28.0	28.3	30.0	33.5	37.1	37.5	38.7	37.4	31.7	32.8	27.3	25.4	26.2	27.5	29.0	30.3	32.2	31.6	30.8
2. Defence	38.3	35.6	35.5	35.5	34.0	33.2	31.1	29.5	28.2	31.2	31.3	31.7	30.7	31.6	32.8	32.9	33.6	33.9	34.4	36.7	37.5
3. Public order and safety	16.3	18.9	20.2	21.4	21.7	22.2	22.1	22.0	22.2	23.0	23.0	25.1	27.9	28.6	30.0	31.5	31.8	32.1	32.5	33.6	34.3
4. Economic affairs	38.1	35.1	32.8	34.7	34.5	34.0	32.5	31.2	28.0	25.0	26.8	29.4	33.6	36.0	37.6	37.3	38.6	39.8	39.9	48.1	44.7
of which: enterprise and economic development	13.0	11.3	8.3	8.0	7.9	6.7	6.2	5.8	5.6	3.9	5.6	6.0	6.2	6.9	6.9	7.2	7.1	6.9	7.1	15.6	8.9
of which: science and technology	2.0	2.0	1.9	2.1	2.2	1.6	1.6	1.8	1.8	1.7	1.7	1.7	2.1	2.5	2.6	2.8	3.3	3.0	3.3	3.2	3.4
of which: employment policies	5.9	3.9	4.2	4.3	4.4	4.5	4.2	3.7	3.2	3.7	4.4	4.7	4.0	3.5	3.6	3.5	3.6	3.5	3.4	3.1	3.7
of which: agriculture, fisheries and forestry	4.4	4.4	4.3	4.3	5.5	4.8	5.4	7.2	6.1	5.6	5.3	5.8	7.6	5.8	6.0	6.0	6.1	5.4	5.1	5.4	6.0
of which: transport	12.7	13.6	14.1	16.0	14.5	16.4	15.1	12.6	11.3	10.0	9.8	11.1	13.7	17.3	18.5	17.7	18.5	21.0	21.0	20.8	22.7
5. Environment protection	4.8	5.2	5.3	5.3	4.9	5.4	5.7	4.9	5.2	5.5	6.1	6.3	6.5	7.0	7.1	7.8	9.2	9.8	9.7	9.6	11.2
6. HOUSING AND COMMUNITY AMENITIES	9.2	9.7	10.4	10.5	9.0	8.8	8.4	7.7	6.4	7.0	5.8	6.8	7.5	6.4	7.6	8.8	11.5	12.2	13.2	15.0	15.3
7. Health	40.6	43.9	47.4	50.8	53.0	56.2	57.4	57.1	58.0	59.8	61.8	66.9	72.1	77.4	85.2	91.7	97.3	99.7	104.7	110.0	117.6
8. Recreation, culture and religion	7.0	7.8	7.6	7.6	7.4	7.5	7.6	7.6	8.3	9.2	9.7	9.6	10.3	10.9	11.0	11.0	11.7	12.0	12.5	13.1	13.8
9. Education (includes training)	42.5	45.6	48.0	49.3	50.2	51.6	51.2	50.4	50.2	51.0	52.7	56.7	61.8	64.0	69.4	72.0	75.7	76.9	80.1	82.6	86.7
10. Social protection	110.4	110.7	122.9	135.5	142.2	145.3	149.1	150.6	149.0	146.8	153.7	158.6	165.8	169.8	176.9	181.6	185.8	186.8	192.3	203.6	218.4
EU transactions	- 3.1	- 0.4	- 6.3	- 5.0	- 6.7	- 6.1	- 5.7	- 6.9	- 4.8	- 3.3	- 3.4	- 3.2	- 5.8	- 2.2	- 2.4	- 1.0	- 0.6	- 1.9	- 1.6	- 2.9	0.0
Unallocated(2)	–	–	–	–	–	–	–	–	–	–	–	–	–	–	–	–	–	–	–	–	- 2.4
Total expenditure on services	354.2	354.5	365.1	387.3	393.1	404.8	409.7	403.9	401.4	405.9	413.9	435.6	454.0	471.5	499.7	520.7	544.1	551.6	569.8	602.2	629.5
Accounting adjustments	13.0	14.8	24.5	20.4	21.2	21.5	21.6	17.9	17.6	15.8	14.7	13.4	15.6	20.8	18.2	23.9	24.9	28.5	27.3	27.7	27.3
Total Managed Expenditure (TME)	367.1	369.3	389.6	407.7	414.3	426.3	431.3	421.8	419.0	421.7	428.7	449.1	469.6	492.3	517.9	544.7	569.0	580.1	597.2	629.8	656.8

Source: As Table 15b.

Notes: 1. Real terms figures are the cash figures adjusted to 2008/09 price levels using GDP deflators.

2. Includes allowance for shortfall and departmental unallocated provision.

Table 16 **Departmental Expenditure Limits (DEL) and Annually Managed Expenditure (AME)**

£ million

Department	2002/03 outturn	2003/04 outturn	2004/05 outturn	2005/06 outturn	2006/07 outturn	2007/08 outturn	2008/09 estimated outturn	2009/10 plans	2010/11 plans
Health	58,821	65,991	71,433	76,672	80,622	87,571	93,676	101,955	105,270
Education	13,330	15,386	16,641	18,692	46,145	50,146	52,347	57,125	57,517
Defence	29,317	31,089	29,490	29,843	30,713	33,183	34,295	36,964	37,220
DCLG Local Government	37,598	41,128	43,571	46,560	22,763	22,782	24,772	25,727	25,993
Business, Innovation and Skills	14,302	15,009	15,250	16,699	17,265	18,948	19,785	21,959	20,986
Transport	9,643	10,974	10,665	11,354	13,103	12,839	12,657	13,962	12,730
Home Office	7,847	8,510	8,749	9,087	9,100	9,450	9,850	10,329	10,003
DCLG Communities	4,662	7,996	8,543	8,968	8,928	10,161	11,170	13,404	9,937
Justice	8,234	7,637	8,413	8,352	8,561	9,414	9,727	9,849	9,203
Work and pensions	7,211	7,966	8,200	8,158	7,818	7,949	7,876	9,156	8,824
International Development	3,434	3,718	3,845	4,488	4,863	5,186	5,617	6,631	7,619
Chancellor's Departments	4,053	4,366	4,455	4,621	4,701	4,442	4,545	4,632	4,111
Energy and Climate Change		785	1,126	1,925	2,374	2,158	1,955	3,113	3,113
Environment, Food and Rural Affairs	2,516	2,560	2,589	2,785	2,885	2,877	2,863	3,074	2,756
Cabinet Office	1,251	1,652	1,388	1,583	1,741	1,912	2,132	2,323	2,288
Foreign and Commonwealth Office	1,513	1,535	1,726	1,840	1,850	1,963	2,173	2,260	2,127
Culture, Media and Sport	1,187	1,342	1,280	1,442	1,643	1,933	2,271	2,007	1,957
Independent Bodies	672	682	757	778	682	721	783	833	1,003
Law Officers' Departments	518	582	647	656	698	716	722	720	687
Scotland	17,929	19,915	20,741	22,465	24,537	26,485	26,915	28,534	28,401
Wales	9,654	10,532	11,126	11,903	12,688	13,442	14,076	15,131	15,177
Northern Ireland	7,467	7,621	8,099	8,524	8,820	9,563	10,175	10,915	10,719
Modernisation Funding	–	–	–	–	–	–	–	–	200
DEL Reserves/Allowance for shortfall	–	–	–	–	–	–	–	- 2,600	2,100
Departmental Expenditure Limits	241,159	266,977	278,733	297,396	312,500	333,841	350,382	378,000	380,000
Annually Managed Expenditure	179,883	188,618	213,644	226,610	237,546	248,693	279,462	291,260	316,800
of which social security benefits	113,604	117,801	124,781	129,621	133,463	140,474	151,196	164,840	169,878
Total Managed Expenditure	421,042	455,595	492,377	524,006	550,046	582,534	629,844	669,260	696,800

Source: Pubic Expenditure, Cm 7890, HM Treasury, 2010.

Note: Figures are the sum of resource and net capital DEL for each department. They are net of depreciation and do not include local authority self-financed expenditure.

Section 3 Compendium of tables

Dwellings, stock condition and households

Table 17a **Dwellings by tenure in England, Scotland and Wales**

Thousands

England

	1971	1976	1981	1986	1991	1992	1993	1994	1995	1996	1997	1998	1999	2000	2001	2002	2003	2004	2005	2006	2007	2008	2009
Owner-occupiers	8,503	9,570	10,773	12,015	13,397	13,539	13,646	13,766	13,886	13,983	14,111	14,308	14,518	14,701	14,838	14,942	15,088	15,210	15,312	15,390	15,449	15,409	15,396
+ Privately rented		2,332	2,044	1,953	1,767	1,806	1,867	1,929	1,998	2,073	2,125	2,121	2,086	2,089	2,133	2,197	2,285	2,389	2,525	2,673	2,866	2,976	3,136
	3,122																						
+ Housing association		281	410	475	608	646	714	779	857	942	985	1,040	1,146	1,273	1,424	1,492	1,651	1,702	1,802	1,842	1,886	2,142	2,211
+ Local authority	4,586	4,985	4,798	4,439	3,899	3,844	3,760	3,666	3,565	3,470	3,401	3,309	3,178	3,012	2,812	2,706	2,457	2,335	2,166	2,086	1,987	1,870	1,820
= All dwellings	16,211	17,168	18,025	18,882	19,671	19,836	19,987	20,139	20,305	20,468	20,622	20,778	20,927	21,075	21,207	21,337	21,481	21,636	21,805	21,990	22,189	22,398	22,564

Wales

	1971	1976	1981	1986	1991	1992	1993	1994	1995	1996	1997	1998	1999	2000	2001	2002	2003	2004	2005	2006	2007	2008	2009
Owner-occupiers	540	631	680	761	837	847	854	862	870	878	891	888	915	903	905	932	925	950	952	955	968	974	955
+ Privately rented			105	98	97	98	99	101	102	104	100	112	94	117	127	110	130	125	133	137	135	136	164
	151	131																					
+ Housing association			24	25	28	30	35	38	42	45	48	50	52	54	55	57	57	64	65	66	67	89	107
+ Local authority	276	284	290	254	222	219	216	213	210	207	204	201	197	193	188	183	177	162	158	156	154	132	113
= All dwellings	967	1,046	1,099	1,138	1,184	1,194	1,204	1,214	1,224	1,233	1,243	1,251	1,258	1,267	1,275	1,282	1,289	1,302	1,308	1,314	1,323	1,331	1,339

Scotland

	1971	1976	1981	1986	1991	1992	1993	1994	1995	1996	1997	1998	1999	2000	2001	2002	2003	2004	2005	2006	2007	2008	2009
Owner-occupiers	569	645	718	884	–	1,132	1,176	1,217	1,258	1,293	1,327	1,366	1,400	1,435	1,446	1,479	1,514	1,544	1,555	1,570	1,587	1,590	1,612
+ Privately rented			191	154	–	154	154	154	155	155	154	154	154	155	169	179	180	184	208	225	233	263	263
	305	234																					
+ Housing association			36	50	–	57	62	67	77	91	99	115	121	131	139	143	238	251	251	251	261	269	268
+ Local authority	948	1,042	1,027	962	–	816	783	755	721	692	668	630	608	583	553	531	416	389	374	362	347	330	326
= All dwellings	1,822	1,921	1,970	2,050	–	2,160	2,175	2,193	2,210	2,230	2,248	2,266	2,283	2,303	2,307	2,332	2,349	2,369	2,389	2,408	2,427	2,452	2,469

Table 17b **Dwellings by tenure in England, Scotland and Wales**

Percentages

	1971	1976	1981	1986	1991	1992	1993	1994	1995	1996	1997	1998	1999	2000	2001	2002	2003	2004	2005	2006	2007	2008	2009
England																							
Owner-occupiers	52.5	55.7	59.8	63.6	68.1	68.3	68.3	68.4	68.4	68.3	68.4	68.9	69.4	69.8	70.0	70.0	70.2	70.3	70.2	70.0	69.6	68.8	68.2
+ Privately rented	19.3	13.6	11.3	10.3	9.0	9.1	9.3	9.6	9.8	10.1	10.3	10.2	10.0	9.9	10.1	10.3	10.6	11.0	11.6	12.2	12.9	13.3	13.9
+ Housing association		1.6	2.3	2.5	3.1	3.3	3.6	3.9	4.2	4.6	4.8	5.0	5.5	6.0	6.7	7.0	7.7	7.9	8.3	8.4	8.5	9.6	9.8
+ Local authority	28.3	29.0	26.6	23.5	19.8	19.4	18.8	18.2	17.6	17.0	16.5	15.9	15.2	14.3	13.3	12.7	11.4	10.8	9.9	9.5	9.0	8.3	8.1
= All dwellings	100.0	100.0	100.0	100.0	100.0	100.0	100.0	100.0	100.0	100.0	100.0	100.0	100.0	100.0	100.0	100.0	100.0	100.0	100.0	100.0	100.0	100.0	100.0
Wales																							
Owner-occupiers	55.8	60.3	61.9	66.9	70.7	70.9	70.9	71.0	71.1	71.2	71.7	71.0	72.7	71.3	71.0	72.7	71.8	73.0	72.8	72.7	73.2	73.2	71.3
+ Privately rented	15.6	12.5	9.6	8.6	8.2	8.2	8.2	8.3	8.3	8.4	8.0	9.0	7.5	9.2	10.0	8.6	10.1	9.6	10.2	10.4	10.2	10.2	12.2
+ Housing association			2.2	2.2	2.4	2.5	2.9	3.1	3.4	3.6	3.9	4.0	4.1	4.3	4.3	4.4	4.4	4.9	5.0	5.0	5.1	6.7	8.0
+ Local authority	28.5	27.2	26.4	22.3	18.8	18.3	17.9	17.5	17.2	16.8	16.4	16.1	15.7	15.2	14.7	14.3	13.7	12.4	12.1	11.9	11.6	9.9	8.4
= All dwellings	100.0	100.0	100.0	100.0	100.0	100.0	100.0	100.0	100.0	100.0	100.0	100.0	100.0	100.0	100.0	100.0	100.0	100.0	100.0	100.0	100.0	100.0	100.0
Scotland																							
Owner-occupiers	31.2	33.6	36.4	43.1	–	52.4	54.1	55.5	56.9	58.0	59.0	60.3	61.3	62.3	62.7	63.4	64.5	65.2	65.1	65.2	65.4	64.8	65.3
+ Privately rented	16.7	12.2	9.7	7.5	–	7.1	7.1	7.0	7.0	7.0	6.9	6.8	6.7	6.7	7.3	7.7	7.7	7.8	8.7	9.3	9.6	10.7	10.7
+ Housing association			1.8	2.4	–	2.6	2.9	3.1	3.5	4.1	4.4	5.1	5.3	5.7	6.0	6.1	10.1	10.6	10.5	10.4	10.8	11.0	10.9
+ Local authority	52.0	54.2	52.1	46.9	–	37.8	36.0	34.4	32.6	31.0	29.7	27.8	26.6	25.3	24.0	22.8	17.7	16.4	15.7	15.0	14.3	13.5	13.2
= All dwellings	100.0	100.0	100.0	100.0	–	100.0	100.0	100.0	100.0	100.0	100.0	100.0	100.0	100.0	100.0	100.0	100.0	100.0	100.0	100.0	100.0	100.0	100.0

Table 17c Dwellings by tenure in Great Britain, Northern Ireland and the United Kingdom

Thousands

	1971	1976	1981	1986	1992	1993	1994	1995	1996	1997	1998	1999	2000	2001	2002	2003	2004	2005	2006	2007	2008	2009
Great Britain																						
Owner-occupiers	9,612	10,846	12,171	13,660	15,518	15,676	15,845	16,014	16,154	16,329	16,562	16,833	17,039	17,189	17,353	17,527	17,700	17,818	17,915	18,004	17,973	17,963
+ Privately rented	3,578	2,978	2,340	2,205	2,058	2,120	2,184	2,255	2,332	2,379	2,387	2,334	2,361	2,429	2,486	2,595	2,698	2,866	3,035	3,234	3,375	3,563
+ Housing association			470	550	733	811	884	976	1,078	1,132	1,205	1,319	1,458	1,618	1,692	1,946	2,018	2,118	2,159	2,214	2,500	2,586
+ Local authority	5,810	6,311	6,115	5,655	4,879	4,759	4,634	4,496	4,369	4,273	4,140	3,983	3,788	3,553	3,420	3,050	2,886	2,698	2,604	2,488	2,332	2,259
= All dwellings	19,000	20,135	21,094	22,070	23,190	23,366	23,546	23,739	23,931	24,113	24,295	24,469	24,645	24,788	24,951	25,120	25,303	25,500	25,712	25,939	26,181	26,372
Northern Ireland																						
Owner-occupiers	–	245	271	323	376	384	395	411	409	422	434	446	455	488	481	491	501	505	508	523	524	517
+ Privately rented	–	59	38	22	20	21	21	21	22	23	26	27	32	37	47	54	61	68	76	69	97	96
+ Housing association	–	–	3	6	10	11	12	13	14	15	15	16	17	19	20	21	22	22	23	24	26	28
+ NIHE	–	177	190	184	167	164	161	155	152	148	142	137	131	129	120	113	100	102	99	97	83	97
= All dwellings	–	481	501	536	573	580	590	600	597	608	618	626	636	674	668	679	684	698	706	713	730	738
United Kingdom																						
Owner-occupiers	–	11,091	12,442	13,983	15,894	16,060	16,240	16,425	16,563	16,751	16,996	17,279	17,494	17,677	17,834	18,018	18,201	18,323	18,423	18,527	18,497	18,480
+ Privately rented	–	3,037	2,378	2,227	2,078	2,141	2,205	2,276	2,354	2,402	2,413	2,361	2,393	2,466	2,533	2,649	2,759	2,934	3,111	3,303	3,472	3,659
+ Housing association			473	556	743	822	896	989	1,092	1,147	1,220	1,335	1,475	1,637	1,712	1,967	2,040	2,140	2,182	2,238	2,526	2,614
+ Local authority	–	6,488	6,305	5,839	5,046	4,923	4,795	4,651	4,521	4,421	4,282	4,120	3,919	3,682	3,540	3,163	2,986	2,800	2,703	2,585	2,415	2,356
= All dwellings	–	20,616	21,595	22,606	23,763	23,946	24,136	24,339	24,528	24,721	24,913	25,095	25,281	25,462	25,619	25,799	25,987	26,198	26,418	26,652	26,911	27,110

Table 17d Dwellings by tenure in Great Britain, Northern Ireland and the United Kingdom

Percentages

	1971	1976	1981	1986	1992	1993	1994	1995	1996	1997	1998	1999	2000	2001	2002	2003	2004	2005	2006	2007	2008	2009
Great Britain																						
Owner-occupiers	50.6	53.9	57.7	61.9	66.9	67.1	67.3	67.5	67.5	67.7	68.2	68.8	69.1	69.3	69.5	69.8	70.0	69.9	69.7	69.4	68.7	68.1
+ Privately rented			11.1	10.0	8.9	9.1	9.3	9.5	9.7	9.9	9.8	9.5	9.6	9.8	10.0	10.3	10.7	11.2	11.8	12.5	12.9	13.5
	(18.8)	(14.8)																				
+ Housing association			2.2	2.5	3.2	3.5	3.8	4.1	4.5	4.7	5.0	5.4	5.9	6.5	6.8	7.7	8.0	8.3	8.4	8.5	9.5	9.8
+ Local authority	30.6	31.3	29.0	25.6	21.0	20.4	19.7	18.9	18.3	17.7	17.0	16.3	15.4	14.3	13.7	12.1	11.4	10.6	10.1	9.6	8.9	8.6
= All dwellings	100.0	100.0	100.0	100.0	100.0	100.0	100.0	100.0	100.0	100.0	100.0	100.0	100.0	100.0	100.0	100.0	100.0	100.0	100.0	100.0	100.0	100.0
Northern Ireland																						
Owner-occupiers	–	50.9	54.1	60.3	65.6	66.2	66.9	68.5	68.5	69.4	70.2	71.2	71.5	72.4	72.0	72.4	73.2	72.4	71.9	73.3	71.8	70.1
+ Privately rented	–	12.3	7.6	4.1	3.5	3.6	3.6	3.5	3.7	3.8	4.2	4.3	5.0	5.5	7.0	7.9	8.9	9.8	10.7	9.6	13.3	13.0
+ Housing association	–	0.0	0.6	1.1	1.7	1.9	2.0	2.2	2.3	2.5	2.4	2.6	2.7	2.8	3.0	3.1	3.2	3.2	3.3	3.4	3.6	3.8
+ NIHE	–	36.8	37.9	34.3	29.1	28.3	27.3	25.8	25.5	24.3	23.0	21.9	20.6	19.1	18.0	16.6	14.7	14.6	14.1	13.7	11.4	13.2
= All dwellings	–	100.0	100.0	100.0	100.0	100.0	100.0	100.0	100.0	100.0	100.0	100.0	100.0	100.0	100.0	100.0	100.0	100.0	100.0	100.0	100.0	100.0
United Kingdom																						
Owner-occupiers	–	53.8	57.6	61.9	66.9	67.1	67.3	67.5	67.5	67.8	68.2	68.9	69.2	69.4	69.6	69.8	70.0	69.9	69.7	69.5	69.7	69.5
+ Privately rented			11.0	9.9	8.7	8.9	9.1	9.4	9.6	9.7	9.7	9.4	9.5	9.7	9.9	10.3	10.6	11.2	11.8	12.4	11.8	12.4
	–	(14.7)																				
+ Housing association			2.2	2.5	3.1	3.4	3.7	4.1	4.5	4.6	4.9	5.3	5.8	6.4	6.7	7.6	7.8	8.2	8.3	8.4	8.3	8.4
+ Local authority	–	31.5	29.2	25.8	21.2	20.6	19.9	19.1	18.4	17.9	17.2	16.4	15.5	14.5	13.8	12.3	11.5	10.7	10.2	9.7	10.2	9.7
= All dwellings	–	100.0	100.0	100.0	100.0	100.0	100.0	100.0	100.0	100.0	100.0	100.0	100.0	100.0	100.0	100.0	100.0	100.0	100.0	100.0	100.0	100.0

Sources: Housing Statistics (various editions), Scottish Government and Welsh Assembly Government.

Notes: 1. For years up to 1990, all figures are for the December of the year shown. For England and Wales, from 1991, figures are those for March of the year shown. For Scotland, from 1992 to 2000, figures are those from December of the previous year and from 2001 onwards are for March of the year shown. For Northern Ireland, figures from 1992 to 2001 are for the December of the previous year and figures from 2002 are for March of the year shown.

2. Owner-occupiers includes shared owners and long leaseholders. Private renting includes renting with a job or business. Local authority tenants includes new town tenants. NIHE is the Northern Ireland Housing Executive. Figures in brackets are for housing association and private rented dwellings combined. Separate figures are not available for those years.

3. 2008 and 2009 tenure split figures for England (other than for local authority) are estimates because official (DCLG) figures were not available at the time of collation. The housing association figure for 2008 is drawn from local authority HSSA returns.

4. The 2009 figure for housing associations is based on 2008, uprated to allow for stock transfers and housing association new build completions. The splits between owner-occupied and private rented sector dwellings for 2008 and 2009 are based on the tenure breakdowns published in the English Housing Survey 2008/09 headline report, with annual changes as shown in that document applied pro rata to the DCLG 'all private' dwellings estimates for 2008 and 2009 (as in DCLG Live Table 104).

Table 18 **Gross fixed capital formation in dwellings**

£ million

	1970	1975	1980	1985	1990	1991	1992	1993	1994	1995	1996	1997	1998	1999	2000	2001	2002	2003	2004	2005	2006	2007	2008	2009
Private sector	1,069	2,725	6,115	9,683	16,867	15,577	16,246	17,124	18,285	18,860	20,205	22,017	23,317	23,921	25,604	27,085	31,455	34,804	40,927	43,845	49,273	51,865	46,310	35,475
+ Public sector	801	1,957	2,559	2,536	4,181	2,762	2,579	2,768	2,948	2,804	2,311	1,911	1,905	1,779	1,790	2,721	3,044	3,658	3,372	3,645	4,058	3,902	3,982	4,083
= Whole economy	1,870	4,682	8,674	12,219	21,048	18,339	18,825	19,892	21,233	21,664	22,516	23,928	25,222	25,700	27,394	29,806	34,499	38,462	44,299	47,490	53,331	55,767	50,292	39,558
Gross Domestic Product (£ billion)	51.7	106.7	233.2	361.8	570.3	598.7	622.1	654.2	693.0	733.3	781.7	830.1	879.1	928.7	976.5	1,021.8	1,075.6	1,139.7	1,203.0	1,254.1	1,328.4	1,404.8	1,445.6	1,392.7
Gross fixed capital formation in dwellings as a percentage of Gross Domestic Product	3.6	4.4	3.7	3.4	3.7	3.1	3.0	3.0	3.1	3.0	2.9	2.9	2.9	2.8	2.8	2.9	3.2	3.4	3.7	3.8	4.0	4.0	3.5	2.8

Sources: UK National Accounts, Economic & Labour Market Review, UK Economic Accounts and Office for National Statistics.
Notes: All figures at current market prices.

Table 19a **Housing starts in England**

	1970	1975	1980	1985	1990	1995	1996	1997	1998	1999	2000	2001	2002	2003	2004	2005	2006	2007	2008	2009
Local authorities	100,709	110,335	27,869	18,076	6,533	579	492	310	98	166	106	183	162	302	170	184	290	200	390	150
+ New towns	9,065	14,968	5,541	567	–	–	–	–	–	–	–	–	–	–	–	–	–	–	–	–
+ Government departments	2,461	654	224	175	108	13	–	–	–	–	–	–	–	–	–	–	–	–	–	–
= Total public sector	112,235	125,957	33,634	18,818	6,641	592	492	310	98	166	106	183	162	302	170	184	290	200	390	150
+ Housing associations	8,111	18,768	13,154	10,362	14,111	25,232	22,629	21,191	17,375	16,895	13,021	11,104	11,726	11,623	14,278	15,839	17,540	15,510	18,430	17,370
+ Private sector	148,318	129,777	84,123	144,301	112,717	110,409	121,590	136,069	131,887	130,898	131,389	136,322	137,176	147,519	162,153	161,106	159,380	150,640	86,150	60,710
= All dwellings	268,664	274,502	130,911	173,481	133,469	136,233	144,711	157,570	149,360	147,959	144,516	147,609	149,064	159,444	176,601	177,129	177,200	166,350	104,960	78,220

Table 19b **Housing completions in England**

	1970	1975	1980	1985	1990	1995	1996	1997	1998	1999	2000	2001	2002	2003	2004	2005	2006	2007	2008	2009
Local authorities	118,943	103,403	67,337	22,483	13,873	782	511	290	243	54	87	160	177	177	131	182	290	350	440	370
+ New towns	9,245	11,487	6,973	703	–	–	–	–	–	–	–	–	–	–	–	–	–	–	–	–
+ Government departments	1,993	1,435	525	98	142	5	–	–	–	–	–	–	–	–	–	–	–	–	–	–
= Total public sector	130,181	116,325	74,835	23,284	14,015	787	511	290	243	54	87	160	177	177	131	182	290	350	440	370
+ Housing associations	8,176	13,652	19,299	11,298	13,821	30,888	27,025	20,966	19,901	17,775	16,681	14,502	13,309	12,822	16,604	17,535	20,660	22,100	25,650	25,260
+ Private sector	153,436	131,481	110,232	135,457	136,063	125,466	121,550	128,237	122,855	123,467	118,330	114,845	123,317	131,059	137,330	141,737	139,910	152,100	115,830	92,530
= All dwellings	291,793	261,458	204,366	170,039	163,899	157,141	149,086	149,493	142,999	141,296	135,098	129,507	136,803	144,058	154,065	159,454	160,860	174,530	141,930	118,160

Table 19c **Housing starts in Wales**

	1970	1975	1980	1985	1990	1995	1996	1997	1998	1999	2000	2001	2002	2003	2004	2005	2006	2007	2008	2009
Local authorities	4,849	8,294	2,343	770	338	45	25	3	58	0	62	60	15	14	34	1	10	0	10	0
+ New towns	155	705	96	121	–	–	–	–	–	–	–	–	–	–	–	–	–	–	–	–
+ Government departments	24	74	7	2	–	–	–	–	–	–	–	–	–	–	–	–	–	–	–	–
= Total public sector	5,028	9,073	2,446	893	338	45	25	3	58	0	62	60	15	14	34	1	10	0	10	0
+ Housing associations	105	279	384	579	2,216	2,416	2,124	1,575	1,022	876	976	709	599	484	407	390	320	580	280	850
+ Private sector	8,612	7,386	5,033	7,232	7,654	6,762	6,699	7,498	7,397	8,435	8,314	8,372	8,866	9,399	8,922	8,639	9,180	9,840	5,440	3,910
= All dwellings	13,745	16,738	7,863	8,704	10,208	9,223	8,848	9,076	8,477	9,311	9,352	9,141	9,480	9,897	9,363	9,030	9,510	10,420	5,730	4,790

Table 19d **Housing completions in Wales**

	1970	1975	1980	1985	1990	1995	1996	1997	1998	1999	2000	2001	2002	2003	2004	2005	2006	2007	2008	2009
Local authorities	6,513	7,332	3,493	992	610	176	59	1	30	0	17	98	2	20	2	56	0	0	10	0
+ New towns	173	635	209	81	–	–	–	–	–	–	–	–	–	–	–	–	–	–	–	–
+ Government departments	66	94	2	2	–	–	–	–	–	–	–	–	–	–	–	–	–	–	–	–
= Total public sector	6,752	8,061	3,704	1,075	610	176	59	1	30	0	17	98	2	20	2	56	0	0	10	0
+ Housing associations	73	275	917	607	1,685	2,542	2,557	2,124	1,472	823	958	823	758	391	544	312	357	410	510	910
+ Private sector	8,648	8,900	5,932	6,563	8,111	7,083	7,728	6,766	6,381	7,177	7,644	7,609	7,403	7,850	8,348	7,411	8,361	9,100	6,950	5,450
= All dwellings	15,473	17,236	10,553	8,245	10,406	9,812	10,350	8,891	7,883	8,000	8,619	8,530	8,163	8,261	8,894	7,779	8,718	9,520	7,460	6,340

Table 19e **Housing starts in Scotland**

	1970	1975	1980	1985	1990	1995	1996	1997	1998	1999	2000	2001	2002	2003	2004	2005	2006	2007	2008	2009
Local authorities	25,714	14,938	4,281	2,017	886	393	135	132	62	158	81	60	15	–	–	6	28	432	122	410
+ New towns	2,014	3,683	1,155	190	720	127	–	–	–	–	–	–	–	–	–	–	–	–	–	–
+ Government departments	289	493	5	59	5	–	–	–	–	–	–	–	–	–	–	–	–	–	–	–
= Total public sector	28,017	19,114	5,441	2,266	1,611	520	135	132	62	158	81	60	15	–	–	6	28	432	122	410
+ Housing associations	347	592	1,261	1,487	2,111	5,095	4,646	3,562	3,625	3,875	4,259	4,456	3,339	3,544	4,442	4,892	4,998	5,526	5,818	6,520
+ Private sector	8,141	11,965	9,681	14,095	16,639	17,537	17,414	19,446	15,896	18,609	18,731	18,392	18,862	20,693	23,015	21,310	23,334	21,203	16,194	9,350
= All dwellings	36,505	31,671	16,383	17,848	20,361	23,152	22,195	23,140	19,583	22,642	23,071	22,908	22,216	24,237	27,457	26,208	28,360	27,161	22,134	16,270

Table 19f **Housing completions in Scotland**

	1970	1975	1980	1985	1990	1995	1996	1997	1998	1999	2000	2001	2002	2003	2004	2005	2006	2007	2008	2009
Local authorities	31,570	19,148	6,167	2,610	1,046	491	292	177	139	81	95	72	51	53	–	–	6	28	195	420
+ New towns	2,790	3,636	1,288	201	666	674	–	–	–	–	–	–	–	–	–	–	–	–	–	–
+ Government departments	302	402	33	17	69	–	–	–	–	–	–	–	–	–	–	–	–	–	–	–
= Total public sector	34,662	23,186	7,488	2,828	1,781	1,165	292	177	139	81	95	72	51	53	–	–	6	28	195	420
+ Housing associations	244	766	881	1,148	1,963	4,854	2,566	4,507	1,911	4,009	3,440	4,252	3,979	3,474	3,097	4,649	3,941	4,034	4,109	5,810
+ Private sector	8,220	10,371	12,242	14,435	16,459	18,521	18,422	17,877	18,355	19,407	18,187	18,080	19,116	20,128	21,875	20,640	21,291	21,640	18,057	11,450
= All dwellings	43,126	34,323	20,611	18,411	20,203	24,540	21,280	22,561	20,405	23,497	21,722	22,404	23,146	23,655	24,972	25,289	25,238	25,702	22,361	17,670

Table 19g **Housing starts in Great Britain**

	1970	1975	1980	1985	1990	1995	1996	1997	1998	1999	2000	2001	2002	2003	2004	2005	2006	2007	2008	2009
Local authorities	131,272	133,567	34,493	20,863	7,757	1,017	652	445	218	324	249	303	192	316	204	191	328	632	522	560
+ New towns	11,234	19,356	6,792	878	720	127	–	–	–	–	–	–	–	–	–	–	–	–	–	–
+ Government departments	2,774	1,221	236	236	113	13	–	–	–	–	–	–	–	–	–	–	–	–	–	–
= Total public sector	145,280	154,144	41,521	21,977	8,590	1,157	652	445	218	324	249	303	192	316	204	191	328	632	522	560
+ Housing associations	8,563	19,639	14,799	12,428	18,438	32,743	29,399	26,328	22,022	21,646	18,256	16,269	15,664	15,651	19,127	21,121	22,858	21,616	24,528	24,740
+ Private sector	165,071	149,128	98,837	165,628	137,010	134,708	145,703	163,013	155,180	157,942	158,434	163,086	164,904	177,611	194,090	191,055	191,894	181,683	107,784	73,970
= All dwellings	318,914	322,911	155,157	200,033	164,038	168,608	175,754	189,786	177,420	179,912	176,939	179,658	180,760	193,578	213,421	212,367	215,070	203,931	132,824	99,270

Table 19h **Housing completions in Great Britain**

	1970	1975	1980	1985	1990	1995	1996	1997	1998	1999	2000	2001	2002	2003	2004	2005	2006	2007	2008	2009
Local authorities	157,026	129,883	76,997	26,085	15,529	1,449	862	468	412	135	199	330	230	250	133	238	296	378	645	790
+ New towns	12,208	15,758	8,470	985	666	674	–	–	–	–	–	–	–	–	–	–	–	–	–	–
+ Government departments	2,361	1,931	560	117	211	5	–	–	–	–	–	–	–	–	–	–	–	–	–	–
= Total public sector	171,595	147,572	86,027	27,187	16,406	2,128	862	468	412	135	199	330	230	250	133	238	296	378	645	790
+ Housing associations	8,493	14,693	21,097	13,053	17,469	38,284	32,148	27,597	23,284	22,607	21,079	19,577	18,046	16,687	20,245	22,496	24,958	26,544	30,269	31,980
+ Private sector	170,304	150,752	128,406	156,455	160,633	151,070	147,700	152,880	147,591	150,051	144,161	140,534	149,836	159,037	167,553	169,788	169,562	182,840	140,837	109,430
= All dwellings	350,392	313,017	235,530	196,695	194,508	191,493	180,716	180,945	171,287	172,793	165,439	160,441	168,112	175,974	187,931	192,522	194,816	209,752	171,751	142,200

Table 19i **Housing starts in Northern Ireland**

	1970	1975	1980	1985	1990	1995	1996	1997	1998	1999	2000	2001	2002	2003	2004	2005	2006	2007	2008	2009
Northern Ireland																				
Housing Executive	7,826	6,218	2,901	2,352	1,059	994	1,015	817	261	95	22	32	–	–	–	–	–	–	–	–
+ Government departments	92	129	11	1	–	–	–	–	–	–	–	–	–	–	–	–	–	–	–	–
= Total public sector	7,918	6,347	2,912	2,353	1,059	994	1,015	817	261	95	22	32	–	–	–	–	–	–	–	–
+ Housing associations	31	2	112	395	773	810	887	1,094	1,329	1,599	1,169	1,067	630	673	1,133	1,044	1,145	610	1,450	990
+ Private sector	4,083	3,931	3,338	7,199	5,704	7,975	8,250	9,115	8,869	9,174	9,963	12,146	11,347	12,479	13,354	13,748	14,105	12,370	5,910	6,490
= All dwellings	12,032	10,190	6,362	9,947	7,536	9,779	10,152	11,026	10,459	10,868	11,154	13,245	11,977	13,152	14,487	14,792	15,250	12,980	7,380	7,480

Table 19j **Housing completions in Northern Ireland**

	1970	1975	1980	1985	1990	1995	1996	1997	1998	1999	2000	2001	2002	2003	2004	2005	2006	2007	2008	2009
Northern Ireland																				
Housing Executive	7,692	4,885	2,507	3,233	1,299	1,305	890	1,075	683	196	77	25	19	–	–	–	–	–	–	–
+ Government departments	86	203	56	2	15	–	–	–	–	–	–	–	–	–	–	–	–	–	–	–
= Total public sector	7,778	5,088	2,563	3,235	1,314	1,305	853	1,075	683	196	77	25	19	–	–	–	–	–	–	–
+ Housing associations	18	55	325	595	442	737	805	747	813	1,118	915	1,505	891	930	413	998	1,041	1,040	1,140	1,350
+ Private sector	4,038	3,776	3,568	6,940	6,163	6,790	6,579	8,346	8,581	8,183	10,420	12,120	12,937	13,584	15,143	16,065	16,924	12,660	9,670	8,090
= All dwellings	11,834	8,919	6,456	10,770	7,919	8,832	8,274	10,168	10,077	9,497	11,412	13,650	13,847	14,514	15,556	17,063	17,965	13,710	10,800	9,430

Note: The 1970 figures for the Northern Ireland Housing Executive include new town starts and completions, before their transfer to the NIHE in 1972 and 1973.

Table 19k **Housing starts in the United Kingdom**

	1970	1975	1980	1985	1990	1995	1996	1997	1998	1999	2000	2001	2002	2003	2004	2005	2006	2007	2008	2009
Local authorities	139,098	139,785	37,394	23,215	8,816	2,011	1,667	1,262	479	419	271	335	192	316	204	191	328	632	522	560
+ New towns	11,234	19,356	6,792	878	720	127	–	–	–	–	–	–	–	–	–	–	–	–	–	–
+ Government departments	2,866	1,350	247	237	113	13	–	–	–	–	–	–	–	–	–	–	–	–	–	–
= Total public sector	153,198	160,491	44,433	24,330	9,649	2,151	1,667	1,262	479	419	271	335	192	316	204	191	328	632	522	560
+ Housing associations	8,594	19,641	14,911	12,823	19,211	33,553	30,286	27,422	23,351	23,245	19,425	17,336	16,294	16,324	20,260	22,165	24,003	22,226	25,978	25,730
+ Private sector	169,154	153,059	102,175	172,827	142,714	142,683	153,953	172,128	164,049	167,116	168,397	175,232	176,251	190,090	207,444	204,803	205,999	194,053	113,694	80,460
= All dwellings	330,946	333,101	161,519	209,980	171,574	178,387	185,906	200,812	187,879	190,780	188,093	192,903	192,737	206,730	227,908	227,159	230,320	216,911	140,204	106,750

Table 19l **Housing completions in the United Kingdom**

	1970	1975	1980	1985	1990	1995	1996	1997	1998	1999	2000	2001	2002	2003	2004	2005	2006	2007	2008	2009
Local authorities	164,718	134,768	79,504	29,318	16,828	2,754	1,752	1,543	1,095	331	276	355	249	250	133	238	296	378	645	790
+ New towns	12,208	15,758	8,470	985	666	674	–	–	–	–	–	–	–	–	–	–	–	–	–	–
+ Government departments	2,447	2,134	616	119	226	5	–	–	–	–	–	–	–	–	–	–	–	–	–	–
= Total public sector	179,373	152,660	88,590	30,422	17,720	3,433	1,715	1,543	1,095	331	276	355	249	250	133	238	296	378	645	790
+ Housing associations	8,511	14,748	21,422	13,648	17,911	39,021	32,953	28,344	24,097	23,725	21,994	21,082	18,937	17,617	20,658	23,494	25,999	27,584	31,409	33,330
+ Private sector	174,342	154,528	131,974	163,395	166,796	157,860	154,279	161,226	156,172	158,234	154,581	152,654	162,773	172,621	182,696	185,853	186,486	195,500	150,507	117,520
= All dwellings	362,226	321,936	241,986	207,465	202,427	200,325	188,990	191,113	181,364	182,290	176,851	174,091	181,959	190,488	203,487	209,585	212,781	223,462	182,551	151,640

Sources: Housing Statistics; Scottish Government: Department for Social Development, Northern Ireland.

Table 20a **Right to buy in England**

	Total sales 1980 to 1985	Total sales 1986 to 1990	1991	1992	1993	1994	1995	1996	1997	1998	1999	2000	2001	2002	2003	2004	2005	2006	2007	2008	2009	Cumulative total 1980 to 2009
Local authorities	52,706	102,785	18,752	19,825	16,353	17,170	13,209	11,062	15,559	13,568	12,902	13,704	12,973	15,755	17,452	12,787	11,086	8,800	7,272	4,709	1,610	400,039
+ New towns	6,828	9,908	1,304	984	977	1,347	1,282	246	0	0	0	0	0	0	0	0	0	0	0	0	0	22,876
+ Housing associations	13,105	21,681	2,638	2,712	2,457	2,611	2,145	1,715	1,810	1,380	1,325	1,231	1,122	1,588	3,246	2,416	1,947	1,671	1,518	1,075	541	69,934
= Total	72,639	134,374	22,694	23,521	19,787	21,128	16,636	13,023	17,369	14,948	14,227	14,935	14,095	17,343	20,698	15,203	13,033	10,471	8,790	5,784	2,151	492,849

Table 20b **Right to buy in Wales**

	Total sales 1980 to 1985	Total sales 1986 to 1990	1991	1992	1993	1994	1995	1996	1997	1998	1999	2000	2001	2002	2003	2004	2005	2006	2007	2008	2009	Cumulative total 1980 to 2009
Local authorities	41,736	38,872	3,382	2,716	2,715	3,008	2,265	2,017	2,562	2,500	3,369	3,420	3,389	4,213	6,838	4,897	2,004	1,324	995	267	90	132,579
+ New towns	2,581	294	20	32	35	25	26	3	0	0	0	0	0	0	0	0	0	0	0	0	0	3,016
+ Housing associations	187	708	101	75	64	99	78	73	70	114	97	102	57	75	86	167	80	43	22	64	20	2,382
= Total	44,504	39,874	3,503	2,823	2,814	3,132	2,369	2,093	2,632	2,614	3,466	3,522	3,446	4,288	6,924	5,064	2,084	1,367	1,017	331	110	137,977

Table 20c **Right to buy in Scotland**

	Total sales 1980 to 1985	Total sales 1986 to 1990	1991	1992	1993	1994	1995	1996	1997	1998	1999	2000	2001	2002	2003	2004	2005	2006	2007	2008	2009	Cumulative total 1980 to 2009
Local authorities	52,706	102,785	18,752	19,825	16,353	17,170	13,209	11,062	15,559	13,568	12,902	13,704	12,973	15,755	17,452	12,787	11,086	8,800	7,272	4,709	1,610	400,039
+ New towns	6,828	9,908	1,304	984	977	1,347	1,282	246	0	0	0	0	0	0	0	0	0	0	0	0	0	22,876
+ Housing associations	13,105	21,681	2,638	2,712	2,457	2,611	2,145	1,715	1,810	1,380	1,325	1,231	1,122	1,588	3,246	2,416	1,947	1,671	1,518	1,075	541	69,934
= Total	72,639	134,374	22,694	23,521	19,787	21,128	16,636	13,023	17,369	14,948	14,227	14,935	14,095	17,343	20,698	15,203	13,033	10,471	8,790	4,709	2,151	491,774

Table 20d **Right to buy in Great Britain**

	Total sales 1980 to 1985	Total sales 1986 to 1990	1991	1992	1993	1994	1995	1996	1997	1998	1999	2000	2001	2002	2003	2004	2005	2006	2007	2008	2009	Cumulative total 1980 to 2009
Local authorities	607,318	660,714	73,548	63,986	60,256	65,177	49,434	44,860	57,996	55,914	67,483	71,980	67,097	78,494	95,694	76,174	42,982	29,474	21,527	9,566	3,590	2,303,264
+ New towns	15,023	14,338	1,501	1,182	1,192	1,417	1,309	249	0	0	0	0	0	0	0	1	0	0	0	0	0	36,212
+ Housing associations	21,282	37,618	4,610	3,456	3,187	3,541	2,815	4,168	6,380	5,904	8,672	8,433	9,399	12,133	17,862	11,253	8,387	6,554	4,690	2,139	1,361	183,844
= Total	643,623	712,670	79,659	68,624	64,635	70,135	53,558	49,277	64,376	61,818	76,155	80,413	76,496	90,627	113,556	87,427	51,370	36,028	26,217	10,630	4,951	2,522,245

Source: Housing Statistics; Scottish Government, Welsh Assembly Government.

Notes: Figures include shared ownership sales. Scottish housing association figures include right to buy and some voluntary sales by Scottish Homes. Figures for housing association sales in England from 1996 onwards are for the financial year, and include the preserved right to buy, but not the right to acquire. The Scottish housing association figures from 2006 are for financial years. The Welsh figures for 2009 are estimates based on data for the first three-quarters of the year.

Table 21 **Changes in the regional stock of dwellings by tenure**

	Stock of dwellings (000s)										Percentage change in stock				
	31 March 1991					31 March 2009					1991-2009				
Region	Owner-occupied	Private renting	Housing association	Public sector	Total	Owner-occupied	Private renting	Housing association	Public sector	Total	Owner-occupied	Private renting	Housing association	Public sector	Total
North East	646	59	35	332	1,072	–	–	–	–	–	–	–	–	–	–
Yorkshire & The Humber	1,326	170	46	479	2,021	–	–	–	–	–	–	–	–	–	–
North West	1,898	189	115	591	2,792	–	–	–	–	–	–	–	–	–	–
West Midlands	1,399	143	57	480	2,079	–	–	–	–	–	–	–	–	–	–
East Midlands	1,158	134	28	314	1,634	–	–	–	–	–	–	–	–	–	–
East	1,498	191	54	350	2,093	–	–	–	–	–	–	–	–	–	–
London	1,691	369	148	703	2,912	–	–	–	–	–	–	–	–	–	–
South East	2,336	299	88	376	3,099	–	–	–	–	–	–	–	–	–	–
South West	1,446	212	36	274	1,968	–	–	–	–	–	–	–	–	–	–
England	13,397	1,767	608	3,899	19,671	15,396	3,136	2,211	1,820	22,564	14.9	77.5	263.7	- 53.3	14.7
+ Wales	837	97	28	222	1,184	955	164	107	113	1,339	14.1	69.1	282.1	- 49.1	13.1
+ Scotland	1,101	153	53	838	2,145	1,612	263	268	326	2,469	46.4	71.9	405.7	- 61.1	15.1
= Great Britain	15,175	2,177	689	4,959	23,000	17,963	3,563	2,586	2,259	26,372	18.4	63.7	275.3	- 54.4	14.7
+ Northern Ireland	348	20	9	160	537	517	96	28	97	738	48.6	380.0	211.1	- 39.4	37.4
= United Kingdom	15,523	2,197	698	5,119	23,537	18,480	3,659	2,614	2,356	27,110	19.1	66.6	274.5	- 54.0	15.2

Sources: Housing Statistics, Department for Communities and Local Government, Scottish Government, and Welsh Assembly Government.

Note: Public sector housing comprises local authority, new town and Northern Ireland Housing Executive dwellings. English regional stock figures by tenure are not yet available beyond 2007.

Table 22 **Amenities and central heating in Great Britain 2001**

Percentages

Tenure	North East	North West	Yorkshire & The Humber	East Midlands	West Midlands	East	London	South East	South West	England	Wales	Scotland	Great Britain
Households with central heating													
With sole use of bath/shower & W.C.	85.9	88.0	86.6	93.9	88.6	94.5	91.5	93.6	89.9	91.2	92.3	92.7	91.3
Without sole use of bath/shower & W.C.	0.2	0.2	0.3	0.2	0.2	0.3	0.7	0.3	0.3	0.3	0.2	0.2	0.3
All households with central heating	96.1	88.2	96.9	94.1	88.8	94.8	92.2	93.9	90.2	91.5	92.5	92.8	91.6
Households without central heating													
With sole use of bath/shower & W.C.	3.9	11.7	12.9	5.8	11.1	5.1	7.4	6.0	9.6	8.4	7.4	7.1	8.2
Without sole use of bath/shower & W.C.	0.0	0.1	0.1	0.1	0.1	0.1	0.4	0.1	0.2	0.2	0.2	0.1	0.2
All households without central heating	3.9	11.8	13.1	5.9	11.2	5.2	7.8	6.1	9.8	8.5	7.5	7.2	8.4
All Households (thousands)	1,066	2,813	2,065	1,732	2,154	2,232	3,016	3,287	2,086	20,451	1,209	2,192	23,853

Source: Housing and Households: 2001 Census and other sources, Office of the Deputy Prime Minister, 2003.

Table 23a **English housing conditions: the Decent Homes Standard**

Thousands

Tenure	Decent Homes (Unfitness-based)												Decent Homes (HHSRS-based)					
	1996			2001			2004			2006			2006			2008		
	Decent	Non-decent	All	Decent	Non-decent	All	Decent	Non-decent	All	Decent	Non-decent	All	Decent	Non-decent	All	Decent	Non-decent	All
Social sector																		
Local authority	1,600	1,869	3,469	1,637	1,174	2,812	1,519	816	2,335	1,391	695	2,086	1,410	676	2,086	1,359	625	1,984
Housing association	493	448	941	952	472	1,424	1,228	437	1,665	1,414	436	1,850	1,385	465	1,850	1,507	444	1,951
All social sector	2,092	2,318	4,410	2,589	1,647	4,236	2,748	1,252	4,000	2,805	1,131	3,936	2,794	1,142	3,936	2,866	1,069	3,935
Private sector																		
Owner-occupied	8,391	5,535	13,927	10,483	4,316	14,798	11,213	4,066	15,279	11,738	3,704	15,442	10,107	5,335	15,442	10,165	4,842	15,007
Private rented	752	1,246	1,998	1,072	1,101	2,172	1,340	994	2,334	1,556	1,055	2,611	1,388	1,223	2,611	1,847	1,449	3,296
All private sector	9,144	6,781	15,925	11,554	5,416	16,970	12,553	5,060	17,613	13,294	4,759	18,053	11,495	6,558	18,053	12,012	6,291	18,303
Of which vulnerable households in the private sector:																		
Owner-occupied	880	929	1,809	1,285	784	2,069	1,617	691	2,308	1,767	675	2,442	1,543	905	2,448	1,428	760	2,188
Private rented	196	504	701	256	356	623	347	342	689	378	336	714	334	408	742	429	447	876
All private sector vulnerable	1,076	1,483	2,509	1,542	1,151	2,692	1,963	1,033	2,996	2,145	1,012	3,157	1,877	1,313	3,190	1,857	1,207	3,064
All tenures	11,236	9,099	20,335	14,143	7,063	21,207	15,301	6,312	21,613	16,099	5,890	21,989	14,490	7,700	22,190	15,204	7,360	22,564

Source: English House Condition Survey 2005: Headline Report; English Housing Survey Headline Report 2008/09.

Notes: Decent homes are those that meet the fitness standard; are in a reasonable state of repair; have reasonably modern facilities and services and provide a reasonable degree of thermal comfort. From 2006 onwards the Decent Homes Standard was revised with the new Housing Health and Safety Rating System replacing the fitness standard as one of components of the Decent Homes Standard. Data for both definitions is provided for 2006. Vulnerable households are defined as households in receipt of at least one of the principal means-tested or disability related benefits, including tax credits. Precise definitions vary from year-to-year, reflecting reforms to the new range of tax credits introduced since 2001. No estimates are included for households that are eligible for, but do not claim, those means-tested benefits or tax credits.

Table 23b **English housing conditions: the Decent Homes Standard**

Percentages

Tenure	Decent Homes (Unfitness-based)												Decent Homes (HHSRS-based)					
	1996			2001			2004			2006			2006			2008		
	Decent	Non-decent	All	Decent	Non-decent	All	Decent	Non-decent	All	Decent	Non-decent	All	Decent	Non-decent	All	Decent	Non-decent	All
Social sector																		
Local authority	46.1	53.9	100.0	58.2	41.7	100.0	65.1	34.9	100.0	66.7	33.3	100.0	67.6	32.4	100.0	68.5	31.5	100.0
Housing association	52.4	47.6	100.0	66.9	33.1	100.0	73.8	26.2	100.0	76.4	23.6	100.0	74.8	25.2	100.0	77.2	22.8	100.0
All social sector	47.4	52.6	100.0	61.1	38.9	100.0	68.7	31.3	100.0	71.3	28.7	100.0	71.0	29.0	100.0	72.8	27.2	100.0
Private sector																		
Owner-occupied	60.2	39.7	100.0	70.8	29.2	100.0	73.4	26.6	100.0	76.0	24.0	100.0	65.4	34.6	100.0	67.7	32.3	100.0
Private rented	37.6	62.4	100.0	49.4	50.7	100.0	57.4	42.6	100.0	59.6	40.4	100.0	53.2	46.8	100.0	56.0	44.0	100.0
All private sector	57.4	42.6	100.0	68.1	31.9	100.0	71.3	28.7	100.0	73.6	26.4	100.0	63.7	36.3	100.0	65.6	34.4	100.0
Of which vulnerable households in the private sector:																		
Owner-occupied	48.6	51.4	100.0	62.1	37.9	100.0	70.1	29.9	100.0	72.4	27.6	100.0	63.0	37.0	100.0	65.3	34.7	100.0
Private rented	28.0	71.9	100.0	41.1	57.1	100.0	50.4	49.6	100.0	52.9	47.1	100.0	45.0	55.0	100.0	49.0	51.0	100.0
All private sector vulnerable	42.9	59.1	100.0	57.3	42.8	100.0	65.5	34.5	100.0	68.0	32.0	100.0	58.8	41.2	100.0	60.6	39.4	100.0
All tenures	55.3	44.7	100.0	66.7	33.3	100.0	70.8	29.2	100.0	73.2	26.8	100.0	65.3	34.7	100.0	67.4	32.6	100.0

Table 24a **English housing conditions: average energy efficiency (SAP) ratings**

Rating out of 100

Tenure	1996	2001	2003	2004	2005	2006	2007	2008
Private sector								
Owner-occupied	41.1	44.4	45.0	45.6	46.1	46.9	48.1	49.6
Private rented	37.9	41.9	44.4	45.7	46.0	46.6	48.1	50.2
All private sector	40.7	44.1	44.9	45.6	46.1	46.8	48.1	49.7
Social sector								
Local authority	45.7	49.6	52.0	53.9	55.3	55.8	56.2	58.0
Housing association	50.9	56.4	56.7	57.3	58.9	59.3	59.5	60.3
All social sector	46.8	51.9	53.9	55.3	56.9	57.4	57.8	59.2
All tenures	42.1	45.7	46.6	47.4	48.1	48.7	49.8	51.4

Source: English Housing Survey 2008, DCLG.

Note: SAP ratings are energy cost ratings determined by the government's Standard Assesment Procedure. It is an index based on calculated annual space and water heating costs for a standard heating regime expressed on a scale of 1 (highly inefficient) to 100 (highly efficient).

Table 24b **English housing conditions: Energy Performance Certificate (EPC) Bands in 2008**

Bands	Owner-occupied		Private rented		Private sector		Local authority		Housing association		Social sector		Whole stock	
	Thousands	%	Thousands	%	Thousands	%	Thousands	%	Thousands	%	Thousands	%	Thousands	%
Band A/B (81-100)	19	0.1	18	0.5	37	0.2	15	0.8	25	1.3	41	1.0	77	0.3
Band C (69-80)	908	6.0	366	11.1	1,273	7.0	398	20.1	558	28.6	956	24.3	2,229	10.0
Band D (55-68)	5,004	33.3	1,096	33.3	6,100	33.3	921	46.4	843	43.2	1,764	44.8	7,865	35.4
Band E (39-54)	6,279	41.8	1,141	34.6	7,420	40.5	492	24.8	398	20.4	890	22.6	8,310	37.4
Band F (21-38)	2,288	15.2	472	14.3	2,760	15.1	118	5.9	94	4.8	212	5.4	2,972	13.4
Band G (1-20)	510	3.4	204	6.2	714	3.9	39	2.0	33	1.7	72	1.8	786	3.5
Total	15,007	100.0	3,296	100.0	18,304	100.0	1,984	100.0	1,951	100.0	3,935	100.0	22,239	100.0

Source: English Housing Survey 2008, DCLG.

Note: The EPC Bands are based on SAP ratings (shown in brackets).

Table 25a **Welsh housing conditions: unfit dwellings**

Thousands

	Old definition of unfitness				Current definition of unfitness			
	1973	1976	1981	1986	1986	1993	1998	2004
Fit	837.3	917.8	936.0	949.0	821.7	980.5	1,059.1	1,151.4
Unfit	147.5	100.2	90.9	71.7	199.0	151.2	98.2	57.7
Total	984.8	1,018.0	1,026.9	1,020.7	1,020.7	1,131.7	1,157.3	1,209.1
Percentage unfit	15.0	9.8	8.9	7.0	19.5	13.4	8.5	4.8

Source: Living in Wales 2004 – Report on Unfitness and Repairs, National Assembly for Wales website, 2005.

Note: Unfitness is measured against eleven factors (disrepair, dampness, structural stability, food preparation, heating, lighting, WC, bath/shower/wash basin, ventilation, drainage, water supply). Before 1989 unfitness was judged in terms of the condition of the property. Post-1989 a dwelling is defined as unfit if it fails to meet a satisfactory standard for any any individual factor. The change in definition significantly increased the number of dwellings defined as unfit.

Table 25b **Welsh housing conditions: stock condition by tenure in 2004**

Percentages

Tenure	Stock condition				
	Unfit	Defective	Acceptable	Satisfactory	All conditions
Owner-occupied	4.3	19.9	34.9	41.0	100.0
Private rented	12.2	28.2	39.9	19.6	100.0
Local authority	3.4	26.8	46.9	23.0	100.0
Housing association	2.3	13.5	23.3	60.9	100.0
All tenures	4.8	21.4	36.6	37.2	100.0

Source: Living in Wales 2004 – Report on Unfitness and Repairs, National Assembly for Wales website, 2005.
Note: Figures are for occupied first homes only.

Table 26a **Scottish dwellings below the tolerable standard**

Tenure	Dwellings below tolerable standard	
	Number (000s)	% Incidence
1996		
Private	18	1.3
Social	3	0.5
Total	21	1.0
2002		
Private	17	1.2
Social	3	0.4
Total	20	1.0
2004/05		
Private	13	1.0
Social	1	2.5
Total	14	0.4
2008		
Private	14	0.8
Social	0	0.0
Total	14	0.6

Sources: Scottish House Condition Surveys 1996, 2002, 2004/05 and 2008.

Table 26b **Dwellings failing the Scottish Housing Quality Standard**

	Reason for failing Scottish Housing Quality Standard (SHQS)					
	Below tolerable standard	Serious disrepair	Energy inefficient	Lack modern facilities and services	Not healthy, safe and secure	All SHQS failures
	Thousands					
2002						
Private housing	18	65	1,081	19	417	1,182
Social housing	3	27	451	17	161	501
All housing	20	92	1,532	36	577	1,683
2008						
Private housing	14	57	927	193	398	1,115
Social housing	0	15	256	142	160	387
All housing	14	71	1,183	335	558	1,503
	Percentages					
2002						
Private housing	1	4	70	1	27	77
Social housing	1	4	69	3	25	77
All housing	1	4	70	2	26	77
2008						
Private housing	1	3	55	11	23	66
Social housing	0	2	40	22	25	61
All housing	1	3	51	14	24	64

Sources: Scottish House Condition Surveys 2002 and 2008.

Notes: Dwellings require full central heating (not including electric storage heaters) to qualify as energy efficient. The lower numbers of dwellings shown as lacking modern facilities and services in 2002 are a consequence of the limited scope of the 2002 survey, which preceded the development of the SHQS. The 2002 survey did not cover numbers of sockets in kitchens, safety of gas and oil systems, kitchen layout, storage and safety, or disrepair of attached garages. It is not believed that these additions materially affect the overall estimated numbers of SHQS failures in 2002.

Table 27a **NI house condition survey: key indicators 1979 to 2009**[1]

	1979		1984		1987		1991		1996		2001		2006		2009	
	Number	%	Number	%	Number	%	Number	%	Number	%	Number	%	Number	%	Number	%
Unfit dwellings	66,210	14.1	51,330	10.4	42,900	8.4	50,360	8.8	43,970	7.3	31,570	4.9	24,100	3.4	17,500	2.4
Dwellings lacking one or more basic amenities	84,130	17.8	45,130	9.2	28,330	5.5	19,100	3.3	17,600	2.9	15,660	2.4	–	–	–	–

Sources: Housing Statistics 2005-06 (and earlier volumes), Northern Ireland Department for Social Development, House Condition Survey 2006, Northern Ireland Housing Executive; Northern Ireland House Condition Survey 2009 (preliminary findings)

Note: 1. Due to changes in definition, data for unfit dwellings in the 1991 and later surveys are not directly comparable with those in the earlier surveys.

Table 27b **NI house condition survey: dwellings without central heating**

	1991		1996		2001		2006		2009	
	Number	%	Number	%	Number	%	Number	%	Number	%
Dwelling type										
Terraced house	47,610	23	28,800	14	10,450	5	1,840	1	2,570	1.1
Bungalow	n/a	n/a	16,910	12	7,740	5	2,950	2	830	0.5
Semi-detached house	19,330	14	9,480	9	3,850	3	1,800	1	290	0.2
Detached house	n/a	n/a	12,630	14	7,800	7	2,660	2	1,480	1.1
Flats	11,640	25	8,870	21	2,330	5	3,530	6	2,290	3.8
Dwelling tenure										
Owner-occupied	44,710	87	38,760	10	13,510	3	2,830	1	1,880	0.4
NIHE	32,030	80	14,560	10	2,900	3	620	1	790	0.9
Housing associations	1,020	90	610	5	50	0	0	0	0	0.0
Private rented and other	15,120	47	11,090	29	5,020	10	770	1	910	0.7
Vacant	16,170	47	13,670	47	10,690	34	8,560	21	3,880	8.9
All dwellings	109,040	19	78,690	13	32,170	5	12,780	2	7,460	1.0

Source: As 27a.

Note: Percentage figures show percentage of all dwellings in each category that have central heating.

Table 27c **NI house condition survey: Standard Assessment Procedure (SAP) ratings**

	1991	1996	2001	2006	2009
Average SAP rating by dwelling tenure					
Owner-occupied	29	44	53.8	51.2	56.4
NIHE	26	39	49.3	59.6	61.4
Housing associations	35	41	66.5	69.1	70.5
Private rented	8	27	45.3	51.8	56.6
Tied and other	n/a	44	45.3	51.8	n/a
All dwellings	27	41	51.8	52.4	57.0
Average SAP rating by dwelling type					
Bungalow	n/a	n/a	48.3	45.8	51.8
Terraced	23	39	53.4	55.5	59.3
Semi-detached	32	45	53.6	53.3	58.0
Detached	28	43	50.5	49.3	54.4
Flat	37	36	54.9	63.0	65.2
All dwellings	27	41	51.8	52.5	57.0

Source: As 27a.

Table 28 **Private sector improvement and disabled facilities grants**

£ million

	1990	1991	1992	1993	1994	1995	1996	1997	1998	1999	2000	2001	2002	2003	2004	2005	2006	2007	2008
Improvement grants																			
England	316.7	281.6	349.9	361.3	385.6	336.7	316.5	232.1	233.6	235.1	232.2	268.2	307.3	246.6	229.8	231.5	266.2	236.7	245.0
Scotland	117.2	107.1	109.5	99.2	87.4	78.5	70.1	49.3	46.2	42.4	34.3	40.5	35.2	36.5	40.3	56.3	51.7	43.8	47.8
Wales	85.0	94.3	143.1	156.2	137.1	148.7	146.7	132.6	111.2	91.5	71.6	47.1	57.2	53.7	56.1	51.7	63.3	31.5	28.5
Total improvement grants (A)	518.9	483.0	602.5	616.7	610.1	563.9	533.3	414.0	391.0	369.0	338.1	357.0	397.8	334.3	326.4	333.0	384.5	315.3	321.3
Disabled facilities grants																			
England	68.3	52.3	61.8	70.4	86.7	96.3	99.0	60.4	104.7	113.6	122.7	133.6	166.5	202.0	210.3	221.3	232.8	250.1	284.8
Wales	0.1	4.5	9.5	12.2	11.8	14.8	15.7	19.1	20.5	21.7	24.8	27.6	28.7	30.3	28.5	35.4	40.5	37.6	34.4
Total disabled facilities grants (B)	68.4	56.8	71.3	82.6	98.5	111.1	114.7	79.5	125.2	135.3	147.5	161.2	195.2	232.3	238.8	256.7	273.3	287.7	319.2
Total all grants (A+B)	587.3	539.8	673.8	699.3	708.6	675.0	648.0	493.5	516.2	504.3	485.6	518.2	593.0	566.6	565.2	589.7	657.8	603.0	640.5

Sources: Housing and Construction Statistics, Welsh Housing Statistics, Scottish Housing Statistics Bulletins.

Notes: Includes grants under 1985, 1989 and 1996 Acts for repairs and improvements. Disabled facilities grants under the 1989 and 1996 Acts only apply in England and Wales.

The 1985 Act continues to operate in Scotland, and makes no separate provision for disabled facilities grants. From 2003, figures are for the twelve months beginning in April of each year.

Table 29a **Renovation grants paid to private owners under the Local Government and Housing Act 1989, the Housing (Scotland) Act 1987, the Housing Act 1985 and earlier acts**

Number of grants

	1980-1984	1985-1989	1990	1991	1992	1993	1994	1995	1996	1997	1998	1999	2000	2001	2002	2003	2004	2005	2006	2007	2008	2009
North East	50,334	36,470	7,157	1,445	4,549	4,009	4,609	4,805	4,950	1,696	68	39	38	–	–	–	–	–	–	–	–	–
Yorkshire & Humberside	75,432	59,049	14,473	10,311	9,812	10,131	9,721	9,326	9,684	4,710	654	109	31	–	–	–	–	–	–	–	–	–
North West	110,879	94,227	13,253	4,297	13,737	12,118	13,997	13,740	16,534	7,896	910	112	56	–	–	–	–	–	–	–	–	–
East Midlands	73,191	55,214	10,418	8,514	8,403	7,930	9,888	9,618	8,064	4,584	545	77	39	–	–	–	–	–	–	–	–	–
West Midlands	58,696	55,073	11,707	12,330	10,044	8,044	10,126	9,454	9,498	5,129	1,290	610	111	–	–	–	–	–	–	–	–	–
East Anglia	32,743	30,071	4,280	854	6,204	6,727	7,796	8,488	8,996	4,509	472	81	144	–	–	–	–	–	–	–	–	–
Greater London	103,152	89,877	10,916	7,412	7,442	8,024	9,504	11,236	11,910	6,987	1,402	311	329	–	–	–	–	–	–	–	–	–
Rest of South East	120,809	94,413	13,102	3,440	11,463	11,812	12,410	15,504	14,832	6,544	780	114	112	–	–	–	–	–	–	–	–	–
South West	71,131	47,774	7,598	8,632	8,514	9,506	11,091	10,916	10,802	4,299	531	189	85	–	–	–	–	–	–	–	–	–
England	696,367	562,168	96,786	85,240	83,060	80,757	91,238	93,087	95,230	46,354	6,652	1,642	945	–	–	–	–	–	–	–	–	–
Wales	82,732	95,181	26,545	21,139	16,629	16,067	14,703	17,315	17,347	12,116	3,168	901	270	–	–	–	–	–	–	–	–	–
Scotland	161,572	166,612	23,557	23,478	24,934	21,194	22,091	19,036	15,800	13,585	12,711	12,822	11,333	12,414	11,755	11,978	12,594	13,570	14,088	11,832	12,825	11,492
Great Britain	940,671	823,961	146,888	129,857	124,623	118,018	128,032	129,438	128,377	72,055	22,531	15,365	12,548	12,414	11,755	11,978	12,594	13,570	14,088	11,832	12,825	11,492

Sources: Housing Statistics, Welsh Housing Statistics.

Notes: 1. No new grants were made under the 1985 Act in England and Wales after June 1990; although payments continued for grants made before that date.

Figures on the residual numbers of grants paid in England and Wales ceased to be collected at the end of June 1995 and end of December 1996 respectively.

2. The 1989 Act grants system for England and Wales started in July 1990, apart from Minor Works Assistance, which started in April 1990. The 1989 Act does not apply in Scotland.

Figures for the years before 1992 are only available for standard regions, not for government office regions. 1990 and 1991 figures are therefore only shown for the government office and standard regions with the same boundaries.

3. Figures for Scotland are for financial years from 2008.

Table 29b **Renovation grants paid to private owners under the Housing Grants, Construction and Regeneration Act 1996 and Regulatory Reform Order 2002**

Number of grants

	Renewal grants											Disabled facilities grants										
	1996/97-1998/99	1999/2000	2000/01	2001/02	2002/03	2003/04	2004/05	2005/06	2006/07	2007/08	2008/09	1996/97-1998/99	1999/2000	2000/01	2001/02	2002/03	2003/04	2004/05	2005/06	2006/07	2007/08	2008/09
North East	13,200	3,760	3,357	4,071	4,056	2,480	3,080	2,630	6,700	4,560	7,460	4,050	1,610	1,678	1,867	2,366	2,150	2,260	2,230	2,790	3,020	3,350
Yorkshire & The Humber	31,160	10,480	10,165	6,380	6,275	7,030	11,130	11,760	11,300	12,730	12,420	6,272	2,090	2,385	2,516	2,773	4,430	3,350	3,520	3,530	3,720	4,520
North West	67,580	31,860	29,781	24,245	17,287	17,250	18,870	18,230	23,970	26,650	36,840	10,886	3,580	4,429	4,344	4,535	5,340	5,460	5,870	6,190	6,500	7,600
East Midlands	19,720	9,310	7,570	6,880	5,785	5,680	6,070	5,490	4,830	6,250	5,500	4,966	1,790	2,053	2,163	2,197	2,640	2,890	3,070	3,310	3,390	3,610
West Midlands	38,620	16,280	8,352	8,074	6,810	6,200	5,050	4,770	19,020	16,310	21,050	6,767	2,160	2,190	2,397	5,129	7,840	9,390	3,780	4,270	3,940	4,220
East	24,290	11,550	8,599	7,180	6,540	5,780	4,710	4,270	4,260	4,770	6,180	7,318	2,720	2,755	2,742	2,704	3,050	3,460	4,150	4,260	4,200	4,190
London	34,550	11,550	12,010	9,096	7,854	7,220	7,730	7,870	7,990	10,840	7,650	5,861	2,190	2,284	2,127	2,350	3,220	2,900	2,850	3,120	3,130	3,440
South East	35,260	14,490	11,473	9,361	8,348	6,360	5,180	4,880	6,050	8,140	9,920	10,547	3,570	3,694	3,693	4,253	4,580	5,020	5,450	5,610	5,840	6,070
South West	23,730	11,150	7,600	6,777	4,991	6,400	6,260	6,210	12,960	10,680	11,350	7,566	3,010	3,263	3,663	3,795	3,940	3,820	4,030	4,190	4,380	4,780
England	288,120	120,420	98,907	82,064	67,946	64,400	68,080	66,100	97,080	100,910	118,370	64,230	22,720	24,731	25,512	30,102	37,170	38,550	34,940	37,270	38,130	41,780
Wales	18,249	10,893	10,021	9,573	9,555	9,497	7,906	8,010	10,481	8,213	8,328	6,612	4,190	4,770	4,248	4,917	4,428	4,593	5,268	5,899	5,830	7,525
Great Britain	306,369	131,313	108,928	91,637	77,501	73,897	75,986	74,110	107,561	109,123	126,698	70,842	26,910	29,501	29,760	35,019	41,598	43,143	40,208	43,169	43,960	49,305

Sources: Housing Statistics, Welsh Housing Statistics.

Notes: The 1996 Act's system of grants started in December 1996 in England and Wales and the Regulatory Reform (Housing Assistance)(England and Wales) Order 2002 took effect from 18 July 2003.

Disabled facilities grants include both mandatory and discretionary grants. Renewal grants include renovation grants, HMO grants, common parts grants and home repairs assistance grants.

Table 30a **Property characteristics by tenure in Great Britain in 2008**

Percentages of households

	Owner-occupiers			Social rented			Private rented			Total
	Owned outright	With mortgage	All owners	Local authority	Housing association	All social rented	Unfurnished	Furnished	All private rented	
Property type										
Houses:										
Detached	39	27	32	1	1	1	13	6	12	24
Semi-detached	34	35	34	24	25	24	21	14	20	31
Terraced	19	30	25	31	30	30	34	35	35	27
All houses:	92	91	92	56	56	56	69	56	66	82
Flats:										
Purpose-built	6	6	6	42	40	41	18	30	20	14
Converted	2	2	2	2	4	3	13	14	13	3
All flats:	8	9	8	44	44	44	31	44	34	18
Total	100	100	100	100	100	100	100	100	100	100

Source: General Lifestyle Survey 2008, Office for National Statistics.
Notes: Flats includes maisonettes. Figures do not total precisely due to rounding.

Table 30b **Property age by tenure in Great Britain in 2004**

Percentages of households

	Owner-occupiers			Social rented			Private rented			Total
	Owned outright	With mortgage	All owners	Local authority	Housing association	All social rented	Unfurnished	Furnished	All private rented	
Property age										
Pre-1919	20	22	21	4	10	6	37	39	40	20
1919 - 1944	20	19	20	20	10	16	18	21	18	19
1945 - 1964	24	19	21	39	23	33	13	13	13	23
1965 - 1984	24	22	23	31	25	29	15	14	15	24
1985 or later	11	18	15	6	32	15	17	14	16	15
Total	100	100	100	100	100	100	100	100	100	100

Source: General Household Survey 2004, Office for National Statistics.
Notes: Figures may not total precisely because of rounding.

Table 31a **Tenure profile of heads of household by age in Great Britain**

Percentages

| Item | Owner-occupiers | | Rented | | | | | All tenures |
	Owned outright	With mortgage	Local authority	Housing association	Private: Unfurnished	Furnished	With job or business	
Ages at 1980								
Under 25	0	4	4	7	4	40	7	4
25 - 29	1	13	7	11	5	24	11	8
30 - 44	8	48	22	15	13	20	32	26
45 - 64	40	33	36	20	27	10	43	34
65 - 74	32	2	21	25	26	4	6	17
75 or over	20	0	12	23	25	2	1	10
All ages	100	100	100	100	100	100	100	100
Ages at 1990								
Under 25	0	3	6	8	9	37	6	4
25 - 29	0	13	9	10	9	24	16	9
30 - 44	5	46	20	20	22	23	36	28
45 - 59	22	30	17	14	10	8	28	23
60 - 69	33	6	20	15	16	4	12	16
70 - 79	26	1	19	22	20	2	2	13
80 or over	13	0	9	12	13	1	1	6
All ages	100	100	100	100	100	100	100	100
Ages at 2000								
Under 25	0	2	7	7	12	29	–	4
25 - 29	0	10	7	6	17	20	–	7
30 - 44	6	48	26	29	36	34	–	31
45 - 59	23	33	20	20	19	9	–	26
60 - 69	30	6	13	11	6	3	–	14
70 - 79	28	2	17	16	6	3	–	12
80 or over	12	0	9	11	5	2	–	6
All ages	100	100	100	100	100	100	–	100
Ages at 2008								
Under 25	0	2	4	5	12	19	–	3
25 - 29	0	7	7	5	15	27	–	6
30 - 44	5	48	25	27	38	25	–	29
45 - 59	23	36	23	24	20	17	–	28
60 - 69	30	5	15	14	5	5	–	15
70 - 79	27	1	14	13	6	5	–	12
80 or over	15	0	13	12	4	4	–	8
All ages	100	100	100	100	100	100	–	100

Sources: General Household Surveys 1980 and 1990; General Lifestyle Survey 2008, Office for National Statistics.

Note: For 2000 and 2008 figures for private lettings with a job or business are included within the figures for private unfurnished and furnished lettings. The 2008 figures are also for the 'household reference person', which has replaced the old concept of household head.

Table 31b **Tenure profile of heads of household by sex and marital status in Great Britain**

Percentages

| Item | | Owner-occupiers | | Rented | | | | | All tenures |
		Owned outright	With mortgage	Local authority	Housing association	Private: Unfurnished	Furnished	With job or business	
Sex & marital status at 1980									
Men:	Married	20	40	31	1	4	1	3	100
	Single	17	22	25	1	11	22	3	100
	Widowed	35	5	45	2	9	1	2	100
	Divorced/separated	9	34	36	1	9	8	3	100
	All men	20	37	31	1	5	2	3	100
Women:	Married	13	41	32	2	2	10	2	100
	Single	30	9	30	3	12	13	3	100
	Widowed	36	3	46	3	11	0	0	100
	Divorced/separated	13	16	58	3	6	3	1	100
	All women	30	8	44	3	10	4	1	100
Total		23	30	34	1	6	3	3	100
Sex & marital status at 1990									
Men:	Married	24	54	16	1	2	1	2	100
	Single	14	39	20	3	8	14	2	100
	Widowed	42	9	39	3	5	0	1	100
	Divorced/separated	12	40	29	4	7	6	3	100
	All men	23	49	18	2	3	2	2	100
Women:	Married	35	30	22	9	0	0	4	100
	Single	19	22	35	7	7	8	2	100
	Widowed	44	6	39	4	6	1	0	100
	Divorced/separated	12	30	44	4	6	2	1	100
	All women	30	16	39	5	6	3	1	100
Total		25	41	24	3	4	2	2	100

contd...

Table 31b (continued)

Percentages

Item		Owner-occupiers		Rented					All tenures
		Owned outright	With mortgage	Local authority	Housing association	Private: Unfurnished	Furnished	With job or business	
Sex & marital status at 2000									
Men:	Married	32	52	8	3	4	1	–	100
	Cohabiting	7	63	10	3	12	5	–	100
	Single	15	39	16	6	11	14	–	100
	Widowed	54	9	23	7	5	2	–	100
	Divorced/separated	13	38	22	8	12	7	–	100
	All men	27	48	11	4	6	4	–	100
Women:	Married	23	51	15	3	6	1	–	100
	Cohabiting	7	51	19	7	10	6	–	100
	Single	14	28	27	12	11	8	–	100
	Widowed	57	5	23	10	4	0	–	100
	Divorced/separated	17	33	28	11	10	2	–	100
	All women	28	29	23	9	8	3	–	100
Total		27	41	16	6	7	3	–	100
Sex & marital status at 2008									
Men:	Married	38	48	5	3	4	1	–	100
	Cohabiting	7	62	5	5	17	4	–	100
	Single	21	35	12	12	12	7	–	100
	Widowed	71	3	13	9	4	0	–	100
	Divorced/separated	22	33	16	14	12	3	–	100
	All men	33	44	7	6	7	2	–	100
Women:	Married	28	51	9	6	5	1	–	100
	Cohabiting	8	50	13	7	18	3	–	100
	Single	15	30	19	17	14	5	–	100
	Widowed	62	5	13	14	5	1	–	100
	Divorced/separated	21	32	18	18	10	2	–	100
	All women	30	31	14	13	9	2	–	100
Total		32	39	10	9	8	2	–	100

Sources: General Household Surveys 1980 and 1990; General Lifestyle Survey 2008, Office for National Statistics.

Notes: The 2000 and 2008 figures distinguish between married and cohabiting; for earlier years married includes cohabiting. They also include private lettings with a job or business within furnished and unfurnished lettings. They are also for the household reference person.

Table 31c **Tenure profile of heads of household by socio-economic group and economic activity status in Great Britain**

Percentages

| Item | Owner-occupiers | | Rented | | | | | All tenures |
	Owned outright	With mortgage	Local authority	Housing association	Private: Unfurnished	Furnished	With job or business	
Socio-economic group at 1980								
Professional	3	8	0	4	0	9	8	4
Employers/managers	10	24	3	3	4	9	25	12
Intermediate non-manual	4	11	2	4	5	17	8	6
Junior non-manual	5	10	6	7	6	18	13	8
Skilled manual	15	34	27	19	17	21	23	25
Semi-skilled manual	6	8	14	8	9	10	21	10
Unskilled manual	2	1	5	3	3	5	0	3
Economically inactive	56	4	42	52	55	11	1	33
Total	100	100	100	100	100	100	100	100
Socio-economic group at 1990								
Professional	2	10	0	0	2	8	8	5
Employers/managers	9	24	2	4	7	11	26	14
Intermediate non-manual	4	14	2	5	6	14	10	8
Junior non-manual	3	7	4	4	6	10	6	5
Skilled manual	12	30	15	12	20	17	20	21
Semi-skilled manual	3	7	11	10	9	9	26	8
Unskilled manual	1	1	4	1	3	4	0	2
Economically inactive	66	7	61	63	48	26	5	38
Total	100	100	100	100	100	100	100	100

contd...

Table 31c (continued)

Percentages

| Item | Owner-occupiers | | Rented | | | | | All tenures |
	Owned outright	With mortgage	Local authority	Housing association	Private: Unfurnished	Furnished	With job or business	
Socio-economic group at 2000								
Professional	3	9	1	1	7	16	–	6
Employers/managers	8	26	2	3	12	15	–	15
Intermediate non-manual	5	15	3	6	11	13	–	10
Junior non-manual	4	10	7	8	11	13	–	8
Skilled manual	10	22	10	10	15	12	–	15
Semi-skilled manual	3	8	10	9	10	7	–	7
Unskilled manual	1	2	3	4	3	3	–	2
Economically inactive	67	8	65	59	32	22	–	38
Total	100	100	100	100	100	100	–	100
Socio-economic classification at 2008[1]								
Large employers and higher managerial	2	10	1	0	3	3	–	5
Higher professional	5	13	0	1	10	11	–	8
Lower managerial and professional	10	32	5	6	20	21	–	19
Intermediate	4	8	4	3	8	6	–	6
Small employers and own account	6	8	2	4	8	5	–	6
Lower supervisory and technical	4	10	4	4	7	7	–	6
Semi-routine	3	7	13	10	12	11	–	7
Routine	4	6	7	8	8	8	–	6
Never worked/long-term unemployed	0	0	3	3	0	5	–	1
Economically inactive	63	6	62	61	22	24	–	36
Total	100	100	100	100	100	100	–	100

Sources: General Household Surveys 1980, 1990; General Lifestyle Survey 2008, Office for National Statistics.

Notes: Excludes members of the armed forces, economically active full-time students and those who were unemployed and had never worked. For 2008, 'Never worked and long-term unemployed' are included as a separate category. Skilled manual includes own account non-professionals. Semi-skilled manual includes personal service. 2000 and 2008 figures include private lettings with a job or business within unfurnished and furnished lettings. They are also for the household reference person.

1. From April 2001 the National Statistics Socio-economic classification (NS-SEC) was introduced for all official statistics and surveys. It has replaced Social Class based on Occupation and Socio-economic Groups (SEG).

Table 32a **Race by tenure in Great Britain (2005, 2006 and 2007 combined)**

Percentages

	White	Indian	Pakistani/ Bangladeshi	Black	Other	All ethnic minorities	Total
Tenure							
Outright owner	32	25	23	8	15	17	31
Owner with mortgage	40	49	40	30	32	35	40
Rented:							
Local authority or							
housing association	19	10	24	46	28	27	19
Private, unfurnished	7	7	5	9	13	12	8
Private, furnished	2	10	5	6	13	10	3
Total	100	100	100	100	100	100	100

Source: General Household Survey 2007, Office for National Statistics.

Table 32b **Race by dwelling type in Great Britain (2004, 2005 and 2006 combined)**

Percentages

Dwelling type	White	Indian	Pakistani/ Bangladeshi	Black	Other	All ethnic minorities	Total
House:							
Detached	23	15	4	5	12	9	22
Semi-detached	32	31	21	15	21	21	31
Terraced	27	26	54	31	25	32	28
Flats:							
Purpose-built	14	23	16	41	33	31	16
Converted	3	5	5	9	9	8	4
Other	0	0	0	0	0	0	0
Total	100	100	100	100	100	100	100

Sources: General Household Surveys 2004,2005 & 2006; unpublished data from analysis of GHS datasets.

Table 32c **Race by occupation standards in Great Britain (2004, 2005 and 2006 combined)**
Percentages

Level of occupation against the Bedroom Standard	White	Indian	Pakistani/ Bangladeshi	Black	Other	All ethnic minorities	Total
Two or more below standard	0	1	5	2	0	2	0
One below standard	2	3	12	13	3	8	2
Equals standard	24	33	36	42	43	39	25
One above standard	37	31	27	27	31	29	37
Two or more above standard	37	32	21	16	22	22	36

Source: General Household Surveys 2004,2005 & 2006; authors analysis of GHS datasets.

Table 33 **Tenure, cars, consumer durables and second dwellings in Great Britain**
Percentage of households with specified durables in 2008

Item	Rented					Owner-occupiers		All households
	Local authority	Housing association	Other unfurnished	Rented furnished	Rent free	In process of purchasing	Outright owner	
No car	64	52	32	48	42	9	23	26
One car	30	37	49	40	39	41	50	43
Two or more cars	6	11	19	12	19	50	27	31
Central heating	96	97	88	93	96	96	95	95
Washing machine	89	88	95	92	93	99	97	96
Tumble dryer	47	48	45	37	55	69	58	59
Microwave	90	91	88	90	95	94	92	92
Dishwasher	11	11	17	15	36	53	42	38
CD player	77	78	83	74	82	93	85	86
Home computer	61	91	76	76	56	91	61	72
Internet connection	55	87	63	73	51	87	55	66
Telephone	98	95	74	68	95	95	98	90
Mobile phone	69	88	84	90	64	88	69	79
Satellite receiver	77	92	77	62	76	92	77	82
Video recorder	79	71	56	39	68	71	79	70
Second dwelling	1	0	3	3	2	7	5	5

Source: Living Costs and Food Survey 2008, National Statistics.

Table 34 **Employment status of household heads by tenure**

Percentages

Year	Tenure	In employment:			Unemployed	Retired	Other economic inactive	Total
		Full-time	Part-time	All				
1981	Outright owners	37	4	42	3	44	11	100
	Homebuyers	92	1	93	3	2	2	100
	Council renting	43	4	47	9	28	15	100
	Housing association	42	4	46	6	34	14	100
	Private, unfurnished	51	4	56	4	30	10	100
	Private, furnished	65	1	66	9	5	20	100
	All tenures	58	3	62	5	24	10	100
1991	Outright owners	26	6	32	3	58	7	100
	Homebuyers	86	3	89	4	4	4	100
	Council renting	25	5	30	11	40	19	100
	Housing association	29	5	34	9	42	15	100
	Private, unfurnished	54	5	59	6	28	8	100
	Private, furnished	56	5	61	12	4	23	100
	All tenures	54	4	59	6	27	9	100
2001/02	Outright owners	26	6	32	1	63	5	100
	Homebuyers	86	5	92	1	4	4	100
	Council renting	22	9	31	5	36	28	100
	Housing association	24	10	34	5	34	27	100
	Private, unfurnished	60	8	67	3	14	16	100
	Private, furnished	61	9	69	5	3	22	100
	All tenures	54	7	61	2	27	10	100
2008	Outright owners	26	11	37	1	57	6	100
	Homebuyers	86	7	93	1	3	3	100
	Social renters	24	9	34	6	31	29	100
	Private renters	60	10	70	4	9	16	100
	All tenures	53	9	62	2	26	10	100

Sources: Housing trailers to the 1981 & 1991 Labour Force Surveys, Survey of English Housing 2001/02 and 2008.

Notes: Unemployed includes households that believe no work is available. Equivalent figures for 1984, 1988, and 1993/4 to 2005/06 can be found in earlier editions of the Review. From 2001/02 figures relate to the 'household reference person' rather than the head of household. The results of the 2008 survey did not distinguish council from housing association tenants and private renters were not divided between furnished and unfurnished.

Table 35 **Employment status of recently moving household heads by tenure in 1984, 1991, 2001/02 and 2009**

Percentages

Year	Tenure	In employment: Full-time	Part-time	All employed	Unemployed	Retired	Other economic inactive	Total
1984	Outright owner	31	5	36	9	31	19	100
	Buying with mortgage	94	1	95	3	–	2	100
	Council	29	5	33	24	17	26	100
	Housing association	40	12	52	16	12	10	100
	Private, unfurnished	74	4	77	11	3	11	100
	Private, furnished	52	4	56	16	1	28	100
	All tenures	64	3	67	11	7	14	100
1991	Outright owner	37	5	42	6	42	8	100
	Buying with mortgage	93	2	94	3	1	2	100
	Council	28	3	31	22	20	27	100
	Housing association	30	6	35	13	28	24	100
	Private, unfurnished	75	4	79	9	2	9	100
	Private, furnished	55	4	59	11	1	28	100
	All tenures	64	3	67	10	8	15	100
2001/02	Outright owner	28	15	43	2	48	7	100
	Buying with mortgage	94	3	97	1	1	2	100
	Council	20	9	29	10	16	45	100
	Housing association	24	12	36	11	16	37	100
	Private, unfurnished	70	8	77	4	4	15	100
	Private, furnished	59	10	69	5	0	25	100
	All tenures	63	7	71	4	8	17	100
2009	Outright owner	34	12	46	2	38	14	100
	Buying with mortgage	89	5	94	2	1	2	100
	Council	23	11	34	15	13	39	100
	Housing association	29	9	39	13	15	33	100
	Private, unfurnished	66	9	75	8	2	15	100
	Private, furnished	58	12	70	7	1	22	100
	All tenures	59	10	68	8	5	19	100

Sources: Housing trailers to the 1984 and 1991 Labour Force Surveys, Survey of English Housing 2001/02, Annual Population Survey 2009.

Notes: 'Other economic inactive' includes people who were permanently sick or disabled, in full-time education or looking after the family at home. The figures for 2001/02 and 2009 are for the household reference person.

Table 36 **Incomes of household heads by tenure in Great Britain**

£ per week

Tenure	1972	1976	1980	1984	1988	1992	1996	2000	2004	2007	2008
Owners:											
Outright owner	25	59	81	107	157	194	225	281	367	417	440
With mortgage	39	96	142	195	267	320	380	461	555	664	643
Tenants:											
Local authority	22	58	68	76	93	110	131	140	178	204	203
Housing association	–	54	66	88	94	120	145	164	203	221	201
Private, unfurnished	19	48	60	77	110	149	223	262	406	375	398
Private, furnished	21	57	87	89	161	170	222	333	260	376	418

Source: General Household Surveys 1972 to 2007; General Lifestyle Survey 2008.

Notes: Income figures are mean averages for usual gross income of household heads. Local authority tenants includes tenants of new towns. In 2000, the GHS switched from 'head of household' to 'household reference person'. Under this revised definition the highest earning joint householder, rather than the male joint householder, is defined as the 'household reference person'. Because of this, there is a discontinuity in the series.

Table 37 **Tenure and sources of income in 2008**

Sources of income		Tenant households					Homeowner households		
	Local authority	Housing association	Other unfurnished	Rented furnished	Rent free	In process of purchasing	Outright owner	All owners
	£	£	£	£	£	£	£	£
Household weekly income:								
Gross	281	354	877	568	418	998	577	768
Disposable	255	314	710	469	356	788	488	625
	%	%	%	%	%	%	%	%
Percentage from:								
Wages & salaries	43	51	72	80	65	80	41	72
Self-employment	4	2	6	5	5	11	9	6
Investments	0	0	13	1	2	2	7	11
Pensions & annuities	4	5	1	0	5	2	21	1
Social security	48	41	8	5	21	4	21	8
Other sources	1	1	1	10	2	1	0	2
Total	100	100	100	100	100	100	100	100

Source: Family Spending 2009, Office for National Statistics.

Notes: Pensions and annuities exclude social security benefits. Social security benefits exclude housing benefit and council tax benefit.

Table 38 **Tenure and gross weekly household income in Great Britain in 2008**

Percentages of households in each gross income decile group

Income decile group	Lower income boundary	Tenant households					Homeowner households		All households
		Local authority	Housing association	Other unfurnished	Rented furnished	Rent free	In process of purchasing	Outright owner	
	£	%	%	%	%	%	%	%	%
Lowest		36	15	10	4	4	4	28	100
Second	146	21	16	9	1	1	6	46	100
Third	224	17	16	9	2	1	12	44	100
Fourth	305	10	10	11	2	1	25	42	100
Fifth	408	8	6	11	1	2	34	37	100
Sixth	522	5	7	9	4	1	46	28	100
Seventh	664	4	4	8	3	1	56	24	100
Eighth	817	2	2	8	3	0	64	20	100
Ninth	1,026	1	2	5	1	2	69	20	100
Highest	1,356	0	1	4	1	0	72	23	100
All		11	8	8	2	1	39	31	100

Source: Family Spending 2009, Office for National Statistics.

Section 3   Compendium of tables

Private housing

Table 39a **Numbers of property transactions in England and Wales**

Thousands

Year	1980	1981	1982	1983	1984	1985	1986	1987	1988	1989	1990	1991	1992	1993	1994	1995	1996	1997	1998	1999	2000	2001	2002	2003	2004	2005	2006[1]	2007	2008	2009
Transactions	1,267	1,351	1,542	1,669	1,760	1,743	1,801	1,937	2,148	1,580	1,398	1,306	1,136	1,196	1,274	1,135	1,242	1,440	1,347	1,469	1,433	1,458	1,586	1,341	1,786	1,529	1,609	1,563	889	847

Sources: Economic Trends, Inland Revenue Statistics, Inland Revenue, HMRC.
Note: 1. From 2006, only transactions of £40,000 or more are counted by HMRC. The equivalent figures for 2006 and 2007, consistent with the data for earlier years, were 1,777 and 1,793.

Table 39b **Residential property transactions in England and Wales**

Year	1986	1987	1988	1989	1990	1991	1992	1993	1994	1995	1996	1997	1998	1999	2000	2001	2002	2003	2004	2005	2006[1]	2007	2008	2009
All property transactions (000s)	1,801	1,937	2,148	1,580	1,398	1,306	1,136	1,196	1,274	1,135	1,242	1,440	1,347	1,469	1,433	1,458	1,586	1,341	1,786	1,529	1,609	1,563	889	847
Residential property transactions (000s)	1,600	1,744	1,990	1,467	1,283	1,225	1,032	1,114	1,168	1,047	1,122	1,296	1,220	1,368	1,327	1,343	1,450	1,204	1,627	1,379	1,475	1,423	787	769
Residential properties as a percentage of all property transactions (%)	88.8	90.0	92.6	92.8	91.8	93.8	90.8	93.1	91.7	92.2	90.3	90.0	90.6	93.1	92.6	92.1	91.4	89.5	90.1	90.2	91.7	91.0	88.5	90.8

Sources: Inland Revenue Statistics, Economic Trends, Housing and Construction Statistics, HMRC.
Note: 1. From 2006, only transactions of £40,000 or more are counted by HMRC.

Table 40 **Numbers of mortgage advances per year in Great Britain**

Thousands

	1980	1985	1990	1995	1996	1997	1998	1999	2000	2001	2002	2003	2004	2005	2006	2007	2008	2009
Building societies	675	1,073	780	513	589	396	230	304	311	225	247	196	173	181	248	231	104	104
+ Banks		176	333	346	431	674	678	757	734	965	1,061	967	882	808	892	756	368	469
+ Insurance companies	18	19	26															
+ Local authorities	16	23	8															
+ Other specialist lenders				50	65	116	127	82	68	68	113	202	205	209	289	269	44	24
= Total	709	1,291	1,147	909	1,085	1,186	1,035	1,143	1,113	1,257	1,422	1,363	1,262	1,197	1,428	1,260	516	598

Sources: Housing and Construction Statistics (annual volumes) for 1980 to 1990; Bank of England 1991 onwards.
Notes: The 1980 figures are for England and Wales only and exclude council house sales. Thereafter, figures are for Great Britain, and include council house sales.
        Abbey National Plc figures included with the bank's figures from July 1989. The Bank of England data from 1991 onwards also reflects the continuing trend for building societies to convert to banks. The figures for banks and other specialist lenders for the years 1991 to 1997 are understood to include remortgage advances as well as loans for house purchase. From 1998 the data relates solely to advances for house purchase.

Table 41 **Gross and net advances secured on dwellings per year in the United Kingdom**

£ million

	1980	1985	1990	1995	1996	1997	1998	1999	2000	2001	2002	2003	2004	2005	2006	2007	2008	2009
Gross advances in year																		
Building societies	9,614	26,491	40,915	33,714	39,838	27,797	20,716	25,872	24,924	25,904	34,994	46,300	46,864	43,516	52,591	51,692	37,483	18,574
+ Banks	–	–	18,737	21,239	28,727	44,602	62,262	78,648	83,335	119,765	162,423	194,959	202,756	201,833	234,390	247,147	192,940	118,458
+ Insurance companies	1,870	1,829	698	119	291	210	345	616	538	773	869	412	109	5	106	104	964	507
+ Local and central government			491	206	249	236	245	347	264	275	374	271	113	342	407	644	1,225	1,063
+ Other specialist lenders	–	–	8,992	2,010	2,555	4,382	5,808	9,220	10,734	13,410	22,079	35,397	41,435	42,585	57,861	63,172	21,411	5,032
= Total	11,484	28,320	69,833	57,288	71,660	77,227	89,376	114,703	119,795	160,127	220,739	277,339	291,277	288,281	345,355	362,759	254,023	143,634
Net advances in year																		
Building societies	5,722	14,711	24,185	9,169	12,854	11,278	7,865	10,567	8,931	6,406	10,215	18,664	17,077	13,062	16,446	12,891	4,958	-7,368
+ Banks	500	4,223	6,409	7,689	6,651	11,897	15,119	21,492	19,481	31,094	48,928	47,579	42,844	33,233	29,984	13,826	-42,879	43,135
+ Insurance companies	1,060	-241	210	-377	-166	-58	114	-646	168	43	-165	209	34	-428	-212	-3	778	415
+ Local and central government			-424	-159	-146	-1,099	-155	106	11	97	206	186	4	252	340	522	1,191	1,030
+ Other specialist lenders	–	–	2,914	-1,156	-88	1,814	2,288	6,360	12,164	16,251	19,642	34,443	40,779	45,090	63,952	81,042	76,646	-25,733
= Total	7,368	19,118	33,294	15,166	19,105	23,832	25,231	37,879	40,755	53,891	78,826	101,081	100,738	91,209	110,510	108,278	40,694	11,479
Amount outstanding at end of period																		
Building societies	42,696	97,213	176,661	223,237	223,905	97,578	106,331	113,497	106,990	113,413	123,638	142,312	160,116	173,204	189,687	202,666	208,345	189,711
+ Banks	2,880	21,111	85,677	139,956	158,210	305,687	320,565	345,032	386,334	418,645	467,601	511,049	543,063	575,797	605,793	627,026	586,771	732,329
+ Insurance companies	6,865	8,137	4,521	1,881	1,715	1,657	1,771	1,125	1,293	1,336	1,171	1,380	1,414	986	774	771	1,549	1,964
+ Local and central government			3,846	1,819	1,673	313	526	630	625	722	928	1,114	1,118	1,370	1,680	2,201	3,392	4,422
+ Other specialist lenders	–	971	24,038	24,012	24,090	26,107	27,440	34,692	41,202	57,234	81,834	118,737	171,805	215,662	280,825	354,553	426,221	307,088
= Total	52,441	127,432	294,743	390,905	409,593	431,342	456,633	494,976	536,444	591,350	675,172	774,592	877,516	967,019	1,078,759	1,187,218	1,226,279	1,235,515

Source: Financial Statistics – all figures from 1990 onwards. Compendium of Housing Finance Statistics 1997, Council of Mortgage Lenders - figures for 1980 and 1985.

Notes: From 1993 includes lending to housing associations. The figures for banks and building societies reflect the process of building society demutualisation by some building societies.

Table 42a Advances to first-time buyers

Year	1970	1975	1980	1985	1990	1995	1996	1997	1998	1999	2000	2001	2002	2003	2004	2005	2006	2007	2008	2009
Number of loans (000s)	330	305	318	570	413	419	435	512	525	592	500	568	532	370	358	372	401	357	194	199
Average dwelling price (A) (£)	4,330	9,549	17,533	23,742	45,234	46,489	48,693	52,674	61,344	71,623	75,840	85,021	103,754	109,336	131,693	141,299	145,970	159,494	163,208	165,512
Average advance (B) (£)	3,464	7,292	12,946	20,260	37,332	41,389	43,867	46,567	50,921	57,383	60,451	67,037	80,306	82,553	100,065	110,638	120,612	130,565	124,191	114,607
Average annual income (C) (£)	1,766	3,753	7,749	10,466	17,016	18,697	19,723	20,919	22,746	25,277	26,259	28,489	31,988	28,723	32,437	35,937	40,253	41,901	41,479	40,971
Average advance as % of dwelling price (B/A)	80.0	76.4	73.8	85.3	82.5	89.0	90.1	88.4	83.0	80.1	79.7	78.8	77.4	75.5	76.0	78.3	82.6	81.9	76.1	69.2
Ratio average advance/ average income (B/C)	1.96	1.94	1.67	1.94	2.19	2.21	2.22	2.23	2.24	2.27	2.30	2.35	2.51	2.87	3.08	3.08	2.98	3.12	2.99	2.80
Interest rates (%)	8.6	11.1	14.9	13.0	14.3	7.5	6.5	7.3	6.9	5.9	6.2	5.0	4.5	4.1	5.6	5.0	5.3	6.1	5.6	4.2
Average monthly repayment (D) (£)	22.27	53.16	122.6	173.43	381.02	288.29	281.45	321.27	347.83	359.89	402.00	396.86	451.32	445.79	628.41	654.98	735.73	860.42	779.92	624.61
Average repayment as % of average income (12xD/C)	15.1	17.0	19.0	19.9	26.9	18.5	17.1	18.4	18.4	17.1	18.4	16.7	16.9	18.6	23.2	21.9	21.8	24.6	22.6	18.3

Sources: Housing Finance, Compendium of Housing Finance Statistics, Council of Mortgage Lenders.

Notes: All figures relate to the UK. For years to 1993 the data is for building societies only. Average income data subject to variation in recording by different societies. From 1989 Q3 to 1993 Abbey National are excluded from data on the number of building society loans, but retained for other columns. From 1994 data is from the wider Survey of Mortgage Lenders, which has now become the Regulated Mortgage Survey. Average mortgage payments are calculated on the basis of a conventional 25 year mortgage, and on the basis of the average mortgage rates for the year, adjusted to net repayments allowing for changes in tax and MITR rates, and the impact of the £30,000 limit on relief against the average advance. For the years to 1996 mortgage rates are average year end building society rates. From 1997 mortgage rates are average fourth quarter rates for all mortgage lenders.

Table 42b Annual changes in house prices, mortgage advances and incomes for first-time buyers

Percentages

Year	1970	1975	1980	1985	1990	1995	1996	1997	1998	1999	2000	2001	2002	2003	2004	2005	2006	2007	2008	2009
Average dwelling price	5.7	5.7	17.5	7.1	13.8	- 3.6	4.7	8.2	16.5	16.8	5.9	12.1	22.0	5.4	20.4	7.3	3.3	9.3	2.3	1.4
Average advance	6.9	11.0	14.7	7.8	13.3	3.2	6.0	6.2	9.3	12.7	5.3	10.9	19.8	2.8	21.2	10.6	9.0	8.3	- 4.9	- 7.7
Average income	9.2	14.2	23.2	7.3	11.7	1.4	5.5	6.1	8.7	11.1	3.9	8.5	12.3	- 10.2	12.9	10.8	12.8	3.4	- 1.0	- 1.2

Source and Notes: As Table 42a.

Table 42c **Advances to moving owner-occupiers**

Year	1970	1975	1980	1985	1990	1995	1996	1997	1998	1999	2000	2001	2002	2003	2004	2005	2006	2007	2008	2009
Number of loans (000s)	210	345	358	505	367	377	513	615	563	660	622	745	865	882	887	647	722	658	323	320
Average dwelling price (A) (£)	5,838	13,813	28,959	39,390	76,170	87,196	91,193	96,303	101,250	111,203	122,140	131,803	138,967	165,126	190,983	209,304	239,042	258,459	262,880	259,559
Average advance (B) (£)	3,854	7,409	13,359	23,300	45,180	55,977	58,507	62,182	64,918	71,717	78,590	84,181	88,707	101,241	114,036	128,688	148,784	161,294	157,348	149,439
Average annual income (C) (£)	2,168	4,299	8,688	12,702	22,479	28,088	29,468	30,533	31,693	33,961	35,197	37,675	38,134	38,664	40,734	47,314	56,774	60,054	61,665	61,244
Average advance as percentage of dwelling price (B/A)	66.0	53.6	46.1	59.2	59.3	64.2	64.2	64.6	64.1	64.5	64.3	63.9	63.8	61.4	59.7	61.5	62.2	62.4	59.9	57.6
Ratio average advance/ average income (B/C)	1.78	1.72	1.54	1.83	2.00	1.99	1.99	2.04	2.05	2.11	2.23	2.26	2.33	2.62	2.80	2.72	2.62	2.69	2.55	2.44
Interest rates (%)	8.6	11.1	14.9	13.0	14.3	7.5	6.5	7.3	6.9	5.9	6.2	5.0	4.5	4.1	5.6	5.0	5.3	6.1	5.6	4.2
Average monthly repayment (D) (£)	24.78	54.01	126.51	199.45	478.02	397.41	381.59	436.04	447.07	452.49	522.62	498.35	498.53	547.67	716.15	761.83	907.58	1,062.93	988.15	814.44
Average repayment as percentage of average income (12xD/C)	13.7	15.1	17.5	18.8	25.5	17.0	15.5	17.1	16.9	16.0	17.8	15.9	15.7	17.0	21.1	19.3	19.2	21.2	19.2	16.0

Sources and Notes: As Table 42a.

Table 42d **Annual changes in house prices, mortgage advances and incomes for moving owner-occupiers**

Percentages

Year	1970	1975	1980	1985	1990	1995	1996	1997	1998	1999	2000	2001	2002	2003	2004	2005	2006	2007	2008	2009
Average dwelling price	13.4	9.8	20.3	7.3	6.8	2.8	4.6	5.6	5.1	9.8	9.8	7.9	5.4	18.8	15.7	9.6	14.2	8.1	1.7	- 1.3
Average advance	11.4	14.8	12.9	8.5	10.1	1.6	4.5	6.3	4.4	10.5	9.6	7.1	5.4	14.3	12.4	12.8	15.6	8.4	- 2.4	- 5.0
Average income	9.1	16.2	22.3	8.5	16.2	4.2	4.9	3.6	3.8	7.2	3.6	7.0	1.2	1.4	5.4	16.2	20.0	5.8	2.7	- 0.7

Sources and Notes: As Table 42a.

Table 43a **Mortgage cost to income ratios for first-time buyers**

	1986	1990	1991	1992	1993	1994	1995	1996	1997	1998	1999	2000	2001	2002	2003	2004	2005	2006	2007	2008	2009
North East	16.6	21.8	19.5	17.3	15.9	15.7	16.3	15.8	17.5	16.8	14.9	15.8	14.8	13.9	15.1	19.4	18.9	20.4	22.9	20.6	16.3
Yorkshire & The Humber	18.1	23.6	21.6	18.6	16.9	17.5	17.8	15.9	18.3	17.5	16.2	17.0	15.0	14.6	15.6	20.0	19.6	21.0	23.6	21.4	17.3
North West	18.1	23.5	21.7	19.1	17.9	17.6	18.0	16.8	18.7	17.6	15.9	17.0	15.3	15.0	16.3	20.7	20.2	21.1	23.6	21.4	17.3
West Midlands	18.8	25.8	23.6	19.2	17.6	18.1	18.2	16.4	18.9	18.2	16.4	17.7	16.3	15.9	17.3	21.8	21.2	21.8	24.3	21.9	17.8
East Midlands	18.6	27.1	22.7	18.4	17.0	17.6	17.8	16.2	18.0	17.6	15.9	16.9	15.8	16.7	17.6	21.7	20.7	21.3	24.0	21.7	17.2
East	21.5	30.6	24.7	20.0	18.2	18.8	19.0	17.1	18.9	18.8	17.2	18.9	17.1	17.3	20.0	24.5	22.8	22.6	25.4	23.3	18.5
London	23.3	30.9	25.8	20.6	18.7	19.3	20.2	18.7	20.3	19.9	18.7	20.7	18.8	18.9	21.1	25.7	23.5	22.4	25.6	23.8	19.2
South East	22.4	31.4	25.3	20.5	18.4	19.3	19.7	18.0	19.6	19.4	18.1	20.1	17.5	18.7	20.7	25.4	23.4	22.8	25.8	23.8	19.1
South West	21.4	30.0	24.1	19.7	18.3	18.7	19.4	17.6	19.6	19.5	17.7	18.8	17.6	18.1	19.1	23.8	22.9	22.6	25.4	23.0	18.6
Wales	18.7	23.7	20.3	17.8	16.8	17.2	17.5	16.2	18.1	18.0	16.1	16.8	15.4	15.4	16.0	20.4	20.2	21.0	23.6	21.4	17.6
Scotland	18.1	18.0	17.3	14.5	14.2	15.0	15.6	15.1	16.9	16.7	15.8	15.9	14.4	14.8	14.1	19.1	18.2	18.5	21.4	19.6	16.3
Northern Ireland	16.9	19.2	16.0	13.7	13.2	14.6	15.1	13.9	17.2	17.4	16.3	17.5	15.8	14.1	16.5	20.1	19.5	20.9	25.1	22.8	18.6
United Kingdom	20.1	26.9	23.0	19.1	17.5	18.0	18.5	17.1	19.0	18.6	17.1	18.4	16.7	16.9	18.6	23.2	21.9	21.8	24.6	22.6	18.3

Sources: As for Table 42, except that data up to 1992 only is from the BSA 5% sample survey, with data for later years from the wider Survey of Mortgage Lenders/Regulated Mortgage Survey.

Note: Data is for government office regions. Mortgage costs are computed based on a 25 year repayment mortgage.

Table 43b **Mortgage cost to income ratios for moving owner-occupiers**

	1986	1990	1991	1992	1993	1994	1995	1996	1997	1998	1999	2000	2001	2002	2003	2004	2005	2006	2007	2008	2009
North East	17.2	21.7	20.1	17.1	16.1	16.1	15.4	15.2	16.3	15.4	14.6	15.3	14.1	14.6	15.4	19.3	18.2	18.4	20.1	18.2	14.6
Yorkshire & The Humber	17.6	22.7	21.0	17.7	16.6	17.0	16.4	15.3	16.3	16.2	15.0	16.1	14.6	14.8	15.5	19.4	18.4	18.7	20.7	18.6	15.0
North West	17.6	23.9	21.5	18.7	16.6	17.1	16.5	14.9	16.6	15.8	15.2	16.4	14.9	14.4	15.6	19.5	18.3	18.8	20.7	18.7	15.2
West Midlands	18.3	25.3	22.0	18.4	17.0	17.4	16.8	15.1	17.2	16.7	15.7	17.6	15.9	15.7	16.8	20.7	19.1	19.3	21.4	19.1	15.5
East Midlands	17.8	24.6	21.7	18.0	16.1	17.2	15.8	14.8	16.6	16.4	14.6	17.0	15.3	15.1	16.3	20.5	18.7	19.1	20.6	18.6	15.2
East	19.7	27.0	23.3	19.0	16.8	17.6	17.3	15.3	17.0	16.7	16.1	18.3	16.2	16.1	17.7	22.3	20.0	19.2	21.4	19.5	16.3
London	21.6	27.4	23.6	19.0	17.1	17.9	17.1	16.2	17.4	17.8	16.6	19.6	17.0	17.2	19.0	22.6	20.4	19.2	21.5	19.1	16.4
South East	20.9	28.9	23.8	19.6	17.9	18.4	18.2	16.2	17.8	17.6	16.6	19.2	16.9	16.9	18.5	22.7	20.4	20.0	21.9	20.1	16.9
South West	19.8	25.6	22.1	18.6	16.9	17.6	16.8	15.5	17.1	17.2	16.2	18.1	16.4	15.4	17.7	21.8	19.6	19.3	21.2	19.4	16.1
Wales	18.1	23.7	20.6	18.0	16.2	16.6	16.8	14.5	16.5	15.8	14.6	16.3	14.6	14.2	15.5	19.1	18.2	18.0	19.9	18.2	14.9
Scotland	18.1	23.0	19.6	16.5	16.6	16.3	16.4	15.1	16.2	16.0	14.6	15.8	13.8	13.7	14.5	18.1	17.2	18.2	20.8	18.8	14.8
Northern Ireland	17.4	20.1	16.3	14.2	14.5	15.6	15.0	14.3	15.8	15.1	14.5	16.2	14.7	15.1	14.5	17.4	17.3	18.7	21.7	19.4	16.2
United Kingdom	19.0	25.5	22.1	18.3	16.9	17.5	17.0	15.5	17.1	16.8	15.8	17.8	15.9	15.7	17.0	21.1	19.3	19.2	21.2	19.2	16.0

Source and Notes: As Table 43a.

Table 44a **Average endowment payments for households with endowment policies**

£ per week

Country	1994/95	1995/96	1996/97	1997/98	1998/99	1999/00	2000/01	2001/02	2002/03	2003/04	2004/05	2005/06	2006	2007	2008
England	16.12	15.95	16.84	18.64	18.98	19.59	22.30	22.77	21.98	22.88	22.37	23.24	24.62	21.81	23.39
Scotland	13.77	14.72	15.40	17.06	14.28	17.56	17.56	18.75	18.56	17.38	19.41	18.28	18.20	19.60	16.25
Wales	11.62	14.37	14.46	15.15	16.54	16.59	16.00	15.81	15.40	18.14	14.90	24.55	20.70	19.00	17.60
Northern Ireland	8.32	12.09	11.42	11.98	13.46	12.81	12.95	11.59	17.28	16.78	–	18.64	9.12	14.40	17.70
United Kingdom	15.54	15.42	16.21	18.22	18.15	19.27	21.51	21.90	21.65	21.95	21.36	22.23	23.34	21.10	22.82

Table 44b **Percentage of homebuying households with endowment policies**

Percentages

Country	1994/95	1995/96	1996/97	1997/98	1998/99	1999/00	2000/01	2001/02	2002/03	2003/04	2004/05	2005/06	2006	2007	2008
England	66.6	67.8	65.2	63.9	63.8	61.5	53.9	51.6	43.8	38.9	30.3	25.6	22.9	19.1	15.4
Scotland	76.9	81.7	72.8	76.7	75.0	73.2	55.1	66.9	52.7	39.9	39.1	36.4	32.0	20.0	22.2
Wales	61.2	67.2	68.4	66.4	71.7	67.8	41.8	56.7	54.6	47.3	35.7	18.2	18.2	26.3	22.0
Northern Ireland	79.1	78.8	77.6	76.0	87.2	58.5	24.4	50.0	46.7	40.4	–	20.0	20.0	20.0	20.0
United Kingdom	67.4	69.1	66.2	65.3	65.4	62.9	52.9	53.1	45.1	39.6	31.4	26.6	23.6	19.8	15.9

Table 44c **Average endowment payment per household with mortgage**

£ per week

Country	1994/95	1995/96	1996/97	1997/98	1998/99	1999/00	2000/01	2001/02	2002/03	2003/04	2004/05	2005/06	2006	2007	2008
England	10.74	10.81	10.98	11.91	12.11	12.05	12.02	11.75	9.63	8.90	6.78	5.95	5.64	4.17	3.60
Scotland	10.59	12.03	11.21	13.09	10.71	12.85	9.68	12.54	9.78	6.93	7.59	6.65	5.82	3.92	3.61
Wales	7.11	9.66	9.89	10.06	11.86	11.25	6.69	8.96	8.41	8.58	5.32	4.47	3.77	5.00	3.87
Northern Ireland	6.58	9.53	8.86	9.10	11.74	7.49	3.16	5.80	8.07	6.78	–	3.73	1.82	2.88	3.54
United Kingdom	10.47	10.66	10.73	11.90	11.87	12.12	11.38	11.63	9.76	8.69	6.71	5.91	5.51	4.18	3.63

Source: Original analysis of Family Expenditure Survey and Expenditure and Food Survey database; supplied by Office for National Statistics.

Note: The figures for Scotland, Wales and Northern Ireland from 2000/01 may be distorted by small sample sizes and those for Northern Ireland for 2004/05 are omitted for that reason. In Tables 44a and 44c, figures for Northern Ireland exclude endowment policies from before 1984. From 2006 the reporting period for the Expenditure and Food Survey became the calendar year.

Table 45 **Homeowners' housing wealth, borrowing and equity**

| | USA | France | Germany | United Kingdom | | | | | | | | | |
	1989	1984	1988	1980	1985	1990	1995	2000	2005	2006	2007	2008	2009
Billions (of the national currency)													
Gross Domestic Product	5,132	4,362	2,111	233	362	570	733	977	1,254	1,326	1,399	1,448	1,396
Value of owner-occupied stock	6,500	4,189	2,850	287	514	1,082	1,023	1,858	3,126	3,452	3,793	3,423	3,551
House purchase debt	1,900	701	427	53	127	295	390	535	967	1,079	1,187	1,226	1,234
'Free equity'	4,600	3,488	2,420	234	387	787	633	1,323	2,159	2,373	2,606	2,197	2,315
Percentages													
Value of stock as % of GDP	127	96	135	123	142	190	140	190	249	260	271	236	254
Debt as a % of GDP	37	16	20	23	35	52	53	55	77	81	85	85	88
Free equity as a % of GDP	90	80	115	100	107	138	86	135	172	179	186	152	153

Sources: Figures for USA, France and Germany from *House Prices, Land Prices, The Housing Market and House Purchase Debt in Britain and Other Countries*, A. Holmans, Department of the Environment.

Note: UK figures updated and revised. They differ from the figures in Table 6, as they have been adjusted to exclude values for non-corporate private landlords included within the personal sector.

Table 46a **Private sector regional land prices per hectare**

£ thousands

Region	1981	1982	1983	1984	1985	1986	1987	1988	1989	1990	1991	1992	1993	1994	1995	1996	1997	1998	1999	2000	2001	2002
North	76.3	79.6	71.9	80.2	121.6	123.0	105.2	120.7	277.8	216.5	322.2	237.1										
North East										280.0	275.0	248.1	250.5	260.0	280.0	300.0	320.0	350.0	379.0	407.0	435.0	619.0
North West	84.9	75.3	97.5	81.6	100.8	124.7	146.1	197.3	393.7	309.2	326.3	311.5										
North West										329.9	325.3	309.2	272.4	263.2	301.1	332.5	325.0	350.0	410.0	480.0	580.0	702.0
Yorkshire & The Humber	61.4	78.1	85.5	96.2	115.4	107.3	122.3	174.8	252.8	355.0	324.9	301.8	251.6	282.7	348.5	367.8	335.0	365.0	390.0	435.0	490.0	542.0
West Midlands	124.1	91.5	130.9	130.9	125.1	150.4	220.4	393.6	458.8	495.6	370.0	360.0	335.0	355.3	434.0	375.6	447.8	500.0	620.0	685.0	810.0	905.0
East Midlands	63.7	72.4	75.5	101.1	94.2	115.7	178.4	313.7	396.0	376.0	315.0	290.0	275.0	296.7	310.0	325.0	340.0	360.0	420.0	490.0	580.0	699.0
East Anglia	71.0	75.8	83.1	94.7	149.1	153.7	273.5	452.5	547.1	405.4	235.6	261.0										
East										631.3	349.4	379.6	360.0	420.7	452.3	519.7	554.9	600.0	780.0	980.0	1,250.0	1,612.0
London	390.1	486.0	754.6	600.5	888.2	1,532.5	2,133.4	2,169.0	3,091.1	2,209.0	1,606.9	1,458.7	1,325.0	1,450.0	1,530.0	1,600.0	1,800.0	2,000.0	2,200.0	3,000.0	4,000.0	5,080.0
South East	168.1	180.5	218.4	286.6	378.9	407.0	605.9	820.9	762.9	583.0	603.7	556.0										
South East										545.0	520.0	480.0	450.0	539.3	595.3	654.0	785.2	875.1	1,075.0	1,295.0	1,750.0	1,903.0
South West	78.9	94.5	138.3	121.7	197.1	194.7	309.1	496.0	493.7	450.0	375.0	325.0	340.1	420.0	424.8	463.7	460.5	479.6	533.0	674.0	925.0	1,049.0
England	112.0	119.4	155.1	150.7	199.7	240.9	346.9	460.9	453.3	432.1	379.2	347.6	339.1	389.9	413.3	441.0	443.6	470.9	557.3	655.7	821.7	975.7
Wales	31.6	48.8	49.2	74.5	89.0	76.7	83.8	97.8	191.5	222.6	155.0	177.6	167.5	241.7	190.1	281.7	292.2	394.5	440.0	590.0	690.0	812.0

Sources: Housing Statistics, Department of Transport, Local Government and the Regions.

Notes: Data for the years to 1992 are provided for standard statistical regions. From 1990 data is provided for government office regions. In many cases these are co-terminus. Where government office regions have different boundaries these are shown in italics, immediately below the standard region they most resemble. The data in this series for the years from 1990 was significantly revised by DTLR to remove inconsistencies with Valuation Office data, and should be treated with caution. Figures for 1999 onwards are provisional.

Table 46b **Average valuations of residential building land with outline planning permission**

£ per hectare

Region	1995	1996	1997	1998	1999	2000	2001	2002	2003	2004	2005	2006	2007	2008	2009	2010
North East	447,355	429,038	449,256	451,594	463,628	507,716	543,095	628,027	963,727	1,268,944	1,814,916	1,849,953	2,217,356	2,218,662	1,445,834	1,124,891
North West	446,819	451,278	461,990	524,644	573,469	631,495	744,421	815,127	1,109,197	1,400,273	2,004,171	2,226,536	2,380,971	2,406,641	1,742,192	1,363,558
Yorkshire & The Humber	497,042	489,102	532,931	553,062	578,089	632,403	688,803	752,958	1,003,824	1,653,153	2,209,222	2,302,058	2,407,292	2,448,155	1,595,780	1,254,610
East Midlands	397,096	396,022	427,096	497,444	529,256	616,392	811,441	937,115	1,342,793	1,562,098	1,767,812	1,808,203	1,873,741	1,892,275	1,214,710	1,066,995
West Midlands	597,383	599,984	637,614	772,089	826,416	961,625	1,155,503	1,284,108	1,533,093	1,809,564	2,037,488	2,141,222	2,222,459	2,363,523	1,802,878	1,599,129
East	735,231	732,264	808,907	898,870	947,453	1,342,715	1,637,111	1,837,117	2,445,760	2,731,248	2,920,667	3,134,875	3,411,406	3,682,312	2,487,748	2,297,946
South East	862,368	854,106	1,008,744	1,225,825	1,392,684	1,862,731	2,185,985	2,420,759	2,746,040	2,856,647	3,119,845	3,440,685	3,955,960	4,013,138	2,582,609	2,330,145
London	2,107,732	2,140,519	2,486,641	3,059,363	3,484,825	4,244,864	5,490,647	6,929,675	7,668,101	7,957,084	8,380,322	9,126,040	9,320,976	10,490,053	7,007,053	6,283,593
South West	591,412	604,577	677,361	858,503	948,178	1,160,049	1,352,397	1,519,247	1,829,808	2,024,036	2,225,509	2,381,163	2,691,328	2,851,832	1,932,990	1,568,997
England	812,328	816,828	921,288	1,098,965	1,223,258	1,514,834	1,873,027	2,208,799	2,609,360	2,888,647	3,244,959	3,508,352	3,748,465	4,005,118	2,700,537	2,360,338

Source: Department for Communities and Local Government website.

Note: Valuations for the years to 2003 are for the Spring of each year. From 2004 they are for the January of each year. This table replaces the series in Table 46a which is no longer being updated.

Table 47a **Average regional house prices**

£

Region	1970	1975	1980	1985	1990	1995	1996	1997	1998	1999	2000	2001	2002	2003	2004	2005	2006	2007	2008	2009
North	3,942	9,601	17,710	22,786	43,655	47,060	51,684	53,332	57,776	63,424	65,145	71,153	79,439	101,561	127,291	137,229	143,097	154,761	161,325	159,790
Yorkshire & Humberside	3,634	9,058	17,689	23,338	47,231	54,356	55,867	60,019	62,214	67,416	72,176	76,368	88,126	114,253	137,317	148,014	158,247	170,203	173,158	176,040
North West	4,184	9,771	20,092	25,126	50,005	56,533	57,701	63,622	65,514	71,901	78,415	82,623	92,693	115,447	139,635	149,599	157,947	170,477	175,054	174,626
East Midlands	3,966	9,989	18,928	25,539	52,620	55,060	58,855	61,930	66,155	72,437	79,323	87,280	104,835	132,013	154,493	161,487	164,336	176,255	177,025	172,415
West Midlands	4,490	10,866	21,663	25,855	54,694	62,123	64,320	67,803	71,864	79,757	88,431	97,650	112,313	137,371	161,846	168,904	177,182	185,048	185,260	184,900
East Anglia	4,515	11,528	22,808	31,661	61,427	60,971	61,819	69,764	74,808	79,349	92,628	103,964	129,395	153,666	174,363	184,966	194,243	206,745	210,971	198,177
Greater London	6,882	14,918	30,968	44,301	83,821	89,528	94,065	105,809	114,783	142,321	163,577	182,325	207,246	241,864	272,886	282,548	305,544	342,122	351,494	338,120
Rest of South East	6,223	14,664	29,832	40,487	80,525	80,939	85,767	92,833	103,797	117,753	137,354	152,538	175,727	211,056	232,390	239,251	251,400	271,981	279,730	269,320
South West	4,879	12,096	25,293	32,948	65,378	65,096	68,034	73,004	80,203	89,217	104,233	118,639	142,403	174,482	197,926	204,686	213,586	230,885	230,085	220,404
Wales	4,434	10,083	19,363	25,005	46,464	52,978	54,898	58,372	60,902	67,483	72,285	79,628	88,261	109,661	138,141	149,979	157,457	169,848	169,948	165,659
Scotland	5,002	11,139	21,754	26,941	41,744	53,143	56,674	57,883	63,585	69,312	69,961	73,570	77,655	103,641	118,932	129,631	137,192	158,798	168,593	174,433
Northern Ireland	4,387	10,023	23,656	23,012	31,849	42,810	47,678	53,309	59,376	66,267	72,514	79,885	83,829	95,217	110,188	129,229	169,259	229,701	218,282	184,282
United Kingdom	4,975	11,787	23,596	31,103	59,785	65,644	70,626	76,103	81,774	92,521	101,550	112,835	128,265	155,627	180,248	190,760	204,813	223,405	227,765	226,064

Sources: Housing Finance, Council of Mortgage Lenders and DCLG website. Derived from the DoE/BSA 5% sample survey; from 1993 the wider Survey of Mortgage Lenders and from 2005 the Regulated Mortgage Survey.

Notes: The average prices are not adjusted for changes in the mix of properties mortgaged to building societies and other mortgage lenders. There is a discontinuity in the series between 1992 and 1993, due to the switch to the wider Survey of Mortgage Lenders. Data for England is for standard statistical regions.

Table 47b **Average regional house prices**

Mix-adjusted index (2002 Quarter 1 = 100)

Region	1970	1975	1980	1985	1990	1995	1996	1997	1998	1999	2000	2001	2002	2003	2004	2005	2006	2007	2008	2009
North	5.3	12.5	25.7	34.6	66.7	71.0	73.5	78.4	81.7	88.3	92.0	96.4	111.6	135.6	170.4	188.6	201.0	216.7	214.5	–
North East										87.7	91.4	95.2	42.6	137.9	173.9	191.0	203.9	218.6	215.5	200.7
Yorkshire & Humberside	4.4	10.8	22.3	31.8	67.4	68.6	70.7	74.5	77.0	81.7	85.8	92.2	111.5	134.3	163.3	179.4	194.1	209.6	205.6	190.7
North West	4.7	10.9	24.0	32.0	67.6	67.2	68.2	73.0	76.0	81.3	87.2	96.3	112.9	133.5	162.1	179.0	190.9	205.2	201.5	–
North West										82.6	88.3	96.6	112.6	133.0	161.7	178.9	190.7	205.4	202.0	188.5
East Midlands	4.2	10.3	21.0	30.5	63.2	60.0	63.3	66.1	72.0	74.8	83.0	92.1	115.1	141.0	160.8	169.9	175.8	188.0	182.8	168.2
West Midlands	4.4	10.2	21.0	27.1	60.2	59.5	61.2	64.9	69.8	75.3	85.0	92.5	112.6	132.8	153.4	163.1	170.8	181.3	176.6	164.8
East Anglia	3.8	9.2	18.9	27.8	54.6	49.8	50.0	54.7	61.8	65.3	78.1	84.8	110.2	130.2	142.6	147.4	153.6	167.0	163.9	–
East of England										68.9	81.0	90.4	110.3	129.9	139.2	143.4	149.2	162.8	161.6	148.1
Greater London	3.3	7.4	16.4	25.6	51.0	46.0	47.3	54.3	62.3	76.9	90.8	100.3	110.3	120.3	128.9	132.6	142.1	164.0	165.2	151.3
Rest of South East	3.7	8.6	18.4	27.6	54.5	47.9	50.1	55.7	63.9	71.3	85.1	94.6	110.4	127.8	135.8	139.1	145.3	160.2	159.7	–
South East										71.9	85.9	94.8	110.4	127.0	135.2	138.1	144.6	159.9	159.3	145.9
South West	3.7	9.1	19.7	27.5	54.6	49.8	51.9	56.2	62.4	69.5	81.0	91.6	113.1	133.4	147.5	152.7	160.5	175.4	171.8	158.1
Wales	4.8	11.0	22.5	31.7	63.8	62.4	65.2	68.9	72.2	77.9	82.2	91.9	110.7	133.2	165.4	184.3	197.7	213.9	209.5	192.3
Scotland	6.0	13.5	27.2	40.0	64.2	76.9	79.2	83.8	88.5	90.5	93.2	97.2	109.8	124.9	151.4	169.5	188.8	216.6	222.6	213.8
Northern Ireland	5.1	11.2	26.7	32.3	42.1	55.4	60.2	66.9	74.0	81.2	90.1	99.3	109.5	119.1	131.7	149.7	184.7	260.3	236.6	196.3
United Kingdom	4.0	9.4	20.0	28.8	57.4	54.8	56.7	62.0	68.8	76.7	87.7	95.1	111.2	128.7	143.9	151.8	161.4	179.0	177.3	163.5

Sources: Compendium of Housing Finance Statistics, Council of Mortgage Lenders, derived from the Regulated Mortgage Survey (and its predecessor surveys).

Notes: The indexes are adjusted for changes in the mix of properties mortgaged to building societies (to 1993) and mortgage lenders (subsequent years). This discontinuity has little impact on the mix-adjusted house price for the UK, but there is some variable impact on the regional indices. Data in England is for standard statistical regions from 1970; with data for government office regions from 1999 (names in italics). Standard and government office regions are identical for Yorkshire & Humberside, East and West Midlands, London and the South West. Where standard and government offices differ the government office region figures are shown immediately below the standard region they most resemble.

Table 48 **Median regional house prices for first-time buyers by size of dwelling in 2009**

£

Region	1 bedroom	2 bedrooms	3 bedrooms	4 bedrooms	5 bedrooms or more	All sizes
North East	77,000	94,000	117,725	170,000	237,500	110,000
Yorkshire & The Humber	80,000	100,000	121,000	170,000	220,000	116,000
North West	82,500	97,500	125,000	175,000	200,000	116,000
West Midlands	83,000	108,000	130,000	190,000	275,000	125,000
East Midlands	74,500	98,500	122,000	175,000	229,000	115,000
East	110,000	136,000	160,000	225,000	370,000	150,000
London	172,500	215,000	245,000	360,000	615,000	220,000
South East	123,000	158,000	183,000	275,000	457,500	170,000
South West	100,000	134,500	157,500	226,000	325,000	148,500
Wales	92,500	105,500	120,000	172,750	249,725	117,000
Scotland	95,000	110,000	130,000	201,000	285,000	115,000
Northern Ireland	86,500	101,000	122,500	180,000	250,000	125,000
United Kingdom	125,000	134,500	150,000	220,000	315,000	145,000

Sources: Department for Communities and Local Government; analysis commissioned from the sample Survey of Mortgage Lenders/Regulated Mortgage Survey.

Notes: Figures are for sales to first-time buyers, excluding sitting tenants. Cases where the number of rooms, rather than bedrooms, were reported are excluded. Figures for properties with one bedroom or five or more bedrooms may be unreliable, because of small sample sizes.

Table 49 **Average regional mortgage repayments**

£ per week

Region	1980	1985	1986	1987	1988	1989	1990	1991	1992	1993	1994	1995	1996	1997	1998	1999	2000
North	16.30	21.27	26.07	28.81	28.29	33.50	40.14	44.34	38.81	35.37	34.59	40.92	42.17	47.43	58.64	50.56	62.22
North West	15.48	23.13	25.42	29.51	26.54	35.20	45.05	49.68	46.91	37.93	41.86	43.70	49.91	53.30	58.55	56.69	65.68
Yorkshire & The Humber	14.14	24.22	25.45	25.28	26.46	33.24	42.97	47.49	44.24	37.22	40.34	44.51	43.78	47.25	62.04	53.01	61.85
West Midlands	18.82	25.85	27.49	29.00	29.92	40.46	46.92	51.46	48.42	43.46	41.16	48.85	48.79	57.44	65.69	69.23	72.70
East Midlands	15.89	22.32	25.77	25.06	30.72	39.21	50.30	48.34	54.41	42.61	43.62	49.01	48.47	52.93	61.68	57.72	69.53
East Anglia	19.63	27.13	31.49	35.89	38.80	50.50	61.83	50.36	55.22	50.56	47.24	52.55	57.57	55.05	66.56	60.29	80.65
London	23.00	38.48	43.53	51.86	56.37	79.66	89.56	89.35	78.70	76.05	71.56	67.16	74.31	86.49	97.83	105.08	124.31
South East	23.70	36.85	39.53	46.15	50.79	66.52	81.76	76.08	75.19	65.10	62.88	68.38	70.38	79.09	88.89	94.13	113.62
South West	18.58	28.29	32.41	35.47	38.79	49.46	67.80	62.97	61.97	47.11	51.09	49.92	53.02	59.56	64.85	68.99	73.76
Wales	17.74	24.07	27.26	29.57	27.15	37.63	49.79	43.37	42.37	42.65	33.64	43.87	50.52	54.28	58.73	52.43	56.60
Scotland	24.18	31.11	32.12	33.50	37.17	43.72	48.65	52.69	49.05	39.79	40.17	42.17	47.74	51.70	58.65	56.52	71.61
Northern Ireland	18.00	27.61	23.36	24.69	26.36	42.20	36.89	44.09	35.01	32.15	27.47	37.64	32.66	41.17	44.17	44.14	51.79
United Kingdom	19.50	29.07	31.94	35.81	37.83	49.82	60.39	60.27	57.65	49.49	49.04	52.47	56.13	61.69	70.78	70.68	83.20

Sources: Family Expenditure Surveys; Office for National Statistics. Data for years to 1992 extracted from FES database by Anthony Murphy, Northern Ireland Economic Research Centre.

Notes: Repayments include both capital and interest, and are the average for all home-buyers with outstanding mortgages. Endowment and life insurance premiums are not included. After 2000 this data is no longer available by standard statistical regions.

Table 50 **Average mortgage repayments including endowment payments**

£ per week

	1996/97	1997/98	1998/99	1999/00	2000/01	2001/02	2002/03	2003/04	2004/05	2005/06	2006	2007	2008
North East	54.39	59.62	70.10	62.14	73.90	76.78	73.74	61.85	78.65	68.41	78.51	86.27	107.38
North West	59.07	62.62	69.22	66.30	77.03	79.61	83.03	85.08	89.03	84.06	91.24	93.92	110.68
Yorkshire & The Humber	53.89	56.69	72.19	61.99	72.61	72.98	67.99	80.67	86.34	90.55	87.74	99.72	94.82
West Midlands	58.74	70.02	76.97	80.83	86.16	86.20	82.11	99.19	89.48	110.48	101.31	106.77	112.25
East Midlands	58.48	63.49	71.46	67.85	79.35	91.01	85.87	92.01	91.59	97.04	106.60	96.16	100.59
East	73.83	72.43	89.49	89.24	109.61	109.73	115.58	122.32	117.86	123.97	126.17	130.48	138.58
London	87.40	99.81	111.19	118.10	136.34	141.12	138.60	141.97	131.20	136.36	147.15	173.30	183.77
South East	87.10	95.75	106.10	112.54	133.43	124.80	133.34	127.88	125.06	144.78	148.13	134.33	165.01
South West	63.05	72.99	76.84	81.21	87.11	101.40	101.49	116.37	99.87	106.48	104.07	116.74	116.60
England	68.61	75.55	85.15	85.98	98.59	101.65	101.79	106.70	103.72	110.99	114.08	118.04	128.43
Wales	60.33	64.26	70.67	63.74	65.16	71.21	65.13	88.68	71.51	76.77	88.05	96.77	85.61
Scotland	58.83	64.71	69.31	69.49	83.78	78.37	76.96	79.86	80.70	84.81	93.07	97.57	96.12
Northern Ireland	41.46	50.16	55.95	51.53	56.97	51.83	70.57	70.61	52.81	79.15	91.53	74.30	90.33
United Kingdom	66.98	73.62	82.75	82.72	95.49	97.80	97.41	102.72	99.04	106.66	110.08	114.23	122.64

Sources: Family Expenditure Survey and Expenditure and Food Survey; Office for National Statistics.

Note: Repayments include capital, interest and endowment premiums, and are the average for all homebuyers with outstanding mortgages. From 2006 the reporting period for the Expenditure and Food Survey became the calendar year. For 2008, endowment premiums for North East England, London, Wales and Northern Ireland are based on fewer than 20 recording households, consequently their figures should be regarded with extra caution.

Table 51 Mortgage arrears and repossessions

Year	1980	1985	1990	1991	1992	1993	1994	1995	1996	1997	1998	1999	2000	2001	2002	2003	2004	2005	2006	2007	2008	2009
Number of mortgages at year end (000s)	6,210	7,717	9,415	9,815	9,922	10,137	10,410	10,521	10,637	10,738	10,821	10,987	11,177	11,251	11,368	11,452	11,515	11,608	11,746	11,852	11,667	11,401
Repossessions during year	3,480	19,300	43,900	75,500	68,600	58,600	49,200	49,400	42,600	32,800	33,900	29,900	22,900	18,200	12,000	8,500	8,200	14,500	21,000	25,900	40,000	47,700
Cases in mortgage arrears																						
12+ months arrears	–	13,100	36,100	91,700	147,000	151,800	117,100	85,200	67,000	45,200	34,900	29,500	20,800	19,700	16,500	12,600	11,000	15,000	15,700	15,300	29,500	65,300
6 - 12 months arrears	15,500	57,100	123,100	183,600	205,000	164,600	133,700	126,700	101,000	73,800	74,000	57,100	47,900	43,200	34,100	31,000	29,900	38,600	34,900	40,500	72,000	88,700
3 - 6 months arrears	–	–	–	–	–	193,700	169,100	177,900	139,300	117,800	129,100	96,700	95,300	81,400	66,600	55,800	60,500	69,400	64,900	71,700	117,400	106,600
3 - 5 months arrears	–	97,000	206,600	305,500	275,400	242,050	191,590	–	–	–	–	–	–	–	–	–	–	–	–	–	–	–
2 months arrears	–	140,000	237,500	269,800	207,800	198,400	135,840	–	–	–	–	–	–	–	–	–	–	–	–	–	–	–

Sources: Compendium of Housing Finance Statistics & Housing Finance, Council of Mortgage Lenders; Janet Ford, *Roof* (figures for 2 & 3-5 months arrears for years 1985 to 1994).

Notes: Properties taken into possession include those voluntarily surrendered. The CML 3-6, 6-12 & 12+ months arrears figures are for the end of the year. The Janet Ford survey figures for 2 & 3-5 months arrears are for March of the year. Her survey of mortgage arrears figures has now been discontinued from publication following the introduction of the CML 3-6 months arrears series. Changes in the mortgage rate have the effect of changing monthly repayments and hence the number of months in arrears which a given amount represents.

Table 52 Court actions for mortgage repossessions in England and Wales

Year & Quarter	2005				2006[1]				2007[1]				2008[1]				2009[1]				2010
	Q1	Q2	Q3	Q4	Q1[1]	Q2	Q3	Q4	Q1[1]	Q2	Q3	Q4	Q1[1]	Q2	Q3	Q4	Q1	Q2	Q3	Q4	Q1
Actions entered	25,870	28,475	29,990	31,019	33,246	32,989	34,445	30,578	34,818	33,189	34,977	34,741	40,873	39,072	38,047	24,749	23,968	26,419	24,938	18,208	18,487
Suspended orders	7,915	9,774	10,342	9,667	21,297	21,475	23,296	21,950	22,578	21,695	23,391	22,990	26,199	29,586	29,284	26,694	16,522	19,042	21,115	15,556	13,908
Orders made	6,126	8,550	9,352	9,118																	

Source: Mortgage possession statistics, Lord Chancellor's Department, Department for Constitutional Affairs, Ministry of Justice.

Note: 1. From 2007, and for revisions of earlier figures, the published statistics no longer distinguish suspended orders from other orders made.

Table 53a **Court orders for mortgage repossession: actions entered 1990-1995**

Region	Numbers						Percentage of the total for England and Wales					
	1990	1991	1992	1993	1994	1995	1990	1991	1992	1993	1994	1995
North	4,943	6,917	6,064	4,639	3,742	3,762	3.4	3.7	4.3	4.0	4.3	4.3
Yorkshire & Humberside	10,434	14,146	10,280	8,447	7,619	7,402	7.2	7.6	7.2	7.3	8.7	8.4
East Midlands	11,036	13,468	10,110	7,672	6,045	6,456	7.6	7.2	7.1	6.6	6.9	7.3
East Anglia	5,558	6,237	5,012	3,884	2,974	2,816	3.8	3.3	3.5	3.3	3.4	3.2
Greater London	29,291	35,265	25,681	21,250	15,545	12,135	20.2	18.9	18.1	18.3	17.7	13.8
South East	35,673	44,610	33,780	27,698	19,896	18,650	24.5	23.9	23.8	23.8	22.6	21.2
South West	12,209	16,694	12,544	11,742	7,355	7,063	8.4	8.9	8.8	10.1	8.4	8.0
West Midlands	13,596	17,693	13,974	10,299	8,614	8,217	9.4	9.5	9.8	8.9	9.8	9.3
North West	14,974	21,384	17,158	14,103	11,726	12,325	10.3	11.5	12.1	12.1	13.3	14.0
Wales	7,636	10,235	7,588	6,447	4,442	5,344	5.3	5.5	5.3	5.5	5.1	6.1
England and Wales	145,350	186,649	142,191	116,181	87,958	84,170	100	100	100	100	100	100

Sources: Answers to Parliamentary Questions – 12/12/91 & 13/2/92; Mortgage possession statistics, Lord Chancellor's Department.

Table 53b **Court orders for mortgage repossession: suspended orders 1990-1995**

Region	Numbers						Percentage of the total for England and Wales					
	1990	1991	1992	1993	1994	1995	1990	1991	1992	1993	1994	1995
North	1,997	3,368	4,216	3,385	2,820	2,522	4.1	4.9	6.2	5.4	6.2	5.5
Yorkshire & Humberside	3,002	5,103	4,763	4,540	3,154	3,604	6.2	7.4	7.0	7.3	6.9	7.9
East Midlands	3,610	4,480	4,946	4,233	3,185	3,273	7.4	6.5	7.2	6.8	7.0	7.2
East Anglia	1,420	1,991	1,752	2,237	1,291	1,222	2.9	2.9	2.6	3.6	2.8	2.7
Greater London	12,076	13,051	12,444	10,640	8,399	6,705	24.8	18.9	18.2	17.1	18.4	14.7
South East	11,112	17,223	16,832	15,154	10,797	10,696	22.8	24.9	24.6	24.3	23.7	23.5
South West	3,406	5,786	5,182	5,189	3,473	3,428	7.0	8.4	7.6	8.3	7.6	7.5
West Midlands	4,456	6,475	6,384	5,488	4,372	4,223	9.1	9.4	9.3	8.8	9.6	9.3
North West	5,329	8,112	8,123	7,802	5,800	6,347	10.9	11.7	11.9	12.5	12.7	13.9
Wales	2,382	3,457	3,673	3,598	2,253	2,703	4.9	5.0	5.4	5.8	4.9	5.9
England and Wales	48,790	69,046	68,315	62,266	45,544	44,723	100	100	100	100	100	100

Source: As Table 53a.

Table 53c **Court orders for mortgage repossession: orders made 1990-1995**

	Numbers						Percentage of the total for England and Wales					
Region	1990	1991	1992	1993	1994	1995	1990	1991	1992	1993	1994	1995
North	1,549	2,192	2,138	1,652	1,322	1,179	2.8	3.0	3.6	3.8	4.1	3.7
Yorkshire & Humberside	3,792	5,741	4,171	2,892	2,320	2,222	6.9	7.8	7.1	6.7	7.2	6.9
East Midlands	3,828	5,224	4,346	2,752	2,361	2,122	7.0	7.1	7.4	6.4	7.3	6.6
East Anglia	2,299	3,060	2,328	1,804	1,141	1,101	4.2	4.1	4.0	4.2	3.6	3.4
Greater London	11,146	14,400	11,409	8,825	6,797	6,046	20.4	19.5	19.4	20.5	21.2	18.8
South East	15,422	18,561	14,222	10,484	7,956	7,634	28.2	25.1	24.2	24.4	24.8	23.8
South West	4,812	6,468	5,085	4,056	2,537	2,419	8.8	8.8	8.7	9.4	7.9	7.5
West Midlands	4,582	6,940	5,235	3,358	2,600	2,365	8.4	9.4	8.9	7.8	8.1	7.4
North West	4,708	7,312	6,331	4,897	3,618	3,815	8.6	9.9	10.8	11.4	11.3	11.9
Wales	2,580	3,958	3,403	2,297	1,485	1,632	4.7	5.4	5.8	5.3	4.6	5.1
England and Wales	54,718	73,856	58,668	43,017	32,137	30,535	100	100	100	100	100	100

Sources: As Table 53a.

Table 53d **Court orders for mortgage repossession: actions entered 1996-2009**

	Numbers														Percentage of the total for England and Wales			
Region	1996	1997	1998	1999	2000	2001	2002	2003	2004	2005	2006	2007	2008	2009	1996	2000	2005	2009
North East	3,493	3,015	4,298	4,191	4,037	3,426	3,107	3,077	3,468	5,580	7,083	8,073	8,526	5,762	4.4	5.5	4.8	6.2
Yorkshire & The Humber	7,649	6,881	8,209	8,082	7,766	6,958	6,150	5,994	6,624	10,187	11,967	13,753	14,691	10,051	9.6	10.6	8.8	10.7
East Midlands	5,861	4,928	6,383	6,788	5,669	5,414	4,714	4,856	5,778	8,667	10,168	10,751	11,394	7,257	7.3	7.8	7.5	7.8
East	8,268	6,672	8,498	7,342	6,167	5,507	5,362	6,408	7,856	11,285	12,038	12,422	12,768	8,404	10.4	8.5	9.8	9.0
London	11,389	9,181	11,365	9,996	8,158	7,367	8,707	10,706	13,535	21,160	21,863	20,090	19,470	12,932	14.3	11.2	18.3	13.8
South East	11,647	9,131	11,189	9,371	8,585	8,170	7,986	9,489	11,483	16,559	17,433	16,975	17,195	11,441	14.6	11.8	14.4	12.2
South West	6,412	5,690	7,251	7,000	5,154	4,364	4,081	4,565	5,414	7,853	8,514	8,601	9,427	6,334	8.0	7.1	6.8	6.8
West Midlands	7,578	6,691	8,095	9,483	9,748	7,569	6,275	7,381	8,622	12,188	14,764	16,176	16,446	9,958	9.5	13.4	10.6	10.6
North West	12,640	10,954	14,160	13,866	12,396	11,652	10,685	10,193	10,682	15,316	19,204	21,681	23,084	15,111	15.8	17.0	13.3	16.2
Wales	4,921	3,930	5,388	5,489	5,294	4,539	4,668	4,360	4,394	6,559	8,214	9,203	9,740	6,283	6.2	7.3	5.7	6.7
England and Wales	79,858	67,073	84,836	81,608	72,974	64,966	61,735	67,029	77,856	115,354	131,248	137,725	142,741	93,533	100	100	100	100

Source: Mortgage possession statistics, Ministry of Justice.
Note: Figures in Tables 53d, e & f are for government office regions; figures in Tables 53a, b & c are for standard statistical regions.

Table 53e Court orders for mortgage repossession: suspended orders 1996-2009

Region	Numbers														Percentage of the total for England and Wales			
	1996	1997	1998	1999	2000	2001	2002	2003	2004	2005	2006	2007	2008	2009	1996	2000	2005	2009
North East	2,045	1,577	2,298	2,325	1,882	1,598	1,224	1,230	1,237	1,820	2,561	2,523	3,105	1,966	4.7	5.9	4.8	6.0
Yorkshire & The Humber	3,844	3,471	4,300	4,087	3,664	3,180	2,451	2,240	2,374	3,472	4,200	4,136	5,400	3,305	8.9	11.6	9.2	10.0
East Midlands	3,036	2,563	3,085	2,774	2,436	2,421	1,798	1,806	2,060	2,848	3,262	3,431	3,978	2,359	7.0	7.7	7.6	7.2
East	4,030	2,982	3,891	3,475	2,462	2,212	1,967	2,198	2,606	3,759	3,868	3,511	4,614	2,991	9.3	7.8	10.0	9.1
London	6,435	4,659	5,327	4,493	3,081	2,651	2,703	3,170	3,911	6,428	6,681	5,783	6,928	4,985	14.8	9.7	17.0	15.1
South East	6,644	5,388	5,812	4,403	3,864	3,416	2,879	3,208	3,769	5,379	5,731	5,056	5,932	4,154	15.3	12.2	14.3	12.6
South West	3,280	2,730	3,035	2,831	2,339	1,797	1,662	1,613	1,834	2,667	2,789	2,479	3,501	2,058	7.6	7.4	7.1	6.2
West Midlands	3,839	3,368	3,757	4,054	3,652	3,481	2,526	2,805	3,062	4,246	5,031	4,974	6,349	3,541	8.8	11.5	11.3	10.7
North West	7,605	5,541	6,459	5,989	5,702	5,026	4,477	3,933	3,749	4,997	6,466	6,822	8,560	5,327	17.5	18.0	13.3	16.2
Wales	2,670	2,353	2,814	2,217	2,571	2,119	1,859	1,733	1,487	2,082	2,610	2,759	3,727	2,260	6.1	8.1	5.5	6.9
England and Wales	43,428	34,632	40,778	36,648	31,653	27,901	23,546	23,936	26,089	37,698	43,199	41,474	52,094	32,946	100	100	100	100

Source and note: As Table 53d.

Table 53f Court orders for mortgage repossession: orders made 1996-2009

Region	Numbers														Percentage of the total for England and Wales			
	1996	1997	1998	1999	2000	2001	2002	2003	2004	2005	2006	2007	2008	2009	1996	2000	2005	2009
North East	1,157	974	1,171	1,068	1,102	1,145	832	807	865	1,444	2,433	2,941	3,686	2,791	4.2	5.4	4.4	7.1
Yorkshire & The Humber	2,558	2,316	3,068	2,971	2,391	2,154	1,704	1,646	1,701	2,875	4,074	4,974	6,299	4,582	9.2	11.7	8.7	11.7
East Midlands	2,008	1,708	1,716	1,772	1,604	1,450	1,301	1,217	1,555	2,653	3,655	3,990	5,285	3,198	7.2	7.9	8.0	8.1
East	3,391	2,529	2,632	2,216	1,628	1,406	1,275	1,531	1,994	3,260	4,373	4,434	5,421	3,557	12.2	8.0	9.8	9.1
London	4,813	3,426	3,516	3,362	2,073	1,817	2,310	2,777	3,821	6,660	8,054	7,656	7,720	4,812	17.3	10.2	20.1	12.2
South East	3,968	3,120	3,410	2,709	2,621	1,934	1,822	2,183	2,900	4,663	5,566	5,969	6,512	4,568	14.3	12.9	14.1	11.6
South West	2,372	1,928	2,077	2,026	1,307	1,065	1,011	1,025	1,407	2,283	2,827	3,005	3,768	2,634	8.5	6.4	6.9	6.7
West Midlands	2,082	1,996	2,357	2,277	2,303	2,107	1,682	1,750	2,204	3,355	4,860	5,648	7,144	4,079	7.5	11.3	10.1	10.4
North West	4,039	3,254	3,670	3,685	3,714	3,377	3,016	2,679	2,738	4,135	6,317	7,525	9,803	6,506	14.5	18.2	12.5	16.6
Wales	1,387	1,273	1,660	1,460	1,644	1,367	1,249	1,131	1,135	1,818	2,660	3,038	4,031	2,562	5.0	8.1	5.5	6.5
England and Wales	27,775	22,524	25,277	23,546	20,387	17,822	16,202	16,746	20,320	33,146	44,819	49,180	59,669	39,289	100	100	100	100

Source and note: As Table 53d.

Table 54a Types of letting in the private rented sector

Thousands

Type of letting	Exclusive of non-private lodgers			Inclusive of non-private lodgers														
	1988	1990	1993/94	1993/94	1994/95	1995/96	1996/97	1997/98	1998/99	1999/00	2000/01	2001/02	2002/03	2003/04	2004/05	2005/06	2006/07	2007/08
Assured	–	360	375	378	367	374	331	321	254	275	213	272	384	221	254	306	310	340
Assured shorthold	–	140	825	826	877	945	1,074	1,165	1,223	1,241	1,221	1,233	1,129	1,481	1,584	1,730	1,781	1,864
Protected shorthold & pre-89 assured	60	40	–	–	–	–	–	–	–	–	–	–	–	–	–	–	–	–
All assured	60	540	1,199	1,204	1,244	1,319	1,406	1,486	1,478	1,517	1,434	1,505	1,514	1,702	1,838	2,036	2,091	2,204
Regulated, registered rent	470	320	245	245	172	167	128	121	107	79	62	66	67	59	59	48	56	–
Regulated, unregistered rent	600	270	162	162	139	105	114	84	81	75	60	51	59	81	67	68	84	–
All regulated	1,070	590	407	407	311	272	242	205	188	154	122	117	127	140	125	114	139	120
Not accessible to the public, rent paid	240	230	146	146	187	204	193	141	156	215	180	112	153	137	172	195	206	–
Not accessible to the public, rent free	270	250	230	230	244	223	223	208	231	229	202	196	201	212	187	167	183	–
All not accessible to the public	510	480	375	375	431	428	417	349	387	444	382	308	354	349	359	362	389	304
Resident landlord	110	90	73	158	181	209	198	178	169	151	192	162	176	164	186	135	144	127
Other	60	90	22	22	30	26	18	38	25	40	56	38	51	13	17	33	33	14
Total	1,810	1,790	2,077	2,166	2,197	2,254	2,280	2,255	2,247	2,305	2,186	2,129	2,221	2,368	2,526	2,681	2,796	2,770

Sources: Housing in England, 1996/97, 2000/01 & 2003/04, Office for National Statistics and Communities and Local Government.

Notes: 'Non-private lodgers' are lodgers who are members of owner-occupier or social rented sector households. Such lettings were not identified in the 1988 and 1990 surveys.

Lettings not accessible to the public include tied tenancies, lettings of student residences, and lettings at low rents to friends and relatives. Pre-1989 protected shorthold lettings have been grouped with the various forms of assured tenancies, but legally they are a form of regulated tenancy.

Table 54b Types of letting in the private rented sector

Percentages

Type of letting	Exclusive of non-private lodgers			Inclusive of non-private lodgers														
	1988	1990	1993/94	1993/94	1994/95	1995/96	1996/97	1997/98	1998/99	1999/00	2000/01	2001/02	2002/03	2003/04	2004/05	2005/06	2006/07	2007/08
Assured	–	20	18	17	17	17	15	14	11	12	10	13	17	9	10	11	11	12
Assured shorthold	–	8	40	38	40	42	47	52	54	54	56	58	51	63	63	65	64	67
Protected shorthold & pre-89 assured	4	2	–	–	–	–	–	–	–	–	–	–	–	–	–	–	–	–
All assured	4	30	58	56	57	59	62	66	66	66	66	71	68	72	73	76	75	80
Regulated, registered rent	26	18	12	11	8	7	6	5	5	3	3	3	3	2	2	2	2	–
Regulated, unregistered rent	33	15	8	8	8	8	5	4	4	3	3	2	3	3	3	3	3	–
All regulated	59	33	20	19	14	12	11	9	8	7	6	5	6	6	5	4	5	4
Not accessible to the public, rent paid	13	13	7	7	9	9	8	6	7	9	8	5	7	6	7	7	7	–
Not accessible to the public, rent free	15	14	11	11	11	10	10	9	10	10	9	9	9	9	7	6	7	–
All not accessible to the public	28	27	18	17	20	19	18	15	17	19	17	14	16	15	14	13	14	11
Resident landlord	6	4	4	7	8	9	9	8	8	7	9	8	8	7	7	5	5	5
No security	4	5	1	1	1	1	1	2	1	2	3	2	2	1	1	1	1	1
Total	100	100	100	100	100	100	100	100	100	100	100	100	100	100	100	100	100	100

Sources and Notes: See Table 54a.

Table 55 **Buy to let loans**

	1998	1999	2000	2001	2002	2003	2004	2005	2006	2007	2008	2009
Loans outstanding												
Number	28,700	73,200	120,300	185,000	275,500	417,500	576,700	699,400	835,900	1,025,500	1,157,000	1,223,000
Value (£m)	2,000	5,400	9,100	14,700	24,200	39,000	56,900	73,100	93,200	120,600	137,800	145,300
Average (£)	70,000	74,000	76,000	79,000	88,000	93,000	99,000	105,000	111,000	118,000	119,000	119,000
New gross lending												
Number	–	44,400	48,400	72,200	130,000	187,600	226,000	223,100	319,200	346,000	222,700	93,500
Value (£m)	–	3,100	3,900	6,900	12,200	19,200	22,700	24,500	37,000	44,600	27,200	8,500
Average (£)	–	70,000	81,000	96,000	94,000	102,000	100,000	110,000	116,000	129,000	122,000	91,000
Of which:												
New house purchases												
Number	–	–	–	–	85,030	117,120	143,870	120,460	170,830	183,300	102,810	55,780
Value (£m)	–	–	–	–	8,030	11,600	14,060	12,630	19,590	23,100	12,030	4,700
Average (£)	–	–	–	–	94,000	99,000	98,000	105,000	115,000	126,000	117,000	84,000
Remortgages & Other												
Number	–	–	–	–	44,970	70,480	82,130	102,640	148,370	162,700	119,890	37,740
Value (£m)	–	–	–	–	4,170	7,600	8,640	11,870	17,410	21,500	15,170	3,790
Average (£)	–	–	–	–	93,000	108,000	105,000	116,000	117,000	132,000	127,000	100,000
Mortgages 3+ months in arrears (%)	0.70	0.50	0.47	0.55	0.40	0.33	0.54	0.65	0.58	0.73	2.31	2.00

Source: Council of Mortgage Lenders.

Note: Loans outstanding are those at the end of each period. Lending figures have been grossed to cover all lenders and estimated where actual figures were not provided. Results for the years to 2004 may be compared over time but care should be taken with pre-2000 figures. There is a discontinuity from 2005 as an additonal large lender started to submit data from that time.

Section 3   Compendium of tables

Social housing expenditure plans

Table 56 **Territorial analysis of identifiable government expenditure in the UK**

£ million

	1985/86	1990/91	1991/92	1992/93	1993/94	1994/95	1995/96	1996/97	1997/98	1998/99	1999/00	2000/01	2001/02	2002/03	2003/04	2004/05	2005/06	2006/07	2007/08	2008/09	2009/10 plans
Housing expenditure (A)																					
England	3,099	3,549	4,314	4,791	3,905	3,890	3,620	3,396	2,708	3,274	2,756	3,495	4,152	3,485	4,441	5,821	7,788	8,488	9,516	11,181	12,266
Wales	135	323	345	425	388	383	397	359	297	281	212	206	253	287	294	281	405	467	509	644	562
Scotland	624	649	718	640	646	664	587	582	475	473	459	1,050	1,412	1,264	1,258	986	1,406	1,679	1,746	1,787	1,914
Northern Ireland	346	245	255	261	237	226	257	241	238	301	275	521	611	595	710	866	956	889	1,130	1309	1205
United Kingdom	4,204	4,766	5,631	6,117	5,177	5,164	4,861	4,579	3,718	4,330	3,702	5,270	6,428	5,631	6,702	7,955	10,555	11,523	12,902	14,921	15,947
All government expenditure (B)																					
England	84,557	124,499	143,581	160,448	170,116	178,402	189,320	193,280	193,971	203,221	215,318	229,425	255,696	274,196	300,093	322,385	342,903	358,076	379,399	409,516	435,222
Wales	5,565	8,495	9,367	11,438	11,982	12,549	13,334	13,678	13,801	14,327	15,036	16,004	17,460	19,023	20,636	21,626	23,027	24,164	25,309	27,563	28,243
Scotland	11,682	16,308	17,885	20,833	22,229	23,275	24,224	24,680	24,901	25,349	27,274	28,777	31,770	33,848	36,805	38,427	41,792	43,875	46,409	48,650	51,345
Northern Ireland	4,318	6,107	6,725	7,476	8,023	8,315	8,692	9,081	9,279	9,647	10,080	11,182	11,831	12,618	13,414	14,272	15,030	15,618	16,863	17,975	18,715
United Kingdom	106,122	155,410	177,558	200,195	212,351	222,541	235,570	240,719	241,953	252,544	267,709	285,387	316,758	339,685	370,949	396,711	422,762	441,734	467,981	503,704	533,525
Housing share of government expenditure (A/B) (percentages)																					
England	3.7	2.9	3.0	3.0	2.3	2.2	1.9	1.8	1.4	1.6	1.3	1.5	1.6	1.3	1.5	1.8	2.3	2.4	2.5	2.7	2.8
Wales	2.4	3.8	3.7	3.7	3.2	3.1	3.0	2.6	2.2	2.0	1.4	1.3	1.4	1.5	1.4	1.3	1.8	1.9	2.0	2.3	2.0
Scotland	5.3	4.0	4.0	3.1	2.9	2.9	2.4	2.4	1.9	1.9	1.7	3.6	4.4	3.7	3.4	2.6	3.4	3.8	3.8	3.7	3.7
Northern Ireland	8.0	4.0	3.8	3.5	3.0	2.7	3.0	2.7	2.6	3.1	2.7	4.7	5.2	4.7	5.3	6.1	6.4	5.7	6.7	7.3	6.4
United Kingdom	4.0	3.1	3.2	3.1	2.4	2.3	2.1	1.9	1.5	1.7	1.4	1.8	2.0	1.7	1.8	2.0	2.5	2.6	2.8	3.0	3.0

Sources: Public Expenditure Analyses, Cm 1520, Cm 1920, Cm 2219, Cm 2519, Cm 2821, Cm 3201, Cm 3601, Cm 3901, Cm 4201, Cm 4601, Cm 5101, Cm 5401, Cm 5901, Cm 6201, Cm 6521, Cm 6811, Cm 7091, HC489 & Cm7630, Cm7890.

Notes: Identifiable government expenditure is net of housing capital receipts, which are treated as 'negative expenditure' rather than income. Housing expenditure excludes housing benefit subsidy.

Table 57a **Gross social housing investment in Great Britain**

£ million (cash)

	1979/80	1980/81	1985/86	1986/87	1987/88	1988/89	1989/90	1990/91	1991/92	1992/93	1993/94	1994/95	1995/96	1996/97	1997/98	1998/99	1999/00	2000/01	2001/02	2002/03	2003/04	2004/05	2005/06	2006/07	2007/08	2008/09	2009/10
England	3,508	3,403	3,837	3,802	4,111	4,451	6,132	4,356	4,554	5,117	4,986	4,429	3,873	3,686	3,172	3,211	3,127	3,582	3,989	4,848	5,371	5,724	6,150	6,461	7,073	7,533	7,854
Wales	153	146	180	239	293	295	376	371	370	457	432	419	411	370	314	300	255	250	259	277	271	307	335	353	344	334	359
Scotland	382	477	594	649	829	895	894	867	855	895	929	976	945	737	585	610	625	639	690	731	682	857	966	1,086	1,100	1,037	1,279
Great Britain	4,043	4,026	4,611	4,690	5,233	5,641	7,402	5,594	5,779	6,469	6,347	5,824	5,229	4,793	4,071	4,121	4,007	4,471	4,938	5,856	6,325	6,888	7,451	7,900	8,517	8,904	9,492

Sources: See Tables 58, 63, 75, 76, 81 and 82.
Note: Figures exclude private finance. See source tables for further notes.

Table 57b **Gross social housing investment in Great Britain at constant prices**

£ million (2009/10 prices)

	1979/80	1980/81	1985/86	1986/87	1987/88	1988/89	1989/90	1990/91	1991/92	1992/93	1993/94	1994/95	1995/96	1996/97	1997/98	1998/99	1999/00	2000/01	2001/02	2002/03	2003/04	2004/05	2005/06	2006/07	2007/08	2008/09	2009/10
England	13,102	10,632	8,581	8,221	8,438	8,596	11,034	7,276	7,145	7,738	7,329	6,409	5,458	5,013	4,197	4,156	3,964	4,488	4,894	5,769	6,201	6,446	6,788	6,938	7,383	7,636	7,854
Wales	571	456	403	517	601	570	677	620	581	691	635	606	579	503	415	388	323	313	318	330	313	346	370	379	359	339	359
Scotland	1,427	1,490	1,328	1,403	1,702	1,728	1,609	1,448	1,341	1,353	1,366	1,412	1,332	1,002	774	789	793	801	847	870	788	965	1,067	1,166	1,148	1,051	1,279
Great Britain	15,100	12,579	10,312	10,141	10,741	10,894	13,320	9,344	9,067	9,782	9,329	8,427	7,369	6,519	5,386	5,334	5,080	5,602	6,059	6,969	7,302	7,757	8,225	8,483	8,889	9,025	9,492

Sources: See Tables 58, 63, 75, 76, 81 and 82.
Note: Figures exclude private finance. See source tables for further notes.

Table 58 **Local authority gross investment plans, including use of capital receipts and RCCOs, in Great Britain**

£ million

	1986/87	1990/91	1991/92	1992/93	1993/94	1994/95	1995/96	1996/97	1997/98	1998/99	1999/00	2000/01	2001/02	2002/03	2003/04	2004/05	2005/06	2006/07	2007/08	2008/09	2009/10
England																					
Capital provision	1,614	1,875	2,061	1,964	1,792	1,572	1,459	1,326	1,151	1,323	1,320	1,968	2,491	2,709	2,770	2,834	3,277	3,234	3,085	3,019	2,621
Local resources	1,380	1,245	746	751	1,273	1,235	1,138	1,192	1,249	1,190	1,086	811	619	1,119	715	1,153	1,307	1,273	1,923	1,882	1,634
Total	2,993	3,122	2,812	2,721	3,065	2,807	2,597	2,518	2,400	2,513	2,406	2,779	3,110	3,828	3,485	3,987	4,534	4,507	5,008	4,901	4,255
Wales																					
Capital provision	142	184	194	263	254	267	262	257	210	216	201	194	199	209	207	211	211	208	207	191	179
Local resources	45	71	43	21	37	25	43	14	33	17	-8	1	3	10	14	31	46	59	40	47	39
Total	187	255	238	283	292	292	305	271	243	233	193	195	202	219	221	242	258	267	247	238	217
Scotland																					
Borrowing and grants	312	322	311	268	286	310	300	245	232	239	216	227	255	237	239	200	217	261	222	299	470
Local resources	141	299	276	308	305	315	292	188	152	179	193	197	183	221	136	277	300	283	285	250	179
Total	453	621	587	576	591	625	592	433	384	418	410	424	438	457	374	477	517	544	508	549	649
Great Britain																					
Capital provision	2,068	2,381	2,566	2,500	2,331	2,140	2,021	1,828	1,593	1,778	1,737	2,389	2,945	3,155	3,216	3,245	3,705	3,703	3,514	3,509	3,270
Local resources	1,566	1,615	1,065	1,080	1,615	1,575	1,473	1,394	1,434	1,386	1,271	1,009	805	1,350	865	1,461	1,653	1,615	2,248	2,179	1,851
Total	3,634	3,996	3,631	3,580	3,946	3,715	3,484	3,222	3,027	3,164	3,009	3,398	3,750	4,504	4,080	4,706	5,309	5,318	5,763	5,688	5,121

Sources: See tables for local authority gross investment in each country, except for England 2008/09 and 2009/10 total figures only from Local Government Financial Statistics England 2010.

Notes: England split between capital provision and local resources estimated for 2008/09 and 2009/10 on basis of 2007/08 figures.

Capital provision includes all supported borrowing, and capital grants, including provision for the Estates Action and ALMO programmes in England. Local resources comprise the use of capital receipts and RCCOs (revenue contributions to capital outlay; in Scotland, capital funded from current revenue). Welsh capital provision figures include capital vired to Housing for Wales for local authority housing association schemes (for the years to 1997/98). Scottish figures for 1995/96 and 1996/97 exclude provision for transfers of existing new town stock. Scottish figures do not include new Community Ownership and the Fuel Poverty programmes introduced in 1999/00. Scottish figures for years from 1998/99 include estimated borrowing/capital receipts split for funding of non-HRA investment.

Table 59 **Housing associations' gross investment expenditure, including use of private finance, in Great Britain**

£ million

	1986/87	1987/88	1988/89	1989/90	1990/91	1991/92	1992/93	1993/94	1994/95	1995/96	1996/97	1997/98	1998/99	1999/00	2000/01	2001/02	2002/03	2003/04	2004/05	2005/06	2006/07	2007/08	2008/09	2009/10
England																								
Homes and Communities Agency	809	864	881	1,034	1,234	1,732	2,369	1,843	1,530	1,183	1,078	684	607	638	717	775	921	1,817	1,678	1,600	1,951	2,064	2,632	3,599
Local authority grants	145	156	128	308	193	179	286	388	331	354	327	363	335	328	400	410	499	249	69	–	–	–	–	–
Private finance	0	25	125	250	250	700	1,100	1,275	1,475	1,475	1,475	1,175	1,025	875	1,050	600	800	1,600	1,400	1,200	1,700	1,800	2,000	2750
Total	954	1,045	1,134	1,592	1,677	2,611	3,755	3,506	3,336	3,012	2,880	2,222	1,967	1,841	2,167	1,785	2,220	3,666	3,147	2,800	3,651	3,864	4,632	6,349
Wales																								
Welsh Assembly Gov't capital programme	52	63	66	73	102	115	163	131	122	100	92	66	68	68	55	58	55	52	65	78	86	96	96	142
Local authority grants	0	2	7	17	14	17	11	10	5	6	7	2	–	–	–	–	–	–	–	–	–	–	–	–
Private finance	0	8	8	22	33	53	73	70	68	76	75	45	42	42	36	36	34	32	46	56	63	70	70	104
Total	52	72	80	112	149	186	247	211	195	183	174	116	109	110	90	93	89	84	111	134	150	166	166	246
Scotland																								
Scottish Government capital programme	114	132	164	203	195	220	255	263	269	279	256	174	165	172	181	193	192	235	255	360	454	500	416	548
Local authority grants	–	–	–	–	11	8	3	10	–	–	–	–	–	–	–	–	–	–	–	–	–	–	–	–
Private finance	0	0	0	5	43	42	63	73	81	118	92	74	85	105	116	119	94	131	185	247	309	308	334	375
Total	114	132	164	208	249	271	321	346	350	397	348	248	250	277	297	312	286	366	440	607	763	808	750	923
Great Britain																								
HCA and government funding	975	1,059	1,111	1,310	1,531	2,067	2,787	2,237	1,921	1,562	1,426	924	840	878	953	1,026	1,168	2,104	1,998	2,038	2,491	2,660	3,144	4,289
Local authority grants	145	158	135	325	218	204	286	388	331	354	327	363	335	328	400	410	499	249	69	–	–	–	–	–
Private finance	0	33	133	277	326	795	1,236	1,418	1,624	1,669	1,642	1,294	1,152	1,022	1,202	755	928	1,763	1,631	1,503	2,072	2,178	2,404	3,229
Total	1,120	1,249	1,378	1,912	2,075	3,068	4,323	4,063	3,881	3,592	3,402	2,586	2,326	2,228	2,554	2,191	2,595	4,116	3,698	3,541	4,563	4,838	5,548	7,518

Sources: See Tables 62, 63, 64, 76 & 83. English private finance figures are authors' estimates based on grant levels and outturn grant rates.

Notes: English figures include HAG on deferred interest, but exclude expenditure under the rough sleepers, ERCF and other 'non-ADP' programmes. In Scotland and Wales, councils provided their funding for housing associations through Communities Scotland and the Welsh Assembly Government. Historic Scottish figures exclude provision for NLF repayments, expenditure on Scottish Homes' properties and 'GRO' grants to private developers.

The Homes and Communties Agency took over from the Housing Corporation as state funder of housing associations in England in 2008/09. The 2008/09 figures for England relate solely to the National Affordable Housing Programme. In Wales and Scotland housing association grant was formerly distributed via Housing For Wales and via Communities Scotland and Scottish Homes.

Table 60 **Receipts from council and new town house sales**

£ million

	1980/81	1981/82	1982/83	1983/84	1984/85	1985/86	1986/87	1987/88	1988/89	1989/90	1990/91	1991/92	1992/93	1993/94	1994/95	1995/96	1996/97	1997/98	1998/99	1999/00	2000/01	2001/02	2002/03	2003/04	2004/05	2005/06	2006/07	2007/08	2008/09	Cumulative total
England																														
Local authorities	655.9	1,240.7	1,768.7	1,316.4	1,107.7	1,061.1	1,237.4	1,697.2	2,652.5	2,700.4	1,616.3	1,089.2	841.4	1,022.9	945.6	670.7	732.7	923.5	911.0	1,374.0	1,426.0	1,566.0	2,210.0	2,936.0	2,575.0	1,544.0	1,145.0	934.0	234.0	40,135.3
New towns	29.4	38.5	43.0	49.9	49.0	31.2	43.3	62.3	98.1	73.8	21.9	16.6	4.7	4.1	-	-	-	-	-	-	-	-	-	-	-	-	-	-	-	565.8
Total	685.3	1,279.2	1,811.7	1,366.3	1,156.7	1,092.3	1,280.7	1,759.5	2,750.6	2,774.2	1,638.2	1,105.8	846.1	1,027.0	945.6	670.7	732.7	923.5	911.0	1,374.0	1,426.0	1,566.0	2,210.0	2,936.0	2,575.0	1,544.0	1,145.0	934.0	234.0	40,701.1
Wales																														
Local authorities	12.1	92.3	111.0	61.4	45.4	43.3	54.4	58.7	113.2	151.9	72.1	50.1	41.8	45.6	49.3	38.9	35.1	48.8	42.9	61.4	62.1	63.9	96.1	169.6	138.3	76.7	64.8	46.0	15.9	1,963.1
New towns	2.3	4.7	10.2	4.5	3.4	3.2	0.3	0.5	1.1	1.1	1.2	1.0	0.8	0.8	0.5	0.6	-	-	-	-	-	-	-	-	-	-	-	-	-	36.2
Total	14.4	97.0	121.2	65.9	48.8	46.5	54.7	59.2	114.3	153.0	73.3	51.1	42.6	46.4	49.8	39.5	35.1	48.8	42.9	61.4	62.1	63.9	96.1	169.6	138.3	76.7	64.8	46.0	15.9	1,999.3
Scotland																														
Local authorities	23.7	61.3	101.3	121.3	116.0	104.8	116.4	166.3	254.3	300.6	256.7	239.3	251.4	237.0	244.3	186.6	196.2	228.0	193.7	214.4	215.4	221.2	309.0	272.1	274.8	285.4	257.1	235.2	127.6	5,811.4
New towns	12.2	16.5	15.5	22.4	21.3	16.3	19.6	26.2	29.2	48.2	37.0	25.4	22.7	25.0	29.2	21.0	3.7	-	-	-	-	-	-	-	-	-	-	-	-	391.4
Total	35.9	77.8	116.8	143.7	137.3	121.1	136.0	192.5	283.5	348.8	293.7	264.7	274.1	262.0	273.5	207.6	199.9	228.0	193.7	214.4	215.4	221.2	309.0	272.1	274.8	285.4	257.1	235.2	127.6	6,202.8
Great Britain																														
Local authorities	691.7	1,394.3	1,981.0	1,499.1	1,269.1	1,209.2	1,408.2	1,922.2	3,020.0	3,152.9	1,945.1	1,378.6	1,134.6	1,305.5	1,239.2	896.2	964.0	1,200.3	1,147.6	1,649.8	1,703.5	1,851.1	2,615.1	3,377.7	2,988.1	1,906.1	1,466.9	1,215.2	377.5	47,909.8
New towns	43.9	59.7	68.7	76.8	73.7	50.7	63.2	89.0	128.4	123.1	60.1	43.0	28.2	29.9	29.7	21.6	3.7	-	-	-	-	-	-	-	-	-	-	-	-	993.4
Total	735.6	1,454.0	2,049.7	1,575.9	1,342.8	1,259.9	1,471.4	2,011.2	3,148.4	3,276.0	2,005.2	1,421.6	1,162.8	1,335.4	1,268.9	917.8	967.7	1,200.3	1,147.6	1,649.8	1,703.5	1,851.1	2,615.1	3,377.7	2,988.1	1,906.1	1,466.9	1,215.2	377.5	48,903.2

Sources: Housing Statistics, Department for Communities and Local Government; Welsh Housing Statistics, Welsh Assembly Government; Statistical Bulletin, Scottish Government.

Note: Receipts shown are the selling price of dwellings sold net of discounts. They comprise initial receipts plus the value of any mortgages granted by the local authority or new town.

Table 61 UK local authority housing revenue accounts[3]

£ million

	1970	1975	1980	1985	1990	1991	1992	1993	1994	1995	1996	1997	1998	1999	2000	2001	2002	2003	2004	2005	2006	2007	2008	2009
Income																								
Rent on dwellings:																								
Paid by tenants[1]	576	935	1,778	2,063	2,813	3,085	2,924	2,740	2,608	2,927	2,984	2,645	3,305	3,178	3,073	2,932	2,789	2,534	2,141	2,000	1,933	1,878	1,901	1,715
Rent rebates[1]	–	237	541	2,190	3,003	3,442	4,193	4,799	5,272	5,350	5,428	5,485	5,372	5,350	5,284	5,277	5,232	5,120	5,159	5,249	5,344	5,430	5,389	5,522
Rent on other properties	22	36	75	108	183	192	212	229	222	219	215	209	216	230	224	227	228	225	228	224	229	229	221	212
Subsidies:																								
Central government[2]	155	700	1,715	537	1,132	1,175	1,030	914	741	765	725	710	744	491	379	304	236	234	113	140	74	- 5	- 126	- 132
Local authorities[2]	96	213	516	578	129	–	–	1	–	–	3	1	1	16	21	9	17	18	23	30	25	19	18	24
Imputed	–	–	–	–	–	–	–	–	–	–	–	–	–	–	–	–	–	–	–	–	–	–	–	–
Other income[4]	6	13	133	393	409	419	400	402	393	372	368	374	506	489	450	586	665	765	718	704	731	814	884	1093
Total	896	2,134	4,758	5,869	7,669	8,313	8,759	9,085	9,236	9,633	9,723	9,424	10,144	9,754	9,431	9,335	9,167	8,896	8,382	8,347	8,336	8,365	8,287	8,434
Expenditure																								
Supervision and management	75	271	649	1,084	1,631	1,741	1,855	1,950	2,010	2,134	2,156	2,196	2,218	2,241	2,243	2,297	2,349	2,373	2,487	2,592	2,715	2,716	2,755	2,757
Repairs	135	370	1,015	1,558	2,253	2,373	2,491	2,563	2,540	2,737	2,755	2,761	2,771	2,678	2,615	2,505	2,431	2,329	2,233	2,263	2,307	2,232	2,246	2,273
Debt interest (net)	562	1,254	2,715	2,447	2,306	2,048	1,834	2,012	2,172	2,254	2,350	2,116	2,040	1,923	1,744	1,720	1,607	1,391	1,210	1,073	953	849	816	828
Capital repayments	100	161	306	449	591	603	1,021	996	864	800	1424	721	713	721	861	866	2,041	2,400	967	1,025	970	1,559	2,228	1,062
Other current expenditure	16	17	63	184	326	391	413	383	316	270	238	226	242	339	334	321	288	263	247	307	433	316	313	326
Balance	8	61	10	147	562	1,157	1,145	1,181	1,334	1,367	838	1,404	2,160	1,904	1,701	1,626	451	140	1,238	1,087	958	693	- 71	1,188
Total	896	2,134	4,758	5,869	7,669	8,313	8,759	9,085	9,236	9,633	9,723	9,424	10,144	9,754	9,431	9,335	9,167	8,896	8,382	8,347	8,336	8,365	8,287	8,434

Source: United Kingdom National Accounts (1980-2007 editions), Office for National Statistics.

Notes: 1. Prior to April 1983, supplementary benefit in respect of rent was generally paid direct to tenants. After that date it became housing benefit automatically paid direct to the local authority. As a result of that change those payments transfer from the rent paid by tenants to the rent rebate line. The rent rebate scheme was first introduced in 1972.

2. From April 1990, local authority subsidies were ended in England and Wales. Equivalent amounts were then included in the calculation of central government subsidy under transitional arrangements. Restrictions on local authority subsidies, leading to their phased reduction, applied from 1981/82 onwards in Scotland.

3. Figures in this table are derived from a different source than those for individual countries within the UK, and direct comparisons cannot be made.

4. The main components of this heading are: interest income, heating charges and other sources. These have all been increasing in recent years.

Table 62a Housing capital investment in England

£ million (cash)

	1980/81	1981/82	1982/83	1983/84	1984/85	1985/86	1986/87	1987/88	1988/89	1989/90	1990/91	1991/92	1992/93	1993/94	1994/95	1995/96	1996/97	1997/98	1998/99	1999/00	2000/01
Gross housing investment																					
Local authority investment:																					
+ New build & acquisitions	1,008	760	736	743	792	704	612	625	782	932	544	431	211	252	105	71	65	50	48	51	50
+ HRA stock renovation	670	620	962	1,148	1,280	1,315	1,521	1,742	1,904	2,953	1,721	1,483	1,561	1,710	1,708	1,550	1,452	1,436	1,557	1,496	1,746
+ Housing association	170	142	134	138	147	120	145	156	128	308	193	179	286	388	331	354	327	329	339	330	433
+ Private renovation	263	321	550	1,040	869	581	519	534	458	489	488	545	527	594	565	581	622	481	494	465	529
+ Homeownership	611	776	830	477	391	276	196	188	300	417	176	174	136	121	98	41	52	105	112	79	19
+ Urban programme	9	14	23	25	22	27	24	25	34	26	42	29	33	46	–	–	–	–	–	–	–
= Local authority total	2,729	2,633	3,235	3,571	3,501	3,023	3,017	3,270	3,604	5,124	3,164	2,841	2,754	3,111	2,807	2,597	2,518	2,400	2,550	2,420	2,777
+ New towns	165	115	71	85	81	56	40	50	46	39	32	27	18	12	17	20	–	–	–	–	–
+ Housing Corporation	508	521	755	734	697	711	715	752	791	935	1,232	1,732	2,369	1,843	1,530	1,183	1,078	684	607	638	717
+ HATS	–	–	–	–	–	–	–	–	–	–	–	10	27	78	92	93	90	89	90	83	86
+ Other	0	2	4	15	7	4	3	3	2	3	2	6	12	11	11	15	12	3	3	0	0
= Total gross investment (A)	3,403	3,271	4,065	4,405	4,286	3,794	3,775	4,077	4,444	6,100	4,430	4,616	5,181	5,055	4,457	3,908	3,698	3,176	3,250	3,141	3,580
Capital receipts																					
Local authority	1,037	1,684	2,491	2,156	1,941	1,838	2,034	2,369	3,423	3,319	2,395	1,549	1,432	1,830	1,542	1,324	1,073	1,290	1,608	2,082	1,997
+ New towns	19	38	63	84	88	64	98	143	226	207	111	195	47	166	61	68	–	–	–	–	–
+ Housing Corporation	13	29	76	110	86	101	129	117	139	125	78	93	63	48	43	31	540	671	4	0	6
+ Other	4	2	0	0	1	2	2	4	2	2	0	0	0	0	0	0	0	0	0	0	0
= Total capital receipts (B)	1,073	1,754	2,630	2,351	2,117	2,004	2,262	2,633	3,790	3,653	2,584	1,837	1,542	2,044	1,646	1,423	1,613	1,961	1,612	2,082	2,003
Net housing investment																					
Local authority	1,692	949	744	1,415	1,560	1,185	983	901	182	1,805	769	1,292	1,322	1,281	1,265	1,273	1,445	1,110	942	338	780
+ New towns	146	77	8	1	-7	-8	-58	-93	-180	-168	-79	-168	-29	-154	-44	-48	–	–	–	–	–
+ Housing Corporation	495	492	679	624	611	610	586	635	652	810	1,154	1,639	2,306	1,795	1,487	1,153	538	13	603	638	711
+ HATS	–	–	–	–	–	–	–	–	–	–	–	10	27	78	92	93	90	89	90	83	86
+ Other	-3	2	4	14	6	3	1	-1	0	1	2	6	12	11	11	15	22	–	–	–	–
+ Total net investment (A–B)	2,330	1,517	1,436	2,054	2,169	1,790	1,513	1,444	654	2,447	1,846	2,779	3,638	3,011	2,811	2,486	2,095	1,212	1,635	1,059	1,577

Sources: Public Expenditure Plans, Department of Transport, Local Government and the Regions.

Notes: Local authority capital receipts are shown gross of loans to purchasing council tenants, which are also included as expenditure in the homeownership row. Expenditure for the Housing Corporation for the years to 1989/90 excludes capitalised interest, capitalised interest, which has only been added to the Corporation's expenditure total since then. Local authority stock renovation includes the Estate Action programme.

Table 62b **Housing capital investment in England at constant prices**

£ million (2000/01 prices)

	1980/81	1981/82	1982/83	1983/84	1984/85	1985/86	1986/87	1987/88	1988/89	1989/90	1990/91	1991/92	1992/93	1993/94	1994/95	1995/96	1996/97	1997/98	1998/99	1999/00	2000/01
Gross housing investment																					
Local authority investment:																					
+ New build & acquisitions	2,451	1,688	1,529	1,477	1,495	1,221	1,007	962	1,124	1,242	684	525	251	295	120	78	72	54	50	52	50
+ HRA stock renovation	1,629	1,377	1,998	2,281	2,416	2,280	2,502	2,682	2,736	3,936	2,162	1,805	1,854	2,004	1,946	1,713	1,604	1,539	1,623	1,524	1,746
+ Housing association	413	315	278	274	278	208	238	240	184	411	242	218	340	455	377	391	361	353	353	336	433
+ Private renovation	640	713	1,142	2,066	1,641	1,007	854	822	658	652	613	663	626	696	644	642	687	516	515	474	529
+ Homeownership	1,486	1,724	1,724	948	738	479	322	289	431	556	221	212	162	142	112	45	57	113	117	80	19
+ Urban programme	22	31	48	50	42	47	39	38	49	35	53	35	39	54	0	0	0	0	0	0	0
= Local authority total	6,637	5,849	6,719	7,097	6,609	5,242	4,962	5,035	5,179	6,830	3,975	3,457	3,271	3,647	3,199	2,869	2,782	2,572	2,659	2,465	2,777
+ New towns	401	255	147	169	153	97	66	77	66	52	40	33	21	14	19	22	0	0	0	0	0
+ Housing Corporation	1,235	1,157	1,568	1,459	1,316	1,233	1,176	1,158	1,137	1,246	1,548	2,108	2,814	2,160	1,744	1,307	1,191	733	633	650	717
+ HATS	–	–	–	–	–	–	–	–	–	–	–	12	32	91	105	103	99	95	94	85	86
+ Other	0	4	8	30	13	7	5	5	3	4	3	7	14	13	13	17	13	3	3	0	0
= Total gross investment (A)	8,276	7,266	8,442	8,754	8,091	6,579	6,209	6,278	6,386	8,131	5,566	5,618	6,153	5,925	5,079	4,318	4,086	3,404	3,389	3,199	3,580
Capital receipts																					
Local authority	2,522	3,741	5,173	4,285	3,664	3,187	3,345	3,648	4,919	4,424	3,009	1,885	1,701	2,145	1,757	1,463	1,186	1,383	1,677	2,120	1,997
+ New towns	46	84	131	167	166	111	161	220	325	276	139	237	56	195	70	75	0	0	0	0	0
+ Housing Corporation	32	64	158	219	162	175	212	180	200	167	98	113	75	56	49	34	597	719	4	0	6
+ Other	10	4	0	0	2	3	3	6	3	3	0	0	0	0	0	0	0	0	0	0	0
= Total capital receipts (B)	2,609	3,896	5,462	4,672	3,997	3,475	3,720	4,055	5,446	4,869	3,247	2,236	1,831	2,396	1,876	1,572	1,782	2,102	1,681	2,120	2,003
Net housing investment																					
Local authority	4,115	2,108	1,545	2,812	2,945	2,055	1,617	1,387	262	2,406	966	1,572	1,570	1,502	1,442	1,406	1,597	1,190	982	344	780
+ New towns	355	171	17	2	- 13	- 14	- 95	- 143	- 259	- 224	- 99	- 204	- 34	- 181	- 50	- 53	0	0	0	0	0
+ Housing Corporation	1,204	1,093	1,410	1,240	1,153	1,058	964	978	937	1,080	1,450	1,995	2,739	2,104	1,695	1,274	594	14	629	650	711
+ HATS	–	–	–	–	–	–	–	–	–	–	–	12	32	91	105	103	99	95	94	85	86
+ Other	- 7	4	8	28	11	5	2	- 2	0	1	3	7	14	13	13	17	24	0	0	0	0
+ Total net investment (A–B)	5,666	3,370	2,982	4,082	4,095	3,104	2,488	2,224	940	3,262	2,319	3,382	4,321	3,529	3,203	2,747	2,315	1,299	1,705	1,079	1,577

Sources and Notes: As Table 62a.

Table 63 Housing capital provision in England

£ million

	1985/86 outturn	1986/87 outturn	1987/88 outturn	1988/89 outturn	1989/90 outturn	1990/91 outturn	1991/92 outturn	1992/93 outturn	1993/94 outturn	1994/95 outturn	1995/96 outturn	1996/97 outturn	1997/98 outturn	1998/99 outturn	1999/00 outturn	2000/01 outturn	2001/02 outturn	2002/03 outturn	2003/04 outturn	2004/05 outturn	2005/06 outturn	2006/07 outturn	2007/08 outturn
Housing Corporation/HCA																							
Gross (A)	841	809	864	881	1,034	1,234	1,732	2,369	1,843	1,530	1,183	1,078	684	607	638	717	775	921	1,817	1,678	1,600	1,951	2,064
– Capital receipts	105	132	124	143	127	78	93	63	48	43	31	40	17	4	3	6	3	5	18	20	25	34	59
– Mortgage portfolio receipts												500	654										
= Net Housing Corporation (B)	737	677	740	738	907	1,154	1,639	2,306	1,795	1,487	1,153	538	13	603	635	711	772	916	1,799	1,658	1,575	1,918	2,005
Local authorities																							
Supported borrowing	1,586	1,423	1,362	1,178	908	1,384	1,441	1,194	1,020	872	820	751	666	987	1,024	1,820	684	945	821	746	911	885	897
+ ALMO borrowing																		56	321	643	888	891	887
+ Major Repairs Allowance																	1,665	1,593	1,526	1,440	1,327	1,337	1,180
+ Capital grants	138	146	150	197	325	311	352	422	415	327	323	297	260	222	225	84	103	102	97	5	101	121	121
+ Estates Action		45	75	140	190	180	268	348	357	373	316	252	174	96	67	64	39	13	5	–	–	–	–
+ Estates Renewal Challenge Fund												26	51	18	4								
Total capital provision (C)	1,721	1,613	1,588	1,514	1,424	1,877	2,066	1,970	1,792	1,572	1,459	1,326	1,151	1,323	1,320	1,968	2,491	2,709	2,770	2,834	3,227	3,234	3,085
+ LA 'self-financed' expenditure	1,275	1,380	1,659	2,056	3,674	1,245	746	751	1,273	1,235	1,138	1,192	1,249	1,190	1,086	811	619	1,119	715	1,153	1,307	1,273	1,923
= Gross LA capital (D)	2,996	2,993	3,247	3,570	5,098	3,122	2,812	2,721	3,065	2,807	2,597	2,518	2,400	2,513	2,406	2,779	3,110	3,828	3,485	3,987	4,534	4,507	5,008
HATS (E)							10	27	78	92	93	90	88	90	83	86	104	99	69	59	16	3	1
Total central government capital provision (B+C+E)	2,458	2,290	2,328	2,252	2,331	3,031	3,715	4,303	3,666	3,151	2,705	1,954	1,252	2,017	2,038	2,765	3,367	3,764	4,638	4,551	4,818	5,155	5,091
Total gross capital (A+D+E)	3,837	3,802	4,111	4,451	6,132	4,356	4,554	5,117	4,986	4,429	3,873	3,686	3,172	3,210	3,127	3,582	3,989	4,848	5,371	5,724	6,150	6,461	7,073

Sources: Cm 5405, Office of the Deputy Prime Minister (and earlier equivalents). Local authority capital expenditure and receipts England 2008-09 Final Outturn, DCLG website.

Notes: Credit approvals are shown net of provision for the Estates Action Programme. This is shown separately, as from 1994/95 the programme was switched to the Single Regeneration Budget.

Capital grants include Gypsy site grant and other minor capital programmes. Table does not include PFI, or housing elements within the New Deal for Communities programme. For data for more recent years, see Commentary Chapter 4.

Table 64 **Homes and Communities Agency National Affordable Housing Programme** (formerly Housing Corporation Approved Development Programme)

£ million

Item	1991/92 outturn	1992/93 outturn	1993/94 outturn	1994/95 outturn	1995/96 outturn	1996/97 outturn	1997/98 outturn	1998/99 outturn	1999/00 outturn	2000/01 outturn	2001/02 outturn	2002/03 outturn	2003/04 outturn	2004/05 outturn	2005/06 outturn	2006/07 outturn	2007/08 outturn	2008/09 outturn	2009/10 outturn	2010/11 plans
Housing for rent	1,525	2,199	1,539	1,246	948	851	541	506	558	620	687	807	–	–	–	–	–	–	–	–
+ Housing for sale	87	124	290	280	234	216	160	115	79	97	88	114	–	–	–	–	–	–	–	–
+ HAG on deferred interest	118	45	14	3	1	1	0	0	0	0	0	0	–	–	–	–	–	–	–	–
+ Other capital expenditure	2	1	1	1	0	0	1	0	0	0	0	1	–	–	–	–	–	–	–	–
= Gross capital expenditure	1,732	2,369	1,843	1,530	1,183	1,068	702	621	638	717	775	921	1,818	1,654	1,599	1,951	2,064	2,620	3,599	4,541
– ADP/NAHP capital receipts	93	63	48	43	31	37	17	4	1	5	2	5	6	19	25	34	59	9	52	98
– Non-ADP/NAHP capital receipts						500	654		2	1	1									
= Net capital expenditure	1,639	2,306	1,795	1,487	1,153	531	31	617	634	711	772	916	1,811	1,635	1,574	1,918	2,005	2,610	3,547	4,443

Sources: Cms 1508, 3207, 3607 & 4204; Housing Corporation Investment Bulletins 1999 to 2004; The Housing Corporation; Homes and Communities Agency.

Notes: Housing for rent figures include major repairs, Mini-HAG, Rough Sleepers Initiative and City Challenge, but exclude ERCF. Housing for sale includes Purchase Grant from 1996/97.

Non-ADP receipts are loan receipts, including those, in 1996/97 and 1997/98, from the sale of the Housing Corporation loans portfolio. 2003/04 and 2004/05 figures include all Homeless Directive Initiatives, Starter Homes Initiative, Thames Gateway and Safer Communities programmes. They do not include Transitional Local Authority Social Housing Grant or Rent Restructuring Grant. Annual Accounts from 2003/04 to 2005/06 do not provide a split between grants for rent and grants for sale (other than through some designated sales schemes).

Table 65 **Housing Corporation planned revenue expenditure**

£ million

Item	1989/90 outturn	1990/91 outturn	1991/92 outturn	1992/93 outturn	1993/94 outturn	1994/95 outturn	1995/96 outturn	1996/97 outturn	1997/98 outturn	1998/99 outturn	1999/00 outturn	2000/01 outturn	2001/02 outturn	2002/03 outturn	2003/04 outturn	2004/05 outturn	2005/06 outturn	2006/07 outturn	2007/08 outturn
Supported Housing Management Grant	29	39	62	95	98	128	123	136	135	121	135	125	127	163	0	0	0	0	0
+ Other grants and subsidies	25	29	42	41	48	72	75	82	73	29	19	18	28	20	11	19	6	6	8
+ Running costs	20	24	25	28	30	31	31	32	29	28	30	31	34	36	37	42	44	45	47
= Total revenue expenditure	74	91	129	164	176	231	229	250	237	177	184	174	189	219	48	61	50	52	56

Sources: Cms 1508, 3207, 3607 & 3906, Housing Corporation. All figures from 1997/98 onwards are from the Housing Corporation.

Notes: Supported Housing Management Grant replaced Special Needs Management Allowance, which previously replaced Hostel Deficit Grant. 'Other grants and subsidies' includes the grants for Corporation Tax relief, Rough Sleepers Initiative, ERCF revenue funding, and Innovation and good practice grants.

Table 66a **Local authority housing capital expenditure in England by region**
£ million

Region	1993/94	1995/96	2000/01	2001/02	2002/03	2003/04	2004/05	2005/06	2006/07	2007/08	2008/09	2009/10	2010/11 planned	2011/12 proposed	2012/13 proposed
North East	163.6	154.9	160.8	182.2	191.5	231.2	274.2	344.8	381.6	383.3	292.7	376.2	389.2	256.0	151.1
Yorkshire & The Humber	270.3	272.7	277.7	323.8	351.9	369.2	535.7	707.9	682.2	700.1	679.8	582.0	606.4	309.4	289.4
North West	402.6	385.2	378.2	399.8	417.3	551.9	658.9	724.4	647.8	622.2	528.4	509.8	495.0	361.3	302.2
East Midlands	205.1	184.8	172.3	202.1	239.0	256.9	289.5	300.0	280.1	255.6	255.7	275.7	338.4	260.0	251.4
West Midlands	319.1	270.0	257.4	304.9	306.8	320.6	358.7	448.2	477.4	517.5	572.2	540.6	513.4	377.8	298.8
East	326.8	207.1	224.4	275.4	307.0	270.5	413.1	277.0	278.3	256.6	237.1	250.8	300.1	238.0	188.7
London	712.0	701.3	795.0	848.5	938.1	981.9	1,049.8	1,137.0	1,130.1	1,081.4	1,111.6	1,250.4	1,418.6	991.9	806.1
South East	364.6	353.5	321.0	375.0	439.9	298.1	314.8	317.9	298.3	319.9	328.9	340.9	374.1	326.4	256.7
South West	242.6	215.4	191.5	217.1	232.1	187.4	192.7	219.3	223.5	236.5	218.4	195.7	323.7	180.4	130.5
England	3,006.6	2,744.8	2,778.3	3,128.8	3,423.8	3,467.7	4,087.4	4,476.5	4,399.3	4,373.1	4,224.7	4,322.1	4,667.9	3,301.2	2,674.9

Table 66b **Local authority regional shares of housing capital expenditure in England**
Percentages

Region	1993/94	1995/96	2000/01	2001/02	2002/03	2003/04	2004/05	2005/06	2006/07	2007/08	2008/09	2009/10	2010/11	2011/12	2012/13
North East	5.4	5.6	5.8	5.8	5.6	6.7	6.7	7.7	8.7	8.8	6.9	8.7	8.3	7.8	5.6
Yorkshire & The Humber	9.0	9.9	10.0	10.3	10.3	10.6	13.1	15.8	15.5	16.0	16.1	13.5	13.0	9.4	10.8
North West	13.4	14.0	13.6	12.8	12.2	15.9	16.1	16.2	14.7	14.2	12.5	11.8	10.6	10.9	11.3
East Midlands	6.8	6.7	6.2	6.5	7.0	7.4	7.1	6.7	6.4	5.8	6.1	6.4	7.2	7.9	9.4
West Midlands	10.6	9.8	9.3	9.7	9.0	9.2	8.8	10.0	10.9	11.8	13.5	12.5	11.0	11.4	11.2
East	10.9	7.5	8.1	8.8	9.0	7.8	10.1	6.2	6.3	5.9	5.6	5.8	6.4	7.2	7.1
London	23.7	25.5	28.6	27.1	27.4	28.3	25.7	25.4	25.7	24.7	26.3	28.9	30.4	30.0	30.1
South East	11.5	11.8	11.6	12.0	12.8	8.6	7.7	7.1	6.8	7.3	7.8	7.9	8.0	9.9	9.6
South West	8.1	7.8	6.9	6.9	6.8	5.4	4.7	4.9	5.1	5.4	5.2	4.5	6.9	5.5	4.9
England	100.0	100.0	100.0	100.0	100.0	100.0	100.0	100.0	100.0	100.0	100.0	100.0	100.0	100.0	100.0

Sources: Housing Investment Programme data, Housing Strategy Statistical Appendixes, Department for Communities and Local Government.

Notes: Figures for 1993/94 relate to cash expenditure, while later years are accruals.

Table 67a **Area-based regeneration programmes of the 1980s and 1990s: dwellings completed or improved**

	1987/88	1988/89	1989/90	1990/91	1991/92	1992/93	1993/94	1994/95	1995/96	1996/97	1997/98	1998/99	1999/00	1987/88 to 1999/00	Five-year output	Lifetime outputs Rounds 1-5 forecast
Estate Action	47,000	79,400	63,700	49,500	62,600	69,200	66,000	46,178	26,313	20,239	10,997	6,956	–	548,083	–	–
City Challenge	–	–	–	–	–	–	–	–	26,038	28,989	13,277	–	–	–	110,154	–
Single Regeneration Budget	–	–	–	–	–	–	–	–	6,960	20,530	36,090	60,680	55,983	–	–	308,000
Total	47,000	79,400	63,700	49,500	62,600	69,200	66,000	46,178	59,311	69,758	60,364	67,636	55,983	548,083	110,154	308,000

Sources: Cms 1508, 1908, 2207, 2507, 2807, 3207, 3607, 3906, 4204, 4604 & 5105; Department of Transport, Local Government and the Regions.

Notes: The vast majority of homes enumerated here were improved rather than newly constructed under these programmes. The programmes were discontinued during the late 1990s.

Table 67b **English Partnerships**

Housing units facilitated	1999/00 actual	2000/01 actual	2001/02 actual	2002/03 actual	2003/04 actual	2004/05 actual	2005/06 actual	2006/07 actual	2007/08 actual
In-year outputs	2,858	3,800	1,638	1,456	1,903	2,518	3,182	4,248	6,632
Lifetime outputs from projects approved in year	4,450	7,000	1,950	3,504	–	–	–	–	–

Sources: Cm 5105; Corporate Plan 2001/02 to 2003/04, Annual Reports, English Partnerships.

Note: Lifetime outputs were not reported after 2002/03.

Table 68a **Large Scale Voluntary Transfers of council housing in England, 1988-2010**

Financial year	Dwellings	Gross transfer price (£m)	Transfer transactions			Loan facilities at transfer (£m)	Setup costs (£m)	Treasury levy (£m)
			Partial	Whole stock	All			
1988/89	11,176	98.4		2	2	130.7	2.9	–
1989/90	14,405	102.2		2	2	123.5	3.0	–
1990/91	45,552	414.4		11	11	708.4	21.9	–
1991/92	10,791	92.1		2	2	176.5	4.9	–
1992/93	26,325	238.0		4	4	319.0	12.2	–
1993/94	30,103	270.5	1	9	10	455.3	13.8	22.5
1994/95	40,234	403.0	4	8	12	741.9	22.0	52.9
1995/96	44,871	481.1	3	10	13	966.7	23.1	50.0
1996/97	22,248	192.5	1	4	5	419.5	10.8	9.6
1997/98	32,982	259.7	11	5	16	682.2	14.1	–
1998/99	73,900	483.9	14	10	24	1,239.3	20.6	–
1999/2000	97,385	658.7	13	13	26	1,512.4	48.6	58.3
2000/01	134,219	795.0	2	16	18	1,892.0	37.7	55.6
2001/02	35,390	377.7	1	7	8	647.5	15.7	56.3
2002/03	167,270	545.9	9	15	24	2,114.3	73.3	31.7
2003/04	38,635	140.8	3	7	10	409.5	16.5	81.0
2004/05	101,511	200.4	6	10	16	1,231.5	44.0	8.2
2005/06	46,653	114.8	11	8	19	807.0	15.3	9.4
2006/07	75,753	105.7	12	10	22	1,354.0	45.5	9.7
2007/08	93,594	244.1	13	18	31	3,183.9	38.8	31.2
2008/09	41,961	8.0	5	4	9	1,337.7	16.0	–
2009/10	23,575	5.6	3	3	6	447.7	8.9	0.7
Total	1,208,533	6,232.5	112	178	290	20,900.5	509.3	477.0

Source: Homes and Communities Agency stock transfers dataset.

Table 68b **Large Scale Voluntary Transfers of council housing in England with negative prices and/or overhanging debt, 1996-2010**

Financial year	Negative value transfers							Overhanging debt only (positve value transfers)					Total public funding (£m)		
	Dwellings	Transfer transactions			ERCF grant (£m)	Gap funding (£m)	Overhanging debt write-off (£m)	Dwellings	Transfer transactions			Overhanging debt write-off (£m)	Gap funding (incl. ERCF grant (£m))	Overhanging debt write-off (£m)	Total
		Partial	Whole stock	All					Partial	Whole stock	All				
1996/97	1,769	1	–	1				–	–	–	–				
1997/98	8,577	9	–	9	132.2			–	–	–	–		132.2	0.0	132.2
1998/99	19,022	13	–	13	151.2			–	–	–	–		151.2	0.0	151.2
1999/2000	16,980	10	–	10	207.0			5,330	–	1	1	21.0	207.0	21.0	228.0
2000/01	1,859	1	–	1				42,770	–	3	3	255.2	0.0	255.2	255.2
2002/03	17,179	7	–	7			108.7	98,280	–	6	6	439.5	0.0	548.2	548.2
2003/04	4,397	3	–	3				12,397	–	2	2	90.9	0.0	90.9	90.9
2004/05	9,759	5	1	6		17.0	101.8	73,506	1	5	6	489.7	17.0	591.5	608.5
2005/06	18,021	8	3	11		88.3	240.0	14,391	3	2	5	145.9	88.3	385.9	474.2
2006/07	37,226	11	3	14		174.1	449.1	18,052	1	4	5	96.7	174.1	545.8	719.9
2007/08	44,413	11	5	16		385.3	1,132.1	8,780	1	3	4	29.5	385.3	1,161.6	1,546.9
2008/09	30,175	4	2	6		230.5	476.6	9,660	1	1	2	47.8	230.5	524.5	755.0
2009/10	22,333	3	2	5		119.5	135.5	–	–	–	–		119.5	135.5	255.0
Total	231,710	86	16	102	490.4	1,014.7	2,643.9	283,166	7	27	34	1,616.2	1,505.1	4,260.1	5,765.2

Source: Homes and Communities Agency stock transfers dataset.

Note: Transfers completed prior to 1996 could proceed only if they were both positive value transactions and there was no overhanging debt remaining after payment of the transfer receipt. ERCF is the Estates Renewal Challenge Fund – see Table 63.

Table 69 **Local authority housing revenue accounts in England**

£ million

	1990/91	1991/92	1992/93	1993/94	1994/95	1995/96	1996/97	1997/98	1998/99	1999/00	2000/01	2001/02	2002/03	2003/04	2004/05	2005/06	2006/07	2007/08	2008/09
Income																			
Gross rent from dwellings	4,888	5,449	6,022	6,424	6,636	6,802	6,942	6,991	6,938	6,841	6,725	6,700	6,486	6,315	5,985	6,019	6,051	6,066	5,475
+ Other rents	164	169	190	205	190	188	180	179	178	188	189	194	194	192	188	189	189	186	161
+ Housing subsidy	3,486	3,687	3,958	4,059	4,069	3,853	3,790	3,634	3,298	3,041	2,769	4,053	3,860	3,730	770	884	791	698	492
+ Interest income	259	207	182	146	139	150	134	137	146	98	120	230	295	612	598	576	491	731	1,356
+ LA subsidy (sums directed)	1	3	2	1	4	3	3	5	7	9	9	5	18	20	24	31	24	18	21
+ Other income	323	419	323	339	350	341	353	348	360	337	475	530	569	704	615	662	659	738	855
= Total income	9,122	9,934	10,677	11,174	11,389	11,337	11,402	11,293	10,917	10,513	10,288	11,713	11,423	11,575	8,187	8,275	8,208	8,437	8,359
Expenditure																			
Supervision and management	1,471	1,594	1,683	1,781	1,833	1,817	1,873	1,900	1,964	1,950	2,317	2,002	2,029	2,099	2,225	2,317	2,381	2,385	2,148
+ Repairs	1,971	2,010	2,119	2,174	2,233	2,203	2,214	2,189	2,201	2,124	2,044	1,905	1,840	1,818	1,736	1,786	1,788	1,756	1,618
+ Revenue to capital	269	438	390	334	463	622	542	462	390	319	220	215	194	214	194	272	284	276	264
+ Charge for capital	2,707	2,461	2,437	2,515	2,488	2,270	2,219	2,204	2,149	2,011	1,871	3,377	3,297	3,395	3,072	3,013	2,903	3,091	4,245
+ Gross rebates	2,468	2,946	3,526	3,947	4,133	4,271	4,351	4,307	4,225	4,144	3,956	3,968	3,915	3,790	0	0	0	0	0
+ Transfers	23	21	39	18	22	34	62	55	68	77	94	76	54	51	681	627	670	696	681
+ Other expenditure	279	381	416	310	235	171	165	185	191	195	197	180	184	189	175	254	222	235	179
= Total expenditure	9,187	9,850	10,610	11,080	11,406	11,388	11,436	11,302	11,186	10,820	10,700	11,724	11,513	11,554	8,083	8,269	8,249	8,438	9,136
Balances																			
End of year balances	317	463	595	730	752	729	687	692	656	618	593	571	483	606	663	817	–	–	–
Changes in balances	- 66	131	143	106	7	- 55	- 43	- 8	- 67	- 56	- 14	- 12	- 90	20	- 10	- 5	–	–	–
Average number of dwellings (000s)	3,969	3,872	3,802	3,713	3,616	3,518	3,436	3,355	3,244	3,095	2,912	2,759	2,582	2,396	2,250	2,126	2,036	1,960	–

Source: Communities and Local Government, taken from local authority subsidy claim forms, grossed up for missing authorities.

Notes: Repair expenditure includes net transfers to repair accounts. Housing subsidy comprises basic housing subsidy plus housing benefit subsidy. For an analysis of housing subsidy see Table 70.

The total income and expenditure figures exclude balances. Figures for end of year balances, and changes in balances, do not tally as they reflect the revisions made in each year's subsidy claim forms.

From 2001/02 debt charges are shown under resource accounting conventions, and include provision for building depreciation. Stock figures are the average for the beginning and end of the year (the 2007/08 figure is an estimate).

From 2004/05 transfers represent negative housing susbidy for authorities contributing to the national subsidy pool. Net central government subsidy is the positive housing subsidy figure shown as income less the transfer figure shown as expenditure.

Table 70 **Rent 'surpluses', housing subsidy and housing benefit subsidy 1990-2004**

£ million

	1990/91 outturn	1991/92 outturn	1992/93 outturn	1993/94 outturn	1994/95 outturn	1995/96 outturn	1996/97 outturn	1997/98 outturn	1998/99 outturn	1999/00 outturn	2000/01 outturn	2001/02 estimate	2002/03 plans	2003/04 plans
Positive housing subsidy	1,357	1,156	1,003	827	777	644	666	657	539	485	445	983	943	952
− Rent 'surpluses'	201	283	495	706	885	1,051	1,146	1,220	1,320	1,417	1,453	581	640	650
= Net housing subsidy	1,156	873	508	121	-108	-408	-481	-563	-781	-932	-1,008	402	303	302
Gross rent rebates	2,505	2,877	3,453	4,005	4,250	4,431	4,455	4,345	4,151	4,035	3,920	3,936	4,019	3,915
− Rent 'surpluses'	201	283	495	706	885	1,051	1,146	1,220	1,320	1,417	1,453	581	640	650
= Net rebate subsidy	2,304	2,594	2,958	3,299	3,365	3,380	3,309	3,125	2,831	2,618	2,467	3,355	3,379	3,265
+ Positive housing subsidy	1,357	1,156	1,003	827	777	644	666	657	539	485	445	983	943	952
= Total HRA subsidy	3,661	3,750	3,961	4,126	4,142	4,023	3,975	3,783	3,370	3,103	2,912	4,388	4,322	4,217

Sources: Department of Local Government, Transport and the Regions Annual Reports, Cm 2807, Cm 3207, Cm 3607, Cm 3906, Cm 4204, Cm 4604, Cm 5105 & Cm 5405.

Notes: Rent surpluses are technically described as 'negative housing subsidy entitlements'. The increase in positive housing subsidy in 2001/02 was a consequence of the introduction of major repairs allowances. The subsidy system requiring notional rent surpluses to be set against the costs of rent rebates was abolished at the end of 2003/04.

Table 71a Global housing association accounts: balance sheet

£ million

	Associations with more than 250 properties							Associations with more than 1,000 properties				
	1999/00	2000/01	2001/02	2002/03	2003/04	2004/05	2005/06	2004/05	2005/06	2006/07	2007/08	2008/09
Fixed assets												
Housing properties at cost or valuation	46,512	50,889	52,700	58,331	63,228	67,893	74,033	64,156	70,295	77,426	85,164	94,567
− Capital grants	24,193	25,454	25,486	27,474	29,193	30,276	30,856	28,163	28,891	31,815	34,352	37,363
− Depreciation	219	425	618	742	937	1,188	1,378	1,121	1,304	1,624	1,963	2,376
= Net book value of housing properties	22,100	25,010	26,596	30,115	33,098	36,429	41,799	34,872	40,100	43,987	48,849	54,828
+ Other fixed assets	1,466	1,537	1,261	1,342	1,541	1,786	1,927	1,592	1,695	1,960	2,140	2,587
= Total fixed assets (A)	23,566	26,547	27,857	31,457	34,639	38,215	43,726	36,464	41,795	45,946	50,989	57,415
Current assets												
Cash & short term investments	1,633	1,905	1,630	1,388	1,664	1,418	1,357	1,164	1,081	1,342	1,445	1,953
+ Non-liquid current assets	127	255	261	376	620	692	1,097	656	1,077	1,432	2,421	3,035
+ Other current assets	820	1,330	1,423	2,104	2,305	2,649	2,158	1,698	1,918	2,212	3,063	3,266
= Total current assets (B)	2,580	3,490	3,314	3,868	4,589	4,759	4,612	3,518	4,076	4,986	6,929	8,254
Current liabilities												
Short term loans	259	350	273	362	386	370	569	325	519	512	743	539
+ Bank overdrafts	39	33	36	32	40	38	47	32	43	41	63	24
+ Other current liabilities	1,472	1,890	1,780	2,221	2,452	2,584	2,713	2,361	2,516	2,991	4,489	4,834
= Total current liabilities (C)	1,770	2,273	2,089	2,615	2,878	2,992	3,329	2,718	3,078	3,544	5,295	5,397
Total assets less current liabilities (A+B-C)	24,376	27,764	29,082	32,710	36,348	39,974	44,890	37,257	42,682	47,212	52,444	60,272
Long term creditors and provisions												
Long term loans	15,169	18,067	19,806	21,706	24,186	26,537	28,924	24,773	27,806	30,375	34,156	39,468
+ Other long term creditors	297	371	651	994	885	1,063	1,623	961	1,563	2,353	3,033	3,106
+ Provisions	37	99	91	152	462	544	787	538	781	911	849	1,227
= Total long term creditors and provisions (D)	15,503	18,537	20,548	22,852	25,533	28,144	31,334	26,272	30,150	33,639	38,038	43,801
Reserves												
Accumulated surplus	2,963	3,215	2,964	3,264	3,578	4,154	4,164	3,691	3,590	4,012	4,575	5,420
+ Designated and restricted reserves	1,888	1,961	1,457	1,448	1,525	1,362	1,425	1,131	1,182	1,313	1,304	1,184
+ Revaluation reserves	4,022	4,051	4,113	5,146	5,712	6,299	7,731	6,148	7,521	8,129	8,434	9,444
+ Pension reserves						15	236	15	239	119	92	58
= Total reserves (E)	8,873	9,227	8,534	9,858	10,815	11,830	13,556	10,985	12,532	13,573	14,406	16,106
Total loans, provisions and reserves (D+E)	24,376	27,764	29,082	32,710	36,348	39,974	44,890	37,257	42,682	47,212	52,444	59,907

Sources: 2009 Global Accounts of Housing Associations, Tenant Services Authority, 2009. Also 2001-2008 editions (Housing Corporation and TSA).

Note: Since 2007 the Global Accounts have been limited to the accounts of associations with more than 1,000 properties, while earlier editions were based on those with more than 250 properties.

Table 71b Global housing association accounts: income and expenditure account

£ million

	Associations with more than 250 properties							Associations with more than 1,000 properties				
	1999/00	2000/01	2001/02	2002/03	2003/04	2004/05	2005/06	2004/05	2005/06	2006/07	2007/08	2008/09
Income from social housing lettings												
+ Rents receivable, net of voids	3,742	4,272	4,513	5,050	5,569	6,028	6,588	5,726	6,289	6,774	7,403	8,234
+ Service charges	452	509	554	678	489	503	561	443	495	563	615	709
+ Charges for support services	0	0	0	53	234	235	220	194	181	166	214	208
+ Grants from local authorities and others	265	280	237	302	382	341	388	249	290	295	282	303
+ HC revenue grants	117	130	123	142	31	16	12	13	12	21	14	16
+ HC major repairs grants	9	13	19	15	15	15	16	12	14	19	21	14
= Total income from social housing lettings	4,585	5,204	5,446	6,240	6,720	7,138	7,785	6,637	7,281	7,839	8,548	9,484
+ Net income from other activities	- 38	- 41	- 11	8	32	6	21	1	12	17	30	- 1
+ Surplus on disposal of fixed assets	109	120	196	301	398	460	536	419	499	542	577	336
= Total income	4,656	5,283	5,631	6,549	7,150	7,604	8,342	7,057	7,792	8,397	9,155	9,819
Operating expenditure												
+ Management costs	916	1,116	1,121	1,318	1,372	1,451	1,601	1,321	1,470	1,658	1,913	2,087
+ Maintenance costs	849	1,049	1,256	1,466	1,675	1,686	1,806	1,610	1,738	1,868	2,042	2,308
Major repairs expenditure	449	451	429	527	676	860	1,041	832	1,024	1,044	1,146	1,218
+ Service costs	751	824	771	817	743	781	914	707	825	857	877	983
+ Care/support services	14	19	96	165	287	291	264	209	191	203	203	223
+ Other costs	376	509	504	668	698	749	824	710	771	813	821	1,021
= Total operating expenditure (A)	3,355	3,968	4,177	4,961	5,451	5,818	6,450	5,389	6,018	6,442	7,002	7,840
Interest and other income and expenditure												
Interest payable and other similar charges	1,150	1,315	1,356	1,394	1,439	1,589	1,671	1,515	1,610	1,727	1,957	2,083
− Interest receivable and other income	175	201	123	102	115	147	147	115	134	131	192	192
= Net interest payable (B)	975	1,114	1,233	1,292	1,324	1,442	1,524	1,400	1,476	1,596	1,765	1,891
Other charges (C)	53	67	13	46	99	- 100	48	- 96	49	88	60	- 118
Total expenditure including net interest charges (A+B+C)	4,383	5,149	5,423	6,299	6,874	7,160	8,022	6,693	7,543	8,126	8,827	9,613
Surplus for year before tax	273	134	208	250	276	444	320	364	249	271	328	206
− Tax payable (net of grants)	13	10	29	10	31	10	10	9	8	13	9	3
= Surplus for year after tax	260	124	179	240	245	434	310	364	241	257	319	203

Sources and note: As Table 71a.

Table 72 Rents and earnings in England

£ per week

	1980	1985	1990	1991	1992	1993	1994	1995	1996	1997	1998	1999	2000	2001	2002	2003	2004	2005	2006	2007	2008	2009
Local authorities:																						
Subsidy guideline	8.47	16.12	23.05	24.89	27.34	29.40	31.60	33.88	34.70	35.36	36.35	37.81	39.28	41.18	43.29	45.46	48.15	50.89	56.02	60.16	63.79	66.97
Average rent	7.70	15.54	23.74	27.29	30.57	33.62	35.68	38.31	40.13	41.17	42.25	43.83	45.62	47.87	49.93	51.02	52.90	55.27	57.94	61.63	64.21	66.05
Housing associations:																						
Fair rents	12.52	19.75	29.94	32.73	36.48	38.50	42.15	44.46	48.25	51.35	55.29	56.65	62.73	–	–	–	–	–	–	–	–	–
Assured rents			28.97	33.93	39.03	44.87	45.90	48.42	50.24	51.40	53.16	53.84	54.43	55.46	56.90	58.11	60.45	63.08	65.40	68.13	72.23	75.88
Private tenants:																						
Fair rents	11.18	18.11	29.21	32.02	36.13	38.92	42.73	45.63	50.71	53.69	58.75	60.77	66.52	–	–	–	–	–	–	–	–	–
Market rents			46.67	54.50	58.85	62.27	65.60	68.62	68.90	71.75	72.42	74.19	76.58	88.32	103.10	104.90	106.72	111.47	115.55	–	–	–
All lettings															112.31	122.17	123.48	126.85	135.12	133.27	149.89	–
Average earnings	110.70	172.10	266.70	288.30	308.10	320.90	330.10	340.60	356.00	372.70	389.90	405.40	426.20	451.50	471.70	483.40	515.50	527.70	548.00	561.10	586.40	598.30
Rents as a % earnings:																						
Local authority rents	7.0	9.0	8.9	9.5	9.9	10.5	10.8	11.2	11.3	11.0	10.8	10.8	10.7	10.6	10.6	10.6	10.3	10.5	10.6	11.0	10.9	11.0
H.A. fair rents	11.3	11.5	11.2	11.4	11.8	12.0	12.8	13.1	13.6	13.8	14.2	14.0	14.7	–	–	–	–	–	–	–	–	–
H.A. assured rents			10.9	11.8	12.7	14.0	13.9	14.2	14.1	13.8	13.6	13.3	12.8	12.3	12.1	12.0	11.7	12.0	11.9	12.1	12.3	12.7
Private fair rents	10.1	10.5	11.0	11.1	11.7	12.1	12.9	13.4	14.2	14.4	15.1	15.0	15.6	–	–	–	–	–	–	–	–	–
All private rents															23.8	25.3	24.0	24.0	24.7	23.8	25.6	

Sources: Cm 1908, Cms 288-II, Regional Trends, Determination of Reckonable Income 1988/89, Rent Officer Statistics, Answer to Parliamentary Question 26/7/93. Housing and Construction Statistics, Annual Survey of Hours and Earnings, CORE Quarterly Bulletin, Guide to Local Rents, DCLG. Housing association rents from 2004 are sourced direct from CORE general needs dataset.

Private rents from 2002 onwards for all types of lettings are from the Family Resources Survey.

Notes: Local authority average rents are for the April of each year; the guideline rents refer to the financial year. Housing association assured rents exclude service charges.

1988 housing association fair rents, and private fair and market rent figures are for the second quarter of the year. From 2004 housing association rent figures are for financial years. From 2006 the averages for housing association 'assured rents' include some secure tenancy rents.

Private market rents are those determined by the rent officer when referred for housing benefit purposes. Fair rent figures for 2001 onwards are not available.

Private sector rent figures from 2001 onwards are for financial years. The all lettings figures include rents for regulated as well as assured tenancies; but exlude rent free lettings. Earnings figures are average earnings for England for all adults in full-time work.

Table 73 **Average weekly local authority rents by region**

£ per week

	1988/89	1990/91	1995/96	1996/97	1997/98	1998/99	1999/00	2000/01	2001/02	2002/03	2003/04	2004/05	2005/06	2006/07	2007/08	2008/09	2009/10	2010/11	Increase 1988/89 to 2010/11
																			%
East	18.15	23.88	40.20	41.37	42.71	44.20	45.59	47.78	49.94	51.88	52.48	54.93	57.62	60.15	64.75	66.83	68.13	69.52	383.0
London	22.06	29.10	50.76	52.94	54.23	55.25	58.00	60.17	62.36	64.65	65.11	66.58	69.58	72.77	76.79	79.72	82.43	83.40	378.1
South East	20.11	27.18	44.40	45.96	47.05	48.36	50.55	51.97	53.98	56.34	57.59	59.41	61.61	63.98	67.91	70.83	72.99	74.15	368.7
West Midlands	18.61	23.78	35.34	37.03	37.96	38.83	39.82	41.31	44.68	46.67	47.43	49.28	51.59	54.11	57.32	59.54	61.47	63.27	340.0
South West	18.59	24.21	39.62	40.85	41.45	42.48	43.59	44.99	46.55	48.21	48.54	50.08	51.62	53.61	56.79	59.18	61.44	62.55	336.5
East Midlands	17.82	21.12	32.62	34.20	35.67	36.67	38.05	39.66	41.45	43.63	44.42	45.94	48.27	50.38	53.65	56.00	57.46	58.96	330.9
Yorkshire & The Humber	17.31	19.84	29.75	31.44	32.36	33.64	35.11	36.95	39.44	41.70	42.48	44.18	46.03	48.28	51.74	53.87	55.63	56.89	328.7
North West	18.09	21.98	35.25	37.70	38.38	39.49	40.57	42.24	44.20	45.83	46.53	47.29	48.97	50.79	53.60	55.63	57.19	58.51	323.4
North East	18.25	21.02	32.25	33.37	34.17	35.28	36.76	38.54	40.43	41.52	42.00	43.48	45.56	47.82	51.07	53.09	54.61	56.39	309.0
England	19.01	23.92	38.41	40.13	41.17	42.25	43.83	45.62	47.87	49.93	51.02	52.90	55.27	57.93	61.62	64.21	66.05	67.36	354.3

Source: Department for Communities and Local Government.

Notes: Rent figures from 1996/97 are for April, earlier figures are averages for the financial year. Figures for the North West up to 1998/99 are stock-weighted averages of the figures for Merseyside and the 'North West excluding Merseyside'.

Pre-2003/04 figures may include service charges.

Table 74 **Housing association and local authority rents in England, March 2009**

£ per week

Letting type & size of dwelling	North West	North East	Yorkshire & The Humber	West Midlands	East Midlands	East	London	South East	South West	England
Housing associations										
Net rents										
Bedsits	49.47	51.63	47.39	51.38	50.38	55.67	68.69	60.35	54.23	58.62
One bedroom	56.22	55.48	54.03	59.43	58.14	64.37	78.53	71.15	62.15	64.30
Two bedroom	63.32	60.90	61.39	67.19	67.08	74.66	89.59	83.08	71.81	72.54
Three bedroom	68.73	65.23	66.93	72.09	70.87	83.06	101.03	93.19	79.84	78.51
Four bedroom	75.33	70.14	77.61	82.55	78.95	92.88	112.09	103.11	88.80	91.07
Gross rents										
Bedsits	54.63	58.59	53.88	57.26	58.28	60.21	74.97	66.13	58.77	64.45
One bedroom	59.80	58.54	57.52	63.98	62.95	67.64	84.29	75.16	65.89	68.49
Two bedroom	65.20	62.33	63.37	69.94	68.83	76.37	95.59	85.99	73.72	75.27
Three bedroom	69.35	65.87	67.62	72.76	71.48	83.61	104.66	94.16	80.53	79.53
Four bedroom	76.06	70.70	78.85	83.35	79.84	93.75	115.61	104.39	89.74	92.64
Target rents										
Bedsits	50.03	50.22	47.56	50.39	49.02	56.92	74.91	60.39	53.53	60.56
One bedroom	56.54	55.54	55.13	58.41	57.60	65.20	85.23	71.26	61.87	65.81
Two bedroom	64.31	62.53	63.64	67.09	66.80	75.62	96.15	83.29	71.29	74.13
Three bedroom	71.98	69.15	70.36	75.35	74.14	85.76	108.25	94.85	80.41	81.75
Four bedroom	78.39	75.66	78.76	83.95	82.79	96.07	121.72	104.92	89.22	95.33
Local authorities										
Bedsits	42.13	43.56	43.14	46.30	43.68	49.58	61.11	52.79	45.03	53.40
One bedroom	50.26	47.74	48.54	52.88	49.80	57.60	69.50	61.74	51.92	56.84
Two bedroom	56.45	53.27	53.75	59.09	56.12	66.45	79.50	71.25	58.73	64.05
Three bedroom	62.09	57.96	58.30	67.06	60.61	75.10	90.30	80.71	67.16	70.32
Four bedroom	68.52	62.37	61.62	74.08	66.93	84.12	106.37	87.58	75.17	84.92

Source: Guide to local rents 2009, Cambridge Centre for Housing and Planning Research.

Notes: 1. Housing association target rents are set on the basis of local earnings and capital values. Current rents are being phased towards those levels. Gross rents are inclusive of service charges eligible for housing benefit.

2. Housing association rents are as of 31 March 2009. Local authority rents are estimates for the period 1 April 2009 to 31 March 2010.

Table 75 **Welsh housing capital expenditure**

£ million

	1981/82	1985/86	1990/91	1995/96	1996/97	1997/98	1998/99	1999/00	2000/01	2001/02	2002/03	2003/04	2004/05	2005/06	2006/07	2007/08	2008/09	2009/10
Gross investment																		
Local authorities:																		
HRA acquisitions and new build	44.5	26.2	20.4	11.1	17.6	5.6	7.4	11.1	7.3	11.2	10.5	12.0	10.6	9.6	9.8	5.4	10.0	7.4
+ HRA renovation	24.3	49.7	105.8	89.8	56.2	62.4	77.1	58.7	77.0	85.6	95.6	91.5	119.4	140.4	157.0	144.9	129.5	123.8
+ Enveloping and environmental works	0.3	4.8	26.2	18.3	15.8	15.5	14.8	14.0	11.6	15.0	15.7	26.1	28.7	31.1	25.2	25.3	29.3	26.1
+ Slum clearance	2.0	0.6	0.7	0.7	0.9	0.4	0.7	0.5	0.3	0.5	0.5	0.5	0.4	0.1	0.0	0.0	0.0	0.0
+ Low cost homeownership	0.6	0.4	3.4	7.3	8.8	12.4	5.9	1.1	0.9	0.9	0.0	0.0	0.0	0.3	0.1	0.3	4.7	3.4
+ Improvement grants etc.	18.5	55.3	93.5	177.3	171.7	146.4	126.7	107.8	97.6	88.5	96.9	90.6	83.2	76.0	74.9	71.3	64.6	56.6
+ Private housing loans	5.7	2.4	5.1	0.2	0.1	0.1	0.0	0.0	0.0	0.0	0.0	0.1	0.0	0.0	0.0	0.0	0.0	0.2
= Total local authorities	95.9	139.4	255.1	304.7	271.0	242.8	232.7	193.3	194.7	201.7	219.3	220.9	242.3	257.5	267.0	247.1	238.2	217.4
+ Housing associations	32.3	40.6	116.0	106.4	98.6	71.2	67.4	61.8	54.9	57.7	57.9	50.3	64.6	77.7	86.6	96.4	96.4	142.3
= Total gross investment (A)	128.2	180.0	371.1	411.1	369.6	314.0	300.1	255.1	249.6	259.4	277.2	271.2	306.9	335.2	353.6	343.5	334.6	359.7
Capital receipts:																		
Local authorities	65.5	72.0	87.2	50.6	49.3	56.5	52.4	69.1	70.1	68.5	102.3	176.2	147.7	88.2	75.2	54.9	15.9	7.3
+ Housing associations	1.0	3.8	9.5	6.5	6.7	5.5	2.4	–	–	–	–	–	–	–	–	–	–	–
= Total receipts (B)	66.5	75.8	96.7	57.1	56.0	63.0	54.8	69.1	70.1	68.5	102.3	176.2	147.7	88.2	75.2	54.9	15.9	7.3
Total net investment (A–B)	61.7	104.2	274.4	354.0	313.6	251.0	245.3	186.0	179.5	190.9	174.9	95.0	159.2	247.0	278.4	288.6	318.7	352.4

Sources: Welsh Housing Statistics, Welsh Office, Welsh Assembly Government. Local Government Finance Statistics (capital receipts), Welsh Assembly Government.

Notes: Following devolution, Housing for Wales was merged into the National Assembly for Wales, having taken over from the Housing Corporation from 1989/90. Housing association figures include credit approvals vired from Welsh local authorities. 'HRA acquisitions and newbuild etc.' includes other HRA; 'Improvement grants' includes other non-HRA. Since 1998/99 housing associations have retained sales receipts.

Table 76 **Welsh housing capital plans and investment**

£ million

	1986/87	1990/91	1991/92	1992/93	1993/94	1994/95	1995/96	1996/97	1997/98	1998/99	1999/00	2000/01	2001/02	2002/03	2003/04	2004/05	2005/06	2006/07	2007/08	2008/09	2009/10
Local authorities:																					
Capital provision	141.9	183.9	194.3	262.6	254.2	267.2	261.5	256.6	210.1	215.8	201.1	194.2	199.2	209.2	207.1	211.2	211.2	208.4	207.2	191.0	178.9
+ Net local financial resources	45.4	71.2	43.2	20.8	37.3	24.8	43.2	14.4	32.7	16.9	-7.8	0.5	2.5	10.1	13.8	31.1	46.3	58.2	39.9	46.7	38.6
= Gross investment (A)	187.3	255.1	237.5	283.4	291.5	292.0	304.7	271.0	242.8	232.7	193.3	194.7	201.7	219.3	220.9	242.3	257.5	266.6	247.1	237.7	217.5
+ MRA to transfer landlords (B)																		2.8	4.0	20.2	31.6
Housing associations:																					
Net provision	46.4	92.2	107.4	151.7	122.1	110.8	93.7	85.4	60.2	63.2	68.4	54.9	57.7	54.8	51.6	64.6	77.7	86.4	96.4	96.4	142.3
+ Local authority transfers	0.0	14.3	17.3	11.3	9.5	5.4	6.2	6.5	5.5	1.5	–	–	–	–	–	–	–	–	–	–	–
+ Capital receipts	5.1	9.5	7.8	10.9	9.3	10.8	6.5	6.7	5.5	2.7	–	–	–	–	–	–	–	–	–	–	–
= Gross provision	51.5	116.0	132.5	173.9	140.9	127.0	106.4	98.6	71.2	67.4	61.8	54.9	57.7	54.8	51.6	64.6	77.7	86.4	96.4	96.4	142.3
+ Private finance	0.0	33.0	53.0	73.4	70.4	67.8	76.2	75.1	45.0	42.0	38.0	35.5	35.7	34.0	32.0	46.0	56.0	63.0	70.0	70.0	90.0
= Gross investment (C)	51.5	149.0	185.5	247.3	211.3	194.8	182.6	173.7	116.2	109.4	99.8	90.4	93.4	88.8	83.6	110.6	133.7	149.6	166.4	166.4	232.3
Total gross investment (A+B+C)	238.8	404.1	423.0	530.7	502.8	486.8	487.3	444.7	359.0	342.1	293.1	285.1	295.1	308.1	304.5	352.9	391.2	419.0	417.5	424.3	481.4

Sources: Departmental reports by the Welsh Office; Cms 1916, 2215, 2515, 2815, 3215, 3615, 3915 & 4216, Welsh Housing Statistics, Welsh Assembly Government.

Notes: Local authority provision and investment figures for years to 1998/99 do not include credit approvals vired to Housing for Wales. Net local financial resources include the use of capital receipts and revenue contributions to capital outlay. They are also net of decisions by councils to use 'housing' credit approvals to finance investment in other services. For the years to 2007/08 net local financial resources are balancing figures between capital provision and outturn housing investment.

For 2009/10 they are a rounded estimate based on trends in available receipts and 'unsupported' prudential borrowing.

For the years to 2003/04 capital provision includes capital grants and credit approvals. From 2004/05 capital provsion includes capital grants, major repairs allowance (MRA) and indicative levels of supported prudential borrowing. 'Unsupported' prudential borrowing is included in net local financial resources. Housing association provision figures are outturn for years to 2006/07. Private finance figures are estimates.

Table 77 Welsh local authority housing revenue accounts

£ thousands

		1990/91	1991/92	1992/93	1993/94	1994/95	1995/96	1996/97	1997/98	1998/99	1999/00	2000/01	2001/02	2002/03	2003/04	2004/05	2005/06	2006/07	2007/08	2008/09	2009/10
Income:																					
Net rents from dwellings		115,295	123,899	124,512	123,746	125,355	129,612	128,193	130,283	132,839	134,434	131,811	130,329	124,326	127,277	–	–	–	–	–	–
Rent rebates	+	165,042	183,517	208,729	227,062	244,050	256,362	270,126	263,098	260,803	260,827	271,373	273,495	249,880	261,469	–	–	–	–	–	–
Total rent from dwellings	=	280,337	307,416	333,241	350,808	369,405	385,974	398,319	393,381	393,642	395,261	403,184	403,824	374,206	388,746	391,296	387,186	412,078	420,168	387,304	312,530
Rents from land etc.	+	2,934	3,407	3,674	3,813	3,851	3,861	3,606	4,404	4,850	4,463	4,290	5,545	4,932	5,264	5,394	5,080	5,318	4,698	4,663	3,341
Government subsidy	+	164,945	175,843	188,590	189,972	194,272	192,357	191,758	183,220	168,823	168,034	180,161	180,122	180,545	184,903	- 81,918	- 85,656	- 99,111	- 100,150	- 94,213	- 85,846
Supporting People services	+	–	–	–	–	–	–	–	–	–	–	–	–	–	–	5,998	5,415	5,850	6,185	4,274	3,972
Sums transferred into the HRA	+	5,854	86	136	118	113	108	97	94	98	99	107	98	96	75	31	31	0	0	0	0
Credit to the HRA	+	14,867	11,036	8,084	6,229	5,971	5,478	4,585	2,746	3,174	3,051	2,750	2,342	2,027	2,018	1,663	1,635	1,518	1,551	2,215	1,287
Other transfers	+	7,491	1,442	159	206	845	251	325	517	387	79	105	99	51	51	548	551	535	- 243	1,411	- 207
Other income	+	5,711	8,705	10,646	10,236	9,162	8,419	8,242	13,831	17,065	18,647	15,991	15,759	14,071	16,573	16,095	16,139	16,755	18,958	17,366	14,850
Credit balance from previous year	+	24,591	21,439	25,513	34,745	37,390	38,595	29,456	36,013	30,545	25,820	28,348	34,850	38,579	50,181	46,375	49,482	48,973	54,779	64,321	54,907
Total income	=	506,730	529,374	570,043	596,127	621,009	635,043	636,388	634,206	618,584	615,454	634,936	642,639	614,507	647,811	385,482	379,863	391,916	405,946	387,341	304,834
Expenditure:																					
Supervision & management		59,992	67,017	73,320	74,229	76,896	81,153	84,805	86,702	86,460	89,697	99,937	99,660	98,871	101,038	104,284	107,440	117,514	121,367	109,107	95,800
Repairs & maintenance	+	114,214	112,164	112,337	119,648	123,655	126,290	124,467	123,173	121,285	113,018	121,935	124,233	125,127	133,846	133,462	137,698	131,324	142,149	134,130	121,029
Supporting People services	+	–	–	–	–	–	–	–	–	–	–	–	–	–	6,199	5,635	5,127	4,675	4,720	4,392	
Expenditure for capital purposes	+	46,701	31,753	36,213	23,719	25,163	25,264	25,120	28,304	33,353	32,748	32,859	23,481	13,207	5,415	4,134	6,808	9,508	11,650	19,094	16,059
Capital financing charges	+	96,539	106,265	102,049	101,501	108,939	108,991	101,392	98,803	87,563	80,573	80,851	84,300	83,476	93,026	80,282	68,908	62,405	57,632	46,309	36,245
Other expenditure/transfers	+	2,803	2,586	2,650	7,535	3,711	3,149	3,075	4,519	3,917	6,420	4,071	5,341	6,074	7,360	7,306	7,717	10,938	11,456	10,551	7,920
Rent rebates	+	165,042	183,517	208,729	227,062	244,050	256,362	270,126	263,098	260,803	260,827	271,373	273,495	249,880	261,469	–	–	–	–	–	–
Debit balance from previous year	+	–	559	–	5,043	–	4,378	2,926	1,302	–	611	284	678	523	–	–	–	363	–	–	0
Balance at year end	+	21,439	25,513	34,745	37,390	38,595	29,456	24,477	28,837	25,556	31,747	28,888	32,437	37,977	44,397	46,581	45,550	48,610	59,099	65,575	61,705
Total expenditure	=	506,730	529,374	570,043	596,127	621,009	635,043	636,388	634,538	618,936	615,640	638,197	643,625	615,136	646,552	382,248	379,756	385,426	408,028	389,486	343,150

Source: Welsh Housing Statistics and Welsh Assembly Government.

Note: The 'notional' rent surpluses historically applied towards the cost of rent rebates are now transferred to the Welsh Assembly Government. In turn, the WAG budget is reduced each year to compensate HM Treasury for the contribution no longer made from rents toward the costs of rent rebates. Figures from 2004/05 onwards are estimates from 2nd Advance HRAS forms.

Table 78 **Housing subsidy and housing benefit subsidy in Wales 1990-2004**

£ million

	1990/91	1991/92	1992/93	1993/94	1994/95	1995/96	1996/97	1997/98	1998/99	1999/00	2000/01	2001/02	2002/03	2003/04
Basic housing subsidy:														
Positive entitlements	17.8	7.6	5.2	3.8	3.2	2.3	0.6	0.7	0.0	0.1	0.4	0.5	1.1	1.9
− Negative entitlements	10.5	17.4	25.5	41.2	54.2	69.7	76.5	80.8	91.8	93.1	87.8	87.2	91.9	83.7
= Net housing subsidy	7.3	- 9.8	- 20.3	- 37.4	- 51.0	- 67.4	- 75.9	- 80.1	- 91.8	- 93.0	- 87.4	- 86.7	- 90.8	- 81.8
Gross rent rebate subsidy	165.9	184.4	210.7	228.2	245.9	258.1	265.8	261.6	260.4	261.2	263.5	267.5	274.0	269.0
− Negative basic housing subsidy entitlements	10.5	17.4	25.5	41.2	54.2	69.7	76.5	80.8	91.8	93.1	87.8	85.6	91.9	83.7
= Net rent rebate subsidy	155.4	167.0	185.2	187.0	191.7	188.4	189.3	180.8	168.6	168.1	175.7	181.9	182.1	185.3
Combined housing subsidy	173.2	174.6	190.4	190.7	194.8	190.7	189.9	181.5	168.6	168.2	176.1	182.4	183.5	187.2

Source: National Assembly for Wales, derived from housing subsidy claims.

Notes: The combined housing subsidy is conventionally presented as the sum of positive basic housing subsidy entitlements and net rent rebate subsidy. Alternatively it could be expressed as the sum of net basic housing subsidy entitlements and gross rent rebate subsidy. This would make the role of negative housing subsidy entitlements more explicit.

Table 79 **Rents and earnings in Wales**

£ per week

	1981	1982	1983	1984	1985	1990	1991	1992	1993	1994	1995	1996	1997	1998	1999	2000	2001	2002	2003	2004	2005	2006	2007	2008	2009
Local authorities:																									
Subsidy guideline						22.98	24.73	27.31	29.12	31.31	33.58	34.50	35.24	36.21	37.47	38.94	40.93	42.36	43.72	45.51	47.59	49.77	52.57	55.82	58.67
Average rent	11.43	13.93	14.55	15.51	16.53	23.49	26.44	29.21	31.32	33.44	35.35	37.29	38.68	39.14	40.81	42.01	43.80	43.72	44.89	47.99	50.06	52.80	55.44	58.09	61.33
Housing associations:																									
Fair rents	13.53	15.19	16.17	17.77	18.67	30.08	32.02	34.60	35.37	38.52	40.08	42.71	44.75	46.68	–	–	–	–	–	–	–	–	–	–	–
Assured rents						30.73	34.64	39.55	42.51	43.43	42.16	42.44	41.87	42.47	43.59	–	–	–	–	–	–	–	–	–	–
All rents																45.17	46.26	48.07	49.61	51.15	52.99	55.21	58.23	62.06	65.40
Private renting:																									
Unfurnished fair rents	10.10	11.15	11.77	13.29	14.12	23.87	26.65	29.29	31.51	34.08	35.63	39.18	40.57	41.35	–	–	–	–	–	–	–	–	–	–	–
Unfurnished market rents						35.38	42.25	46.37	51.13	53.92	58.65	57.26	59.04	60.59	58.81	59.65	–	–	–	–	–	–	–	–	–
All private rents																75.08	73.85	78.45	83.91	109.44	97.09	99.73	–		
Average earnings	119.40	130.20	139.40	149.20	160.30	232.10	252.20	270.90	281.20	291.40	301.30	313.00	330.10	343.90	353.60	368.40	381.80	399.70	414.50	441.70	460.80	476.10	484.10	506.70	515.80
Rent as a % earnings:																									
Local authority rents	9.6	10.7	10.4	10.4	10.3	10.1	10.5	10.8	11.1	11.5	11.7	11.9	11.7	11.4	11.5	11.4	11.5	10.9	10.8	10.9	10.9	11.1	11.5	11.5	11.9
HA fair rents	11.3	11.7	11.6	11.9	11.6	13.0	12.7	12.8	12.6	13.2	13.3	13.6	13.6	13.6	–	–	–	–	–	–	–	–	–	–	–
HA assured rents						13.2	13.7	14.6	15.1	14.9	14.0	13.6	12.7	12.3	12.3	–	–	–	–	–	–	–	–	–	–
HA all rents																12.3	12.1	12.0	12.0	11.6	11.5	11.6	12.0	12.2	12.7
Private fair rents	8.5	8.6	8.4	8.9	8.8	10.3	10.6	10.8	11.2	11.7	11.8	12.5	12.3	12.0	–	–	–	–	–	–	–	–	–	–	–
Unfurnished market rents						15.2	16.8	17.1	18.2	18.5	19.5	18.3	17.9	17.6	16.6	16.2	–	–	–	–	–	–	–	–	–
All private market rents																18.8	17.8	17.8	18.2	23.0	20.1	19.7			

Sources: Welsh Assembly Government, Welsh Housing Statistics, Housing and Construction Statistics, Regional Trends, Rent Officer Statistics, New Earnings Surveys, Community Housing Cymru.
Private rent figures from 2002 are from the Family Resources Survey.

Notes: The housing association assured tenancy rents derived from the Welsh 'CORE' data are mean rents net of service charges for the financial year – the Welsh CORE system no longer operates. The housing association fair rent figures are inclusive of service charges and are derived from Housing and Construction Statistics and Rent Officer Statistics. Housing association 'all rent' figures are derived from Welsh Housing statistics, those for 2000 to 2002 are stock-weighted using 2001 Census data. Housing association fair rent and private rent figures for 1998 are for the second quarter of the year. Private market rents are those determined by the rent officer when referred for the purposes of housing benefit. These, and the private fair rent figures, are no longer published. Private rent figures for all lettings (except those that are rent free) are for financial years. Earnings figures are average earnings for Wales for all adults in full-time work.

Table 80 **Scottish gross housing investment**

£ million

	1980/81	1985/86	1990/91	1991/92	1992/93	1993/94	1994/95	1995/96	1996/97	1997/98	1998/99	1999/00	2000/01	2001/02	2002/03	2003/04	2004/05	2005/06	2006/07	2007/08	2008/09	2009/10
Cash	477	594	942	958	895	929	976	945	737	586	610	625	640	691	731	738	921	1,031	1,086	1,100	1,032	1,279
2009/10 prices	1,490	1,328	1,573	1,503	1,353	1,366	1,412	1,331	1,002	775	790	792	802	848	870	852	1,037	1,138	1,166	1,148	1,046	1,279
GDP deflator	32.0	44.7	59.9	63.7	66.1	68.0	69.1	71.0	73.5	75.6	77.3	78.9	79.8	81.5	84.0	86.6	88.8	90.6	93.1	95.8	98.7	100.0

Sources: Scottish Government outturn figures and returns from local authorities.

Notes: Gross outturn capital expenditure by local authorities, by new towns, and by the Scottish Government (historically, Communities Scotland and its predecessors). Includes estimates for the use of capital receipts and revenue for local authority capital investment. Excludes transfer payments for new town stock sold to local authorities, NLF repayments, corporation tax and housing association use of private finance. Excludes current expenditure.

Table 81 **Scottish housing investment by agency**

£ million

	1986/87	1990/91	1991/92	1992/93	1993/94	1994/95	1995/96	1996/97	1997/98	1998/99	1999/00	2000/01	2001/02	2002/03	2003/04	2004/05	2005/06	2006/07	2007/08	2008/09	2009/10 provisional
Gross investment:																					
Local authorities[1]	453	621	587	576	591	625	592	432	384	418	410	414	438	457	374	477	517	544	508	549	649
+ New towns	28	43	33	34	35	37	35	10	–	–	–	–	–	–	–	–	–	–	–	–	–
+ Housing Corporation	114																				
+ SSHA	54																				
+ Communities Scotland[2]		203	235	283	303	311	316	293	201	192	201	208	216	209	255	277	386	490	537	437	569
+ Other programmes[3]				2	1	3	1	1	1	0	14	18	37	65	109	167	128	52	55	46	61
= Total gross investment (A)	649	867	855	895	929	976	945	737	586	610	625	640	691	731	738	921	1,031	1,086	1,100	1,032	1,279
Capital receipts:																					
Local authorities[4]		297	270	293	284	290	252	166	71	62	67	62	65	67	70	181	204	198	190	124	61
+ New towns	26	47	36	4	5	7	7	6	4	–	–	–	–	–	–	–	–	–	–	–	–
+ Communities Scotland[2,5]		68	65	64	65	68	85	107	–	–	–	–	–	–	–	–	–	–	–	–	–
= Total capital receipts (B)	204	412	371	361	354	365	344	279	75	62	67	62	65	67	70	181	204	198	190	117	61
Loan repayments[6] (C)		10	132	254	4	2	2	2	2	2	2	2	2	2	2	–	–	–	–	–	–
= Net investment (A–B–C)	445	445	352	280	571	609	599	456	509	546	556	576	623	661	666	740	827	888	910	915	1,218

Sources: Scottish Government outturn figures and returns from local authorities.

Notes: 1. Gross local authority investment includes both HRA and non-HRA components (see Table 82). However, figures for 1995/96 and 1996/97 exclude £107 million and £83 million, respectively - sums associated with purchase of new town stock. These expenditures are also excluded from the new towns' capital receipts figures.

2. Scottish Homes prior to November 2001. From 1996/97 receipts were used to pay debts. Following the abolition of Communities Scotland in April 2008 the programme for 2008/09 was taken over by the Scottish Government for 2008/09.

3. This includes Fuel poverty and Community Ownership capital payments.

4. In 1996/97 Scottish authorities were required to set aside 25 per cent of gross capital receipts against HRA debt. In 1997/98 the set aside requirement was increased to 75 per cent. Set aside was then abolished in 2004/05.

5. 1988/89 receipt figure is for predecessor bodies.

6. Loan repayments from 2001/02 are extrapolations of previous years' figures.

Table 82 **Provision for local authority housing investment in Scotland**

£ million

	1984/85	1985/86	1990/91	1991/92	1992/93	1993/94	1994/95	1995/96	1996/97	1997/98	1998/99	1999/00	2000/01	2001/02	2002/03	2003/04	2004/05	2005/06	2006/07	2007/08	2008/09	2009/10 provisional	2010/11 forecast
HRA investment	254	291	492	476	449	471	490	469	339	320	352	345	351	367	401	312	364	427	462	453	501	606	647
Financed by:																							
Borrowing	121	169	200	205	145	171	182	184	157	172	177	156	168	188	184	180	94	133	184	150	240	410	432
Capital receipts	132	122	290	265	289	279	283	245	160	79	73	69	67	75	78	46	181	204	198	190	124	61	59
Revenue	1	–	2	6	15	21	25	40	22	69	102	120	126	104	139	86	89	90	80	92	123	115	124
Capital grants/ other																				21	14	20	32
Non-HRA investment	167	117	129	111	127	120	135	123	94	64	66	65	63	71	56	62	113	90	82	55	48	43	43
Financed by:																							
Borrowing	141	88	122	106	128	114	119	116	88	60	–	–	–	–	–	–	–	–	–	–	–	–	–
Capital receipts	26	29	7	5	4	5	7	7	6	4	–	–	–	–	–	–	–	–	–	–	–	–	–
Other initiatives:																							
Community Ownership												14	18	18	31	0	40	0	0	0	0	0	
Fuel Poverty[1]														18	34	53	63	63	52	55	51	61	

Sources: Scottish Office, Cms 2814, 3214, 3614, 3914 & 4215, Scottish Government outturn figures and returns from local authorities.

Notes: In 1996/97 Scottish authorities were required to set aside 25 per cent of gross capital receipts against HRA debt. In 1997/98 the set aside requirement was increased to 75 per cent. Set aside was then abolished in 2004/05.

Provision for non-HRA investment is now included within a combined local government services block. HRA borrowing figures for 1995/96 and 1996/97 include £107 and £83 million respectively for the purchase of new town stock. In 2003/04 non-HRA borrowing consent was replaced with grants for investment in private sector housing. For subsequent years they are a balancing figure between total HRA investment and other sources of funding. Capital receipts are for expenditure in the year; not newly available receipts.

Non-HRA investment figures from 2008/09 are for improvement grants expenditure only. The 'forecast' figure for 2010/11 is an estimate based on the previous year's figure.

Other initiatives: an element of the expenditure on Community Ownership is included in the Communities Scotland figure, and expenditure on Empty Homes and Rough Sleepers Initiative is included in the Communities Scotland line in Table 81.

1. Fuel Poverty figures include total spend, including Warm Deal and Central Heating Programme grant and, in 2010-11, the Home Insulation programme. The figure also includes fees and other ad-hoc contracts and payments, including the cost of monitoring and inspection of contracts and funding for Energy Action Scotland. Note that currently most of the programme is paid to the private sector rather than to local authorities.

Table 83 **Scottish Homes, Communities Scotland, Scottish Government capital grants and private finance for affordable housing development**
£ million

Programme	1989/90	1990/91	1991/92	1992/93	1993/94	1994/95	1995/96	1996/97	1997/98	1998/99	1999/00	2000/01	2001/02	2002/03	2003/04	2004/05	2005/06	2006/07	2007/08	2008/09	2009/10
Housing associations:																					
Capital programme (A)	202.6	194.8	220.4	255.1	263.1	268.6	278.5	255.5	173.8	165.1	171.7	181.1	193.4	191.5	234.6	255.3	359.5	454.3	500.4	415.6	547.8
+ Private finance (B)	5.4	42.9	42.3	62.5	72.5	81.4	118.0	92.4	73.8	85.0	105.3	116.2	118.9	93.9	131.3	145.4	223.8	296.7	296.8	319.4	356.1
= Total housing associations (Y)	208.0	237.7	262.7	317.6	335.6	350.0	396.5	347.9	247.6	250.1	283.0	297.3	312.3	285.4	365.9	400.7	583.3	751.0	797.2	735.0	903.9
Environmental etc. programmes (C)	–	–	–	11.7	11.1	9.4	8.6	7.9	5.5	6.6	7.8	7.7	10.4	8.6	9.5	9.9	17.7	29.0	32.0	17.8	16.6
Private developers (D)	2.0	8.1	14.6	15.8	28.4	33.1	29.2	29.9	21.4	20.2	21.9	18.7	11.7	8.6	11.2	11.5	9.2	6.3	5.0	3.3	4.5
+ Private finance (E)	4.5	37.0	44.8	68.5	76.0	102.7	90.0	98.9	63.6	78.6	93.2	50.7	6.7	35.2	63.8	39.7	22.9	12.0	11.1	14.2	18.7
= Total private developers (Z)	6.5	45.1	59.4	84.3	104.4	135.8	119.2	128.8	85.0	98.8	115.1	69.4	18.4	43.8	75.0	51.2	32.1	18.3	16.1	17.5	23.2
Total capital programme (A+C+D)	204.6	202.9	235.0	282.6	302.6	311.1	316.3	293.3	200.7	191.9	201.4	207.5	215.5	208.7	255.3	276.7	386.4	489.6	537.4	436.7	568.9
Total private finance (B+E)	9.9	79.9	87.1	131.0	148.5	184.1	208.0	191.3	137.4	163.6	198.5	166.9	125.6	129.1	195.1	185.1	246.7	308.7	307.9	333.6	374.8
Total capital investment (Y+C+Z)	214.5	282.8	322.1	413.6	451.1	495.2	524.3	484.6	338.1	355.5	405.9	374.4	341.1	337.8	371.9	372.9	633.1	798.3	845.3	770.3	943.7

Source: Scottish Homes Investment Bulletin, Scottish Homes, Communities Scotland, Scottish Government.

Notes: Grants to housing associations and private developers are for both rent and sale schemes. Capital programme figures exclude investment in Scottish Homes dwellings and PES transfers from Scottish local authorities. They also exclude revenue grants. For the years prior to 1992/93 separate figures for expenditure on private developer and other environmental and social programmes are not available, and they are both included in the private developers' figures.

Table 84 Scottish local authorities consolidated housing revenue account

£ million

Item	1987/88 outturn	1990/91 outturn	1995/96 outturn	1996/97 outturn	1997/98 outturn	1998/99 outturn	1999/00 outturn	2000/01 outturn	2001/02 outturn	2002/03 outturn	2003/04 outturn	2004/05 outturn	2005/06 outturn	2006/07 outturn	2007/08 outturn	2008/09 outturn	2009/10 outturn	2010/11 estimate
Expenditure:																		
Loan charges	429	519	501	502	479	452	415	392	375	308	238	217	206	196	189	185	187	223
+ Supervision & management	78	114	147	170	176	187	196	202	215	230	179	187	200	212	206	233	239	252
+ Repairs & maintenance	212	255	345	345	370	384	395	409	440	449	349	345	352	348	348	349	357	354
+ Capital funded from revenue	0	2	40	22	69	102	120	126	104	139	86	89	90	80	107	124	120	113
+ Other expenditure	23	44	45	87	49	51	61	65	70	79	63	61	63	64	62	55	53	53
= Total	743	934	1,078	1,126	1,143	1,176	1,186	1,194	1,204	1,205	915	899	911	899	912	945	956	995
Income:																		
Rental income	630	812	946	1,020	1,071	1,091	1,086	1,093	1,089	1,078	838	842	850	837	831	849	880	903
+ Housing support grant	42	58	22	19	16	13	10	10	9	10	8	9	8	6	6	6	6	5
+ General fund contribution	41	8	- 3	- 2	0	- 21	- 10	- 5	- 3	- 8	- 2	- 2	- 7	- 22	- 3	- 1	- 1	0
+ Other income	31	60	78	67	58	63	67	65	87	95	62	58	68	80	67	77	71	72
= Total	744	939	1,044	1,104	1,146	1,146	1,154	1,163	1,182	1,174	907	907	919	902	901	932	956	980

Source: Scottish Office Statistical Bulletins and Scottish Government.

Notes: Excludes balances brought and carried forward, and transfers to and from repair and renewals funds. General fund contributions are shown net of HRA transfers to general funds. Rental income relates to dwellings only; rents from garages etc. are included within other income.

Following stock transfer, 2003/04 and later figures exclude Glasgow, Dumfries and Galloway and Scottish Borders. From 2006/07 they exclude Argyll & Bute and Eilean Sinr, and from 2007/08 they exclude Inverclyde.

Table 85 Average costs, rents and subsidies in Scottish housing revenue accounts

	1980/81	1985/86	1990/91	1991/92	1992/93	1993/94	1994/95	1995/96	1996/97	1997/98	1998/99	1999/00	2000/01	2001/02	2002/03	2003/04	2004/05	2005/06	2006/07	2007/08	2008/09	2009/10
Average annual cost per house (£)	688	826	1,240	1,351	1,405	1,463	1,609	1,640	1,782	1,946	2,029	2,092	2,179	2,282	2,373	2,331	2,375	2,527	2,639	2,772	2,759	2,916
Percentage of costs met by:																						
Rents etc.	50	77	94	94	95	96	98	97	98	99	99	99	99	99	99	99	99	99	99	99	99	99
+ Housing support grant	37	9	6	6	5	4	2	3	2	1	1	1	1	1	1	1	1	1	1	1	1	1
+ General fund contributions	13	14	–	–	–	–	–	–	–	–	–	–	–	–	–	–	–	–	–	–	–	–
= Total	100	100	100	100	100	100	100	100	100	100	100	100	100	100	100	100	100	100	100	100	100	100

Sources: Convention of Scottish Local Authorities; Scottish Office Statistical Bulletins, Scottish Government.

Table 86 **Rents and earnings in Scotland**

	1981	1985	1990	1991	1992	1993	1994	1995	1996	1997	1998	1999	2000	2001	2002	2003	2004	2005	2006	2007	2008	2009
£ per week																						
Local authorities:																						
Subsidy assumption			21.30	23.97	26.36	30.32	34.86	37.48	38.60	39.38	40.56	41.77	42.61	43.67	44.77	45.88	47.03	49.41	50.65	51.91	54.93	56.30
Average rent	7.67	11.53	20.91	23.13	24.64	26.37	27.71	28.64	31.11	33.60	35.36	36.43	38.05	39.30	40.43	40.89	42.64	44.79	46.23	48.35	50.36	52.83
Housing associations:																						
Fair rents	9.38	18.79	26.37	24.35	26.69	28.60	31.78	34.35	36.38	37.15	39.40	40.01	43.00	45.52	47.12	–	–	–	–	–	–	–
Assured/SST rents			25.72	28.92	30.40	32.96	33.92	35.89	37.68	39.51	41.08	41.46	46.27	48.81	50.69	52.14	50.22	52.37	51.96	56.21	58.32	61.01
Private tenants:																						
Fair rents	8.06	15.17	23.53	25.76	29.60	29.18	–	–	35.67	37.57	40.87	41.70	42.49	–	–	–	–	–	–	–	–	–
Housing benefit rents									55.38	60.00	60.00	63.46	65.00	65.77	69.00	69.23	70.00	75.00	80.00	82.77	–	–
All private rents															78.98	79.72	91.56	96.52	96.46	108.77	104.35	
Average earnings (£ per week)	122.00	165.80	244.00	265.30	286.70	296.80	300.80	313.40	324.90	336.80	350.30	364.90	383.00	404.50	427.00	436.80	459.60	480.80	502.50	512.40	537.70	554.90
Rent as a % earnings:																						
Local authority rents	6.3	7.0	8.6	8.7	8.6	8.9	9.2	9.1	9.6	10.0	10.1	10.0	9.9	9.7	9.5	9.4	9.3	9.3	9.2	9.4	9.4	9.5
HA fair rents	7.7	11.3	10.8	9.2	9.3	9.6	10.6	11.0	11.2	11.0	11.2	11.0	11.2	11.3	11.0	–	–	–	–	–	–	–
HA assured/SST rents			10.5	10.9	10.6	11.1	11.3	11.5	11.6	11.7	11.7	11.4	12.1	12.1	11.9	11.9	10.9	10.9	10.3	11.0	10.8	11.0
Private fair rents	6.6	9.1	9.6	9.7	10.3	9.8	–	–	11.0	11.2	11.7	11.4	11.1	–	–	–	–	–	–	–	–	–
Private benefit rents									17.0	17.8	17.1	17.4	17.0	16.3	16.2	15.8	15.2	15.6	15.9	16.2	–	–
All private rents															18.5	18.3	19.9	20.1	19.2	21.2	19.4	

Sources: Housing and Construction Statistics, Regional Trends, New Earnings Surveys, Annual Survey of Hours and Earnings, Scottish Government, Communities Scotland, Joint Centre for Scottish Housing Research, Family Resources Survey.

Notes: Rent figures are for financial years (e.g. '2009'=2009/10). Earnings figures are for calendar years. Average local authority rents and the subsidy assumption rent levels (used to calculate Housing Support Grant) refer to the financial year; as from 2007/08 the only local authority receiving Housing Support Grant has been the Shetland Islands Council. The housing association assured and fair rent figures from 1990 onwards are derived from SCORE returns and are mean rents inclusive of service charges eligible for housing benefit. Earnings figures are average earnings for Scotland for all adults in full-time work. Housing benefit rents are the median appropriate rents for the calendar year. Scottish rent officer statistics for private sector fair rents, and the 'appropriate' rents in housing benefit cases, were not collated for 1994 or 1995. The private fair rents figures for the years to 1993 are for unfurnished lettings only. The fair and market rent figures from 1996 are for both furnished and unfurnished lettings. The all private rents figures from 2002 are for all lettings (except those that are rent free) and are for financial years.

Table 87 **Financial provision for housing in Northern Ireland**

£ million

	1985/86 outturn	1986/87 outturn	1987/88 outturn	1988/89 outturn	1989/90 outturn	1990/91 outturn	1991/92 outturn	1992/93 outturn	1993/94 outturn	1994/95 outturn	1995/96 outturn	1996/97 outturn	1997/98 outturn	1998/99 outturn	1999/00 outturn	2000/01 outturn	2001/02 outturn	2002/03 outturn	2003/04 outturn	2004/05 outturn	2005/06 outturn	2006/07 outturn	2007/08 outturn	2008/09 outturn	2009/10 plans
Northern Ireland Housing Executive Grant	131	146	157	170	121	127	139	126	127	123	123	136	145	153	153	154	160	183	185	226	160	143	159	165	157
+ Supporting People Programme																			48	49	55	56	61	63	62
+ Net lending	118	96	99	86	80	60	54	59	46	38	40	23	- 3	- 42	- 60	- 85	- 86	- 116	- 120	- 75	- 57	- 124	- 97	- 93	- 88
+ Receipts Initiative													2	13											
+ Chancellor's Initiative														3	8										
= Total	249	242	256	256	201	186	193	185	173	162	163	159	146	127	101	69	74	67	113	200	158	75	123	135	131
+ Housing associations	35	34	34	34	28	25	26	42	30	29	36	34	41	53	56	57	63	69	91	99	145	142	181	128	157
+ Renovation grants and enveloping	60	56	45	42	36	32	32	31	32	34	44	49	46	42	40	42	42	43	41	45	46	44	45	54	36
+ Administration and miscellaneous	2	2	2	2	2	2	2	2	2	2	2	2	2	2	2	2	2	4	3	4	4	4	4	4	4
= Total provision	346	335	337	334	268	246	253	260	239	225	245	243	234	224	199	170	182	183	248	348	353	265	353	321	328

Sources: Northern Ireland Expenditure Plans and Priorities, Cms 1517, 1917, 2216, 2516, 2816, 3216, 3616 & 4217, Department of the Environment for Northern Ireland, Department for Social Development, Northern Ireland Housing Executive.

Notes: The reduction in grant to the Northern Ireland Housing Executive (NIHE) in 1989/90 follows some £366 million of NIHE debt being written off. This had a neutral impact on the NIHE programmes. Provision for voluntary housing is net of capital receipts. NIHE net lending figures from 1997/98 onwards are negative, as debt repayments exceed planned new investment.

Table 88 **Gross housing investment in Northern Ireland**

£ million

	1985/86 outturn	1990/91 outturn	1991/92 outturn	1992/93 outturn	1993/94 outturn	1994/95 outturn	1995/96 outturn	1996/97 outturn	1997/98 outturn	1998/99 outturn	1999/00 outturn	2000/01 outturn	2001/02 outturn	2002/03 outturn	2003/04 outturn	2004/05 outturn	2005/06 outturn	2006/07 outturn	2007/08 outturn	2008/09 outturn	2009/10 outturn
Northern Ireland Housing Executive:																					
New house building	82	39	40	35	35	36	48	42	36	16	8	3	4	1	2	1	0	1	0	0	0
+ Land etc. purchase	9	7	10	9	12	15	11	19	19	17	16	23	30	45	59	7	6	8	6	15	22
+ Estate renovation	79	71	66	71	79	79	73	64	64	61	63	60	60	76	80	92	106	101	95	75	27
+ Other	3	4	3	7	2	3	2	2	2	2	3	4	3	5	4	12	2	2	2	2	8
= Total	173	121	120	122	128	133	134	127	119	96	90	90	97	127	145	112	114	112	103	92	57
+ Voluntary housing	40	37	41	58	49	45	50	48	55	65	68	67	73	81	91	99	145	141	181	144	173
+ Renovation grants and enveloping	60	32	32	30	32	34	44	49	46	42	40	42	42	43	41	45	46	44	45	41	45
+ Warm Homes																12	15	21	23	22	9
= Gross public investment (A)	273	190	193	210	205	212	228	224	220	203	198	199	212	251	277	268	320	318	352	299	294
Capital receipts:																					
Northern Ireland Housing Executive	42	43	34	37	45	56	56	60	71	71	81	108	106	160	179	88	93	161	78	8	18
+ Voluntary housing	5	12	14	16	19	16	15	14	13	12	12	10	10	13	10	11	11	15	8	7	4
= Total (B)	47	55	48	52	64	72	71	74	83	83	93	118	116	173	189	99	104	176	86	15	22
Net public investment (A–B)	226	135	145	158	141	140	158	150	135	120	105	81	96	78	88	169	216	142	266	269	202

Sources: Northern Ireland Expenditure Plans and Priorities, Cms 1517, 1917, 2216, 2516, 2816, 3216, 3616, 3916 & 4217, Department for Social Development.

Note: Renovation grants and enveloping and Warm Homes expenditure are financed from revenue in Northern Ireland.

Table 89 **Rents and earnings in Northern Ireland**

Year	1981/82	1986/87	1987/88	1988/89	1989/90	1990/91	1991/92	1992/93	1993/94	1994/95	1995/96	1996/97	1997/98	1998/99	1999/00	2000/01	2001/02	2002/03	2003/04	2004/05	2005/06	2006/07	2007/08	2008/09	2009/10
Average rent per week (£)																									
Northern Ireland Housing Executive	10.06	14.78	15.34	18.18	19.04	21.13	23.09	25.43	27.57	29.63	31.56	32.62	34.42	35.93	37.52	39.18	40.34	41.53	42.88	44.19	45.73	47.04	48.82	50.81	51.84
Housing associations	–	–	–	–	–	–	–	–	–	–	30.90	34.50	35.50	38.00	40.70	44.12	46.95	52.31	56.05	58.85	61.87	64.82	68.76	73.44	76.96
Private rents	–	–	–	–	–	–	–	–	–	–	–	–	–	–	–	–	–	70.70	72.76	72.66	82.71	79.38	86.01	84.16	–
Average earnings (£)	114.3	161.0	176.4	189.8	206.5	225.6	245.9	269.6	282.4	286.5	300.2	306.2	319.7	332.6	344.9	360.4	375.0	390.1	404.2	431.4	452.2	472.1	474.3	489.0	513.3
Rent as a % earnings																									
Northern Ireland Housing Executive	8.8	9.2	8.7	9.6	9.2	9.4	9.4	9.4	9.8	10.3	10.5	10.7	10.8	10.8	10.9	10.9	10.8	10.6	10.6	10.2	10.1	10.0	10.3	10.4	10.1
Housing associations	–	–	–	–	–	–	–	–	–	–	10.3	11.3	11.1	11.4	11.8	12.2	12.5	13.4	13.9	13.6	13.7	13.7	14.5	15.0	15.0
Private rents	–	–	–	–	–	–	–	–	–	–	–	–	–	–	–	–	–	18.1	18.0	16.8	18.3	16.8	18.1	17.2	–

Sources: Northern Ireland Housing Statistics, Northern Ireland Housing Executive, Regional Trends, Family Resources Survey, Northern Ireland New Earnings Surveys, Annual Survey of Hours and Earnings.

Notes: Earnings figures are average Northern Ireland earnings; figures up to 1997/98 come from the New Earnings Survey, subsequent figures come from the Annual Survey of Hours and Earnings for full-time employees. NIHE rents are for the December of the year. Housing association rent figures include rates and service charges. Private rents are for all types of letting (except those that are rent-free). Due to the small Family Resources Survey sample size for the private rented sector in Nothern ireland, the private rents figures hould be treated with caution.

Section 3　Compendium of tables

Housing needs, homelessness, lettings and housing management

Table 90 Local authority homeless acceptances

Number of households

	1980	1985	1990	1991	1992	1993	1994	1995	1996	1997	1998	1999	2000	2001	2002	2003	2004	2005	2006	2007	2008	2009
Not held to be intentionally homeless																						
England	60,400	91,010	140,350	144,780	142,890	132,380	122,460	117,490	113,590	102,000	104,630	105,370	111,340	117,830	123,840	135,590	127,760	100,170	76,860	64,970	57,510	41,780
+ Scotland	7,038	10,992	14,233	15,500	17,700	17,000	16,000	15,200	15,500	15,600	16,500	18,000	18,200	24,900	27,506	29,995	30,032	31,700	31,326	31,214	33,156	35,239
+ Wales	4,772	4,825	9,226	9,293	9,818	10,792	9,897	8,638	8,334	4,297	4,371	3,695	4,156	5,181	6,437	8,512	10,071	8,376	6,974	6,339	6,226	5,430
= Great Britain	72,210	106,827	163,809	169,573	170,408	160,172	148,357	141,328	137,424	121,897	125,501	127,065	133,696	147,911	157,783	174,097	167,863	140,246	115,160	102,523	96,892	82,449
Held to be intentionally homeless																						
England	2,520	2,970	5,450	6,940	6,350	5,660	4,570	4,920	5,070	4,960	6,120	7,330	8,860	8,420	9,490	12,230	13,640	13,830	11,410	9,920	8,890	6,880
+ Scotland	938	980	1,580	1,800	2,200	2,000	1,800	1,700	1,700	1,800	1,900	2,300	2,400	2,000	1,435	1,146	1,099	1,230	1,430	1,461	1,545	1,404
+ Wales	674	546	737	550	452	333	396	362	815	343	380	476	510	555	608	657	921	976	865	797	627	579
= Great Britain	4,132	4,496	7,767	9,290	9,002	7,993	6,766	6,982	7,585	7,103	8,400	10,106	11,570	10,975	11,533	14,033	15,660	16,036	13,705	12,178	11,062	8,863
All homeless acceptances																						
England	62,920	93,980	145,800	151,720	149,240	138,040	127,030	122,410	118,660	106,960	110,750	112,700	120,200	126,250	133,330	147,820	141,400	114,000	88,270	74,890	66,400	48,660
+ Scotland	7,976	11,972	15,813	17,300	19,900	19,000	17,800	16,900	17,200	17,400	18,400	20,300	20,600	26,900	28,941	31,141	31,131	32,930	32,756	32,675	34,701	36,643
+ Wales	5,446	5,371	9,963	9,843	10,270	11,125	10,293	9,001	9,149	4,640	4,751	4,171	4,666	5,717	7,045	9,201	10,993	9,352	7,839	7,136	6,853	6,009
= Great Britain	76,342	111,323	171,576	178,863	179,410	168,165	155,123	148,311	145,009	129,000	133,901	137,171	145,466	158,867	169,316	188,162	183,524	156,282	128,865	114,701	107,954	91,312

Sources: Department for Communities and Local Government, Scottish Government and Welsh Assembly Government.

Notes: The 1990 figures for Wales include 2,000 households made homeless in Colwyn Bay by flooding in the February of that year. Scottish figures are for priority need homeless and potentially homeless cases only, and figures from 2000 onwards are for financial years (i.e. 2000/01 etc). The England and Wales figures for 1997 and later years reflect the changes in homeless legislation, and no longer include 'non-priority acceptances'.
In 1996 these accounted for 3,310 acceptances in England and 3,501 acceptances in Wales.

Table 91a **Homeless households in temporary accommodation in England**[1]

Number of households

	1980	1985	1986	1987	1988	1989	1990	1991	1992	1993	1994	1995	1996	1997	1998	1999	2000	2001	2002	2003	2004	2005	2006	2007	2008	2009
Bed and breakfast	1,330	5,360	8,990	10,370	10,970	11,480	11,130	12,150	7,630	4,900	4,130	4,500	4,160	4,520	7,240	8,000	9,870	11,860	13,240	8,420	6,450	4,950	4,210	3,530	2,560	1,850
+ Hostels[2]	3,380	4,730	4,610	5,150	6,240	8,020	9,010	9,990	10,840	10,210	9,730	9,660	9,640	8,730	9,760	9,660	10,790	10,680	9,640	10,370	10,060	9,230	7,840	6,620	5,250	4,150
+ Private sector leasing	–	–	–	–	–	–	–	23,740	27,910	23,270	15,800	11,530	10,980	14,040	17,400	19,820	25,260	24,490	33,010	46,310	55,590	54,830	52,120	53,440	47,740	32,430
+ Other[3]	–	5,830	7,190	9,240	12,890	18,400	25,130	14,050	16,690	15,200	15,970	18,450	17,410	17,580	19,390	24,700	27,160	30,480	29,250	29,520	28,920	29,720	25,340	15,910	11,930	14,940
= All temporary accommodation	4,710	15,920	20,790	24,760	30,100	37,900	45,270	59,930	63,070	53,580	45,630	44,140	42,190	44,870	53,790	62,180	73,080	77,510	85,140	94,610	101,030	98,730	89,510	79,500	67,480	53,370
Homeless at home[4]																										
All	–	–	–	–	–	–	–	8,700	10,420	8,640	8,370	8,890	9,500	8,190	9,970	10,450	12,220	12,000	14,800	23,070	20,910	–	–	–	–	–
Main duty accepted	–	–	–	–	–	–	–	–	–	–	–	–	5,470	5,790	6,440	6,580	7,610	8,600	9,760	17,500	16,100	11,570	8,470	8,080	6,070	4,150

Sources: Homelessness Statistics, Department for Communities and Local Government, Hansard 18/4/91, Column 186.

Notes: 1. Under the provisions of the 1985 and the 1996 Housing Acts - figures relate to placements as at calendar year end.

2. Includes women's refuges.

3. Includes dwellings leased by local authorities from private landlords for years prior to 1991.

4. Figures for households accepted as homeless, but that remained in their existing accommodation pending rehousing, were not collected before 1991. Figures for homeless at home cases where the main homeless duty was accepted were only collected from 1997. The wider series of all homeless at home cases was discontinued after March 2005.

Table 91b **Homeless households in temporary accommodation in Wales**

Number of households

	1997	1998	1999	2000	2001	2002	2003	2004	2005	2006	2007	2008	2009
Local authority dwelling	175	288	249	306	344	263	411	430	549	562	354	279	232
Housing association	36	37	34	34	44	25	31	34	49	64	105	121	133
Private sector landlord	37	32	23	40	24	10	23	36	39	40	65	67	73
Private sector leasing	135	145	173	160	99	142	198	337	410	612	725	890	983
Hostel	102	107	84	86	116	137	218	199	360	325	314	340	292
Women's refuges	28	31	30	38	48	46	79	82	65	69	66	88	81
Bed and breakfast	78	69	69	62	111	258	567	772	604	376	240	266	231
Other	27	7	13	15	13	100	138	164	264	242	182	139	0
Homeless at home	74	130	175	170	359	147	613	1,194	1,140	814	536	496	314
Total	692	846	850	911	1,158	1,128	2,278	3,248	3,480	3,104	2,587	2,686	2,339

Source: Welsh Housing Statistics.

Notes: All figures are for homeless households in temporary accommodation at the end of December in each year.

For figures for earlier years (which are for different categories of accommodation) see Welsh Housing Statistics 1997.

Table 91c Homeless households in temporary accommodation in Scotland

Number of households

	1991	1992	1993	1994	1995	1996	1997	1998	1999	2000	2001	2002	2003	2004	2005	2006	2007	2008	2009
Local authority dwelling	1,174	1,262	1,315	1,799	1,851	1,884	1,741	1,859	1,855	1,826	1,968	2,152	2,984	3,537	4,136	4,747	5,164	6,114	6,341
Hostel	1,363	1,384	1,335	1,428	1,648	1,776	1,562	1,465	1,543	1,608	1,512	1,363	1,380	1,586	1,490	1,328	1,242	1,099	1,008
Bed and breakfast	458	616	612	486	449	454	355	360	413	500	502	569	898	1,190	1,516	1,494	1,528	1,609	1,748
Other	160	173	310	72	80	100	114	80	53	61	78	69	141	132	159	416	643	713	956
Total	3,155	3,435	3,572	3,785	4,028	4,214	3,772	3,764	3,864	3,995	4,060	4,153	5,403	6,445	7,301	7,985	8,577	9,535	10,053

Source: Scottish Government Housing Bulletin and Scottish Government website.

Notes: All figures are for homeless households in temporary accommodation at the end of March in each year. Local authority dwellings include Glasgow Housing Association from 2003 and all other housing associations from 2006.

Table 92 Reasons for homelessness in England

Percentages

	1987	1988	1989	1990	1991	1992	1993	1994	1995	1996	1997	1998	1999	2000	2001	2002	2003	2004	2005	2006	2007	2008	2009
Parents, relatives or friends no longer willing or able to accommodate	41	43	43	43	42	42	38	34	29	29	27	27	28	30	33	34	37	38	38	37	36	36	36
Breakdown of relationship with partner	18	19	17	17	16	17	19	20	22	24	25	25	24	23	22	21	20	20	20	20	19	18	20
Loss of private dwelling, including tied accommodation	15	15	16	14	14	15	17	19	20	21	22	23	22	23	22	20	18	18	19	19	20	19	16
Mortgage arrears	9	7	6	9	12	10	8	8	8	7	6	6	5	3	2	1	1	2	2	3	4	4	3
Rent arrears	4	4	5	4	3	2	2	2	2	2	2	3	3	3	3	3	2	2	2	2	2	2	3
Other	13	12	13	13	14	16	16	16	17	17	17	17	19	18	18	22	22	20	19	19	18	20	22

Source: Department for Communities and Local Government, Homelessness Statistics.

Note: Figures may not total to 100, because of rounding.

Table 93 **Homelessness: categories of need in England**

Number of households

	Number of households																				Percentages							
	1990	1991	1992	1993	1994	1995	1996	1997	1998	1999	2000	2001	2002	2003	2004	2005	2006	2007	2008	2009	1990	1995	2000	2005	2006	2007	2008	2009
Priority need households:																												
Households with:																												
Dependent children	84,120	88,950	85,300	76,390	68,620	66,290	63,420	59,380	61,610	62,280	65,330	67,180	66,900	68,840	64,930	52,370	42,000	37,480	34,300	23,850	66	56	59	52	55	58	60	57
Pregnant member	17,470	18,830	18,530	16,500	14,060	13,430	12,930	10,580	10,590	10,350	10,930	11,610	12,000	13,950	14,240	12,090	9,060	7,570	6,460	4,970	14	11	10	12	12	12	11	12
Vulnerable member:																												
Old age	6,570	5,860	6,230	5,920	6,050	5,890	5,510	4,160	3,800	3,850	3,920	4,250	4,330	4,330	3,740	2,530	1,540	1,140	900	600	5	5	4	3	2	2	2	1
Physical handicap	3,950	4,430	5,440	5,400	6,050	6,550	6,250	5,220	5,010	5,160	5,350	6,130	6,760	7,330	6,450	4,970	3,720	3,240	2,770	2,460	3	6	5	5	5	5	5	6
Mental illness	4,220	4,750	6,070	6,490	7,100	7,430	8,180	6,910	7,170	7,610	8,440	10,000	10,540	12,050	11,430	8,060	5,650	4,460	3,870	3,230	3	6	8	8	7	7	7	8
Young	–	–	4,460	4,470	4,090	3,760	3,580	3,170	3,390	3,540	4,400	5,730	6,930	10,860	10,930	8,970	6,750	5,220	4,320	3,000	–	3	4	9	9	8	8	7
Domestic violence	–	–	6,470	7,060	7,370	8,430	8,220	6,380	6,320	6,140	6,450	6,330	6,770	6,210	6,390	4,420	3,180	2,230	1,830	1,600	–	7	6	4	4	3	3	4
Other	9,460	12,610	4,930	4,250	4,170	4,550	4,410	5,080	5,850	5,500	5,440	5,560	8,700	11,140	8,990	6,220	4,610	3,230	2,690	1,900	7	4	5	6	6	5	5	5
Homeless in emergency	2,300	1,820	1,270	1,150	980	1,160	1,090	1,130	910	940	1,070	1,050	950	860	690	560	410	450	380	190	2	1	1	1	1	1	1	0
Total priority need (A)	128,090	137,250	138,700	127,630	118,490	117,490	113,590	102,000	104,630	105,370	111,340	117,830	123,840	135,590	127,760	100,170	76,860	64,970	57,510	41,780	100	100	100	100	100	100	100	100
Non-priority need (B)	12,260	7,530	4,190	4,750	3,970	3,790	3,310	58,000	55,480	55,150	51,610	54,330	60,170	67,120	63,300	48,990	33,910	24,630	17,460	16,230	–	–	–	–	–	–	–	–
Total (A+B)	140,350	144,780	142,890	132,380	122,460	121,280	116,870	160,000	160,110	160,520	162,950	172,160	184,010	202,710	191,060	149,160	110,770	89,600	74,970	58,010	–	–	–	–	–	–	–	–

Source: Department for Communities and Local Government, Homelessness Statistics.

Notes: Separate figures for domestic violence and young person cases are not available for 1991 or earlier years. Percentages do not always add to 100 as a result of roundings. There is a major discontinuity in the figures for acceptances of non-priority need households following the introduction of the Housing Act 1996 provisions in January 1997.

Table 94a **Homelessness by region: homeless acceptances**

Number of households

Region	1991	1992	1993	1994	1995	1996	1997	1998	1999	2000	2001	2002	2003	2004	2005	2006	2007	2008	2009
London	36,310	37,550	31,570	28,690	26,690	25,730	24,370	26,310	28,380	28,230	30,590	28,830	30,510	28,050	22,700	16,240	13,650	13,850	9,970
South East	13,750	13,030	12,630	12,850	13,570	13,700	12,080	12,840	12,620	14,420	14,760	14,220	15,240	13,460	9,990	7,200	5,630	5,050	3,940
South West	9,050	8,990	9,370	9,210	9,960	9,830	8,780	8,910	9,480	11,170	11,380	12,280	11,770	10,100	8,650	5,580	4,690	3,920	3,020
East	8,560	9,300	9,000	8,490	8,730	8,670	8,020	8,660	8,570	9,420	10,310	10,830	11,290	10,680	8,650	7,130	6,040	5,440	3,850
East Midlands	9,730	10,450	10,120	8,890	8,970	8,900	8,070	7,570	7,190	7,350	7,240	8,040	9,140	9,570	7,470	6,100	5,070	4,050	3,020
West Midlands	17,280	17,070	16,440	15,890	17,510	16,240	14,500	14,210	13,340	13,660	14,320	14,780	15,690	15,080	11,860	9,580	9,070	8,950	7,220
Yorkshire & The Humber	12,480	14,430	13,320	11,060	9,930	9,240	8,940	8,440	8,220	9,140	10,330	14,160	16,260	14,590	10,020	8,470	7,520	6,830	4,250
North East	7,870	7,570	6,800	6,060	6,050	5,780	4,420	4,370	4,830	5,060	5,490	6,460	8,020	8,510	6,330	4,980	3,960	3,220	2,300
North West	22,220	20,350	18,380	17,350	16,080	15,500	12,800	13,330	12,770	12,940	13,440	14,260	17,660	17,720	14,530	11,580	9,320	6,200	4,250
England	137,250	138,740	127,630	118,490	117,490	113,590	102,000	104,630	105,370	111,340	117,830	123,840	135,590	127,760	100,170	76,860	64,970	57,510	41,790

Source: Department for Communities and Local Government, Homelessness Statistics.

Notes: Homeless acceptances figures are for priority need households only, and exclude households found to be intentionally homeless. Temporary accommodation figures are for the end of the year, and exclude households that are 'homeless at home' (see Table 91).

Table 94b **Homelessness by region: in temporary accommodation**

Number of households

Region	1991	1992	1993	1994	1995	1996	1997	1998	1999	2000	2001	2002	2003	2004	2005	2006	2007	2008	2009
London	37,130	39,580	33,040	25,990	26,060	24,100	25,120	29,120	35,900	41,540	44,970	51,030	56,950	61,670	63,800	60,960	56,740	49,960	41,190
South East	7,890	8,110	7,190	7,130	6,420	6,550	6,990	8,750	9,060	11,300	12,060	11,120	12,950	13,340	11,870	9,280	6,760	5,050	3,620
South West	2,630	3,020	2,620	2,690	2,540	2,380	2,920	4,380	4,520	5,270	5,280	5,810	6,420	6,410	6,710	5,350	4,450	3,270	2,210
East	3,940	4,200	3,160	2,980	2,750	2,840	3,060	3,560	4,320	4,990	5,730	7,280	7,920	8,350	6,900	5,540	4,390	3,550	2,560
East Midlands	1,810	1,560	1,370	1,470	1,420	1,450	1,270	1,840	1,910	1,830	2,080	2,180	2,630	2,870	2,190	1,930	1,460	1,000	690
West Midlands	2,120	1,660	1,430	1,250	1,220	1,030	1,500	1,600	1,830	2,590	2,030	1,270	1,880	2,600	2,010	1,610	1,450	1,270	1,100
Yorkshire & The Humber	1,620	1,890	1,650	1,330	1,160	1,050	1,150	1,590	1,630	2,310	1,670	2,200	2,350	2,220	2,170	2,070	1,700	1,610	910
North East	430	470	490	430	430	430	710	840	1,090	1,320	1,690	570	770	840	730	470	340	330	150
North West	2,360	2,580	2,630	2,360	2,140	1,970	2,180	2,150	1,960	1,980	2,000	1,860	2,740	2,730	2,340	2,300	2,230	1,450	920
England	59,930	63,070	53,580	45,630	44,140	41,800	44,870	53,790	62,180	73,080	77,510	85,140	94,610	101,030	98,730	89,510	79,500	67,480	53,370

Source and Notes: As Table 94a.

Table 95a **Rough sleepers in 1998 and 2005-2010**

Number of rough sleepers	1998 Local authorities		2005 Local authorities		2006 Local authorities		2007 Local authorities		2008 Local authorities		2009 Local authorities		2010 Local authorities	
	Number	Percentage	Number	Percentage	Number	Percentage	Number	Percentage	Number	Percentage	Number	Percentage	Number	Percentage
No estimate or count	108	30.7	113	31.9	98	27.7	2	0.6	0	0.0	0	0.0	0	0.0
Nil - 10	156	44.3	236	66.7	250	70.6	340	96.0	343	96.6	349	98.6	306	94.2
11 - 20	43	12.2	4	1.1	4	1.1	10	2.8	10	2.8	4	1.1	15	4.6
21 - 30	22	6.3	0	0.0	1	0.3	0	0.0	0	0.0	0	0.0	3	0.9
31 - 40	8	2.3	0	0.0	0	0.0	0	0.0	0	0.0	1	0.3	0	0.0
41 - 50	5	1.4	0	0.0	0	0.0	1	0.3	1	0.3	0	0.0	0	0.0
Over 50	10	2.8	1	0.3	1	0.3	1	0.3	1	0.3	1	0.3	1	0.3
Total	352	100	354	100	354	100	354	100	355	100	354	100	325	100.0

Sources: Shelter Report to Social Exclusion Unit, 1998, and DCLG website.

Table 95b **Rough sleepers by area in 1998 to 2010**

Street count

Authority	1998	1999	2000	2001	2002	2003	2004	2005	2006	2007	2008	2009	2010
Westminster	237	234	227	169	169	133	175	133	173	112	111	110	147
City of London	41	36	40	30	41	36	22	12	25	45	48	38	29
Oxford	39	52	31	24	7	5	7	5	11	11	10	5	16
Kensington and Chelsea	23	28	14	15	6	6	10	12	10	13	12	13	13
Brighton and Hove	44	43	26	20	9	9	9	9	12	12	10	6	12
Lambeth	20	46	47	23	12	11	12	7	9	15	11	13	9
Tower Hamlets	31	10	6	9	2	11	5	..	3	12	7	17	7
Birmingham	56	43	23	19	2	14	7	7	8	5	6	4	6
Bournemouth	44	18	21	14	7	4	12	7	8	5	11	6	6
Exeter	27	19	19	10	7	18	8	8	6	10	15	5	6
Cambridge	30	21	21	16	19	9	3	7	2	6	0	1	6
Camden	59	66	54	38	28	13	5	17	10	6	4	6	5
Liverpool	17	30	19	13	19	19	10	8	9	12	13	9	3
Southwark	31	26	7	13	2	17	6	7	6	11	5	15	3

Source: DCLG Website.

Note: Authorities shown are those with the highest counts in 1998-2009 of those that had rough sleepers on the date of survey in 2010.

Table 96 **Local authority dwelling stock, new dwellings and lettings in England**

Thousands

	1982/83	1985/86	1986/87	1987/88	1988/89	1989/90	1990/91	1991/92	1992/93	1993/94	1994/95	1995/96	1996/97	1997/98	1998/99	1999/00	2000/01	2001/02	2002/03	2003/04	2004/05	2005/06	2006/07	2007/08	2008/09
Stock of dwellings[1]	4,660	4,439	4,366	4,277	4,134	3,991	3,899	3,844	3,760	3,666	3,565	3,470	3,401	3,309	3,178	3,012	2,812	2,706	2,457	2,335	2,166	2,086	1,987	1,882	1,820
Vacant dwellings[2]	114	113	112	103	101	99	83	75	71	70	72	80	81	82	84	87	80	78	63	58	49	43	41	37	35
Vacant dwellings as % of stock	2.4	2.5	2.5	2.4	2.4	2.5	2.1	1.9	1.9	1.9	2.0	2.3	2.4	2.5	2.6	2.9	2.9	2.9	2.5	2.5	2.2	2.1	2.1	2.0	1.9
Completions	27	21	18	15	16	14	13	7	3	1	1	1	0	0	0	0	0	0	0	0	0	0	0	0	0
Lettings3 which are:	439	437	430	426	410	390	401	406	400	405	408	415	422	404	379	354	326	289	273	229	210	189	175	158	152
to existing tenants	184	190	186	184	174	162	161	168	170	170	169	165	162	144	129	118	104	93	82	67	61	56	51	46	45
to new tenants	255	247	244	242	236	228	240	239	230	234	239	250	260	259	249	236	222	197	191	162	149	133	124	111	107
Homeless households as % of new tenants	19	26	27	31	31	35	40	46	45	40	36	34	29	25	25	25	29	32	34	32	34	31	28	28	25

Sources: Department of the Environment Annual Reports, Expenditure Plans, Housing Statistics, Department of Transport, DCLG website.

Notes: 1. Includes dwellings awaiting demolition, and from 1986/87 dwellings owned by authorities outside their own areas. Figures to 1990 are for December; subsequently they are for the end of the financial year.

2. Includes non-secure lettings, and letttings to households displaced by slum clearance.

Table 97a **Lettings to new tenants by local authorities**

Thousands

Region	1980/81	1985/86	1990/91	1991/92	1992/93	1993/94	1994/95	1995/96	1996/97	1997/98	1998/99	1999/00	2000/01	2001/02	2002/03	2003/04	2004/05	2005/06	2006/07	2007/08	2008/09	2009/10
Northern	26.2	24.4	23.0	21.3	22.5	22.2	24.4	27.0	27.9	28.3												
North East			21.3	21.2	20.7	20.6	22.3	24.9	25.8	26.2	25.2	25.4	24.6	20.1	19.0	15.1	14.5	13.0	11	11.5	9.2	9.7
Yorkshire & The Humber	37.7	36.1	31.4	30.8	30.5	29.8	33.6	35.6	37.8	37.6	37.9	38.7	37.1	34.6	36.1	27.2	23.0	17.2	17.3	14.9	15.7	15.6
North West	42.5	42.7	40.2	39.2	36.9	36.6	40.2	43.6	44.3	46.8												
North West			41.9	39.1	38.6	38.2	42.2	45.7	46.5	49.0	48.4	46.0	41.4	36.6	32.7	28.1	24.4	20.0	18.6	14.4	13.6	14.3
East Midlands	23.1	21.6	19.0	18.1	18.1	20.5	20.1	21.3	25.0	25.4	26.0	23.3	22.8	20.4	21.8	16.5	16.6	15.7	15.6	14.6	13.4	13.1
West Midlands	34.0	32.0	29.1	29.0	28.0	29.2	30.1	31.6	33.9	33.7	32.0	29.8	27.8	22.9	20.9	17.6	16.9	15.7	14.4	13.4	13.6	14.6
East Anglia	9.6	11.8	7.4	6.9	6.5	6.2	6.3	6.7	7.3	7.6												
East			17.8	16.3	16.0	17.0	16.7	17.4	18.0	18.2	18.3	17.6	16.9	16.1	14.6	12.9	12.0	12.3	10.5	9.6	8.5	8.3
London	50.1	33.5	43.9	49.4	45.2	44.5	41.5	40.1	40.5	37.3	32.2	28.1	26.6	24.6	23.1	22.5	21.7	19.7	19.1	16.7	17.1	18.2
South East	36.4	29.3	31.4	30.1	29.4	31.0	29.4	29.0	28.8	28.3												
South East			21.1	20.7	19.9	20.2	19.0	18.3	18.1	17.7	17.1	15.6	14.6	12.3	13.5	12.9	11.4	12.1	10.4	9.9	9.2	9.5
South West	15.5	15.6	14.1	14.0	13.1	14.4	13.8	14.6	14.9	14.3	12.9	11.4	10.3	9.9	9.2	9.1	8.5	7.7	7.7	6.6	6.6	6.6
England	275.1	247.0	239.6	238.5	230.2	234.3	239.4	249.8	260.5	259.5	250.0	235.6	222.3	197.5	191.0	162.0	149.1	133.3	124.4	111.4	106.9	109.9

Sources: Housing Statistics, DCLG Website.

Notes: Lettings figures are for lettings to new tenants only, including lettings for non-secure tenancies. The regional figures are compiled from local authority HIP returns, grossed up for incomplete responses. Data for standard statistical regions are shown from 1980/81 to 1997/98, and for government office regions from 1988/89 onwards. Lettings figures from 2003/04 do not include non-secure lettings to homeless households.

Table 97b **Lettings to homeless households**

Percentage of all lettings to new tenants

Region	1980/81	1985/86	1990/91	1991/92	1992/93	1993/94	1994/95	1995/96	1996/97	1997/98	1998/99	1999/00	2000/01	2001/02	2002/03	2003/04	2004/05	2005/06	2006/07	2007/08	2008/09	2009/10
Northern	10	11																				
North East			24	29	27	23	20	18	16	13	12	13	13	16	17	26	26	21	21	18	18	13
Yorkshire & The Humber	10	15	26	31	34	32	27	22	19	18	18	16	19	26	26	33	33	30	26	36	24	17
North West	10	17																				
North West			21	26	26	25	22	20	17	12	11	12	14	16	19	19	27	28	26	22	16	10
East Midlands	10	15	34	45	44	37	33	31	25	19	18	18	21	23	24	24	27	23	21	20	16	12
West Midlands	16	27	42	43	44	37	33	31	28	30	24	24	26	32	36	42	39	33	32	33	29	22
East Anglia	18	15																				
East			40	47	48	42	41	38	36	28	33	32	37	43	48	30	32	27	27	24	21	17
London	27	47	75	76	74	64	60	60	57	51	55	59	64	68	68	52	51	48	41	42	42	37
South East	18	23																				
South East			45	53	54	49	48	49	42	36	41	42	52	55	51	29	32	27	26	27	25	18
South West	23	27	42	46	47	44	41	40	36	27	32	36	45	47	52	42	36	38	30	21	20	12
England	16	23	40	46	45	40	36	34	30	25	25	25	29	32	34	32	34	31	28	28	25	19

Sources and Notes: As Table 97a. Percentages for the years to 1987/88 are for secure lettings to homeless households only. In addition, the majority of the relatively small number of non-secure lettings during that period were made to homeless households. From 1988/89 onwards the percentages relate to both secure and non-secure lettings. This change is necessary to reflect the increasing numbers of non-secure lettings made to new tenants in recent years. In 2003/04 non-secure lettings in England accounted for some 61 per cent of all lettings to new tenants, despite in that year the exclusion of non-secure lettings to homeless households.

Table 98 **Housing association lettings in England**

Thousands

	1980/81	1985/86	1986/87	1987/88	1988/89	1989/90	1990/91	1991/92	1992/93	1993/94	1994/95	1995/96	1996/97	1997/98	1998/99	1999/00	2000/01	2001/02	2002/03	2003/04	2004/05	2005/06	2006/07	2007/08	2008/09	2009/10
Stock	401	464	483	495	512	534	567	608	646	714	779	857	942	985	1,040	1,146	1,273	1,424	1,492	1,651	1,702	1,802	1,842	1,886	2,142	2,211
Lettings	51	62	64	67	70	76	77	86	109	134	132	136	139	145	146	148	150	159	159	144	144	128	127	125	143	138
of which:																										
Existing tenants	9	11	12	13	13	16	15	17	19	22	21	22	32	33	34	36	38	41	42	40	36	32	31	30	38	34
New tenants	42	51	52	54	57	60	62	69	90	112	111	114	107	112	112	111	112	118	117	104	108	96	96	95	105	104
of which :																										
Existing LA tenants	–	–	–	–	–	–	–	–	–	–	–	–	27	29	27	26	24	24	23	19	16	13	12	11	13	13
Statutory homeless	–	–	–	–	–	–	9	15	23	28	26	26	18	13	13	13	14	15	17	17	22	21	23	22	21	17
Lettings to homeless as a % of all lettings to new tenants	–	–	–	–	–	–	14	21	25	25	23	23	17	11	11	12	12	13	14	16	20	22	24	23	20	16

Sources: Answers to Parliamentary Questions 16/7/91 and 2/2/94, Housing Statistics, Cm 2507, Cm 280, Cm 3207 & Cm 3607, DCLG and CORE websites.

Notes: Pre-1989/90 lettings figures are Department of the Environment estimates. New housing association tenants include former council tenants transferring to a housing association letting. However, they exclude former supported housing tenants taking up a general needs tenancy.

Stock figures are for December for years up to 1989/90 and subsequently for the start of the financial year. Lettings to the homeless do not include lettings on non-secure tenancies for which no breakdown is available.

Table 99 **Lettings to new tenants by housing associations by region in England**

	Lettings to new tenants													
Region	1996/97	1997/98	1998/99	1999/00	2000/01	2001/02	2002/03	2003/04	2004/05	2005/06	2006/07	2007/08	2008/09	2009/10
North East	4,701	4,662	5,008	4,476	4,700	6,700	7,106	5,755	6,646	6,091	6,367	6,033	6,916	7,268
Yorkshire & The Humber	7,545	8,537	8,642	8,317	7,658	7,635	8,493	9,045	8,712	9,408	9,184	9,989	10,527	8,985
North West	13,742	15,183	15,494	17,074	18,449	21,028	21,832	20,081	19,653	18,197	19,450	19,158	21,397	21,731
East Midlands	6,579	7,406	7,479	7,452	7,907	7,382	7,178	6,326	7,012	5,764	5,893	5,667	6,540	6,658
West Midlands	8,773	9,661	10,441	11,094	13,280	14,547	14,046	13,180	12,682	11,599	11,118	11,077	12,583	11,358
East	8,414	8,853	8,824	8,301	8,141	7,601	7,980	7,240	8,169	7,546	8,619	8,672	10,012	9,712
London	9,297	8,278	8,307	7,879	7,773	7,982	7,894	6,327	8,607	6,902	7,065	6,890	7,661	7,372
South East	14,139	13,734	13,342	12,820	12,195	12,111	11,523	10,807	12,660	10,825	11,058	10,765	12,016	11,449
South West	6,839	6,926	7,399	8,339	8,677	8,839	7,933	7,053	7,840	6,667	6,932	7,197	8,293	7,606
England	80,029	83,240	84,936	85,752	88,780	93,825	93,985	85,814	91,981	82,999	85,686	85,448	95,945	92,139

Sources: Housing Statistics, DCLG Website (to 2003/04). CORE website 2004/05-2009/10.

Notes: Lettings figures are for general needs lettings to new tenants only, excluding lettings to both existing local authority and housing association general needs tenants (but including lets to former supported housing tenants).

Table 100 **Outputs from the Housing Corporation and Homes and Communities Agency programmes – completions and forecast**

	1990/91 outturn	1995/96 outturn	1996/97 outturn	1997/98 outturn	1998/99 outturn	1999/00 outturn	2000/01 outturn	2001/02 outturn	2002/03 outturn	2003/04 outturn	2004/05 outturn	2005/06 outturn	2006/07 outturn	2007/08 outturn	2008/09 outturn	2009/10 outturn	2010/11 plans
Housing for rent :																	
+ Mixed and public funded	17,610	40,583	29,386	22,843	22,330	19,768	17,755	18,500	-	-	-	-	-	-	-	-	-
+ Short life (Mini-HAG)	990	1,482	2,000	2,777	1,500	1,194	943	894	-	-	-	-	-	-	-	-	-
= Total Rent (A)	18,600	42,065	31,386	25,620	23,830	20,962	18,698	19,394	17,158	16,569	16,349	18,637	23,372	29,557	27,798	30,857	35,825
Sales and incentives :																	
Tenants Incentive Schemes	2,270	6,400	7,029	4,262	2,900	503	158	1,403	-	-	-	-	-	-	-	-	
+ Low cost homeownership	780	10,471	6,966	6,336	6,100	4,032	4,038	2,211	-	-	-	-	-	-	-	-	
= Total sales/incentives (B)	3,050	16,871	13,995	10,598	9,000	4,535	4,196	3,614	4,202	6,458	12,407	17749	18,285	21,538	19,781	22,079	25,675
Total all completions (A+B)	21,650	58,936	45,381	36,218	32,830	25,497	22,894	23,008	21,360	23,027	28,756	36,386	41,657	51,095	47,579	52,936	61,500

Sources: Housing Corporation ADP for 1994/95 and earlier years, Cm 5405 and earlier equivalents, Housing Corporation Investment Bulletins, Annual Reports and Corporate Plans. Homes and Communities Agency Corporate Plan 2009/10-2010/11.

Notes: Mini-HAG and TIS figures include units financed through the special homeless programmes in 1990/91 & 1991/92. Rough Sleepers Initiative and City Challenge schemes are included within the mixed/public funded rent figures. Tenants Incentive Schemes include Purchase Grants from 1996/97 onward. Key worker living includes in Total sales/incentives figures from 2004/05 onwards. See earlier editions of the Review for data for years 1991/92 to 1994/95. The HCA also has programmes (Kickstart and Property and Regeneration) to support the provision of open market homes.

Table 101 **Local authority and housing association lettings to new tenants**

Thousands

	1980/81	1981/82	1982/83	1983/84	1984/85	1985/86	1986/87	1987/88	1988/89	1989/90	1990/91	1991/92	1992/93	1993/94	1994/95	1995/96	1996/97	1997/98	1998/99	1999/00	2000/01	2001/02	2002/03	2003/04	2004/05	2005/06	2006/07	2007/08	2008/09	2009/10
Local authorities	275	251	256	246	240	247	244	242	236	229	240	239	230	234	239	250	260	259	249	236	222	197	191	162	149	133	124	111	107	110
Housing associations	42	43	45	47	49	51	52	54	57	60	62	69	90	112	111	114	107	112	112	111	112	118	117	104	108	96	96	95	105	104
Total	317	294	301	293	289	298	296	296	293	289	302	308	320	346	350	364	367	371	361	347	334	315	308	266	257	229	222	206	212	214

Sources: See Tables 96 & 98.

Notes: From 2003/04 local authority lettings exclude non-secure lettings to homeless households (see Table 96). New housing association tenants include former council tenants transferring to housing associations, but exclude lettings of supported accommodation (and former supported housing tenants taking up general needs tenancies).

The definition of supported housing changed from 2004/05 resulting in a reduction in recorded housing association general needs lettings (see Table 98).

Table 102 **Welsh local authority lettings**

	1980/81	1985/86	1990/91	1991/92	1992/93	1993/94	1994/95	1995/96	1996/97	1997/98	1998/99	1999/00	2000/01	2001/02	2002/03	2003/04	2004/05	2005/06	2006/07	2007/08	2008/09
Stock (000s)	293	257	224	219	216	214	211	208	205	203	199	195	190	185	180	170	160	157	155	143	122
All lettings to new tenants	14,009	13,896	11,530	12,030	11,543	12,547	13,053	13,576	14,555	15,639	15,672	15,347	15,123	14,489	14,348	12,707	11,196	10,090	10,200	9,770	8,202
Lettings to homeless	1,531	2,149	2,473	2,674	2,754	2,471	2,058	1,949	1,681	880	1,269	1,383	1,762	2,200	2,473	2,919	3,299	3,211	3,507	2,999	2,777
Homeless lettings as a % of all lettings	10.9	15.5	21.4	22.2	23.9	19.7	15.8	14.4	11.5	5.6	8.1	9.0	11.7	15.2	17.2	23.0	29.5	31.8	34.4	30.7	33.9

Source: Welsh Housing Statistics.

Notes: Excludes new towns. Stock figures are averages for the financial year.

Table 103 **Scottish local authority lettings**

	1985/86	1990/91	1991/92	1992/93	1993/94	1994/95	1995/96	1996/97	1997/98	1998/99	1999/00	2000/01	2001/02	2002/03	2003/04	2004/05	2005/06	2006/07	2007/08	2008/09	2009/10
Local authorities																					
Lettings to new tenants	45,039	47,480	44,248	41,234	40,262	40,321	41,379	44,468	44,583	45,168	n/a	n/a	37,781	38,191	28,186	26,306	24,267	24,078	21,630	20,369	23,465
Percentage of new lets to homeless	16.3	20.0	21.4	23.8	22.7	20.4	20.5	19.1	20.1	21.2	n/a	n/a	24.2	27.7	34.0	37.1	40.9	43.0	47.9	54.1	52.1
Housing associations																					
Lettings to new tenants	–	–	–	–	–	–	–	–	–	–	–	–	–	–	–	23,825	23,944	23,607	24,038	24,636	24,793
Percentage of new lets to homeless	–	–	–	–	–	–	–	–	–	–	–	–	–	–	–	15.5	16.3	23.6	25.4	26.4	31.0

Source: Scottish Government; Scottish Housing Regulator.

Notes: Lettings to new tenants include waiting list, homeless, National Mobility Scheme and other lettings, but exclude transfers and mutual exchanges. Figures also include lettings of general needs dwellings owned by other agencies to whose stock the local authority has nomination rights. Data was not collected for 1999/2000 and 2000/01.

Table 104 **Northern Ireland lettings and homelessness**

		1980/81	1985/86	1990/91	1991/92	1992/93	1993/94	1994/95	1995/96	1996/97	1997/98	1998/99	1999/00	2000/01	2001/02	2002/03	2003/04	2004/05	2005/06	2006/07	2007/08	2008/09	2009/10
Allocations to new tenants			9,966	12,417	11,637	11,170	10,489	10,280	10,455	8,826	10,164	10,946	10,643	8,496	9,671	8,824	8,766	8,462	7,603	7,978	7,772	7,289	8,132	9,192
of which, homeless	No	–	–	–	–	–	–	–	–	–	–	–	–	3,279	4,088	4,433	4,571	4,434	5,196	5,232	5,339	5,778	6,066
	%	–	–	–	–	–	–	–	–	–	–	–	–	33.9	46.3	50.6	54.0	58.3	65.1	67.3	73.2	71.1	66.0
Homelessness:																							
presenting				9,187	10,081	10,099	9,731	10,068	10,468	11,092	11,672	11,552	10,997	12,694	14,390	16,289	17,230	17,360	20,121	20,013	19,030	18,076	18,664
awarded priority status				4,404	4,158	4,061	3,971	4,014	4,319	4,708	4,956	4,997	5,192	6,457	7,374	8,580	8,594	8,470	9,749	9,744	9,234	8,934	9,914
Placed in temporary accommodation				1,849	1,771	1,790	1,865	1,747	2,151	2,141	2,123	2,249	1,937	2,455	2,542	3,624	4,079	4,177	4,624	3,978	3,897	3,154	3,295

Sources: Northern Ireland Department for Social Development, Northern Ireland Housing Executive.

Notes: Allocations figures are for both NIHE and housing associations, and exclude transfers. Homeless legislation was only extended to Northern Ireland in April 1989.

Numbers placed in temporary accommodation are total placements during the course of the year; not the numbers in temporary accommodation at the end of the year.

Section 3   Compendium of tables

Help with housing costs

Table 105 **Mortgage interest tax relief**

	1970/71	1975/76	1980/81	1985/86	1986/87	1987/88	1988/89	1989/90	1990/91	1991/92	1992/93	1993/94	1994/95	1995/96	1996/97	1997/98	1998/99	1999/00
Basic rate of relief (%)	32	35	30	30	29	27	25	25	25	25	25	25	20	15	15	15	10	10
Cost of tax relief (£m) (A) of which:	298	1,004	2,188	4,750	4,670	4,850	5,400	6,900	7,700	6,100	5,200	4,300	3,500	2,700	2,400	2,700	1,900	1,600
Option mortgage scheme (£m) (B)	13	109	228	–	–	–	–	–	–	–	–	–	–	–	–	–	–	–
In excess of basic rate of income tax (£m)	–	–	130	260	300	400	350	420	470	–	–	–	–	–	–	–	–	–
Number of recipients (000s) (C)	2,960	4,820	5,860	8,100	8,450	8,750	9,200	9,400	9,600	9,700	9,800	10,000	10,400	10,500	10,600	10,700	10,800	10,900
Average tax relief (£) ((A-B)/C)	95	185	335	585	555	555	585	735	800	630	530	430	340	260	230	250	180	150

Sources: Inland Revenue Statistics, Parliamentary Questions.

Notes: The number of recipients is the number of tax units in receipt of mortgage interest tax relief. This does not include households assisted through the Option Mortgage scheme. The 1970/71 and 1975/76 figures are the author's estimates based on 95% of the number of mortgages (the average tax unit to mortgage ratio for the early 1980s); the figures on the number of tax units are not available. The Option Mortgage scheme provided the equivalent of mortgage interest relief (MITR) to lower income households that did not have a sufficient income to attract the tax liability against which MITR could be offset. It operated from 1968 to 1983. Relief at higher rates of income tax was abolished from 1991/92. The 1999/00 figures are provisional. MITR was abolished in April 2000. Some final costs were incurred in the 2000/01 financial year, but the precise figures are not available.

Table 106 **Regional distribution of mortgage interest tax relief**

£ million

	1980/81	1981/82	1982/83	1983/84	1984/85	1985/86	1986/87	1987/88	1988/89	1989/90	1990/91	1991/92	1992/93	1993/94	1994/95	1995/96	1996/97	1997/98	1998/99	1999/00
Northern	80	70	95	100	140	180	200	210	250	310	350	310	230	200	160	130				
North East																110	100	110	80	70
Yorkshire & Humberside	155	150	160	210	260	340	350	360	370	460	510	450	340	300	280	210	190	220	160	130
North West	200	180	215	260	330	440	490	510	530	690	770	640	500	430	340	270				
North West																240	270	300	210	180
East Midlands	115	110	130	180	230	300	320	330	340	430	480	410	340	280	240	190	170	190	130	110
West Midlands	160	190	170	230	280	370	350	360	430	550	620	510	400	340	280	220	200	220	150	130
East Anglia	50	60	75	90	130	170	170	180	220	270	300	250	180	170	140	110				
East																280	240	240	170	140
London	280	290	260	400	500	670	620	650	780	980	1,100	710	740	580	390	310	270	290	200	170
Rest of South East	555	600	650	740	950	1,270	1,220	1,260	1,350	1,750	1,940	1,510	1,390	1,090	880	650				
South East																480	440	510	340	290
South West	140	170	140	230	300	400	380	400	520	660	730	570	480	400	350	260	230	270	180	150
England	1,735	1,820	1,900	2,440	3,120	4,140	4,100	4,260	4,790	6,100	6,800	5,360	4,600	3,790	3,060	2,350	2,090	2,340	1,640	1,380
+ Wales	65	80	80	110	150	200	210	220	180	240	270	230	190	150	130	110	100	110	80	70
+ Scotland	125	120	140	190	260	350	300	310	370	470	530	420	340	300	260	200	180	210	150	130
+ Northern Ireland	35	30	30	40	50	60	60	60	60	90	100	90	70	60	50	40	30	40	30	20
= United Kingdom	1,960	2,050	2,150	2,780	3,580	4,750	4,670	4,850	5,400	6,900	7,700	6,100	5,200	4,300	3,500	2,700	2,400	2,700	1,900	1,600

Sources: Answers to Parliamentary Questions 17/3/93 and 29/11/93; Inland Revenue Statistics.

Notes: Figures exclude the Option Mortgage scheme that operated until 1983/84. Figures from 1996/97 onward are only available for government office regions, while figures for earlier years are for standard regions. For 1995/96 only figures are shown for both standard regions and government office regions. Where the standard and government office regions are identical the data is set out in a single row. Where the government office regions boundaries and/or names differ, the figures are shown in the row(s) below the closest corresponding standard region. The names of government office regions (where they differ from standard regions) are shown inset and in italics. Yorkshire & Humberside changed to Yorkshire & The Humber in the government office regions.

Table 107 **Distribution of mortgage interest tax relief by income band**

Income bands	Cost of mortgage tax relief (£ million) (A)										Numbers receiving tax relief (000s) (B)									
	1990/91	1991/92	1992/93	1993/94	1994/95	1995/96	1996/97	1997/98	1998/99	1999/00	1990/91	1991/92	1992/93	1993/94	1994/95	1995/96	1996/97	1997/98	1998/99	1999/00
£0-5,000	270	260	340	310	310	190	170	220	140	90	490	620	840	840	1,090	980	940	1,020	990	750
£5-10,000	640	420	520	420	360	280	210	210	140	110	1,050	850	1,130	1,120	1,250	1,260	1,160	990	950	970
£10-15,000	1,520	1,170	1,360	1,050	770	550	480	540	300	230	2,060	1,920	2,670	2,540	2,320	2,200	2,110	2,190	1,740	1,570
£15-20,000	1,670	1,450	1,340	1,050	770	590	550	520	360	310	2,110	2,180	2,400	2,330	2,150	2,210	2,370	2,020	2,070	2,090
£20-25,000	1,240	1,120	600	560	520	440	360	460	310	310	1,530	1,600	1,050	1,220	1,360	1,590	1,520	1,730	1,700	2,010
£25-30,000	750	590	300	260	280	260	260	280	220	200	850	870	510	570	720	900	1,040	1,030	1,160	1,300
£30-40,000	770	590	370	320	260	210	200	250	240	180	710	850	610	640	650	740	810	920	1,190	1,130
£40,000 +	840	500	370	330	230	180	170	220	200	170	600	710	590	640	560	620	650	800	1,000	1,070

Table 107 (continued) **Distribution of mortgage interest tax relief by income band**

Income bands	Average tax relief (£ per annum) (A/B)										Percentage of total tax relief by income band									
	1990/91	1991/92	1992/93	1993/94	1994/95	1995/96	1996/97	1997/98	1998/99	1999/00	1990/91	1991/92	1992/93	1993/94	1994/95	1995/96	1996/97	1997/98	1998/99	1999/00
£0-5,000	550	430	410	370	290	200	180	220	150	130	3.5	4.3	6.5	7.2	8.9	7.0	7.1	8.1	7.3	5.6
£5-10,000	610	490	460	380	290	220	180	220	150	120	8.3	6.9	10.0	9.8	10.3	10.4	8.8	7.8	7.3	6.9
£10-15,000	740	610	510	410	330	250	220	240	160	140	19.7	19.2	26.2	24.4	22.0	20.4	20.0	20.0	15.7	14.4
£15-20,000	800	660	560	450	360	260	230	260	180	150	21.7	23.8	25.8	24.4	22.0	21.9	22.9	19.3	18.8	19.4
£20-25,000	810	700	570	460	380	270	240	270	180	150	16.1	18.4	11.5	13.0	14.9	16.3	15.0	17.0	16.2	19.4
£25-30,000	880	680	590	460	390	290	250	270	190	160	9.7	9.7	5.8	6.0	8.0	9.6	10.8	10.4	11.5	12.5
£30-40,000	1,090	690	610	500	410	290	250	280	200	160	10.0	9.7	7.1	7.4	7.4	7.8	8.3	9.3	12.6	11.3
£40,000 +	1,400	700	630	510	400	300	260	280	200	160	10.9	8.2	7.1	7.7	6.6	6.7	7.1	8.1	10.5	10.6

Sources: Inland Revenue Statistics, Parliamentary Questions 12/7/93 and 2/11/93.
Note: The numbers receiving relief are defined as the number of tax units.

Table 108 **Stamp duty on residential dwellings**

£ million

Region	1988/89	1990/91	1991/92	1992/93	1993/94	1994/95	1995/96	1996/97	1997/98	1998/99	1999/00	2000/01	2001/02	2002/03	2003/04	2004/05	2005/06	2006/07	2007/08	2008/09	2009/10
North	15	20	15	5	10	10	15	15													
North East								10	15	15	20	25	30	45	70	95	70	100	95	40	40
North West	50	65	55	20	30	35	35	40													
North West								45	45	55	90	110	140	205	215	240	275	350	355	150	145
Yorkshire & The Humber	40	45	35	15	25	25	25	30	35	40	65	65	70	135	165	225	195	265	260	110	110
East Midlands	55	40	35	15	15	20	20	30	35	40	60	70	75	140	155	220	195	250	255	105	110
West Midlands	60	55	45	20	25	30	30	45	45	55	90	100	120	185	200	265	245	325	320	135	140
East Anglia	45	30	25	10	15	15	15	20													
East								70	85	105	175	205	275	345	400	485	495	675	700	295	350
London	250	145	120	60	110	120	115	165	220	305	595	710	815	945	975	1,195	1,275	1,795	1,895	870	1,035
South East	360	220	175	75	145	170	130	200													
South East								150	190	245	415	475	645	810	815	990	1,055	1,450	1,505	680	810
South West	125	75	60	25	45	45	40	65	75	90	155	180	245	325	420	505	450	640	665	295	340
Wales	25	20	15	10	10	10	10	15	20	20	30	30	40	65	95	110	95	130	130	55	55
Scotland and Northern Ireland	40	55	50	25	35	40	40	50	70	90	140	185	230	325	200	295	250	395	500	220	155
United Kingdom	1,065	770	630	280	465	520	465	675	830	1,065	1,825	2,145	2,690	3,525	3,710	4,620	4,585	6,375	6,680	2,950	3,290

Source: Inland Revenue Statistics 2004, and earlier editions, HM Revenue & Customs website.

Note: Figures for the years to 1996/97 are for standard statistical regions; for 1996/97 and subsequent years' figures are for government office regions. Government office regions that have different boundaries to standard regions are shown in italics below the standard region they replaced. From 2004/05 onwards the data is derived from the Stamp Duty Land Tax database.

Table 109a Subsidies for local authority housing in Great Britain

£ million

	1980/81	1985/86	1990/91	1991/92	1992/93	1993/94	1994/95	1995/96	1996/97	1997/98	1998/99	1999/00	2000/01	2001/02	2002/03	2003/04	2004/05	2005/06	2006/07	2007/08	2008/09
England:																					
Exchequer subsidy	1,423	459	1,156	873	508	121	- 108	- 408	- 481	- 563	- 781	- 932	- 1,008	402	303	302	89	257	121	2	- 189
+ Rate fund transfers	309	277	- 23	- 19	- 25	- 17	- 19	- 28	- 44	- 65	- 80	- 97	- 99	- 24	- 7	- 19	0	0	0	0	0
= Total net subsidy	1,732	736	1,133	854	483	104	- 127	- 436	- 525	- 628	- 861	- 1,029	- 1,107	378	296	283	89	257	121	2	- 189
Wales:																					
Exchequer subsidy	68	9	- 10	- 20	- 37	- 51	- 67	- 76	- 80	- 92	- 93	- 87	- 87	- 91	- 82	- 82	- 82	- 86	- 99	- 100	- 94
+ Rate fund transfers	22	4	0	0	0	0	0	0	0	0	0	0	0	0	0	0	0	0	0	0	0
= Total net subsidy	90	13	- 10	- 20	- 37	- 51	- 67	- 76	- 80	- 92	- 93	- 87	- 87	- 91	- 82	- 82	- 82	- 86	- 99	- 100	- 94
Scotland:																					
Exchequer subsidy	228	44	56	47	36	24	22	19	16	13	11	10	9	10	8	8	9	8	6	5	6
+ Rate fund transfers	80	75	- 1	- 1	- 2	- 2	- 3	- 2	0	0	0	0	0	0	0	0	0	0	0	0	0
= Total net subsidy	308	119	55	47	34	23	19	17	16	13	11	10	9	10	8	8	9	8	6	5	6
Great Britain:																					
Exchequer subsidy	1,719	512	1,202	900	507	94	- 153	- 465	- 545	- 642	- 863	- 1,009	- 1,086	321	229	228	16	179	28	- 93	- 277
+ Rate fund transfers	411	356	- 24	- 20	- 27	- 19	- 22	- 30	- 44	- 65	- 80	- 97	- 99	- 24	- 7	- 19	0	0	0	0	0
= Total net subsidy	2,130	868	1,178	881	480	76	- 175	- 495	- 589	- 707	- 943	- 1,106	- 1,185	297	222	209	16	179	28	- 93	- 277

Sources: See Tables 69, 70, 77, 78 and 84 in the *Review*. Additional information from the Department of Communities and Local Government.

Notes: Figures for transfers between the General Fund and the Housing Revenue Account for the years to 1989/90 are the net result of transfers in and out of the HRA. Figures for housing subsidy in England and Wales from 1990/91 are for net basic housing subsidy (positive housing subsidy entitlements less negative subsidy entitlements). Housing benefit subsidy is not included in this table. Housing subsidy in England increased in 2001/02 with the introduction of major repairs allowances, and again in 2004/05 with the ending of the arrangement where authorities with negative subsidy entitlements were required to meet some or all of the costs of housing benefit for their council tenants. The new arrangements also ended the requirement for a small number of authorities to make transfer payments to the General Fund, as they were still in notional surplus after covering all of the housing benefit costs for their council tenants.

Table 109b General subsidies per local authority dwelling

£ per annum

	1980/81	1985/86	1990/91	1991/92	1992/93	1993/94	1994/95	1995/96	1996/97	1997/98	1998/99	1999/00	2000/01	2001/02	2002/03	2003/04	2004/05	2005/06	2006/07	2007/08	2008/09
England:																					
Exchequer subsidy	286	106	291	225	134	33	- 30	- 116	- 140	- 168	- 241	- 301	- 346	146	117	126	40	121	59	1	- 99
+ Rate fund transfers	62	57	- 5	- 5	- 7	- 5	- 5	- 8	- 13	- 19	- 25	- 31	- 34	- 9	- 3	- 8	0	0	0	0	0
= Total net subsidy	348	163	286	220	127	28	- 35	- 124	- 153	- 187	- 265	- 332	- 380	137	115	118	40	121	59	1	- 99
Wales:																					
Exchequer subsidy	231	39	31	- 46	- 93	- 174	- 243	- 324	- 373	- 398	- 467	- 482	- 463	- 475	- 514	- 506	- 519	- 551	- 643	- 758	- 740
+ Rate fund transfers	75	16	27	0	0	0	0	0	0	0	0	0	0	0	0	0	0	0	0	0	0
= Total net subsidy	306	54	58	- 46	- 93	- 174	- 243	- 324	- 373	- 398	- 467	- 482	- 463	- 475	- 514	- 506	- 519	- 551	- 643	- 758	- 740
Scotland:																					
Exchequer subsidy	255	75	78	77	67	54	37	35	30	26	22	19	18	17	19	20	24	22	17	15	19
+ Rate fund transfers	89	115	11	- 1	- 1	- 3	- 3	- 5	- 3	0	0	0	0	0	0	0	0	0	0	0	0
= Total net subsidy	345	190	90	76	67	51	35	30	27	26	22	19	18	17	19	20	24	22	17	15	19
Great Britain:																					
Exchequer subsidy	279	99	247	191	113	26	- 30	- 104	- 126	- 150	- 213	- 262	- 297	93	68	77	6	68	11	- 38	- 117
+ Rate fund transfers	67	64	- 1	- 4	- 6	- 4	- 5	- 7	- 11	- 16	- 20	- 25	- 27	- 7	- 2	- 6	0	0	0	0	0
= Total net subsidy	345	163	246	186	108	22	- 35	- 111	- 137	- 166	- 233	- 288	- 324	86	66	71	6	68	11	- 38	- 117

Notes: Average figures per dwelling are calculated by dividing the figures in Table 109a by the average HRA stock figures for the year.

Table 110 **Mortgage interest taken into account for income support, jobseeker's allowance and pension credit**

	1980	1981	1982	1983	1984	1986	1987	1988	1989	1990	1991	1992	1993	1994	1995	1996	1997	1998	1999	2000	2001	2002	2003	2004	2005	2006	2007	2008	2009
Average mortgage interest:																													
£ per week	10.18	12.18	13.87	11.93	15.18	18.96	19.31	18.33	24.18	33.41	43.27	43.98	41.92	37.81	39.16	36.97	33.50	37.17	32.91	33.65	35.81	25.50	25.47	25.17	30.55	31.12	36.24	37.91	41.57
£ per annum (A)	529	633	721	620	789	986	1,004	953	1,257	1,737	2,250	2,287	2,180	1,966	2,036	1,922	1,742	1,933	1,711	1,750	1,862	1,326	1,324	1,309	1,589	1,618	1,884	1,971	2,162
Number of claimants (000s) (B)	134	196	235	242	277	356	334	300	281	310	411	499	555	529	499	451	379	334	307	279	260	242	232	232	229	223	215	202	215
Total mortgage interest per annum (£ million) (AxB)	71	124	170	150	219	351	335	286	353	539	925	1,141	1,210	1,040	1,016	867	660	646	525	488	484	321	307	303	364	360	404	398	465

Sources: Annual Statistical Enquiries, Parliamentary Question 9/7/91, Income Support Quarterly Statistics, Jobseeker's Allowance Quarterly Statistics, Pension Credit Statistics.

Notes: All figures are for the May of the year. Figures to 1990 show mortgage interest liabilities taken into account in calculating eligibility for income support, and in earlier years, supplementary benefit.
From 1990 onwards the figures are based on actual help provided, and are net of non-dependant deductions etc. From 1988 to 1995 the average figure for weekly mortgage interest was somewhat depressed by the regulation restricting new claims to 50 per cent of eligible mortgage costs during the first 16 weeks of a claim. The figures from 1996 reflect the further restrictions on initial help with mortgage costs introduced in October 1995. From 1997 onwards the figures also reflect the introduction of the jobseeker's allowance. Figures from 2004 include provision as part of the pension credit scheme. No 1985 figures are available.

Table 111 **Range of mortgage interest taken into account for income support, jobseeker's allowance and pension credit**

Percentage of all claimant cases not affected by restrictions during initial period of claim

Full weekly interest payment liabilities	1990	1991	1992	1993	1994	1995	1996	1997	1998	1999	2000	2001	2002	2003	2004	2005	2006	2007	2008	2009
£0 - £20	42	30	30	32	35	32	33	–	31	36	35	32	47	47	49	41	41	36	35	35
£20 - £40	29	27	28	28	30	30	30	–	31	32	33	32	33	33	32	32	32	32	31	28
£40 - £60	13	18	17	16	16	17	17	–	18	16	18	19	13	13	12	15	15	16	16	15
£60 - £80	7	9	9	9	9	9	10	–	10	8	9	10	4	5	4	6	6	8	8	8
£80 - £100	3	5	6	6	5	6	6	–	5	4	4	5	1	1	1	3	3	3	4	4
£100 +	6	10	10	9	6	6	5	–	4	3	3	4	1	1	1	3	4	6	8	10
Average amount (£ per week)	34.41	46.34	46.01	44.31	39.69	40.49	39.67	–	38.22	37.74	36.75	37.11	26.59	27.15	25.62	31.01	31.52	36.67	38.23	41.56

Source: Department for Work and Pensions.

Notes: Figures are for May of each year and for the years to 1995 show the full weekly interest liabilities of claimant cases not affected by the restrictions applied in the initial period of an income support claim. From 1996 the figures are for actual help provided, and are net of non-dependant deductions etc. From 1998 they include all jobseeker's allowance cases in receipt of housing costs help, including a small number in receipt of partial help due to restrictions during the initial period of a claim. Figures for 1997 are not available. From 2004, pension credit cases are included.

Table 112a **Average mortgage interest taken into account for income support, jobseeker's allowance and pension credit by region: number of cases**

Thousands

Government office region	1990	1991	1992	1993	1994	1995	1996	1997	1998	1999	2000	2001	2002	2003	2004	2005	2006	2007	2008	2009
North East	–	–	–	23	23	23	21	18	16	15	14	13	12	12	12	11	11	11	11	11
North West	–	–	–	73	70	69	64	55	49	46	42	40	36	34	33	32	31	30	29	29
Yorkshire & The Humber	–	–	–	45	44	42	38	32	29	27	25	23	22	20	20	20	20	20	18	20
East Midlands	–	–	–	35	34	32	28	25	22	21	19	17	16	15	14	14	14	14	13	14
West Midlands	–	–	–	55	50	48	44	38	33	30	27	27	25	25	24	23	22	22	19	22
East	–	–	–	55	50	46	41	33	29	26	24	21	19	18	18	18	18	17	16	19
London	–	–	–	81	79	74	67	56	49	44	39	35	32	31	29	27	26	25	24	25
South East	–	–	–	79	72	66	58	46	39	35	30	27	24	23	23	23	23	21	21	22
South West	–	–	–	53	48	43	40	32	26	24	21	20	18	16	17	17	17	16	15	16
England	270	366	447	499	471	443	400	334	292	267	241	222	204	195	191	188	183	174	165	178
Wales	26	27	34	34	33	31	29	25	22	21	19	18	17	17	18	17	16	15	14	15
Scotland	14	18	19	22	24	24	23	20	20	19	19	20	20	20	24	25	25	24	23	23
Great Britain	310	411	499	556	528	499	451	379	334	307	279	260	242	232	232	229	223	215	202	215

Sources: Department for Work and Pensions.

Notes: Figures represent a combined total of income support, income-based jobseeker's allowance and pension credit claimants with mortgage interest payments included in their benefit. Income-based jobseeker's allowance replaced income support for the unemployed in October 1996. Average weekly amounts are housing requirements paid to claimants with mortgage interest payments, and include the amount of allowed mortgage interest together with any other allowable housing costs (such as ground rent). Figures up to and including 1992 are based on a 1% sample. From 1993 figures are based on 5% sample data. Pension credit is included from 2004.

Table 112b **Average mortgage interest taken into account for income support, jobseeker's allowance and pension credit by region: average mortgage interest**

£ per week

Government office region	1990	1991	1992	1993	1994	1995	1996	1997	1998	1999	2000	2001	2002	2003	2004	2005	2006	2007	2008	2009
North East	–	–	–	23.52	23.20	25.42	24.51	22.51	24.89	22.24	24.36	25.87	18.66	18.17	18.13	21.28	22.10	24.86	28.77	31.40
North West	–	–	–	27.00	25.52	27.66	26.77	24.42	27.83	24.89	25.99	28.39	20.38	20.46	20.68	25.14	25.54	29.94	30.75	34.15
Yorkshire & The Humber	–	–	–	27.18	25.93	27.41	26.76	24.33	27.32	25.19	26.09	28.40	20.00	19.53	19.34	23.42	24.58	28.61	31.14	33.25
East Midlands	–	–	–	33.59	30.68	33.25	31.40	29.07	32.92	29.29	29.81	32.45	22.60	22.05	21.97	27.40	28.19	33.99	34.78	38.27
West Midlands	–	–	–	31.91	28.63	30.73	29.16	26.88	30.79	27.87	28.67	30.25	22.02	22.11	22.94	27.84	28.67	33.83	35.48	38.21
East	–	–	–	52.17	46.46	48.15	45.37	40.98	44.84	40.22	40.68	42.87	31.22	31.29	29.73	36.37	38.66	44.24	45.88	52.99
London	–	–	–	63.16	56.45	57.20	54.10	49.21	54.38	47.86	48.87	52.38	37.59	37.44	37.36	45.84	46.17	53.31	54.89	60.50
South East	–	–	–	58.07	52.47	53.41	49.77	45.33	49.70	43.65	44.14	46.29	32.46	32.78	32.54	39.91	39.21	46.04	48.61	51.70
South West	–	–	–	45.42	40.33	41.61	39.48	36.20	39.62	34.89	35.40	38.16	27.46	27.52	27.82	33.42	35.26	41.69	44.62	49.47
England	34.54	44.43	45.25	43.40	39.21	40.52	38.30	34.73	38.46	34.05	34.76	37.01	26.38	26.32	26.28	28.81	28.87	33.79	33.57	37.82
Wales	23.20	33.50	33.46	29.41	26.93	28.36	26.55	24.53	28.55	25.39	26.26	28.97	21.06	21.07	20.62	29.94	30.31	35.20	32.16	34.21
Scotland	30.47	34.36	32.96	27.74	25.51	28.15	26.70	24.09	28.20	25.08	26.97	28.44	20.27	20.82	19.80	22.94	23.27	26.21	30.25	31.03
Great Britain	33.41	43.27	43.98	41.92	37.81	39.16	36.97	33.50	37.17	32.91	33.65	35.81	25.50	25.47	25.17	30.55	31.12	36.24	37.91	41.57

Sources and Notes: As Table 112a.

Table 113 **Housing benefit – numbers of claimants and average claim in Great Britain**

	1980/81	1985/86	1990/91	1991/92	1992/93	1993/94	1994/95	1995/96	1996/97	1997/98	1998/99	1999/00	2000/01	2001/02	2002/03	2003/04	2004/05	2005/06	2006/07	2007/08	2008/09	2009/10
Number of claimants (000s):																						
Rent rebates	1,330	3,710	2,944	2,981	3,023	3,060	3,007	2,953	2,887	2,762	2,664	2,469	2,250	2,103	1,985	1,831	1,819	1,745	1,684	1,625	1,493	1,502
Rent allowances	240	1,150	1,044	1,219	1,315	1,519	1,660	1,798	1,875	1,829	1,811	1,775	1,718	1,764	1,814	1,982	2,124	2,236	2,341	2,416	2,671	2,964
Rate rebates, council tax & community charge benefit	3,350	7,020	6,898	6,506	6,646	5,450	5,606	5,676	5,643	5,491	5,281	5,083	4,756	4,668	4,590	4,653	4,893	4,998	5,088	5,079	5,149	5,519
Average payment (£ per annum):																						
Rent rebates	240	606	1,030	1,184	1,375	1,505	1,654	1,763	1,830	1,893	1,924	2,028	2,137	2,293	2,423	2,493	2,718	2,876	3,047	3,261	3,392	3,497
Rent allowances	199	619	1,323	1,694	1,999	2,268	2,454	2,621	2,735	2,818	2,876	2,943	3,011	3,156	3,411	3,271	3,492	3,648	3,840	4,019	4,318	4,596
Rate rebates, council tax & community charge benefit	82	209	319	178	236	317	332	349	374	406	426	452	489	520	562	629	678	703	740	757	786	811

Sources: Parliamentary Questions 10/3/92 & 13/3/92, Social Security Departmental Reports Cms 2213, 2513, 2813, 3213 & 3613, Social Security Statistics 1991 to 1996, Housing Benefit and Council Tax Benefit Summary Statistics.

Notes: From 1985/86 figures include supplementary benefit cases. This accounts for part of the substantial increase in numbers and the average benefit payment that year. Rate rebate figures are for the years up to 1989/90; community charge benefit figures are for the years 1990/91 to 1992/93 and council tax benefit figures are for 1993/94 onwards. Average benefit payments from 1988/89 onwards are derived from Social Security Statistics and Housing Benefit and Council Tax Benefit Summary Statistics and relate to the August of each year, except for 1991/92 to 1995/96, where May figures are given, and 2008/09 where they are for November. Average figures for numbers of claimants from 1988/89 are derived from the DWP Annual Reports; figures for earlier years are derived from the Parliamentary Questions.

Table 114 Housing benefits expenditure and plans for Great Britain

£ million

	1986/87 outturn	1990/91 outturn	1991/92 outturn	1992/93 outturn	1993/94 outturn	1994/95 outturn	1995/96 outturn	1996/97 outturn	1997/98 outturn	1998/99 outturn	1999/00 outturn	2000/01 outturn	2001/02 outturn	2002/03 outturn	2003/04 outturn	2004/05 outturn	2005/06 outturn	2006/07 outturn	2007/08 outturn	2008/09 outturn	2009/10 estimated outturn	2010/11 plans
Rent rebates																						
England	1,950	2,711	3,351	3,812	4,178	4,355	4,537	4,634	4,536	4,440	4,376	4,287	4,296	4,379	4,216	4,370	4,419	4,505	4,581	4,510	4,583	4,613
+ Scotland	263	404	446	490	528	549	564	617	659	675	682	688	713	743	539	556	562	576	574	592	631	651
+ Wales	134	168	186	210	227	250	261	270	268	266	268	270	273	284	273	274	282	289	299	266	251	199
+ New towns	72	86	85	82	87	76	68	48	33	23	19	13	4	0	0	0	0	0	0	0	0	0
= Total rent rebates	2,419	3,368	4,068	4,593	5,019	5,228	5,430	5,569	5,498	5,405	5,345	5,258	5,282	5,405	5,027	5,200	5,263	5,370	5,454	5,368	5,465	5,463
+ Rent allowances	996	1,779	2,413	3,246	4,189	4,875	5,445	5,810	5,681	5,660	5,719	5,904	6,306	7,231	7,314	7,957	8,666	9,471	10,278	11,735	14,514	16,073
+ Income support: mortgage costs	351	539	925	1,141	1,210	1,040	1,016	867	660	648	527	490	484	321	307	303	364	360	404	398	465	500
= Total housing benefits	3,766	5,686	7,406	8,980	10,418	11,143	11,891	12,246	11,839	11,713	11,591	11,652	12,072	12,957	12,648	13,460	14,293	15,201	16,136	17,501	20,444	22,036
+ Rate rebate, community charge and council tax benefit	1,635	2,115	1,404	1,693	1,940	2,077	2,189	2,311	2,395	2,452	2,511	2,575	2,686	2,834	3,223	3,557	3,774	3,941	4,027	4,234	4,698	5,004
= Total housing & related benefits (A)	5,401	7,801	8,810	10,673	12,358	13,220	14,080	14,557	14,234	14,165	14,102	14,227	14,758	15,791	15,871	17,017	18,067	19,142	20,163	21,736	25,143	27,040
Total all social security benefits	44,323	55,688	66,303	75,257	82,438	84,859	88,707	92,212	93,342	95,557	99,038	101,362	106,691	110,288	105,758	111,072	115,757	119,149	126,049	135,487	147,768	152,544
+ Personal tax credits										140	1,268	3,903	5,048	5,741	9,727	11,601	12,972	14,189	15,404	18,374	21,871	23,349
= Total all benefits and personal tax credits (B)	44,323	55,688	66,303	75,257	82,438	84,859	88,707	92,212	93,342	95,697	100,306	105,265	111,739	116,029	115,485	122,673	128,729	133,338	141,453	153,861	169,639	175,893
All housing benefits as a percentage of total benefits and tax credits (A/B)	12.2	14.0	13.3	14.2	15.0	15.6	15.9	15.8	15.2	14.8	14.1	13.5	13.2	13.6	13.7	13.9	14.0	14.4	14.3	14.1	14.8	15.4

Sources: Department for Work and Pensions Departmental Report 2002, Cm 5424, and earlier equivalent volumes, Benefit Expenditure Tables, DWP website, Annual Statistical Enquiries etc. for income support, and jobseeker's allowance mortgage costs (see Table 110), Public Expenditure Analyses 2010 for Personal Tax Credits.

Notes: Eligible mortgage costs for income support (and jobseeker's allowance) calculation of entitlement for years to 2009/10; authors' estimates for 2010/11. Personal tax credits comprise working families tax credit and disabled tax credit for the years to 2002/03. These are outside the DWP budget, unlike the benefits they replaced. For 2003/04 they comprise the elements of the new working and child tax credits that are defined as public expenditure.

Table 115a **Numbers of recipients and average housing benefit in Great Britain: all cases**

	Numbers of recipients (000s)													Average housing benefit per recipient (£ per week)													
	1988	1990	1995	2000	2001	2002	2003	2004	2005	2006	2007	2009	2010	1988	1990	1995	2000	2001	2002	2003	2004	2005	2006	2007	2009	2010
England:																										
Rent rebates	2,475	2,311	2,380	1,812	1,683	1,607	1,491	1,468	1,455	1,376	1,311	1,214	1,228	16.26	20.18	34.39	42.30	45.40	47.70	49.90	54.00	57.00	61.00	64.72	70.85	69.47
Rent allowances	848	927	1,573	1,530	1,524	1,553	1,670	1,765	1,860	1,982	2,091	2,501	2,816	18.73	25.86	51.51	59.40	60.60	65.80	65.20	68.70	72.70	75.30	78.95	90.11	94.51
Scotland:																										
Rent rebates	496	467	434	349	327	311	232	231	227	219	208	202	207	13.76	17.71	26.25	36.00	37.40	40.10	38.60	42.20	43.70	46.10	49.12	55.89	59.28
Rent allowances	77	86	109	131	134	139	206	216	216	212	222	237	260	19.92	23.13	42.07	46.10	49.30	52.80	47.60	52.30	54.80	54.80	59.79	68.40	72.25
Wales:																										
Rent rebates	161	151	151	127	123	119	115	110	109	108	106	80	76	16.87	20.37	32.23	38.80	40.90	42.70	44.30	46.30	48.30	50.30	53.37	59.40	60.90
Rent allowances	44	55	88	84	83	84	82	90	91	93	95	140	160	17.44	22.24	42.80	49.20	51.70	55.80	55.60	56.50	59.40	62.60	66.24	73.10	76.20
Great Britain:																										
Rent rebates	3,132	2,928	2,964	2,288	2,131	2,038	1,838	1,808	1,788	1,704	1,624	1,496	1,510	15.85	19.80	33.09	41.20	43.90	46.30	48.10	52.00	54.80	58.40	61.98	68.22	67.65
Rent allowances	969	1,067	1,770	1,745	1,741	1,775	1,958	2,071	2,169	2,287	2,408	2,879	3,236	18.78	25.45	50.49	57.60	60.00	64.30	63.00	66.40	70.30	72.90	76.69	87.49	91.83

Sources: Social Security Statistics, Housing Benefit and Council Tax Benefit Summary Statistics, Department for Work and Pensions.

Notes: All figures based on May in each year. Rent rebates cover local authority and new town tenants. Rent allowances cover housing association and private tenants. Figures for 2008 are not available.

Table 115b **Numbers of recipients and average housing benefit in Great Britain: cases also in receipt of income support**

	Numbers of recipients (000s)													Average housing benefit per recipient (£ per week)												
	1988	1990	1995	2000	2001	2002	2003	2004	2005	2006	2007	2009	2010	1988	1990	1995	2000	2001	2002	2003	2004	2005	2006	2007	2009	2010
England:																										
Rent rebates	1,515	1,347	1,505	1,159	1,120	1,106	1,048	1,072	1,068	1,017	974	874	879	18.61	22.98	38.90	46.40	49.20	51.50	53.00	56.70	60.10	64.40	68.10	74.48	72.74
Rent allowances	492	516	1,116	1,019	1,032	1,079	1,179	1,269	1,328	1,411	1,485	1,685	1,867	21.72	31.28	56.40	64.90	67.00	71.60	69.10	72.80	77.10	79.50	83.40	94.55	98.09
Scotland:																										
Rent rebates	280	263	263	217	214	210	161	166	164	160	154	148	151	15.73	20.39	30.40	39.90	40.90	43.70	41.40	45.20	46.40	48.90	52.00	59.15	62.59
Rent allowances	43	44	75	86	92	97	146	160	159	158	166	167	186	24.77	29.54	44.00	50.60	53.90	57.70	52.20	55.40	58.10	57.60	62.70	72.17	75.72
Wales:																										
Rent rebates	97	86	95	83	84	84	83	83	83	84	83	62	58	19.34	23.26	36.70	42.20	43.90	45.70	46.70	48.50	50.70	52.90	56.10	62.35	63.84
Rent allowances	28	31	63	60	61	62	62	69	69	70	72	103	115	19.84	26.15	46.00	52.80	55.30	60.10	58.60	59.50	62.80	66.20	70.30	77.34	80.02
Great Britain:																										
Rent rebates	1,891	1,696	1,863	1,460	1,418	1,400	1,292	1,321	1,315	1,261	1,210	1,084	1,088	18.16	22.60	37.60	45.20	47.60	50.00	51.20	54.70	57.80	61.60	65.20	71.69	70.86
Rent allowances	563	592	1,254	1,166	1,185	1,237	1,387	1,498	1,556	1,640	1,723	1,955	2,168	21.88	30.88	55.10	63.20	65.40	69.90	66.80	70.30	74.50	76.80	80.90	91.74	95.22

Sources: Social Security Statistics, Housing Benefit and Council Tax Benefit Summary Statistics; Department for Work and Pensions.

Notes: All figures based on May in each year. Rent rebates cover local authority and new town tenants. Rent allowances cover housing association and private tenants. Figures for 2008 are not available.

Table 115c **Numbers of recipients and average housing benefit in Great Britain: cases not also in receipt of income support**

	Numbers of recipients (000s)													Average housing benefit per recipient (£ per week)												
	1988	1990	1995	2000	2001	2002	2003	2004	2005	2006	2007	2009	2010	1988	1990	1995	2000	2001	2002	2003	2004	2005	2006	2007	2009	2010
England:																										
Rent rebates	960	964	875	652	564	501	443	395	385	359	336	340	348	12.54	16.28	28.14	35.10	37.80	39.50	42.40	46.60	48.30	51.70	54.90	61.52	61.21
Rent allowances	356	411	445	511	492	474	491	496	534	570	606	816	948	14.59	19.07	38.92	47.50	49.50	52.60	56.00	58.20	61.60	64.90	68.00	80.93	87.46
Scotland:																										
Rent rebates	216	204	175	132	113	101	72	65	63	59	55	54	56	11.22	14.26	21.88	29.40	30.70	32.60	32.10	34.80	36.60	38.50	40.90	46.95	50.38
Rent allowances	34	41	34	45	42	42	60	57	56	54	55	70	74	13.77	16.32	31.66	37.40	39.00	41.50	36.50	43.40	45.40	46.60	51.20	59.39	63.50
Wales:																										
Rent rebates	65	65	57	44	39	35	31	26	25	24	23	18	18	13.18	16.56	27.09	32.60	34.40	35.80	37.90	39.70	40.60	41.50	43.70	49.24	51.41
Rent allowances	16	24	24	24	22	22	20	21	22	23	23	37	45	13.13	17.02	34.41	40.20	41.70	43.50	46.60	46.40	48.80	51.10	53.70	61.28	66.44
Great Britain:																										
Rent rebates	1,241	1,232	1,106	828	716	638	546	487	473	442	414	412	422	12.33	15.95	27.12	34.00	36.50	38.20	40.80	44.60	46.30	49.40	52.50	59.08	59.37
Rent allowances	406	476	503	580	556	538	571	573	613	646	684	924	1,067	14.47	18.72	38.21	46.40	48.40	51.40	53.60	56.30	59.60	62.90	66.10	78.50	84.93

Sources and Notes: See Table 115b.

Table 116a Housing benefit for housing association and private tenants

Thousands

Tenure									Numbers of cases									
	1992	1993	1994	1995	1996	1997	1998	1999	2000	2001	2002	2003	2004	2005	2006	2007	2009[1]	2010[2]
Housing associations	341	426	534	610	723	781	840	897	931	998	1,056	1,244	1,328	1,377	1,449	1,485	1,681	1,783
Private tenants	948	1,050	1,100	1,159	1,155	1,066	971	897	815	743	719	715	744	790	838	923	1,221	1,455
of which:																		
Regulated tenancies	333	278	280	257	217	194	166	144	124	106	95	87	82	76	71	69	54	50
Deregulated tenancies	503	676	765	610	929	869	800	749	687	635	621	626	661	713	766	839	1,167	1,406
Others	111	97	55	9	7	4	2	5	3	2	2	2	1	1	1	16	2	

Sources and Notes: See Table 116b.

Table 116b Average weekly rents and housing benefit for housing association and private tenants

£

	1992	1993	1994	1995	1996	1997	1998	1999	2000	2001	2002	2003	2004	2005	2006	2007	2009[1]	2010
Average weekly rents																		
Housing associations	35.50	39.90	43.60	47.60	50.00	53.40	56.50	58.50	59.80	61.90	66.50	62.10	64.90	68.30	70.70	74.40		
Private tenants	43.90	49.90	54.20	57.90	60.70	62.10	64.30	66.80	67.70	70.00	74.60	76.50	80.80	89.20	93.20	100.70		
Average weekly housing benefit																		
Housing associations	32.20	35.80	39.50	43.10	45.30	48.30	50.80	52.80	54.20	56.70	61.30	58.00	61.00	63.80	65.80	69.10	75.50	77.30
Private tenants	40.70	46.80	51.10	54.40	56.90	58.00	59.30	61.40	62.30	64.40	68.60	71.50	76.80	81.90	85.00	88.90	104.10	109.80

Source: Housing Benefit and Council Tax Benefit Summary Statistics, Department for Work and Pensions.
Notes: Separate statistics for housing association tenants receiving housing benefit have only been collected since May 1992.
All figures are for the May of the year. It should be noted that these figures, particularly for 1992 to 1994, probably underestimate the number of housing association claimants.
1. No figures for 2008 were available and average rents for 2009 and 2010 were not available.
2. Figures for 'Other' private tenancies were not available for 2010.

Table 116c Housing association tenants in receipt of housing benefits

	1981	1982	1983	1984	1985	1986	1987	1988	1989	1990	1991	1992	1993	1994	1995	1996	1997	1998	1999	2000	2001	2002	2003	2004	2005	2006	2007	2009	2010[1]
Thousands	210	220	250	265	285	300	315	320	330	350	375	420	485	540	625	725	783	840	888	929	1,006	1,078	1,226	1,331	1,416	1,461	1,485	1,681	1,783
Percentages	48	50	52	53	54	55	56	54	53	53	53	57	60	61	64	67	69	70	67	64	62	64	63	66	67	68	67	65	65

Source and Notes: Estimates by Alan Holmans for years to 1994. They are estimates of averages for the whole year, and do not therefore exactly match the figures in Table 116a, which are for the May of the year. Also, the administrative figures for the initial years in Table 116a are thought to underestimate the numbers for housing associations.
1. The percentage for 2010 is estimated.

Table 117 **Take-up rates for housing benefit and council tax benefit**

Table 117a **Take-up rates by tenure**

Type of benefit and tenure	Caseload		Expenditure		
	Numbers	Take-up ranges	Total amount claimed	Take-up ranges	Median unclaimed amounts
	000s	%	£m	%	£m
Housing benefit					
Social rented sector tenants	3,030	87 : 93	10,600	91 : 96	765
Private renters	1,000	57 : 69	5,170	66 : 79	1,390
All	4,030	77 : 86	15,770	82 : 90	2,595
Council tax benefit					
Social rented sector tenants	2,900	87 : 94	2,220	90 : 96	175
Private renters	710	68 : 79	560	69 : 81	195
Owner-occupiers	1,400	39 : 44	1,190	41 : 48	1,475
All	5,010	63 : 70	3,960	65 : 73	1,820

Source: Income-related benefits estimates of take-up in 2008/09, Department for Work and Pensions.
Notes: Figures may not sum because of rounding. From 2007/08, figures for housing association tenants have been included with those of local authority tenants, rather than private renters. Median estimates of unclaimed amounts are the mid-point of the ranges published by DWP.

Table 117b **Take-up rates by household type**

Type of benefit and tenure	Caseload		Expenditure		
	Numbers	Take-up ranges	Total amount claimed	Take-up ranges	Median unclaimed amounts
	000s	%	£m	%	£m
Housing benefit					
Couples with children	310	58 : 70	1,400	64 : 79	590
Lone parents	910	81 : 93	4,240	87 : 96	415
Other non-pensioners	1,310	75 : 85	5,000	80 : 90	905
All non-pensioners	2,530	75 : 85	10,640	81 : 90	1,870
Pensioners	1,510	80 : 87	5,140	84 : 91	750
All	4,030	77 : 86	15,770	82 : 90	2,595
Council tax benefit					
Couples with children	340	48 : 57	310	53 : 66	215
Lone parents	860	80 : 90	660	83 : 93	90
Other non-pensioners	1,290	75 : 87	970	75 : 88	235
All non-pensioners	2,490	72 : 81	1,940	74 : 84	530
Pensioners	2,520	56 : 64	2,020	57 : 66	1,265
All	5,010	63 : 70	3,960	65 : 73	1,820

Source and Notes: As Table 117a.

Table 118 **Housing benefit caseload and payments by tenure and region at May 2010**

Region	Number of recipients				Status		Average weekly housing benefit			
	Local authority tenants	Housing association tenants	Private tenants	All tenures	Passported	Non-passported	Local authority tenants	Housing association tenants	Private tenants	All tenures
	000s	000s	000s	000s	000s	000s	£	£	£	£
North East	88	102	67	257	184	73	55.55	66.28	83.78	67.15
North West	107	301	193	602	437	165	57.58	68.96	89.11	73.37
Yorkshire & The Humber	161	127	126	415	295	120	54.15	68.54	83.55	67.47
East Midlands	124	86	95	305	208	97	55.83	72.08	84.93	69.44
West Midlands	152	165	123	441	310	131	61.50	72.41	92.37	74.19
East	103	150	116	369	239	130	66.14	78.69	105.75	83.67
London	303	244	254	803	527	275	97.56	109.96	179.45	127.12
South East	121	202	190	513	318	194	71.21	85.02	116.76	93.53
South West	69	144	140	354	226	127	61.98	74.09	98.04	81.21
England	1,228	1,521	1,303	4,046	2,744	1,312	69.46	79.44	112.30	86.94
Wales	76	86	74	237	173	64	60.93	70.66	82.84	71.36
Scotland	207	176	85	468	337	131	59.31	61.94	94.00	66.58
Great Britain	1,511	1,783	1,463	4,768	3,255	1,507	67.66	77.30	109.82	84.20

Source: Housing Benefit and Council Tax Benefit Summary Statistics, Department for Work and Pensions.

Note: Components may not sum to totals because of rounding and the exclusion of unknown and other small categories.

Table 119 **Escaping the housing benefit poverty trap: gross weekly earnings levels at which housing benefit entitlement ceases**

£ per week

Household type	Housing benefit allowances	Earnings disregards	Child benefit disregards	Rent levels							
				£50	£60	£70	£80	£90	£100	£110	£120
Single person over 25	65.45	5.00	–	*112.80*	*143.08*	194.36	245.65	274.02	296.31	318.61	340.91
Couple over 25	102.75	10.00	–	*119.61*	*163.25*	214.53	265.81	317.10	357.62	379.91	402.21
Lone parent + 1 child under 19	145.22	25.00	20.30	*122.88*	*172.95*	224.23	275.51	326.80	378.05	429.33	470.36
Lone parent + 2 children under 19	202.79	25.00	33.70	166.53	217.82	269.10	320.38	371.63	422.91	474.19	525.48
Couple + 1 child under 19	177.72	10.00	20.30	180.00	231.28	282.56	333.85	385.10	436.38	473.42	495.72
Couple + 2 children under 19	235.29	10.00	33.70	224.87	276.15	327.43	378.68	429.96	481.25	532.53	579.15
Couple + 3 children under 19	292.86	10.00	47.10	269.73	321.02	372.27	423.55	474.83	526.11	577.39	628.68
Couple + 4 children under 19	350.43	10.00	60.20	314.60	365.85	417.13	468.41	519.70	570.98	622.26	675.54

Notes: All figures based on standard income support and housing benefit rates as they apply from April 2010. The figures for lone parent households are for post-April 1998 claimants. Figures are for cases without child care costs eligible for assistance under the working families tax credit scheme. The housing benefit allowances and earnings disregards are set against net earnings (and child benefit and tax credits). For consistency, all figures assume an adult working 30 or more hours per week, although in some cases this implies hourly earnings below the level of the minimum wage at April 2010 (£5.80 per hour).
The cases based on an adult working for 30 hours or more per week at sub-minimum wage rates are shown in *italics*.

Table 120 **Help with housing costs: income support and housing benefits in Northern Ireland**

£ million

	1980/81	1985/86	1986/87	1987/88	1988/89	1989/90	1990/91	1991/92	1992/93	1993/94	1994/95	1995/96	1996/97	1997/98	1998/99	1999/00	2000/01	2001/02	2002/03	2003/04	2004/05	2005/06	2006/07	2007/08	2008/09	2009/10
NIHE tenants	–	–	77	81	87	97	107	120	134	148	165	175	179	181	184	187	179	177	173	170	171	168	166	167	170	176
+ Private and housing association tenants	–	–	15	17	18	23	27	32	40	47	55	65	75	83	89	98	104	120	132	143	165	165	184	197	228	278
= All tenants	5	86	92	98	105	120	134	152	173	195	220	240	254	264	273	285	283	297	305	313	336	333	350	364	398	454
+ Homeowners	–	–	7	9	8	11	14	–	18	17	15	18	20	16	16	13	15	14	12	13	13	13	13	13	21	26
= Total	7	91	99	107	113	131	148	168	191	212	235	258	274	280	289	300	298	311	317	326	349	346	363	377	419	480

Sources: Northern Ireland Expenditure Plans and Priorities, Northern Ireland Social Security Statistical Branch, Northern Ireland Department for Social Development.
Notes: Income support and supplementary benefit figures for help with mortgage costs in Northern Ireland are from surveys undertaken in May each year, except 1997 which is for November.
For years where figures are not available for help with homeowner housing costs, a trend-based estimate has been included in the total help with housing costs figures for Northern Ireland. From 1997/98 figures for help with mortgage costs include assistance given as part of the jobseeker's allowance scheme, as well as income support. From 2008/09 figures for Homeowners includes help under the Income Support, State Pension Credit, Jobseekers and Employment and Support Allowance schemes.

Table 121a **Assistance with housing costs for homeowners, council and private tenants in Great Britain**

£ million

	1980/81	1985/86	1990/91	1991/92	1992/93	1993/94	1994/95	1995/96	1996/97	1997/98	1998/99	1999/00	2000/01	2001/02	2002/03	2003/04	2004/05	2005/06	2006/07	2007/08	2008/09
General subsidies																					
Homeowners	1,925	4,690	7,600	6,010	5,130	4,240	3,450	2,660	2,270	2,660	1,880	1,600	0	0	0	0	0	0	0	0	0
+ Council tenants	2,130	868	1,178	881	480	76	- 175	- 495	- 589	- 707	- 943	- 1,106	- 1,185	297	222	209	16	179	28	- 93	- 277
+ Private tenants			105	135	330	360															
= Total	4,055	5,558	8,883	7,026	5,940	4,676	3,275	2,165	1,681	1,953	937	494	- 1,185	297	222	209	16	179	28	- 93	- 277
Means-tested assistance																					
Homeowners	71	300	539	925	1,141	1,210	1,040	1,016	867	660	646	525	488	484	321	307	303	364	360	404	398
+ Council tenants	841	2,296	3,368	4,068	4,593	5,019	5,228	5,430	5,569	5,495	5,405	5,345	5,258	5,283	5,405	5,025	5,201	5,263	5,368	5,555	5,393
+ Private tenants	145	705	1,388	1,892	2,562	3,188	3,567	3,804	3,820	3,437	3,180	2,966	2,851	2,827	3,040	3,028	3,361	3,723	4,143	4,513	5,280
= Total	1,057	3,301	5,295	6,885	8,296	9,417	9,835	10,250	10,256	9,592	9,231	8,836	8,597	8,594	8,766	8,360	8,865	9,350	9,871	10,472	11,071
All forms of assistance																					
Homeowners	1,996	4,990	8,139	6,935	6,271	5,450	4,490	3,676	3,137	3,320	2,526	2,125	488	484	321	307	278	364	360	404	398
+ Council tenants	2,971	3,164	4,546	4,949	5,073	5,095	5,053	4,935	4,980	4,788	4,462	4,239	4,073	5,580	5,627	5,234	5,217	5,442	5,396	5,462	5,116
+ Private tenants	145	705	1,493	2,027	2,892	3,548	3,567	3,804	3,820	3,437	3,180	2,966	2,851	2,827	3,040	3,028	3,361	3,723	4,143	4,513	5,280
= Total	5,112	8,859	14,178	13,911	14,236	14,093	13,110	12,415	11,937	11,545	10,168	9,330	7,412	8,891	8,988	8,569	8,856	9,529	9,899	10,379	10,794

Sources: See Tables 105, 109, 110, 114 and 116.

Note: All figures are for Great Britain. Figures for means-tested assitance to private tenants exclude estimated costs of rent allowances to housing association tenants (for the years from 1994/95 they are provided by DWP).
General subsidies for home-owners are based solely on mortgage tax relief. They do not include the value of right to buy discounts (see Table 122) or the value of capital gains tax and rental value tax relief (see Commentary Chapter 6). Nor can private sector improvement grants be included in this table as at different times they have been more or less extensively subjected to means-testing.

Table 121b **Assistance with housing costs for homeowners, council and private tenants in Great Britain**

£ million at 2008/09 prices

	1980/81	1985/86	1990/91	1991/92	1992/93	1993/94	1994/95	1995/96	1996/97	1997/98	1998/99	1999/00	2000/01	2001/02	2002/03	2003/04	2004/05	2005/06	2006/07	2007/08	2008/09
General subsidies																					
Homeowners	6,181	10,648	12,946	9,670	7,956	6,473	5,143	3,832	3,193	3,628	2,479	2,078	0	0	0	0	0	0	0	0	0
+ Council tenants	6,840	1,971	2,007	1,418	744	116	- 261	- 713	- 829	- 964	- 1,243	- 1,436	- 1,495	368	271	248	18	200	30	- 97	- 277
+ Private tenants			179	217	512	550															
= Total	13,021	12,618	15,131	11,305	9,212	7,139	4,882	3,119	2,365	2,664	1,236	642	- 1,495	368	271	248	18	200	30	- 97	- 277
Means-tested assistance																					
Homeowners	228	681	918	1,488	1,770	1,847	1,550	1,464	1,220	900	852	682	616	600	391	364	349	407	390	420	398
+ Council tenants	2,701	5,213	5,737	6,545	7,123	7,662	7,793	7,823	7,834	7,494	7,127	6,941	6,632	6,548	6,589	5,954	5,984	5,888	5,821	5,775	5,393
+ Private tenants	466	1,601	2,364	3,044	3,973	4,867	5,317	5,480	5,374	4,687	4,193	3,852	3,596	3,504	3,706	3,588	3,867	4,165	4,492	4,692	5,280
= Total	3,394	7,494	9,020	11,078	12,866	14,376	14,660	14,767	14,427	13,082	12,172	11,475	10,843	10,652	10,686	9,905	10,199	10,460	10,703	10,888	11,071
All forms of assistance																					
Homeowners	6,409	11,329	13,864	11,158	9,726	8,320	6,693	5,296	4,413	4,528	3,331	2,760	616	600	391	364	320	407	390	420	398
+ Council tenants	9,540	7,183	7,744	7,963	7,868	7,778	7,532	7,110	7,005	6,530	5,884	5,505	5,137	6,916	6,860	6,201	6,002	6,088	5,851	5,679	5,116
+ Private tenants	466	1,601	2,543	3,261	4,485	5,417	5,317	5,480	5,374	4,687	4,193	3,852	3,596	3,504	3,706	3,588	3,867	4,165	4,492	4,692	5,280
= Total	16,415	20,112	24,151	22,383	22,079	21,515	19,542	17,886	16,792	15,745	13,408	12,117	9,349	11,020	10,957	10,152	10,189	10,661	10,733	10,791	10,794

Sources and Notes: As Table 121a. Cash figures adjusted by the 'all items' retail price index (CHAW).

Table 122 **Help with housing costs in all tenures in Great Britain**

£ million

	1990/91	1991/92	1992/93	1993/94	1994/95	1995/96	1996/97	1997/98	1998/99	1999/00	2000/01	2001/02	2002/03	2003/04	2004/05	2005/06	2006/07	2007/08
Social housing																		
Council subsidy	1,217	897	510	101	- 155	- 484	- 584	- 674	- 940	- 1,111	- 1,184	321	229	228	16	179	28	- 193
Housing association grant	1,395	2,116	2,984	2,338	1,959	1,640	1,496	1,104	1,040	1,095	1,238	1,320	1,512	1,727	1,400	1,412	1,978	2,129
Housing benefit (council)	3,368	4,068	4,593	5,019	5,228	5,430	5,569	5,495	5,405	5,345	5,258	5,282	5,405	5,027	5,200	5,263	5,371	5,452
Housing benefit (associations)	391	534	722	1,007	1,309	1,640	1,991	2,242	2,480	2,753	3,053	3,486	4,210	4,299	4,613	4,959	5,345	5,787
Total	6,371	7,615	8,809	8,465	8,341	8,226	8,472	8,167	7,985	8,082	8,365	10,409	11,356	11,281	11,229	11,813	12,722	13,175
Private renting																		
BES subsidies	105	135	330	360														
Renovation grants	26	24	30	31	31	28	27	21	20	19	17	18	20	17	16	17	19	15
Housing benefit	1,388	1,892	2,562	3,188	3,567	3,804	3,820	3,437	3,180	2,966	2,851	2,827	3,040	3,028	3,361	3,723	4,143	4,513
Total	1,519	2,051	2,922	3,579	3,598	3,832	3,847	3,458	3,200	2,985	2,868	2,845	3,060	3,045	3,377	3,740	4,162	4,528
Home-owners																		
MITR	7,600	6,010	5,130	4,240	3,450	2,660	2,270	2,660	1,880	1,600	0	0	0	0	0	0	0	0
ISMI	539	925	1,141	1,210	1,040	1,016	867	660	646	525	488	484	321	307	303	364	360	404
Renovation grants	493	459	572	586	580	536	507	393	372	363	326	339	378	317	310	316	365	300
RTB discounts	882	592	485	520	497	359	337	446	464	559	537	474	518	414	185	117	46	24
LCHO grant	108	133	176	357	355	311	290	221	164	122	138	131	236	531	492	647	516	523
Total	9,622	8,119	7,504	6,913	5,922	4,882	4,271	4,380	3,526	3,169	1,489	1,428	1,453	1,569	1,290	1,444	1,287	1,251
Total all tenures	17,512	17,785	19,235	18,957	17,861	16,940	16,590	16,005	14,711	14,236	12,722	14,682	15,869	15,895	15,871	16,963	18,134	17,703

Sources: Tables 27, 60, 64, 76, 83, 121; additional information from Communities Scotland and Welsh Assembly Government.

Note: Renovation grants figures are based on 95 per cent of total private sector grants; 5 per cent are apportioned to the private rented sector. Costs of right to buy discounts are assessed to be those in excess of 32 per cent of vacant possession value (see Contemporary issues Chapter 1 in the 2006/07 edition of the *Review* for a full value for money assessment of the right to buy).

Help with housing costs for home-owners does not include the value of either capital gains tax relief or the non taxation of the rental value of owner-occupied dwellings. See Commentary Chapter 6 for a discussion of the value of those tax reliefs.